Oracle Press™

Oracle9*i* UNIX Administration Handbook

Oracle Press™

Oracle9*i* UNIX Administration Handbook

Donald K. Burleson

McGraw-Hill/Osborne

New York   Chicago   San Francisco
Lisbon   London   Madrid   Mexico City   Milan
New Delhi   San Juan   Seoul   Singapore   Sydney   Toronto

McGraw-Hill/Osborne
2600 Tenth Street
Berkeley, California 94710
U.S.A.

To arrange bulk purchase discounts for sales promotions, premiums, or fund-raisers, please contact **McGraw-Hill**/Osborne at the above address. For information on translations or book distributors outside the U.S.A., please see the International Contact Information page immediately following the index of this book.

Oracle9*i* UNIX Administration Handbook

 4567890 CUS CUS 019876543
ISBN 0-07-222304-9

Publisher
  Brandon A. Nordin

Vice President & Associate Publisher
  Scott Rogers

Acquisitions Editor
  Lisa McClain

Project Editor
  Patty Mon

Acquisitions Coordinator
  Athena Honore

Technical Editor
  Tim Donar

Copy Editor
  Lunaea Weatherstone

Proofreader
  Pam Vevea

Indexer
  Irv Hershman

Computer Designers
  Carie Abrew, Lucie Ericksen

Illustrators
  Michelle Galicia, Michael Mueller, Lyssa Wald

Series Design
  Jani Beckwith

Cover Series Design
  Damore Johann Design, Inc.

This book was composed with Corel VENTURA™ Publisher.

This book is dedicated to the memory of my parents,
Lt. Col. Louis F. Burleson and Virginia G. Burleson.
They taught me to strive for excellence in all endeavors,
and I am grateful for their sacrifices.

About the Author

Donald K. Burleson is an independent Oracle author and consultant with more than 20 years of full-time experience designing and managing complex database systems. Don is one of the world's leading Oracle experts and the author of 13 books and more than 100 articles in national database magazines.

Don also serves as editor-in-chief of *Oracle Internals*, a popular Oracle DBA journal, and consults with numerous Fortune 500 companies. A former adjunct professor emeritus of Information Systems, Don has taught more than 100 computer courses at major universities throughout the United States.

Don is also known for his pioneering efforts in using tiny horses as guides for the blind. Don and his wife Janet founded the charity Guide Horse Foundation to provide free guide horses for the blind, and they have appeared in many national publications including *TIME* magazine, *People* magazine, and television shows such as ABC 20/20 and CNN News. The Guide Horse Foundation maintains a very popular web site at www.guidehorse.org.

Don's web sites are www.dba-oracle.com and www.remote-dba.net. Don can be reached at Don@Burleson.cc. Don Burleson's books include:

Oracle Internals, Tips, Tricks and Techniques for the DBA (CRC Press, 2001)
Oracle High-Performance SQL Tuning (McGraw-Hill/Osborne, Oracle Press, 2001)
Oracle High-Performance Tuning with STATSPACK (McGraw-Hill/Osborne, Oracle Press, 2001)
Unix for the Oracle DBA (O'Reilly & Associates, 2000)
Oracle SAP Administration (O'Reilly & Associates, 1999
Inside the Database Object Model (CRC Press, 1998)
High Performance Oracle Data Warehousing (Coriolis Publishing, 1997)
High Performance Oracle8 Tuning (Coriolis Publishing, 1997)
High Performance Oracle Database Applications (Coriolis Publishing, 1996)
Oracle Databases on the Web (Coriolis Publishing, 1996)
Managing Distributed Databases (John Wiley & Sons, 1994)
Practical Application of Object-Oriented Techniques to Relational Databases (John Wiley & Sons, 1993)

Contents at a Glance

PART III
UNIX Administration for the Oracle DBA

Contents

PART I
UNIX Server Basics

PART II

The Interaction Between Oracle and the UNIX Server

Acknowledgments

Any text of this size and complexity is the result of the dedicated work of many people. As the author, I can take only a small credit for the finished work, and I have many people to thank for their efforts. Foremost, I would like to thank Lisa McClain, Scott Rogers, and Jeremy Judson for their insights and direction in the conception of this book. I also need to thank Athena Honore and Patty Mon for their supreme editorial work and efforts in quality control. Special acknowledgements go to Tim Donar, who reviewed this book, and to my wife Janet Burleson who tolerated the madness of tight deadlines.

Introduction

s of 2002, the vast majority of Oracle databases run in the UNIX environment, and it is not enough for the Oracle professional to master the database internals. Instead, the Oracle DBA must also be familiar with working in a UNIX environment, and they must be able to perform all of the required functions for the Oracle DBA.

UNIX command syntax is among the most cryptic of all environmental languages. Even the most seasoned professionals cannot remember all of the detailed syntax of the more sophisticated commands. Hence, this book is targeted at both seasoned UNIX professionals as well as UNIX neophytes.

This text is the result of my 20+ years of experience with UNIX, and the body of this book is the accumulated UNIX tips and techniques that is specifically geared toward the Oracle DBA in the UNIX environment. In addition to concepts, this book contains working UNIX scripts that provide clear illustrative examples of the use of each command. The intent of this text is to provide the Oracle professional with a general guide and a library of working tools that they can use to solve Oracle problems and tasks in their UNIX environment.

This book was especially challenging because of the dialect differences between the major implementations of UNIX. Commands in IBM's AIX UNIX are often different than Solaris UNIX, and there are also differences between the versions of each UNIX dialect.

To make this text optimal for every Oracle professional, the emphasis is placed on those commands that are common to most UNIX dialects. Whenever possible, I have included specific scripts for each major implementation of UNIX, including Linux, IBM AIX, HP UNIX, Compaq UNIX, and Solaris UNIX.

The organization of this book was also challenging, and I have organized the material into "how-to" chapters so the book can be used as a UNIX reference.

Of course, it is impossible to cover every possible command in every dialect and nuance of UNIX commands. Rather, this book attempts to cover the most commonly-used UNIX commands for the Oracle DBA and show through working scripts how Oracle operates in a UNIX environment.

I work with UNIX and Oracle for a living, and I am always interested in feedback from the readers. If you have a tip, script, or any Oracle-related technique, I invite you to send me an e-mail at don@burleson.cc.

Now, let's get started and take a high-level look at the UNIX language.

PART

I

UNIX Server Basics

CHAPTER 1

Introduction to UNIX

he UNIX operating system has grown from an obscure OS into one of the dominant computing environments in the world. During the 1980s, UNIX gained increasing popularity over mainframe operating systems as new UNIX servers were delivered to customers desiring cheaper platforms for client/server applications. Through the 1990s, UNIX-based systems became larger and more powerful, and UNIX servers finally became capable of supporting large Oracle databases. As an introduction to UNIX for Oracle, this chapter will cover the following topics:

- Introduction to the UNIX architecture

- Introduction to UNIX commands

- Common Oracle UNIX commands

- File management in UNIX

- Directory management in UNIX

- Dissecting complex UNIX commands

This chapter is designed to give the Oracle DBA a broad, sweeping overview of the basic UNIX commands and how they are used in an Oracle server environment. In later chapters, we will drill down into more complex UNIX commands, but this chapter will deal with the basics. We will begin with an overview of simple UNIX commands. By combining UNIX commands, the Oracle DBA is able to create sophisticated management tools and effectively manage their Oracle database.

Let's begin with a brief discussion on the UNIX architecture as it applies to the Oracle database.

Introduction to the UNIX Architecture

At its most basic level, an operating system (OS) is the software program that allows a computer's hardware and software to work together. The OS is responsible for managing the interaction of processes to external devices such as the keyboard, data files, and terminal screen. When an Oracle database runs on a UNIX server, the database software interfaces with UNIX in order to manage the interaction between the database and the data files on disk. The operating system also interacts with the computer's memory.

In addition, Oracle has numerous UNIX structures for holding message logs, trace files, and other housekeeping (see Figure 1-1).

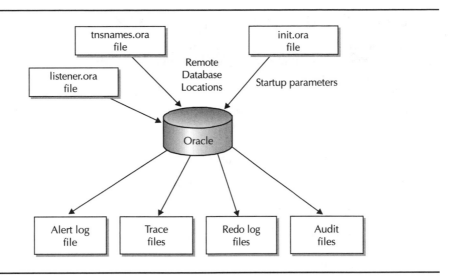

FIGURE 1-1.   *Oracle interacts with the UNIX environment*

We will be exploring the details of the UNIX operating system in Chapter 2, but for now we will just cover the major features of UNIX and how Oracle interacts with UNIX.

Dialects of UNIX

Through the 1990s, UNIX continued to evolve and gain popularity as UNIX servers moved into mainstream data processing. UNIX developed unique dialects, each unique to each UNIX vendor, and today's Oracle professional must be fluent in many different dialects of UNIX.

One of the biggest problems for the Oracle DBA is that it has never been a single, unified UNIX product with total compatibility from one system to another. Most differences have arisen from different versions developed by three major early UNIX dialects: AT&T UNIX, the Berkeley BSD UNIX, and Microsoft's XENIX product.

Today, the most popular dialects of UNIX include Hewlett-Packard UNIX (HP-UX), IBM's UNIX (AIX), Sun UNIX (Solaris), and the popular Linux dialects (Red Hat Linux, SuSe Linux). This book is geared toward all versions of Oracle7, Oracle8, Oracle8i, and Oracle9i, and we include dialects of UNIX including HP-UX, IBM's AIX, Sun's Solaris, and Linux. We will also show some commands in SGI's IRIX and Compaq's Tru64 UNIX and UnixWare.

System Administration in UNIX

Just as the Oracle8 databases were controlled by the values of an initialization file, the UNIX operating system is controlled by several initialization files. These files control the configuration of the Oracle server and the amount of available resources for all tasks that run on the server. The UNIX initialization files control every aspect of the OS environment, and especially those that are related to Oracle performance. These include:

- The setting for the number of semaphores (2x Oracle processes)

- The amount of swap disk (at least double (2x) RAM memory)

- The configuration of the mount points for the disks

- The amount of available RAM memory

Most of the UNIX control facilities are beyond the scope of this text, but it is noteworthy that many of the UNIX system parameters have a direct impact on the performance of the Oracle database. Let's take a closer look at those UNIX control files that impact Oracle.

The UNIX /etc/system File

The /etc/system file controls the setting for numerous UNIX kernel parameters. These parameters have a direct impact on the performance of the Oracle database. At Oracle installation time, the OS-specific installation manual directs the Oracle DBA to the appropriate settings for many of the kernel parameters. Here is a typical /etc/system file for an Oracle server in the Sun Solaris environment:

```
root> cat /etc/system
set shmsys:shminfo_shmmax=4294967295
set shmsys:shminfo_shmmin=1
set shmsys:shminfo_shmseg=10
set semsys:seminfo_semmni=24000
set semsys:seminfo_semmsl=100
set semsys:seminfo_semmns=24000
set semsys:seminfo_semopm=100
set semsys:seminfo_semvmx=32767
set tcp:tcp_conn_hash_size=4096
```

UNIX Access Control Management

In UNIX, a user named **oracle** is generally created to become the owner of the Oracle software on the UNIX server. In addition to the **oracle** user, other UNIX users may be created and granted access to certain Oracle files on the server. Let's begin by understanding how UNIX manages user IDs and groups.

UNIX Group Management   We begin by looking a special file called /etc/group. Each line of the /etc/group file contains group data separated by a colon (:). This file defines each group and contains the following values:

>   **group name   :   group_nbr   : members of the group**

```
root> cat /etc/group
root::0:root
bin::2:root,bin,daemon
mail::6:root
tty::7:root,tty,adm
lp::8:root,lp,adm
nuucp::9:root,nuucp
daemon::12:root,daemon
dba::102:oracle,oradev
mysql::104:
```

Next, let's see how user information is stored inside UNIX.

UNIX User Management   UNIX users are controlled by a special file called /etc/passwd. This file contains a series of strings separated by colons (:). The values are:

>   **username : password : user_nbr : group_nbr : default shell**

```
root> cat /etc/passwd

oracle:x:108:102::/export/home/oracle:/bin/ksh
oradev:x:109:102::/export/home/oradev:/bin/ksh
```

From the above listing you can determine that the **oracle** user has an encrypted password in /etc/shadow, that they are user 108, and they are in group 102. The **oracle** user has /export/home/oracle for a home directory, and they are using the Korn shell as a default shell.

UNIX Passwords on Oracle Servers   UNIX passwords are notoriously vulnerable to hacking. In UNIX, users can change their passwords by invoking the **passwd** command. Note that the listing of /etc/passwd above does not contain the encrypted passwords for the user IDs, and the password column is denoted with an **x**. This indicates that the system administrator is storing the passwords in another special file called /etc/shadow.

Unfortunately, protecting passwords in a /etc/shadow file is not always enough to ensure security. Cracker tools such as John the Ripper can be used to easily crack into these UNIX files, stealing access to the Oracle server, and all database data. To learn how to protect yourself from UNIX password hacking, see the UNIX password cracker at http://www.openwall.com/john/.

Of course, UNIX security is far more than just password management. UNIX security also involves networking, remote shell environments, remote copy facilities, and many other areas.

The Power of Root   In UNIX, the superuser is always called root. The root user may sign on as any UNIX user without supplying a password by using the superuser (**su**) command. For example, the root user can sign on as the **oracle** user by entering **su - oracle**. The root user may also change any password in the system by entering the **passwd** command followed by the user ID. For example, the root user could change the **oracle** user's password by entering **passwd oracle**.

UNIX Connectivity for Oracle   When the Oracle DBA creates their tnsnames.ora file to define remote databases, they often specify the hostname of the foreign server that contains the remote Oracle database. For example, an entry in the tnsnames.ora file for a remote database might look like this:

```
berlin =
     (DESCRIPTION =
       (ADDRESS_LIST =
          (ADDRESS =
            (COMMUNITY = TCP)
            (PROTOCOL = TCP)
          (HOST = humble)
           (PORT = 1521)
           )
       )
      (CONNECT_DATA = (SID = costsys))
     )
```

Here you see a TNS service name of **berlin**, which defines a connection to a remote server named **humble** that contains an Oracle database named **costsys**. When a remote connection request is made from the UNIX server, the /etc/host file is accessed to get the IP address for the **humble** server. From the listing that follows, you see that the **humble** server is located at 192.133.13.12. In sum, the /etc/host file is used to isolate the IP address from the tnsnames.ora file. If the IP address should ever change, the UNIX system administrator only needs to change the IP address in one place:

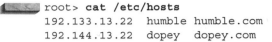
```
root> cat /etc/hosts
192.133.13.22  humble humble.com
192.144.13.22  dopey  dopey.com
```

Next, let's start looking at UNIX commands and begin by exploring their similarity to MS-DOS commands for the PC.

UNIX and DOS Commands

Back in the days before Microsoft Windows dominated the PC market, operating systems were controlled by commands. PC users were required to learn these commands in order to perform tasks. During the 1980s, Microsoft DOS dominated the PC market while the early UNIX command systems were used on larger multiprocessing servers. The main difference between UNIX and DOS is that DOS was originally designed for single-user systems, while UNIX was designed for systems with many users.

While PCs have evolved into GUI interfaces such as Windows, UNIX systems are generally used at a command line, and no dominant GUI has been accepted by the UNIX community. Hence, the Oracle professional must master a bewildering number of cryptic UNIX commands in order to manage their Oracle databases. While several GUI interfaces exist for UNIX they do not have the depth of Windows based system, so the administrator still uses a command line interface most of the time.

One of the most confounding issues for the UNIX neophyte is being confronted with a complex UNIX command. The cryptic nature of UNIX is such that even the most seasoned UNIX professional may have trouble deciphering the purpose of the command.

Let's examine a UNIX command and then see how the command is deciphered by applying a simple set of rules.

Because UNIX and MS-DOS were developed at the same time, they share some common syntax, and the UNIX neophyte will be happy to find many common commands and concepts. Table 1-1 shows some of the commonality between UNIX and MS-DOS commands.

As you can see, being productive with UNIX involves learning many commands and combinations of commands. Rather than attempting to teach you every possible UNIX command, this chapter will focus on those UNIX commands that you will be using to perform basic Oracle database management commands. The next section offers some tips to guide you through the labyrinthine maze of UNIX commands.

Introduction to UNIX Commands

The Oracle professional must know a core set of UNIX commands in order to perform database administration. It is imperative that the Oracle DBA understand how to navigate in UNIX and read and write to UNIX files. We will cover the most

UNIX	MS-DOS	Command Function
cd -	--	Switch between current and last directory
cat	type	Display the contents of a file
cd	cd	Move from one directory to another
cd /u01/test	cd c:\u01\test	Change directory paths
cd ..	cd..	Go up in directory
chmod	attrib	Set file permissions
clear	cls	Clear the screen
cp	copy	Copy a file (or a group of files)
diff	fc	Compare two files
cpio	xcopy	Back up and recover files
date	date	Display the system date
doskey	<ctl> k[3]	Display command history
export PS1='xx'	prompt	Change the command prompt text
find	grep	Find a character string in a file
gzip	dblspace	Compress a data file
ln	--	Form a link to a file
lp	print	Queue a file for printing
lpstat	print	Display the printing queue
ls -al	dir	Display the contents of a directory
mem	lsdev[2]	Display RAM memory
mkdir	md	Create a new subdirectory
move	cp[4]	Move a file to another directory
mv	rename	Rename a file
rm	del	Delete a file (or group of files)
rmdir	rd	Delete an existing directory
setenv[1]	set	Set an environment variable

TABLE 1-1. *UNIX and MD-DOS Commands*

UNIX	MS-DOS	Command Function
sort	sort	Sort lines in a file
ver	uname -a	Display OS version
vi	edit	Create and edit text

[1]C shell command
[2]Solaris command
[3]With **set -o vi** command
[4]No direct UNIX equivalent

TABLE 1-1.   *UNIX and MD-DOS Commands* (continued)

basic UNIX commands for the Oracle professional in this chapter, and subsequent
chapters will get progressively more sophisticated.

UNIX Command Syntax

Commands in UNIX are foreign to the Oracle professional, who is accustomed to
using a GUI to perform database administration. All UNIX commands are entered
from the UNIX command prompt, and there are several noteworthy considerations
about UNIX command syntax.

UNIX Line Continuation Characters

In UNIX, single commands can easily reach hundreds of characters. In order to
prevent command wrapping, it is possible in UNIX to continue a command on
subsequent lines with the backslash (\) character. In the following example, we
show a single UNIX command that scans the last 1,000 lines of the Oracle alert log,
searching for ORA-600 errors and mailing them to the DBA. You can partition this
long UNIX command onto several lines with the \ character:

```
# Note that the command below required $DBA and $ORACLE_HOME to be pre-set

mailx -s 'list of ORA-600 errors from alert log' don@burleson.cc < \

tail -1000 $DBA/$ORACLE_SID/bdump/alert_$ORACLE_SID.log| \
grep ORA-00600
```

Getting Help for UNIX Commands

As we continue our foray into UNIX commands for Oracle, it is critical that you
understand how to find help. All UNIX systems provide manual pages for each and
every UNIX command. This documentation is commonly called the *man pages*.

To see details about the command syntax for any UNIX command, simply preface the command with the **man** command. In the example that follows, you ask UNIX to give you details about the **sort** command:

```
root> man sort
Reformatting page.  Please Wait... done

User Commands                                              sort(1)

NAME
     sort - sort, merge, or sequence check text files

SYNOPSIS
     /usr/bin/sort [ -bcdfimMnru ]  [ -k keydef ]  [ -o output  ]
     [ -S kmem ]  [ -t char ]  [ -T directory ]  [  -y   [ kmem ]
     ]  [ -z recsz ]  [  +pos1    [ -pos2 ]  ]  [ file ... ]

     /usr/xpg4/bin/sort  [  -bcdfimMnru  ]   [   -k keydef  ]    [
     -o output  ]   [ -S kmem ]  [ -t char ]  [ -T directory ]  [
     -y   [ kmem ]  ]  [ -z recsz ]  [  +pos1    [ -pos2 ]  ]   [
     file ... ]

DESCRIPTION
     The sort command sorts lines of all the named files together
     and writes the result on the standard output.

     Comparisons are based on one or  more  sort  keys  extracted
     from  each line of input. By default, there is one sort key,
     the entire input line. Lines are ordered  according  to  the
     collating sequence of the current locale.

OPTIONS
     The following options alter the default behavior:

    /usr/bin/sort
     -c   Checks that the single input file is ordered as speci-
          fied  by  the  arguments and the collating sequence of
          the current locale. The exit code is set and no output
          is produced unless the file is out of sort.
```

You can use the UNIX redirect symbol **>** to save man pages to a file, which you can view at your leisure. In the following example, you write the output from the **man sort** command into a UNIX file called man_sort.lst. Then you use the **grep** utility to search for specific options with the stored text of the man page:

```
root> man sort > man_sort.lst
Reformatting page.  Please Wait... done
```

```
root> grep -i unique man*
     -u    Unique: suppresses all but one in each  set  of  lines
```

As you can see, the > symbol is used to redirect the output from any UNIX command. Let's take a close look at how redirection works in UNIX.

Redirecting UNIX Output

UNIX uses the greater-than (>) and less-than (<) symbols to allow you to redirect the output from a command to a file location. The placement of the > or < depends on the placement of the initial command. In this example, you take the command output from the **ls** command and redirect it into a UNIX file called **man_ls.lst**:

```
root> man ls > man_ls.lst
```

Note that any prior contents of the **man_ls.lst** command will be obliterated because UNIX redirection will always completely rewrite the file. The redirect command **cal** also uses the < operator. In the following example, you take the last ten lines of the Oracle alert log and mail them to the Oracle DBA:

```
mailx -s 'last 10 lines of alert log' don@burleson.cc < \
tail -10 $DBA/$ORACLE_SID/bdump/alert_$ORACLE_SID.log
```

The UNIX redirect command also allows you to append new lines of output into existing files. Let's take a look at how you can append command output into UNIX files.

Appending Data to UNIX Files

UNIX provides the << and >> commands to redirect output onto the end of an existing file. This is very useful when the Oracle DBA wants to keep logs in the UNIX environment. For example, suppose you want to add a notation to the Oracle alert log that you have just checked the recent contents for errors. You could use the following command for this purpose:

```
echo '*****Alert log checked at 2/5/2002 by Don Burleson ****' >> \
$DBA/$ORACLE_SID/bdump/alert_$ORACLE_SID.log
```

You can also use the >> command to append to an existing file of errors. Suppose you are keeping a running list of all Oracle trace file names. You could use the following command to write all new trace file names into a list. Note that the first command line uses a single > to re-create the trace_file_names.lst file, while subsequent redirects use the >> directive to append new entries to this file:

```
ls -al $DBA/$ORACLE_SID/bdump/*.trc  > /tmp/trace_file_names.lst
ls -al $DBA/$ORACLE_SID/udump/*.trc >> /tmp/trace_file_names.lst
ls -al $DBA/$ORACLE_SID/cdump/*.trc >> /tmp/trace_file_names.lst
```

Next, let's look at how to suppress UNIX command output.

Redirecting Output to a NULL Device

When you have a batch job or other Oracle task where the output is not useful, you can use the **/dev/null** device to suppress the output. The **/dev/null** device is the equivalent of the **DD DUMMY** syntax in the JCL language. The **/dev/null** device is commonly used in schedule tasks (using the UNIX **crontab** utility) where the output from the command is not required. In this example, you submit a large batch job and suppress the output.

The ampersand (**&**) tells UNIX to submit the job in the background, and the **2>&1** syntax tells UNIX to redirect the standard error output to standard output. In this example, all possible output from large_file.exe will be suppressed:

```
./large_job.exe & 2>&1 > /dev/null
```

Next, let's look at multiple redirection with the **tee** command.

Using the Tee Command to Redirect Output to Files

The **tee** command is used when you want to display output on the screen and also write the command output to a file. The **tee** command is very useful when you want UNIX script output redirected to several locations. In the following example, you e-mail all errors in the alert log to the DBA and also redirect the output to a file called error.log:

```
mailx -s 'Oracle Alert Log Errors' don@burleson.cc < \
tail -10 $DBA/$ORACLE_SID/bdump/alert_$ORACLE_SID.log | \
grep ORA-|\
tee error.log
```

Now that you understand redirection, let's take a look at how you can connect the output from UNIX commands together.

Piping UNIX Commands

The pipe command is one of the most important commands in UNIX because it allows you to create powerful functions in a single statement. The pipe command is represented with the **|** character. It is used to "connect" the output from one command and send it as input to another command.

For example, suppose you want to list the distinct file owners in a directory. To do this, you must perform three discrete tasks (see Figure 1-2):

1. You must list all files in the directory (**ls -al**).

2. You must parse this output and extract the file owner from the third column of the output (**awk '{ print $2 }'**).

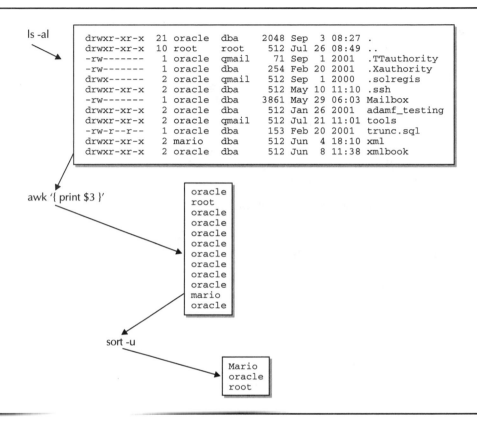

ls -al
```
drwxr-xr-x  21 oracle  dba     2048 Sep  3 08:27 .
drwxr-xr-x  10 root    root     512 Jul 26 08:49 ..
-rw-------   1 oracle  qmail     71 Sep  1 2001  .TTauthority
-rw-------   1 oracle  dba      254 Feb 20 2001  .Xauthority
drwx------   2 oracle  qmail    512 Sep  1 2000  .solregis
drwxr-xr-x   2 oracle  dba      512 May 10 11:10 .ssh
-rw-------   1 oracle  dba     3861 May 29 06:03 Mailbox
drwxr-xr-x   2 oracle  dba      512 Jan 26 2001  adamf_testing
drwxr-xr-x   2 oracle  qmail    512 Jul 21 11:01 tools
-rw-r--r--   1 oracle  dba      153 Feb 20 2001  trunc.sql
drwxr-xr-x   2 mario   dba      512 Jun  4 18:10 xml
drwxr-xr-x   2 oracle  dba      512 Jun  8 11:38 xmlbook
```

awk '{ print $3 }'
```
oracle
root
oracle
oracle
oracle
oracle
oracle
oracle
oracle
oracle
mario
oracle
```

sort -u
```
Mario
oracle
root
```

FIGURE 1-2.   *Piping output from commands*

3. You must then take the list of file owners and remove duplicate entries (**sort -u**).

Using the pipe command, you can tie these three functions together into a single UNIX command, piping the output from one command and sending it as input to the next UNIX command:

```
root> ls -al|awk '{ print $2 }'|sort -u

oracle
root
marion
```

Let's take a closer look at how this works.

First, you execute the **ls -al** command to get the fill details for each file in the directory:

```
root> ls -al
total 928188
drwxr-xr-x  21 oracle    dba           2048 Aug 22 20:47 .
drwxr-xr-x  10 root      root           512 Jul 26 08:49 ..
-rw-------   1 oracle    qmail           71 Sep  1  2000 .TTauthority
-rw-------   1 marion    dba            254 Feb 20  2001 .Xauthority
-rw-------   1 oracle    qmail          437 Aug 12 20:43 .bash_history
drwxr-xr-x  11 oracle    qmail          512 Sep  3  2000 .dt
-rwxr-xr-x   1 oracle    qmail         5111 Sep  3  2000 .dtprofile
```

Next, pipe the output from this command to the **awk** utility to only display the owner of each file:

```
root> ls -al|awk '{ print $2 }'

oracle
root
marion
oracle
oracle
oracle
```

Finally, you pipe the owner list to the UNIX **sort** command to remove duplicate entries:

```
root> ls -al|awk '{ print $2 }'|sort -u

oracle
root
marion
```

Using the Command History File in UNIX

A special file in the UNIX user home directory called .sh_history is used by UNIX to record and allow for fast retrieval of prior commands. For example, if you place the **set -o vi** command in your .profile file, the user can use **<esc> k** to scroll back through your command history, and you can use the **<esc> /** string to quickly display a previous command that contains the string. You can also use the **set -o emacs** command and use the arrow keys to access your command history. Commonly UNIX beginners will use emacs because they have not yet mastered the vi editor commands.

You can also use the UNIX **history** command or **fc** command to display the previous UNIX commands, and you'll see a command number that can be used to retrieve the command:

```
root> history
423     chmod 700 *.file
424     ls -al
425     chmod 404 *.file
426     chmod 400 *.file
427     ls -al
428     sqlplus /
```

Here is a listing of another .sh_history file. Note that it even includes the command that was used to display itself:

```
root> tail -10 .sh_history
cat alert_envtest.log|wc
cat alert_envtest.log|wc -l
cat alert_envtest.log|grep ORA-00600
cat alert_envtest.log|grep ORA-00600|wc -l
echo $DBA
cd
ls -al .s*
tail -10 .sh_history
```

The .sh_history file is commonly used as an audit mechanism, since each and every UNIX command entered by the UNIX user is stored in their .sh_history file. Many shops use it to track the behavior of new Oracle DBAs, since inappropriate or inept UNIX commands are easily spotted.

Here is the script that I use to spy on Oracle DBAs. When run as root, it provides a list of every command executed by everyone on the Oracle server: **audit_commands.ksh**

```
#!/bin/ksh

for user in `cat /etc/passwd|cut -d ':' -f1`
do
    echo "*************************************"
    echo UNIX command security audit for $user
    echo "*************************************"
    cat ~$user/.sh_history
done
```

Let's carefully inspect the behavior of this script.

It lists the /etc/passwd file using **cat /etc/passwd**:

```
root:x:0:0:root:/root:/bin/bash
bin:x:1:1:bin:/bin:
daemon:x:2:2:daemon:/sbin:
news:x:9:13:news:/var/spool/news:
uucp:x:10:14:uucp:/var/spool/uucp:
operator:x:11:0:operator:/root:
piranha:x:60:60::/home/httpd/html/piranha:/dev/null
postgres:x:26:26:PostgreSQL Server:/var/lib/pgsql:/bin/bash
squid:x:23:23::/var/spool/squid:/dev/null
carl:x:500:100:Carl Marx:/home/carl:/bin/bash
pamela:x:501:100:Pamela Zeus:/home/pamela:/bin/bash
olaf:x:512:512::/home/olaf:/bin/bash
mario:x:514:514::/home/mario:/bin/bash
mysql:x:100:101:MySQL server:/var/lib/mysql:/bin/bash
bugz:x:515:515::/etc/httpd/sites/bugz.rovia.com:/bin/bash
oracle:x:516:517::/home/oracle:/bin/bash
afshin:x:522:523::/home/adamf:/bin/bash
celora:x:525:526::/dev/null:/bin/false
weber:x:527:528:Web CVS:/home/webcvs:/bin/bash
```

It extracts the first colon-delimited field using **cut -d':' -f1**:

```
root
bin
daemon
news
uucp
operator
piranha
postgres
squid
carl
pamela
olaf
marion
mysql
bugz
oracle
afshin
celora
weber
```

It then loops through each UNIX user and lists the contents of their .sh_history file. Next, let's take a look at the common UNIX shells and see how they allow you to perform common Oracle maintenance.

UNIX Shells

There are several shells that are available to support UNIX commands. A shell can be thought of as a scripting environment, and each shell has different syntax, so it is important that you know what shell you are using when you enter UNIX commands. In this book, we use the Korn shell, but you can write Oracle scripts using any of the available shells. These include:

- **Bourne shell (sh)**   The Borne shell was the original UNIX command processor, which was developed at AT&T by Stephen R. Bourne in the early 1970s. This is the official shell that is distributed with UNIX systems. The Bourne shell is the fastest UNIX command processor.

- **Bourne Again shell (bash)**   Many UNIX purists prefer the Bourne Again shell, also known as the bash shell.

- **C shell (csh)**   Another command processor, developed by William Joy and others at the University of California in the early 1980s, is known as the C shell. The C shell borrows many concepts from the C language and offers greater versatility than the Bourne shell.

- **Korn shell (ksh)**   Another popular command processor was developed by David Korn in the early 1980s, and is appropriately called the Korn shell. The Korn shell combines many of the best features of the earlier command processors, and it is gaining in popularity among Oracle DBAs. All of the shell scripts in the book are Korn shell scripts.

Your default shell is set in the /etc/passwd file. For example, here you can see that the **root** user has the Bourne shell (**/bin/sh**), the **janet** user uses the Bourne Again shell (**/bin/bash**), the **oracle** user uses the Korn shell (**/bin/ksh**), and the **john** user uses the C shell (**/bin/csh**):

```
root>cat /etc/passwd
root:x:0:1:Super-User:/:/bin/sh
janet:x:100:1::/export/home/janet:/sbin/bash
oracle:x:108:102::/export/home/oracle:/bin/ksh
john:x:108:102::/export/home/john:/bin/csh
```

Each shell has specific syntax and features (see Table 1-2). For the Oracle server environment, the shell chosen is not as important as uniformity. In other words, the Oracle DBA should choose a shell environment and then require that all Oracle UNIX scripts be written in that shell.

Remember, it is quite easy to change your shell environment. You can change your UNIX environment by entering the name of the shell at the UNIX command

Feature	sh	csh	ksh	bash
Job control management		Yes	Yes	Yes
Supports aliases		Yes	Yes	Yes
Supports shell functions	Yes		Yes	Yes
Easy input/output redirection	Yes		Yes	Yes
Command history support		Yes	Yes	Yes
Allows command line editing			Yes	Yes
vi command line editing			Yes	Yes
emacs command line editing			Yes	Yes
Username lookup		Yes	Yes	Yes
Filename completion		Yes	Yes	Yes
Username completion		Yes	Yes	Yes
Hostname completion		Yes	Yes	Yes
History completion				Yes
Can follow symbolic links invisibly			Yes	Yes
Custom prompt			Yes	Yes
Process substitution				Yes
Root can bypass user startup files		Yes		Yes
User can specify startup file			Yes	Yes
Supports list variables		Yes	Yes	
Allows local variables			Yes	Yes

TABLE 1-2. *Features of Each UNIX Shell*

prompt, and you can change the shell for a UNIX script by entering a shell directive as the first line of the script. For example, you can change your shell environment to the Korn shell by entering the **ksh** command, and you can make a UNIX script use the Korn shell by entering **#!/bin/ksh** as the first line of the script. Table 1-3 shows a complete list of commands for changing shell environments.

Interactive shell	Shell Script Command	Shell Name
ksh	#!/bin/ksh	Korn shell
csh	#!/bin/csh	C shell
sh	#!/bin/sh	Bourne shell
bash	#!/bin/bash	Bourne Again shell

TABLE 1-3. *Changing UNIX Shell Environments*

In most Oracle shops, the DBA has a choice of shell environments. As soon as you request a login account for your Oracle server, the first thing the system administrator usually asks you is which shell you prefer.

Using UNIX Command Options

All UNIX commands support from one to many command options. To understand how this works, let's examine the **ls** command. To illustrate the complexity of UNIX commands, the **man ls** command shows that the **ls** command accepts 22 arguments, as shown in Table 1-4:

-a	Lists all entries, including those that begin with a dot (.), which are normally not listed.
-A	Lists all entries, including those that begin with a dot (.), with the exception of the working directory (.) and the parent directory (..).
-b	Forces printing of nonprintable characters to be in the octal \ddd notation.
-c	Uses time of last modification of the i-node.
-C	Multicolumn output with entries sorted down the columns.
-d	If an argument is a directory, lists only its name.
-f	Forces each argument to be interpreted as a directory.
-F	Marks directories with a trailing slash (/), executable files with a *, pipes with a l, and symbolic links with @.
-g	The same as -l, except that the owner is not printed.

TABLE 1-4. *Arguments to the UNIX ls Command*

-I	For each file, prints the i-node number in the first column of the report.
-l	Lists in long format, giving mode, ACL indication.
-L	If an argument is a symbolic link, lists the file or directory the link references rather than the link itself.
-m	Streams output format; files are listed across the page, separated by commas.
-o	The same as -l, except that the group is not printed.
-p	Puts a slash (/) after each filename if the file is a directory.
-q	Forces printing of nonprintable characters in filenames as the character question mark (?).
-r	Reverses the order of sort to get reverse alphabetic or oldest first as appropriate.
-R	Recursively lists subdirectories encountered.
-s	Gives size in blocks, including indirect blocks, for each entry.
-t	Sorts by time stamp (latest first) instead of by name. The default is the last modification time. (See -u and -c.)
-u	Uses time of last access instead of last modification for sorting (with the -t option) or printing (with the -l option).
-x	Multicolumn output with entries sorted across rather than down the page.

TABLE 1-4.   *Arguments to the UNIX **ls** Command* (continued)

One or many of these arguments may be used every time the **ls** command is invoked, and a single minus sign (-) is used to tell Oracle that arguments are being passed to the command. For example, the following is an invocation of the **ls** command using the -**F**, -**a**, -**r**, and -**t** options:

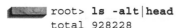
```
root> ls -Fart
.solregis/               1.ksh*                    imp_envtest.lst
```

One common use of the **ls** command in Oracle is used to locate the most recently modified file in a directory. You do this by using the **ls** command with the -**a**, -**l**, and -**t** options, and then pipe the output to the **head** command.

```
root> ls -alt|head
total 928228
```

```
-rw-------    1 oracle   dba        3372 Sep  3 14:43 .sh_history
-rw-r--r--    1 oracle   dba       19159 Sep  3 08:27 man_sort.lst
drwxr-xr-x   21 oracle   dba        2048 Sep  3 08:27 .
-rwxr-xr-x    1 oracle   dba          55 Aug 22 11:56 afiedt.buf
-rw-------    1 oracle   qmail       437 Aug 12 20:43 .bash_history
-rwxr-xr-x    1 oracle   qmail       415 Aug  1 20:37 mail.out
drwxr-xr-x   10 root     root        512 Jul 26 08:49 ..
drwxr-xr-x    3 oracle   dba         512 Jul 26 08:49 book
-rw-r--r--    1 oracle   dba        2198 Jul 26 08:43 sqlnet.log
```

Common Oracle UNIX Commands

Now that you understand the fundamentals of UNIX commands, let's examine common UNIX commands that are used by the Oracle DBA. Many of these commands are used to automate Oracle reporting and make Oracle management simple.

Capturing Server Information with UNIX

For the Oracle DBA who performs reporting functions on multiple servers, capturing the server name is very important. This is especially true in cases where several databases with the same name exist in several servers, and the report must show the server name to properly identify the database.

The most common command to gather server information is the **uname -a** command. Here is an example of the output from this command in Solaris UNIX.

```
root> uname -a
SunOS goofy 5.8 Generic_103634-03 sun4u sparc SUNW,Ultra 00
```

Here is the **uname -a** command on an HP-UX server:

```
root> uname -a
HP-UX penguin B.10.20 A 9000/871 2639229148 two-user license
```

Here you see that the first column is the UNIX dialect (SunOS, HP-UX), the server name (for example, goofy, penguin), the version of the OS, the serial number of the server, and miscellaneous server information.

If you just need the server name for an Oracle report, you can extend the **uname -a** command to capture the server name by using the **awk** utility and parsing out the first column of output:

```
root> uname -a|awk '{ print $2 }'
goofy
```

UNIX also provides the **hostname** command to display the server name:

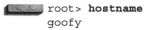
```
root> hostname
goofy
```

Next, let's look at how the **wc** command can be used to monitor the frequency of events in your Oracle database.

The UNIX wc Command

You can use the word count command (**wc**) to display the number of words or lines in a UNIX file. The **wc** command is very useful for the Oracle DBA who is looking to monitor the contents of specific messages with the Oracle alert log.

To illustrate, let's count the number of words in your Oracle alert log:

```
root> cat alert_envtest.log|wc
   108313   741411 5334959
```

Here you see that your Oracle alert log has 180,313 lines, 741,411 words, and 5,334,959 characters. You can use the **wc -l** option to only display the number of lines in a file:

```
root> cat alert_envtest.log|wc -l
   108313
```

You can also use **wc -l** command to count the number of specific messages in the Oracle alert log. Here you are displaying the text of all ORA-600 errors in your alert log using the **cat** and **grep** commands:

```
root> cat alert_envtest.log|grep ORA-00600
ORA-00600: internal error code, arguments: [2655], [0], [1], [], [], []
ORA-00600: internal error code, arguments: [16365], [2208470888], [1], [4]
ORA-00600: internal error code, arguments: [16365], [2209886568], [0], [4]
```

Now, add the **wc -l** command to count the number of ORA-600 errors:

```
root> cat alert_envtest.log|grep ORA-00600|wc -l
   3
```

Capturing Date Information in UNIX

It is also a common practice to capture the date from the UNIX server. Just like Oracle, UNIX dates have a default date format that can be modified according to your needs.

To display the default date in UNIX:

```
root> date
Tue Sep  4 10:29:40 EDT 2001
```

Changing the **date** display format involves invoking the **date** command with a date format mask, very similar to using the Oracle **nls_date_format** to change Oracle dates (see Table 1-5).

As you can see, UNIX has far more date format options than Oracle, and the UNIX date can be displayed in a huge variety of ways.

```
root> date "+DATE: %m/%d/%y%nTIME: %H:%M:%S"
DATE: 09/04/01
TIME: 09:37:49
```

Format	Meaning
%d	Day of the month as a two-digit decimal number (01–31).
%e	Day of the month as a two-character decimal number.
%E	Combined emperor/era name and year.
%H	Hour (24-hour clock) as a two-digit decimal number (00–23).
%I	Hour (12-hour clock) as a two-digit decimal number (01–12).
%j	Day of the year as a three-digit decimal number (001–366).
%m	Month as a decimal two-digit number (01–12).
%M	Minute as a decimal two-digit number (00–59).
%p	Equivalent of either AM or PM. Example shows PM.
%S	Second as a two-digit decimal number.
%t	Tab character.
%u	Weekday as a one-digit decimal number (1–7).
%U	Week number of the year (Sunday as the first day of the week) as a two-digit decimal number (00–53).
%V	Week number of the year (Monday as the first day of the week) as a two-digit decimal number (01–53).
%w	Weekday as a one-digit decimal number (0–6).
%W	Week number of the year (Monday as the first day of the week) as a two-digit decimal number (00–53).

TABLE 1-5. *Formats for the UNIX **date** Command*

Format	Meaning
%x	Current date representation, for example, 01/12/01.
%X	Current time representation, for example, 19:45:58.
%y	Year without century as a two-digit decimal number (00–99).
%Y	Year with century as a four-digit decimal number (1970-2069), for example, 2002.
%Z	Time zone name (or no characters if time zone cannot be determined), for example, PST.

TABLE 1-5. *Formats for the UNIX **date** Command* (continued)

You can also gather the UNIX date from inside a SQL*Plus script. In the example that follows, the SQL*Plus output is spooled to a file using the UNIX date function:

gen.ksh

```
#!/bin/ksh

# First, we must set the environment . . . .
ORACLE_HOME=`cat /etc/oratab|grep ^$ORACLE_SID:|cut -f2 -d':'`
export ORACLE_HOME
PATH=$ORACLE_HOME/bin:$PATH
export PATH

$ORACLE_HOME/bin/sqlplus -s /<<!

spool `hostname`_`date +%d_%m_%y`.lst
select count(*) from dba_data_files;
spool off;

exit
!
```

After running this script, you can issue the UNIX **ls** command, and you'll see that the spool file contains the UNIX hostname and the UNIX date:

```
root> ls -t|head
cheopsdb-02_04_09_01.lst
temp.ksh
get_files.ksh
```

Next, let's look at how you can use UNIX commands to manage connected users.

UNIX User Identification

The UNIX **who** command can be used to show all users who are currently signed on to the UNIX server. Note that the **who** command does not show Oracle users who have connected via the Oracle listener:

```
root> who|head -20
root        ttyp1        Aug 31 19:09
tlmason     ttyp2        Sep  4 08:31
dbogstad    ttyp3        Sep  4 06:33
clarson     ttyp4        Sep  4 07:20
mgeske      ttyp5        Sep  4 06:35
vogden      ttyp6        Sep  4 06:45
crmoore     ttyp7        Sep  4 06:45
yliu        ttyp8        Sep  4 06:47
mbell       ttyp9        Sep  4 06:54
acook       ttypa        Sep  4 06:58
rwestman    ttypb        Sep  4 08:06
eboyd       ttypc        Sep  4 06:58
lhovey      ttypd        Sep  4 07:00
mepeter     ttype        Sep  4 07:10
klong       ttypf        Sep  4 07:02
ldoolitt    ttyq0        Sep  4 07:36
dwilken     ttyq1        Sep  4 08:16
```

You can enhance the **who** command to include a count of all users on your Oracle server. In this example, there are 145 UNIX users connected to this Oracle server:

```
root> who|wc -1
145
```

Locating Files in UNIX

UNIX provides the **which** command for finding the location of executable code in all files specified in the $PATH UNIX variable. In the following example, you can easily find the location of the SQL*Plus executable:

```
root> which sqlplus
/u01/home/oracle/product/9.1.2/bin/sqlplus
```

Remember, the **which** command will only find executables in the UNIX path. It does not universally find any executable on the system.

For nonexecutable files, you can use the UNIX **find** command to locate a particular file. In Chapter 8, we'll extend this command to search for all files that contain specific strings.

```
root> pwd
/
```

```
root> find . -print|grep -i dbmspool.sql
./oracle/product/9.1.2/rdbms/admin/dbmspool.sql
```

In the example above, you **cd** to the root directory (/) and issue a UNIX **find** command to display every file on the Oracle server. Next, you pipe the output of the **find** command to **grep**, which searches for the dbmspool.sql file.

For more details on file management commands, see Chapter 8.

Additional UNIX Utility Commands

UNIX provides many extra utilities to help you execute UNIX commands for Oracle:

- **grep** There is some debate about what grep is an acronym for. Some say that grep stands for generalized regular expression parser, while others insist that grep is short for global regular expression print.

- **awk** The **awk** command name is short for Aho, Weinberger, Kernighan, the folks who created the **awk** utility.

- **sed** The **sed** utility is short for string editor. It is used to replace strings in UNIX files.

Let's take some brief examples of each of these utilities.

Using grep in UNIX

The **grep** utility is a great way to find UNIX files that contain specific strings. It is always a good idea to invoke **grep** with the **-i** option because **grep** will then find your string regardless of the case of the string.

For example, suppose that you want to find an SQL script that recompiles invalid objects:

```
root> grep -i invalid *.sql
MKSTDROL.sql:/* create role for 'invalid' users    */
RUNTHEM.sql:  4  WHERE STATUS = 'INVALID'
add_view.sql:          'IV', 'Library Cache Invalidation',
invalid.sql:Spool run_invalid.sql
invalid.sql:   status = 'INVALID'
invalid.sql:@run_invalid.sql
locks.sql:               'IV', 'Library Cache Invalidation',
```

Using awk in UNIX

The **awk** utility is especially useful for removing a specific column of output from a UNIX command. For example, suppose you need to create a list of UNIX process IDs for all Oracle processes on your server:

```
root> ps -ef|grep -i oracle|awk '{ print $2 }'
23308
25167
```

```
12193
25163
12155
24065
24073
```

Here you start by issuing the **ps -ef** command to get a list of all UNIX processes, and then use **grep** to filter out all processes except those that contain the string **oracle**.

Finally, you use the **awk** utility to extract the second column of output:

```
root> ps -ef|grep -i oracle
    oracle 23308    1  0    May 14 ?        0:06 ora_lgwr_prodb1
    oracle 25167    1  0    Apr 30 ?        0:26 ora_smon_prodc1
    oracle 25163    1  0    Apr 30 ?       41:27 ora_lgwr_prodc1
    oracle 12155    1  0 11:30:43 ?         0:01 oracleprodcars (LOCAL=NO)
    oracle 24065    1  0    Apr 30 ?        0:02 ora_pmon_rman
    oracle 24073    1  0    Apr 30 ?       10:39 ora_ckpt_rman
    oracle 24846    1  0    May 11 ?        0:48 oracleprodc1 (LOCAL=NO)

root> ps -ef|grep -i oracle|awk '{ print $2 }'

23308
25167
12193
25163
12155
24065
24073
```

Using sed in UNIX

The **sed** command is used to make global changes to strings in UNIX files. For example, in the following example you have a utility that will change all strings in a directory from one string to another. This is sort of a "change all" utility within UNIX. The format of the **sed** command is:

sed/oldstring/newstring > new file location

The **sed** utility always makes a new copy of every file it changes, so special care is required to make an in-place change. Note the **sed** line in this script where **sed** changes the old string to the new string in all files in the directory. Note that this script makes a backup of the files in a tmp subdirectory before issuing the change.

chg_all.sh

```
#!/bin/ksh

tmpdir=tmp.$$

mkdir $tmpdir.new

for f in $*
```

```
do
  sed -e 's/oldstring/newstring/g' < $f > $tmpdir.new/$f
done

# Make a backup first!
mkdir $tmpdir.old
mv $* $tmpdir.old/


cd $tmpdir.new
mv $* ../

cd ..
rmdir $tmpdir.new
```

Next, let's take a quick look at various UNIX tools that allow you to view and edit UNIX files.

Viewing and Editing Files in UNIX

UNIX provides several commands and utility programs for viewing the contents of data files. They are often very foreign and cryptic to the UNIX beginner, but it is critical to the effective management of Oracle that you become comfortable with these powerful tools:

- **The vi editor** Pronounced "vee-eye," this is a powerful text-processing program, which, once mastered, is far faster than any text editor known to personal computers. Inside the vi editor, every key (both uppercase and lowercase) performs an editing function. For vi read-only access, files can be accessed using the **view** command.

- **The cat command** The **cat** (concatenate) command, like the MS-DOS **type** command, displays the contents of a file on the screen. For example, entering the command **cat food** would display the entire food file on your screen.

- **The more command** The **more** command is used to display a file one screen at a time. For example, entering the command **more food** would list the food file's first screen. You press the SPACEBAR for the next screen of text.

- **The head command** The **head** command is used to display the first lines of a file. For example, entering the command **head start** would display the first three lines of the start file.

- **The tail command** The **tail** command is used to display the last lines in a file. For example, entering the command **tail gating** would display the last three lines of the gating file.

Let's take a quick look at some of these commands

The UNIX cat Command

In addition to displaying the contents of UNIX files, the **cat** command can be used to join files together. For example, the following command will join together three Oracle trace files and mail them to the DBA:

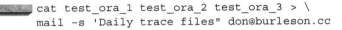

```
cat test_ora_1 test_ora_2 test_ora_3 > \
mail -s 'Daily trace files" don@burleson.cc
```

The UNIX head and tail Commands

The **head** and **tail** commands operate in exactly the same fashion in UNIX, and they are very useful for the Oracle DBA who wants to view only a portion of a UNIX file.

The most common use of the **tail** command for the Oracle DBA is monitoring a file as it becomes full. For example, during an Oracle export, you might want to monitor the new lines being added to the export log file. For this you can use the **tail -f** command to monitor the log:

```
root> tail -f exp_customer.log
```

The **tail** command is also useful for looking at new lines at the bottom of your Oracle alert log. For example, the following command will display the last 100 lines of the Oracle alert log:

```
root> tail -100 $DBA/$ORACLE_SID/bdump/alert_$ORACLE_SID.log|more
```

Note that output of the **tail** command is being piped to the **more** command so that you can view the alert log one page at a time.

Next, let's explore some important UNIX file management commands.

File Management in UNIX

The Oracle DBA is charged with the total maintenance of all of the files that comprise the Oracle software. As such, it is imperative that the Oracle DBA fully understand how to manage UNIX files and directories. This management includes allocating new files, removing old trace and dump files, and managing the growth of the Oracle data files on the server.

The UNIX touch Command

The UNIX **touch** command is used to create an empty file with the proper owners and permissions. This is the equivalent to the IEFBR14 utility on a mainframe computer, where a file is created without any contents.

```
root> touch test.exe

root> ls -al test*

-rw-r-----   1 oracle   dba             0 Aug 13 09:43 test.exe
```

Now let's take a common Oracle example of the **touch** command. First, you enter the UNIX pfile alias that you have placed in your .profile file. This takes you to the location of your Oracle alert log, and the **ls -al** command shows you the file. Note that you are using a more sophisticated command prompt that displays your current working directory. This allows you to see the changes in directory locations.

```
cheops*testsid-/export/home/oracle
root> pfile

cheops*testsid-/u01/app/oracle/admin/testsid/pfile
> ls -al
total 26140
drwxr-xr-x   2 oracle   dba          2048 Jul 18 13:36 .
drwxr-xr-x   9 oracle   dba          2048 Feb 19  2001 ..
-rw-r--r--   1 oracle   dba          2301 Aug 22 13:01 inittestsid.ora
-rw-r--r--   1 oracle   dba          1840 Mar 13 23:00 inittestsid.ora.bkup
```

Next, use the **mv** command to move the alert log to another name. You do this so future **grep** commands will not show old results.

```
cheops*testsid-/u01/app/oracle/admin/testsid/pfile
> mv inittestsid.ora inittestsid.ora.old
```

Now you can re-create an empty alert log file with the **touch** command. Of course, this is not required since Oracle will automatically reallocate the alert log file the first time the DBA needs to write an alert message:

```
cheops*testsid-/u01/app/oracle/admin/testsid/pfile
> touch inittestsid.ora
```

Now the **ls -al** command shows your old and your new alert log files:

```
cheops*testsid-/u01/app/oracle/admin/testsid/pfile
> ls -al
```

```
total 26140
drwxr-xr-x    2 oracle    dba          2048 Sep  4 16:57 .
drwxr-xr-x    9 oracle    dba          2048 Feb 19  2001 ..
-rw-r--r--    1 oracle    dba             0 Sep  4 16:57 inittestsid.ora
-rw-r--r--    1 oracle    dba          1840 Mar 13 23:00 inittestsid.ora.bkup
-rw-r--r--    1 oracle    dba          2301 Aug 22 13:01 inittestsid.ora.old
```

Controlling UNIX File Permission with umask

UNIX has a default permission mask that is used by default by everyone who accesses the Oracle server. This permission mask is known as **umask**, and the value of **umask** controls the default file permissions whenever you create a new UNIX file.

Normally the **umask** is set systemwide in the /etc/profile file so it applies to all users on the system. However, often the Oracle DBA will override the default **umask** by resetting it in their login file (.profile or .cshrc).

The values for **umask** are different depending upon whether the file is executable. The **umask** for the creation of new executable files is calculated based on the value of **umask**. In this case, you have set **umask=022**:

```
 777 Default Permissions
-022 Subtract umask value, for example
-----
 755 Permissions of new file
```

For executable files, the value of **umask** is computed by taking the difference between 777 (read-write-execute) and the actual value of **umask**. The following table illustrates:

umask Value	022	001	143
File permission	755	776	637
Total	777	777	777

In the example that follows, the default **umask** of 022 will leave a file with a permission of 755 (owner read-write-execute, all others read-only) as shown here:

```
root> umask
022

root> touch test.exe

root> ls -al test.exe

-rwxr-xr-x    1 oracle    dba             0 Jan 22 05:36 test.exe
```

For another example, say you wanted all **oracle**-owned files to be completely private, so that only **oracle** could write to them and only members of the DBA group could read them. You would want permissions of 740. To do this, you will reset **umask** to 037:

```
root>umask 037

root>touch test1.txt

root>ls -al test1*

-rw-r-----   1 oracle   dba            0 Aug 13 09:43 test1.txt
```

UNIX umask for Oracle Text Files

The **umask** for the creation of new text files is calculated as follows:

```
 666 Default Permissions
-022 Subtract umask mask, for example
-----
 644 Permissions for new file
```

This example shows that given the default **umask** of 666, and subtracting your sample **umask** value of 022, new text files are created with mode 644, which states that the owner can read and write the file, while members of the group to which the file belongs and everyone else can only read the new file.

The UNIX chmod Command

The UNIX **chmod** command (pronounced "schmod") is used to change the execution permissions of a UNIX file. The **chmod** command is based on the permissions we covered in the **umask** section, and the **chmod** permissions can be assigned either by number (see Table 1-6) or by a letter value.

Owner	Group	World	Meaning
7	7	7	Read + write + execute
6	6	6	Write + execute
5	5	5	Read + execute
4	4	4	Read only

TABLE 1-6.   *The UNIX Numerical File Permissions*

Owner	Group	World	Meaning
2	2	2	Write only
1	1	1	Execute only

TABLE 1-6.   *The UNIX Numerical File Permissions* (continued)

For example, assume that you want to allow all UNIX users in the DBA group to write to your Oracle initialization files. You first need to check the existing permissions:

```
root> ls -al

total 56
drwxr-sr-x   2 oracle    dba            512 Aug 31 1999  ./
drwxr-sr-x   8 oracle    dba            512 Apr 13 08:28 ../
-rw-r--r--   1 oracle    dba            819 May 23 16:11 configPUS1.ora
-rw-r--r--   1 oracle    dba           4435 May 26 15:00 initPUS1.ora
```

Here you see that the **-rw-r--r-** equates to a permission of 644 because **-rw** equals 6 and **r--** equals 4. To add write permissions to the group entry, you must change the permissions from 644 to 664:

```
root> chmod 664 *

root> ls -al

total 56
drwxr-sr-x   2 oracle    dba            512 Aug 31 1999  ./
drwxr-sr-x   8 oracle    dba            512 Apr 13 08:28 ../
-rw-rw-r--   1 oracle    dba            819 May 23 16:11 configPUS1.ora*
-rw-rw-r--   1 oracle    dba           4435 May 26 15:00 initPUS1.ora*
```

You must remember that the default UNIX file permissions are dependent upon the value of the **umask** parameter. To illustrate, let's create several files on the UNIX server:

```
root> umask
022
root> touch t.exe u.ora v.sql
root> ls -al
total 6
drwxr-xr-x   2 oracle    dba            512 Sep  3 15:40 .
drwxr-xr-x  22 oracle    dba           2048 Sep  3 15:40 ..
-rw-r--r--   1 oracle    dba              0 Sep  3 15:40 t.exe
-rw-r--r--   1 oracle    dba              0 Sep  3 15:40 u.ora
-rw-r--r--   1 oracle    dba              0 Sep  3 15:40 v.sql
```

Note that because of the **umask** being equal to 022, each of the files is created with a permission of 644. Let's use the **chmod** command to change the permissions to all of the files to 755:

```
root> chmod 755 *

root> ls -al
total 6
drwxr-xr-x   2 oracle   dba         512 Sep  3 15:40 .
drwxr-xr-x  22 oracle   dba        2048 Sep  3 15:40 ..
-rwxr-xr-x   1 oracle   dba           0 Sep  3 15:40 t.exe
-rwxr-xr-x   1 oracle   dba           0 Sep  3 15:40 u.ora
-rwxr-xr-x   1 oracle   dba           0 Sep  3 15:40 v.sql
```

As we have already noted, the **chmod** command can be used with letter-based permission masks (see Table 1-7).

Let's see how this works. In the absence of a designator (**u**, **g**, or **o**), the **chmod** command makes the change for user, group, and others. In the **chmod** command that follows, you make all .ksh files executable for anyone:

```
root> ls -al
-rw-r--r--   1 oracle   dba           0 Sep  3 15:40 t.exe
-rw-r--r--   1 oracle   dba           0 Sep  3 15:40 u.ora
-rw-r--r--   1 oracle   dba           0 Sep  3 15:40 v.sql

root> chmod +x *

root>ls -al
-rwxr-xr-x   1 oracle   dba           0 Sep  3 15:40 t.exe
-rwxr-xr-x   1 oracle   dba           0 Sep  3 15:40 u.ora
-rwxr-xr-x   1 oracle   dba           0 Sep  3 15:40 v.sql
```

Of course, you do the same operation with the numeric **chmod** command. Since the execution permissions are 644, you use 755 to make all executable:

```
root> ls -al
-rw-r--r--   1 oracle   dba           0 Sep  3 15:40 t.exe
-rw-r--r--   1 oracle   dba           0 Sep  3 15:40 u.ora
-rw-r--r--   1 oracle   dba           0 Sep  3 15:40 v.sql

root> chmod 755 *

root> ls -al
-rwxr-xr-x   1 oracle   dba           0 Sep  3 15:40 t.exe
-rwxr-xr-x   1 oracle   dba           0 Sep  3 15:40 u.ora
-rwxr-xr-x   1 oracle   dba           0 Sep  3 15:40 v.sql
```

User (u)	Group (g)	Others (o)	Meaning
rwx	rwx	rwx	Read + write + execute
rw	rw	rw	Read + write
rx	Rx	rx	Read + execute
wx	wx	wx	Write + execute
r	R	r	Read only
w	W	w	Write only
x	X	x	Execute only

TABLE 1-7.   *The UNIX **chmod** Letter Designations*

As we noted, you can also preface the **chmod** command with a reference to the user (**u**), group (**g**), or others (**o**). For example, consider the following **chmod** command to allow others (**o**) to get write and execute permission:

```
root> ls -al
-rw-r--r--   1 oracle   dba            0 Sep  3 15:40 t.exe
-rw-r--r--   1 oracle   dba            0 Sep  3 15:40 u.ora
-rw-r--r--   1 oracle   dba            0 Sep  3 15:40 v.sql

root> chmod o+wx *

root>ls -al
-rw-r--rwx   1 oracle   dba            0 Sep  3 15:40 t.exe
-rw-r--rwx   1 oracle   dba            0 Sep  3 15:40 u.ora
-rw-r--rwx   1 oracle   dba            0 Sep  3 15:40 v.sql
```

Again, please note that this is equivalent to changing the permissions from 644 to 647 as shown here:

```
root> ls -al
-rw-r--r--   1 oracle   dba            0 Sep  3 15:40 t.exe
-rw-r--r--   1 oracle   dba            0 Sep  3 15:40 u.ora
-rw-r--r--   1 oracle   dba            0 Sep  3 15:40 v.sql

root> chmod 647 *

root> ls -al
-rw-r--rwx   1 oracle   dba            0 Sep  3 15:40 t.exe
```

```
-rw-r--rwx   1 oracle   dba          0 Sep  3 15:40 u.ora
-rw-r--rwx   1 oracle   dba          0 Sep  3 15:40 v.sql
```

You can also use the **chmod** command to revoke permissions on file. In the following example, you revoke all permissions for read, write, and execute access for everyone except the owner. Essentially, you are changing the permissions from 647 to 700:

```
root> ls -al
-rw-r--rwx   1 oracle   dba          0 Sep  3 15:40 t.exe
-rw-r--rwx   1 oracle   dba          0 Sep  3 15:40 u.ora
-rw-r--rwx   1 oracle   dba          0 Sep  3 15:40 v.sql

root> chmod 700 *

root> ls -al
-rwx------   1 oracle   dba          0 Sep  3 15:40 t.exe
-rwx------   1 oracle   dba          0 Sep  3 15:40 u.ora
-rwx------   1 oracle   dba          0 Sep  3 15:40 v.sql
```

TIP
*You can use **chmod** to save an Oracle password in a UNIX file. There are times when you have shell scripts that access Oracle and want to store the Oracle password in a UNIX file, so that only the UNIX **oracle** user can read the file. In this example, you create a file with the Oracle SYSTEM password and **chmod** the file so that only the UNIX **oracle** user can view the contents:*

```
root>echo manager>system_password.file

root> chmod 400 *.file

root> ls -al
-r--------   1 oracle   dba          8 Sep  3 16:17 system_password.file
```

This technique is very useful when you want to write a shell script to access Oracle and you want to keep the password in a single file.

The **chmod** command also has a set of plus operators (**+**) that can be used to add read (**+r**), write (**+w**), or execute (**+x**) to a file. For example, let's assume you are changing some Korn shell scripts and you want to make them unexecutable for everyone until you have completed the change:

```
root> chmod -x *.ksh

root> ls -al *.ksh

-rw-r--r--  1 oracle   dba        205 May 10 09:11 a.ksh
-rw-r--r--  1 oracle   dba        303 May 10 09:11 lert.ksh
-rw-r--r--  1 oracle   dba        312 Jul 19 11:32 back.ksh
-rw-r--r--  1 oracle   dba        567 May 10 09:12 coun.ksh
```

Once the maintenance is complete, the scripts can again be made executable with the **chmod +x** command:

```
root> chmod +x *.ksh

root> ls -al *.ksh

-rwxr-xr-x  1 oracle   dba        205 May 10 09:11 a.ksh*
-rwxr-xr-x  1 oracle   dba        303 May 10 09:11 lert.ksh*
-rwxr-xr-x  1 oracle   dba        312 Jul 19 11:32 back.ksh*
-rwxr-xr-x  1 oracle   dba        567 May 10 09:12 coun.ksh*
```

Next, let's take a look at a very important area of Oracle UNIX administration, the management of UNIX directories.

Directory Management in UNIX

In this section, we cover the UNIX commands that are used to create, manage, and navigate between UNIX directories.

The UNIX pwd Command

The **pwd** command is short for "print working directory," and it tells you where you are located in the UNIX tree structure. For example, here you issue the **pwd** command to see your current directory:

```
root>pwd
/export/home/oracle
```

The **pwd** command is very important, and many Oracle professionals place the **pwd** command in their command prompt so they always know their current directory. This is done by setting the UNIX PS1 system variable:

```
PS1="
`hostname`*\${ORACLE_SID}-\${PWD}
```

```
>"
export PS1
```

Now the UNIX prompt will change to always show you your hostname, the
$ORACLE_SID, and the current working directory:

```
cheops*testsid-/u01/app/oracle/admin/testsid/pfile
>pwd
/u01/app/oracle/admin/testsid/pfile
```

The UNIX ls Command

The UNIX **ls** command is one of the most frequently used UNIX commands.
Without any arguments, the **ls** command will show you a list of all files in your
current directory:

```
root> ls
Mailbox                 invalid.sql                    run_rpt.ksh
ad.sql                  kill_oracle_sessions.ksh       run_trunc.lst
adamf_techeops           l.ksh                          run_trunc.sql
admin                   list.lst                       schools.dmp
afiedt.buf              list2.lst                      scripts
arsd.dmp                lockee.txt                     sql
bksel.lst               lst.lst                        sqlnet.log
```

When you add the **-a** and **-l** arguments, you can see all of the details for each
file in your current working directory:

```
root> ls -al
total 928188
drwxr-xr-x  21 oracle     dba            2048 Aug 22 20:47 .
drwxr-xr-x  10 root       root            512 Jul 26 08:49 ..
-rw-------   1 oracle     qmail           437 Aug 12 20:43 .bash_history
drwxr-xr-x  11 oracle     qmail           512 Sep  3 2000  .dt
-rwxr-xr-x   1 oracle     qmail          4381 Jul 16 13:20 .profile
-rwxr-xr-x   1 oracle     qmail          3648 Sep  1 2000  .profile_old
-rw-------   1 oracle     dba            2264 Sep  3 08:06 .sh_history
drwxr-xr-x   2 oracle     dba             512 May 10 11:10 .ssh
-rw-------   1 oracle     dba            3861 May 29 06:03 Mailbox
-rw-r--r--   1 oracle     dba           12632 Apr 11 16:09 ad.sql
drwxr-xr-x   2 oracle     dba             512 Jan 26 2001  adamf_techeops
drwxr-xr-x   5 oracle     dba             512 Sep  4 2000  admin
-rwxr-xr-x   1 oracle     dba              55 Aug 22 11:56 afiedt.buf
```

Let's take a look at each of the columns in the **ls -al** command so you understand
their meaning (see Table 1-8).

Column	Data
1	File permissions
3	File owner
4	File group
5	File size
6	Last modified date
7	Filename

TABLE 1-8.   *The Columns in the **ls -al** UNIX Command*

The first column is the **ls -al** command which shows the file permissions. The permissions are a set of letters arranged in a group of three: one for the file owner, one for the file group, and another for the world (Figure 1-3).

Let's illustrate how this works with some examples (see Table 1-9).

The third and fourth columns of the **ls -al** command list the owner and group of the file. The file owner is noted in UNIX at the time that the file is initially created. If you have superuser authority (root) you can change the owner and group of any file with the **chown** command.

The fifth column is the file size in bytes, and the last column is the name of the file.

Displaying "Dot" Files in UNIX

The **-a** option of the **ls** command is used to display the dotfiles, which are not normally seen with the **ls** command. There are several dotfiles that are of special interest to the Oracle DBA:

- ■ **Command history files**   These files keep a complete audit of each and every UNIX command issued by the UNIX user. They include .sh_history, .bash_history, and .ksh_history

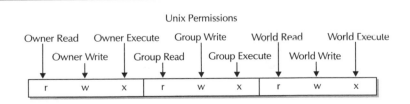

FIGURE 1-3.   *UNIX file permissions*

Permission	Meaning
-rw-------	This file has read-write permissions for the owner.
-rw-r--r--	This file has read-write permissions for the owner.
drwxr-xr-x	This directory has read-write-execute permissions for the owner, read-execute for the group, and read-execute for the world.
-r-xr-----	This file has read-execute permissions for the owner, and read permission for the group.
-r--------	This file has read permission for the owner.
-rw-rw-r--	This file has read-write permissions for the owner and the group, and read permission for the world.

TABLE 1-9. *UNIX File Permission Examples*

■ **Login files** These files contain login scripts that are executed every time the user signs on to UNIX. They include .profile, .cshrc, .kshrc and .bshrc

The UNIX cd Command

The UNIX change directory (**cd**) command is very useful for navigating in your Oracle directory structure. The **cd** command without any arguments takes you to the location of your UNIX home directory. The UNIX home directory is specified in the /etc/passwd file and defines where you will be immediately after a UNIX logon.

```
sting*testc1-/u01/app/oracle/admin/testc1/pfile
>cd

sting*testc1-/export/home/oracle
>
```

When you give **cd** a directory location, you are transferred to that location. In this example, you transfer to the $ORACLE_HOME/rdbms/admin directory:

```
sting*testc1-/export/home/oracle
>cd $ORACLE_HOME/rdbms/admin

sting*testc1-/u01/app/oracle/product/8.1.7_64/rdbms/admin
>
```

UNIX also has a very handy **cd** argument for switching back and forth between two directories. In this example, you use the **cd -** command to bounce back and forth from the pfile directory and the /etc directory:

```
sting*testc1-/u01/app/oracle/admin/testc1/pfile
>cd /etc

sting*testc1-/etc
>cd -
/u01/app/oracle/admin/testc1/pfile

sting*testc1-/u01/app/oracle/admin/testc1/pfile
>cd -
/etc

sting*testc1-/etc
>
```

You can also use the **cd ..** command to go up one level in your directory tree. In this example, you navigate from the pfile directory where the init.ora file is located to the bdump directory where the Oracle alert log is located (see Figure 1-4).

```
sting*testc1-/u01/app/oracle/admin/testc1/pfile
>cd ../bdump

sting*testc1-/u01/app/oracle/admin/testc1/bdump
>
```

Removing UNIX Files and Directories

UNIX provides the **rm** command for removing data files. Of course, the **rm** command can be very dangerous, and most Oracle DBAs make an alias for **rm**, invoking the **rm**

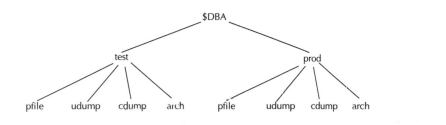

FIGURE 1-4.   *The OFA tree and **cd** navigation*

-i option. The **rm -i** option prompts you to confirm you are certain that you want to remove the file:

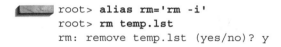

```
root> alias rm='rm -i'
root> rm temp.lst
rm: remove temp.lst (yes/no)? y
```

While UNIX provides an **rmdir** command for removing directories, UNIX also provides the capability to remove entire directories by using the **rm -Rf** command. The **-R** option tells **rm** to recursively cascade through subdirectories, and the **-f** option says to force deletion, even if the permissions do not allow write access. In the example that follows, you can see that the **rm -I** alias warns you if you want to examine the files in the directory before removing them:

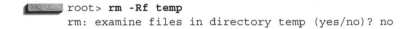

```
root> rm -Rf temp
rm: examine files in directory temp (yes/no)? no
```

CAUTION
*Don't ever try this. To demonstrate the horrible power of the **rm** command, the following command (when executed as root) will permanently remove all files on your entire server!*

```
root> cd /
root> rm -Rf *
```

Now that we have covered the basic UNIX commands, let's take a closer look at how Oracle DBAs use UNIX commands in the Oracle environment.

The Oracle Environment in UNIX

When you log on to UNIX, a special login file is executed to establish your UNIX environment. These login commands perform the following functions:

- Basic UNIX environment commands
- Setting the UNIX command line editor
- Setting Oracle aliases
- Setting a standard UNIX command prompt
- Changing your Oracle UNIX environment

Basic UNIX Environment Commands

There are several things that need to be done when you log on to UNIX. These login commands define your whole environment and are critical to your success in UNIX. Let's start with the basic environment command.

Set Your Shell Environment

Your first choice is which shell you want as your default. Your choices are C shell (**csh**), Bourne shell (**sh**), Korn shell (**ksh**), or the Bourne Again shell (**bsh**). In the following example, you set your default shell to the Korn shell:

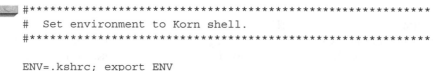

```
#***********************************************************
#   Set environment to Korn shell.
#***********************************************************

ENV=.kshrc; export ENV
```

Set Your umask Parameter

The **umask** parameters set the default file permissions for every file you create in UNIX. In the following example, you set the **umask** to 022:

```
#*************************************************************
#   Set the umask to have 755 for executables and 644 for text
#*************************************************************
umask 022
```

Set Your UNIX Terminal Type

The following command sets the terminal type for your session:

```
#*************************************************************
#   Set the terminal to vt100
#*************************************************************
DBABRV=ora; export DBABRV
ORACLE_TERM=vt100; export ORACLE_TERM
TERM=vt100; export TERM
```

The UNIX Command Line Editor

In UNIX, your login profile file (.profile, .kshrc) issues UNIX commands at logon time to allow you to easily navigate in UNIX. The commands in your logon profile set your terminal type, your command line editor, and other shortcuts that make UNIX navigation easy.

The most important command is the **set -o** command because it defines the command line editor. Let's take a closer look at how the command line editor makes your life in UNIX easier.

UNIX allows you to set the type of command editor. Once set, you can use a variety of shortcuts to quickly redisplay previous UNIX commands. These shortcut commands will greatly reduce the amount of typing at the UNIX prompt, and you can always recognize a UNIX guru because of their use of these command shortcuts. There are two common settings for the command line editor, **emacs** and **vi**.

■ **set -o emacs** This command sets the emacs editor for editing online UNIX commands.

■ **Command completion** The **emaces** setting allows you to complete long filenames by pressing the ESCAPE key twice (<esc><esc>). For example, to **vi** the file oracle_script_for_checking_permissions.ksh, you could enter **vi oracle <esc><esc>**, and the command line will display:

```
root> vi oracle_script_for_checking_permissions.ksh
```

■ **Display previous commands** The emacs editor allows you to view prior commands by pressing the <ctrl> p keys.

■ **set -o vi** This command sets the vi editor for online UNIX commands. Once a command is displayed at the UNIX prompt you can use standard vi commands to edit the command. In addition, the **set -o vi** command allows for easy searches of the UNIX command history.

■ **Command completion** The vi setting allows you to complete long filenames by pressing ESCAPE backslash (<esc> \). For example, to **vi** the file oracle_script_for_checking_permissions.ksh, you could enter **vi oracle <esc> **, and the command line will display:

```
root> vi oracle_script_for_checking_permissions.ksh
```

■ **Display previous commands** The vi editor allows you to view prior commands by pressing the <esc> k key.

■ **Search the command history** You can search for a specific command in your command history and display it on your command line by pressing the ESCAPE key and the forward slash (<esc> /). For example, to redisplay a command that contains ksh, you would enter **<esc> /**, followed by **ksh**. The matching command will then be displayed on your command line.

To automatically set this value, you can place the following code in your login file (.profile, .kshrc, .cshrc):

```
#******************************************************************
# Backspace and Keyboard editor setting
# This setting allows the following shortcuts:
#    <esc> k                 to display command history
#    <esc> \                 for command completion
#    <esc> / searchstring    to find a command in the history file
#******************************************************************
stty erase ^?

set -o vi

export EDITOR=vi
```

Once you have set your basic UNIX environment, you are ready to look at setting your UNIX environment for Oracle.

Oracle Aliases for UNIX

A UNIX alias is a short command that is replaced with a larger command to save typing time. For example, you could create an alias to allow you to count the number of connected users on your oracle server:

```
root> alias numuse='who|wc -l'
root> numuse
463
```

The whole point of UNIX aliases is to save typing. Here is a list of common UNIX aliases that can be added to your UNIX logon file for the UNIX Oracle user. These aliases perform common Oracle functions such as checking the Oracle alert log and transferring quickly between directories.

```
#*******************************
# UNIX aliases for Oracle DBAs
#*******************************
   alias alert='tail -100 \
         $DBA/$ORACLE_SID/bdump/alert_$ORACLE_SID.log|more'
   alias errors='tail -100 \
         $DBA/$ORACLE_SID/bdump/alert_$ORACLE_SID.log|more'
   alias arch='cd $DBA/$ORACLE_SID/arch'
   alias bdump='cd $DBA/$ORACLE_SID/bdump'
   alias cdump='cd $DBA/$ORACLE_SID/cdump'
   alias pfile='cd $DBA/$ORACLE_SID/pfile'
   alias rm='rm -i'
   alias sid='env|grep ORACLE_SID'
   alias admin='cd $DBA/admin'
```

The most important alias here is the alias for the **rm** command. By dynamically replacing **rm** with **rm -i**, you guarantee that you do not accidentally remove an important Oracle file from UNIX.

To illustrate how useful aliases are in Oracle administration, in the following example you can get to your pfile directory in a single command so you can view the contents of your init.ora file:

```
cheops*CPRO-/home/oracle
> pfile
cheops*CPRO-/u01/app/oracle/CPRO/pfile
>ls
initCPRO.ora
```

Aliases can also be used for sophisticated Oracle commands. For example, the following alias can be used to display all Oracle errors in the last 400 lines of the alert log:

```
cheops*testsid-/u01/app/oracle/admin/envtest/pfile
>alias errors='tail -400 $DBA/$ORACLE_SID/bdump/alert_$ORACLE_SID.log|\
    grep ORA-'

cheops*testsid-/u01/app/oracle/admin/envtest/pfile
>errors
ORA-00604: error occurred at recursive SQL level 1
ORA-01089: immediate shutdown in progress - no operations are permitted
ORA-00604: error occurred at recursive SQL level 3
ORA-01089: immediate shutdown in progress - no operations are permitted
```

A Standard UNIX Prompt for Oracle Users

Placing the following code snippet in your **oracle** user login file will give you a standard UNIX prompt that identifies your current server name, the database name your environment is set for (the value of your $ORACLE_SID UNIX variable), and your current working directory. This standard prompt makes it very easy to know where you are when navigating UNIX.

```
#****************************************************************
# Standard UNIX Prompt
#****************************************************************
PS1="
`hostname`*\${ORACLE_SID}-\${PWD}
>"
```

This standardized Oracle UNIX prompt has the advantage of displaying the server name, the ORACLE_SID, and the current directory. The best feature of the standard command prompt is that it also places the command prompt on the next line so you can have a full 80 characters in which to type UNIX commands:

```
cheops*CCPRO-/home/oracle
>pwd

/home/oracle

cheops*CCPRO-/home/oracle
>cd /u01/oradata/CPRO

cheops*CCPRO-/u01/oaradata/CPRO
>
```

Changing Your Oracle Environment in UNIX

One of the confounding problems of UNIX is the bewildering number of things that must be reset every time you change your environment from one Oracle database to another database on the same UNIX server. Oracle provides a command script called **oraenv** to reset your Oracle environment, but it has several problems, and most experienced DBAs issue the following commands to change from one ORACLE_SID to another:

```
export ORAENV_ASK=NO;\
export ORACLE_SID='$DB';\
.TEMPHOME/bin/oraenv;\
export ORACLE_HOME;\
export ORACLE_BASE=\
  `echo ORACLE_HOME | sed -e 's:/product/.*::g'`;\
export DBA=$ORACLE_BASE/admin;\
export SCRIPT_HOME=$DBA/scripts;\
export PATH=$PATH:$SCRIPT_HOME;\
export LIB_PATH=$ORACLE_HOME/lib:$ORACLE_HOME/lib:/usr/lib '
```

Obviously, this is a lot of typing! Rather than reset all of these Oracle variables, experienced DBAs create a UNIX alias with the same name as the ORACLE_SID. When the ORACLE_SID is entered at the command prompt, all of the required commands are executed.

The best solution to the problem of resetting the Oracle environment is to create an alias for every Oracle database on your UNIX server. The following is the login profile code to perform this function:

```
#****************************************************************
# For every Oracle_SID in /var/opt/oracle/oratab,
# create an alias using the SID name.
```

```
# Now, entering the ORACLE_SID at the UNIX prompt will completely set the
# UNIX environment for that SID
#*****************************************************************

for DB in `cat /var/opt/oracle/oratab| \
grep -v \#|grep -v \*|cut -d":" -f1`
do
    alias $DB='export ORAENV_ASK=NO; export ORACLE_SID='$DB'; .
TEMPHOME/bin/oraenv; export ORACLE_HOME; export ORACLE_BASE=`echo
ORACLE_HOME | sed -e 's:/product/.*::g'`; export DBA=$ORACLE_BASE/admin;
xport SCRIPT_HOME=$DBA/scripts; export PATH=$PATH:$SCRIPT_HOME; export
IB_PATH=$ORACLE_HOME/lib:$ORACLE_HOME/lib:/usr/lib '
    done
```

Let's take a close look at how this works. First you have a FOR loop in UNIX. Let's decompose this command and see what it is doing:

```
for DB in `cat /var/opt/oracle/oratab|\
grep -v \#|grep -v \*|cut -d":" -f1`
```

The **for DB in** command means that the script will loop once for each value of $DB.

The argument to the **for DB in** command is enclosed in *graves* (pronounced "gra-vees"), which is the back-tick character (directly above the TAB key on a PC keyboard). Arguments enclosed in graves tell UNIX to execute the command enclosed in the graves and return the result set to UNIX.

In this case, you can see that the command in the graves first performs a **cat** on the var/opt/oracle/oratab file (/etc/oratab in AIX). This lists all databases defined on the UNIX server:

```
root>cat /var/opt/oracle/oratab
test9i:/u01/app/oracle/product/8.1.7_64:Y
testc1:/u01/app/oracle/product/8.1.7_64:Y
#testc2:/u01/app/oracle/product/8.1.7_64:Y
testman:/u01/app/oracle/product/8.1.7_64:Y
```

Next, you see the **grep -v \#** and the **grep -v *** commands. These ignore any lines in the oratab file that are commented out:

```
root>cat /var/opt/oracle/oratab|grep -v \#|grep -v \*
test9i:/u01/app/oracle/product/8.1.7_64:Y
testc1:/u01/app/oracle/product/8.1.7_64:Y
testman:/u01/app/oracle/product/8.1.7_64:Y
```

Next, you issue the **cut -d":" -f1** command. This extracts the first column in the oratab file using a colon (:) as the column delimiter:

```
root>cat /var/opt/oracle/oratab|grep -v \#|grep -v \*|cut -d":" -f1
test9i
testc1
testman
```

You now have a list of valid $ORACLE_SID values. Inside the **for** loop, you create an alias with the value of $DB (the $ORACLE_SID name), and perform all of the required changes to reset the UNIX environment for that database.

Next, let's look at the processes of dissecting complex UNIX commands. It is the job of the Oracle DBA in UNIX to be able to interpret complex UNIX commands so you can understand their meaning and manage the commands.

Dissecting Complex UNIX Commands

UNIX neophytes are often frightened when they see some of the cryptic commands used in UNIX. However, once you learn to use the pipe command to join together UNIX commands, you will have a very powerful tool for creating one-line commands. For example, the following shows a one-line UNIX command that locates and kills all Oracle processes for a specific Oracle database on a server:

```
ps -ef|grep "ora_"|grep $ORACLE_SID|-v grep| \
awk '{ print $2 }'|-exec rm -f {} \;
```

At first glance, this powerful UNIX command appears to be a conglomeration of cryptic letters. However, upon closer examination you can see that this UNIX command is actually a series of commands that are joined together with the pipe operator 1. When viewed this way, your command can be viewed as a connected list of commands

```
ps -ef
|
grep "ora_"
|
grep $ORACLE_SID
|
grep -v grep
|
awk '{ print $2 }'
|
-exec rm -f {} \;
```

By expanding the command onto separate lines (using the 1 character as a delimiter), you can examine each subcommand and see how each successive command refines the output from the prior UNIX command (see Figure 1-5).

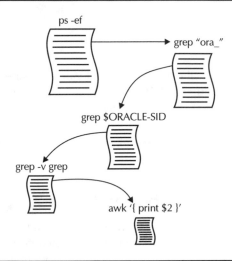

FIGURE 1-5.   *Dissecting a complex UNIX command*

Once you see the individual commands that comprise the whole UNIX script, you are ready to begin understanding each component. From Figure 1-5 you can also see that the result set becomes smaller and more refined with each subsequent command.

Deciphering a Complex UNIX Command

In this example, we will examine a one-line UNIX command that is used to kill all Oracle background processes for a specified database on the UNIX server. As an Oracle DBA, there are times when it is necessary to kill all Oracle processes, or a selected subset of Oracle processes. This is a common UNIX script used by an Oracle DBA who wants to kill all Oracle processes when the Oracle database is locked up, and the database cannot be stopped with the standard Oracle utilities.

CAUTION
Remember that it is only in rare cases where you cannot connect to Oracle that you need to use UNIX to kill your instance. Oracle does not endorse this to stop a database unless a very extreme condition is encountered.

To start, let's look at the syntax of the UNIX **kill** command. The basic format of the UNIX **kill** command is as follows, and a single **kill** command can be used to kill many UNIX processes (PIDs):

```
root> kill -9 process1 process2 process3
```

Since you see that the **kill** command can accept a list of processes, your goal is to gather a list of processes from UNIX and send them as arguments to the **kill** command. To continue the example, the following command will kill all Oracle processes for your server because of the **-exec** syntax.

```
ps -ef|grep "ora_"|grep -v grep|awk '{print $2}'|-exec kill -9 {} \;
```

Let's take a closer look at the steps within this command.

The **ps -ef** UNIX command displays all active processes on the server. However, you want to limit your command to only those processes that are related to the Oracle database.

The **grep "ora_"** command removes all but the Oracle background processes:

```
root> ps -ef|grep "ora_"

oracle 13022     1   0   Sep 30      -   0:18 ora_db02_vald
oracle 14796 42726   0 09:00:46   pts/0  0:00 grep ora_
oracle 17778     1   0   Sep 30      -   0:14 ora_smon_devp
oracle 18134     1   0   Sep 30      -   0:37 ora_snp1_vald
oracle 19516     1   0   Sep 30      -   0:24 ora_db04_prod
oracle 21114     1   0   Sep 30      -   0:37 ora_snp0_devp
oracle 28436     1   0   Sep 30      -   0:18 ora_arch_prod
```

The **grep -v grep** is used to remove the second line from the above output. If you don't specify **grep -v grep**, the subsequent **kill** command will kill your own process. The **grep -v** is the opposite of **grep**. Where **grep** is used to find strings, the **grep -v** command is used to exclude lines with the specified string. In the output that follows, note that the **grep** line is now missing from your output:

```
root> ps -ef|grep "ora_"|grep -v grep

oracle 13022     1   0   Sep 30      -   0:18 ora_db02_vald
oracle 17778     1   0   Sep 30      -   0:14 ora_smon_devp
oracle 18134     1   0   Sep 30      -   0:37 ora_snp1_vald
oracle 19516     1   0   Sep 30      -   0:24 ora_db04_prod
oracle 21114     1   0   Sep 30      -   0:37 ora_snp0_devp
oracle 28436     1   0   Sep 30      -   0:18 ora_arch_prod
```

You now use the UNIX **awk** command. As we have discussed, the **awk** or the **cut** command can be used to extract specific columns from a result set. In this case, you use **awk '{ print $2 }'** to get the second column which is the process ID for these processes. You now have a list of process IDs to send to the **kill** command:

```
root> ps -ef|grep "ora_"|grep -v grep|awk '{ print $2 }'

13022
17778
18134
19516
21114
28436
28956
```

Now you have a clean list of process IDs for the Oracle background processes and you are ready to ship this list to yet another UNIX command. To ship the list to the next command, pipe the list of PIDs to the UNIX **kill** command by using the **-exec** UNIX command. The **-exec** command accepts a list as an argument and performs any UNIX command on the input set.

NOTE
If you are using HP-UX or AIX you can also use the **xargs** *command for this purpose.*

```
ps -ef|grep "ora_"|grep -v grep|awk '{ print $2 }'|-exec kill -9 {} \;
```

Once you have built the complex command, you can encapsulate the command into a single UNIX alias:

```
alias nukem = "ps -ef|grep "ora_"|grep -v grep| \
   awk '{ print $2 }'|-exec rm -f {} \;"
```

Now entering the **alias nukem** alias at the UNIX command prompt will invoke your complex command to kill all Oracle background processes. Of course, the example is for illustration purposes only, since a prudent Oracle DBA would never risk assigning such a dangerous command to an alias.

Conclusion

The purpose of this chapter has been to introduce you to the basic UNIX commands that are used by the Oracle DBA. We have briefly covered the most common UNIX commands and inspected UNIX commands that are used to sample files and directories. The main points of this chapter include:

- Understanding the different dialects of UNIX

- The syntax of common UNIX commands

- Piping together multiple UNIX commands

- UNIX commands for directory and file management

- Setting and changing your Oracle UNIX environment

- Deciphering complex UNIX commands

We are now ready to move on and take a closer look at UNIX server management. The next chapter will cover the internal mechanisms of the UNIX architecture and show the UNIX commands and utilities used by the Oracle DBA to monitor load on the server.

CHAPTER
2

UNIX Server
Management

his chapter is devoted to the management of the Oracle server in a UNIX environment. There are entire books that have been written about using UNIX to monitor a server, but this chapter will concentrate on those tools and techniques that are used by the Oracle DBA to monitor and manage their Oracle UNIX server.

This chapter is organized to begin with an overview of the basics of the UNIX architecture and move quickly into UNIX commands to manage processes, memory, and semaphores. We will also look at UNIX tools and utilities to help you track the performance of your Oracle UNIX server. This chapter will cover the following topics:

- Process internals for UNIX

- Memory management in UNIX

- Process commands in UNIX

- Memory commands in UNIX

- Displaying UNIX kernel parameters

- Displaying system log messages

- UNIX server monitoring

Let's begin by exploring how the UNIX operating system manages processes.

Process Internals for UNIX

The center of the UNIX operating system is called the UNIX kernel. The kernel is used to implement the interface between UNIX processes to all hardware devices such as disks, RAM, and the CPU.

User processes interact with UNIX by making system calls to UNIX. These system calls include base UNIX commands such as **open()**, **read()**, **write()**, **exec()**, **malloc()**, and so on, and these system calls are intercepted by the UNIX kernel and processed according to specific rules (see Figure 2-1).

Let's take a closer look at how a UNIX task operates within the UNIX operating system.

The Run Queue and the Sleep Queue in UNIX

When a UNIX user process communicates with UNIX, the process is placed into a temporary "sleep" state until the system call is completed. This is known as the *sleep queue*, and it is where UNIX tasks wait while UNIX system calls are being serviced on their behalf. The process of a UNIX task sleeping and reawakening is

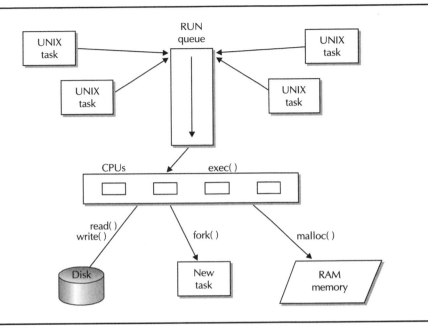

FIGURE 2-1. *User processes interacting with UNIX*

called *context switching.* Active UNIX processes will commonly have context switching as they change from active to waiting states.

All UNIX tasks enter the UNIX run queue whenever they require UNIX services. This is sometimes called the *dispatch queue,* and the run queue is a list of processes that is prioritized by UNIX according to the task's dispatching priority, which is called the *nice* value and is determined by the **priocntl** system call in UNIX (see Figure 2-2).

Let's take a closer look at the interaction between Oracle and UNIX at the process level.

Process Command Execution

To illustrate the communications between UNIX and Oracle, let's use the example of a UNIX script that accesses Oracle to display rollback segment information. Because of the complex details and differences in UNIX dialects, this example has been deliberately oversimplified for illustration purposes.

This script is invoked by passing the ORACLE_SID as an argument to the command such as:

```
./rollstat.ksh myprod
```

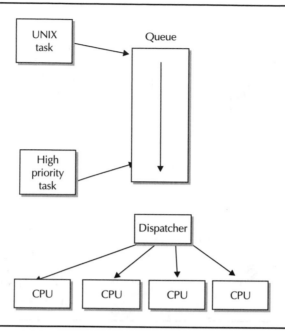

FIGURE 2-2. *The UNIX run queue*

rollstat.ksh

```ksh
#!/bin/ksh

# First, we must set the environment . . . .
export ORACLE_SID=$1
ORACLE_HOME=`cat /etc/oratab|grep ^$ORACLE_SID:|cut -f2 -d':'`
export ORACLE_HOME
PATH=$ORACLE_HOME/bin:$PATH
export PATH

$ORACLE_HOME/bin/sqlplus system/manager<<!

select * from v\$rollstat;

exit
!
echo All Done!
```

Note the reference to the **v$rollstat** view in the UNIX script as **v\$rollstat**. In UNIX, you must place a back-slash character in front of every dollar sign in all SQL commands to tell UNIX that the dollar sign is a literal value and not a UNIX shell command.

When you execute this script in UNIX, the script performs the following UNIX system calls:

1. fork(get_rollstat.ksh)

2. read(/etc/oratab)

3. fork(sqlplus)

4. read(file#,block#)

5. write(v$rollstat contents)

6. write("All Done")

Let's explore how UNIX forks subprocesses in order to service a task.

The Fork System Call

The **fork()** system call directs UNIX to spawn a subtask to service the request. In this case, your Korn shell script will fork two subprocesses (see Figure 2-3).

These forked processes are visible by using the UNIX **ps -ef** command. In the example that follows, you **grep** for all processes owned by **oracle**, and then use the **grep -v** command to remove all Oracle background processes. As you may know, the Oracle background processes (**pmon**, **smon**, **arch**, and so on) are all identified by a UNIX process in the form **ora_*processname_ORACLE_SID***, so that you'll see processes with names like **ora_ smon_testsid**, and **ora_pmon_prod**, and so on.

```
root> ps -ef|grep ora|grep -v ora_

oracle 12624 12622   0 12:07:17 pts/5    0:00 -ksh
oracle 12579 12624   0 12:06:54 ?        0:00 oracletestsid
```

Look closely at the above **ps -ef** listing and note that the first columns are as follows:

- Column 1: Process_owner_name
- Column 2: Process_ID
- Column 3: Parent process_ID

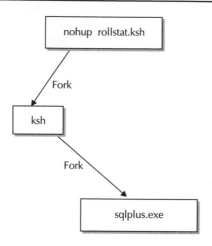

FIGURE 2-3. *Forking a UNIX process*

As you see, whenever a fork occurs, you can track backwards to see the originating process. Here you see that your UNIX session (process 12622) has forked process 12624 when the Korn shell script was started. Process 12624, in turn, has forked process 12579 to manage the connection to SQL*Plus. Here is a step-by-step description of this interaction.

NOTE
The interactions in UNIX are very complicated, and these examples have been made deliberately simple to illustrate the basic concepts.

1. Here you see that the initial task waits in the run queue for service.

2. Upon reaching the head of the run queue, the ksh script is started. It issues the **read()** command to inspect the **/etc/oratab** file and the context switch places it into a sleep state until the I/O is complete.

3. Upon receiving the desired data, the process re-enters the run queue and waits until it can issue the **fork()** command to start SQL*Plus. At this point the context switch is set to sleep until the SQL*Plus process has completed.

4. The SQL*Plus command instructs the Oracle to issue a **read()** command to fetch the desired view information from the RAM memory in the SGA (The V$ views are in RAM, not on disk). Upon completion of the read, a **write()**

command is issued to display the results to the standard out device.
SQL*Plus then terminates and sends a signal back to the owner process.

5. The owner process (ksh) then has a context switch and reawakens. After
   reaching the head of the run queue, it issues a **write()** command to standard
   output to display the "All Done" message.

The UNIX Buffer Cache

Just as Oracle has data buffer caches in RAM memory, UNIX also utilizes a RAM buffer
to minimize unnecessary disk I/O. This buffer is commonly known as the Journal File
System or JFS buffer. When Oracle data is retrieved from the Oracle database, the data
block often travels through several layers of RAM caches (see Figure 2-4).

As we see in Figure 2-4, when Oracle makes a request to fetch a data block, the
Oracle data buffer is first checked to ensure that the block is not already in the Oracle
buffer. If it is not, the UNIX JFS buffer will then be checked for the data block. If the
data block is not in the JFS buffer, the disk array buffer is then checked. Only when
none of these three buffers contains the data block is a physical disk read incurred.

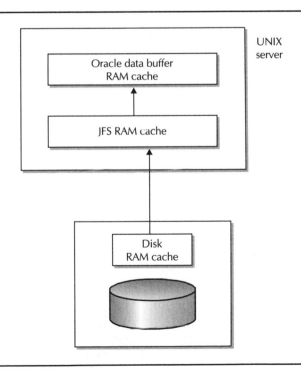

FIGURE 2-4. *Multiple UNIX RAM buffer caches*

The JFS Buffer and Oracle Raw Devices

Because of the high amount of I/O that many Oracle systems experience, many Oracle DBAs consider the use of "raw" devices. A raw device is defined as a disk that bypasses the I/O overhead created by the Journal File System (JFS) in UNIX. The reduction in overhead can improve throughput, but only in cases where I/O is already the bottleneck for the Oracle database. Furthermore, raw devices require a tremendous amount of manual work for both the Oracle administrator and the system administrator. Oracle recommends that raw devices should only be considered when the Oracle database is I/O bound. However, for these types of Oracle databases, raw devices can dramatically improve overall performance. If the database is not I/O bound, switching to raw devices will have no impact on performance.

In many UNIX environments such as AIX, raw devices are called virtual storage devices (VSDs). These VSDs are created from disk physical partitions (PPs), such that a single VSD can contain pieces from several physical disks. It is the job of the system administrator to create a pool of VSDs for the Oracle administrator. The Oracle administrator can then take these VSDs and combine them into Oracle datafiles. This creates a situation where an Oracle datafile may be made from several VSDs. This many-to-many relationship between Oracle datafiles and VSDs makes Oracle administration more challenging.

In summary, raw devices for Oracle databases can provide improved I/O throughput only for databases that are already I/O bound. However, this performance gain comes at the expense of increased administrative overhead for the Oracle administrator. We also know that raw devices will only improve the performance of Oracle databases whose Oracle subsystem is clearly I/O bound. For systems that are not I/O bound, moving to raw devices will not result in any performance gains.

Now that you have a general idea of how UNIX tasks operate, let's take a look at how RAM memory is managed in UNIX.

TIP

On some UNIX systems, DirectIO is available, offering the same performance as raw devices with the added feature of manageability. Oracle8i was the first release to support this feature. Also, Veritas has a product called QuickIO that bypasses the JFS buffers.

Memory Management in UNIX

Most operating systems today possess what is commonly called virtual memory. In a virtual memory configuration it is possible to extend the existing RAM memory with the use of special *swap disk* areas. Memory management in UNIX is critical to the performance of any Oracle database. As you may know from your Oracle DBA 101 training, the RAM regions of Oracle are designed to improve the speed of data access by several orders of magnitude. In other words, RAM is more than 10,000 times faster to access than going to a disk device for the data. Hence, it's important that RAM memory always stays within the actual RAM cache and is not swapped out to the swap disk. Let's take a close look at how this works.

Virtual Memory in UNIX

Virtual memory is an internal "trick" that relies on the fact that not every executing task is always referencing its RAM memory region. Since all RAM regions are not constantly in use, UNIX has developed a paging algorithm that moves RAM memory pages to the swap disk when it appears that they will not be needed in the immediate future (see Figure 2-5).

As memory regions are created, UNIX will not refuse a new task whose RAM requests exceed the amount of RAM. Rather, UNIX will page out the least recently referenced RAM memory page to the swap disk to make room for the incoming request. When the physical limit of the RAM is exceeded, UNIX can wipe out RAM regions because they have already been written to the swap disk.

When the RAM region is removed to swap, any subsequent references by the originating program require UNIX copy *page in* the RAM region to make the memory accessible. UNIX page in operations involve disk I/O and are a source of slow performance. Hence, avoiding UNIX page in operations is an important concern for the Oracle DBA.

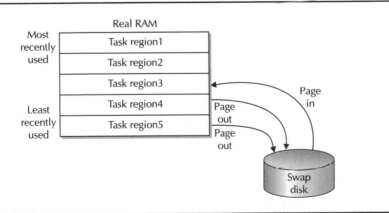

FIGURE 2-5. *RAM demand paging in UNIX*

The Page Out Operation

UNIX will commonly *page out* RAM pages in anticipation of additional demands on the RAM memory region. This asynchronous writing of RAM pages is generally done for all memory regions that are marked as swappable. For details on making the Oracle SGA non-swappable, please see the special **init.ora** parameters described later in this chapter.

In sum, a page out does not cause the RAM memory region to be physically moved out of the RAM, and it is only a preparatory phase. In case UNIX decides to flush the region from RAM, you will have already copied the RAM contents to the swap disk.

Now let's look at what happens when a RAM memory page is purged from physical RAM.

The Page In Operation

A page out is no cause for concern because UNIX has not yet decided to actually remove the region from RAM. However, then UNIX performs a page in, disk I/O is involved, and the requesting tasks will have to wait a long time (milliseconds) while UNIX fetches the region from the swap disk and reloads it into the RAM region.

Hence, RAM page in operations can be disastrous to the performance of Oracle tasks, and the Oracle DBA must constantly be on the lookout for page ins and take appropriate action to remedy the problem.

A section later in this chapter on the **vmstat** utility will show you how to detect page in operations, and you can remedy page in operations in several ways:

- Add additional RAM to the UNIX server

- Reduce the SGA size for your database by lowering the size of the data block buffers

- Mark the critical RAM regions (such as the Oracle SGA) as non-swappable

Now that you understand the basics of RAM management in Oracle, let's take a close look at UNIX commands to manage processes in UNIX.

Jobs of the Oracle DBA and the UNIX System Administrator

In many Oracle shops, computer professionals called system administrators are responsible for the setup, configuration, and tuning of the Oracle database server. The abilities of system administrators vary widely, from excellent support and cooperation to neophyte support and complete non-cooperation.

Because of the tight coupling between database performance and server performance, it is imperative that the Oracle DBA has access to the tools described below. By themselves, the system administrators will not have enough information about what is happening inside the database to properly tune the server. Conversely, the DBA cannot get the information they need to properly configure Oracle if they cannot get access to the server monitor utilities.

Many Oracle shops give **root** access to the DBA so they will have full control over their database server. The system administrator continues to be responsible for the configuration and system software on the server, but the DBA accepts responsibility for setting the kernel parameters and managing the interface layer between Oracle and the operating system environment.

A small minority of shops will restrict access to the **root** account, but these shops will provide the Oracle DBA with access to all of the server monitor tools and system utilities. In either case, it is imperative that the Oracle DBA have access to the system monitor tools.

Process Management Commands in UNIX

This section deals with common UNIX commands to manipulate executing UNIX processes. Let's start with the UNIX **ps** command.

The UNIX ps Command

In Chapter 1, we showed how the **ps** command can be used to display UNIX processes, and we are now ready to look at some more advanced uses of the **ps** command.

This section is designed to provide a basic overview of management of Oracle processes. The basic process management command is the **ps** command. The **ps** command is commonly used to display active processes and the characteristics of active processes.

An inspection of the **ps -ef** command shows the following column values (see Table 2-1).

```
root> ps -ef

UID     PID    PPID   C    STIME      TTY  TIME CMD
oracle 12231     1    0  05:33:06      -   3:15 oracletest (LOCAL=NO)
oracle 24634     1    0  12:57:10      -   4:54 oracletest (LOCAL=NO)
```

Now that you see the general format of the **ps** command, let's look at additional uses of the **ps** command for Oracle.

Col	Header	Description
1	UID	The user ID that owns the process.
2	PID	The process ID for the task.
3	PPID	The parent process. If the parent is 1, the process was created by root.
4	TIME	The current CPU time used by the process.
5	CMD	The UNIX command that is being executed.

TABLE 2-1. *Columns in the **ps -ef** Command*

Display Top CPU Consumers with ps

The following command can be used to display the top CPU consumers on any UNIX server. Note that the **sort +7** command displays the CPU column. This is because the **ps** columns are counted from left to right, with the first column being column 0.

```
root> ps -ef|sort +7|tail
      root    512    1   0   Aug 10  ?       0:53 /usr/lib/osa/bin/arraymon
      root    460    1   0   Aug 10  ?       1:22 /usr/sbin/cron
      root      1    0   0   Aug 10  ?       2:26 /etc/init -
      root    565    1   0   Aug 10  ?       6:12 /usr/bin/perl /pixlog.pl
      root    471    1   0   Aug 10  ?       9:10 /usr/sbin/nscd
   netsaint   765    1   0   Aug 10  ?      27:16 helpdesk/netsaint.cfg
      root    742  572   0   Aug 10  ?      32:04 opt/VRTSvmsa
      root    454    1   0   Aug 10  ?      44:09 /usr/sbin/syslogd
      root      3    0   0   Aug 10  ?     363:12 fsflush
```

Here you see the tasks in order of their total CPU consumption, with the largest value at the end of the list. In cases where a process has been running for more than one day, the display format changes. In these cases, the time format changes and column 6 is the CPU column.

```
root> ps -ef|sort +6|tail
      root   5440  2094   0   05:33:06   -   0:47 /usr/sbin/syslogd
      root   9244     1   0   15:34.21   -   3:26 ./pdimapsvr.ip -D0
      root  10782     1   0   05:73:11   -   4:41 ./pdiconsvr.ip -D0
      root   5990  2094   0   05:01:77   -   5:33 /usr/sbin/snmpd
```

```
root    4312    1   0   08:43:06    -   7:14 /usr/sbin/cron
root    4448 2094   0   02:33:07    -   9:25 /usr/sbin/rwhod
root       1    0   0   02:33:05    - 198:59 /etc/init
root    2450    1   0   01:33:22    - 438:30 /usr/sbin/syncd 60
```

In the real world, the Oracle DBA will issue this command twice, once with column 5 and again with column 6.

Using the ps auxgw Command in HP-UX and AIX

Another approach to finding top CPU consumers on your UNIX server is to use the **ps auxgw** command. The third column of this listing (%CPU) shows the percentage of CPU used. Hence, the following command will display the top CPU users:

```
root> ps auxgw|sort +2|tail
```

```
oracle 14922 0.6 1.0 8300 5720  - A  01:01:46 2:57 oracleprod
oracle 22424 0.6 1.0 8328 6076  - A  07:48:43 0:21 oracleprod
oracle 44518 0.8 1.0 8080 5828  - A  08:47:47 0:02 oracleprod
oracle 20666 1.0 1.0 8304 6052  - A  08:15:19 0:22 oracleprod
oracle 13168 1.6 1.0 8196 5760  - A  05:33:06 3:15 oracleprod
oracle 17402 2.5 1.0 8296 6044  - A  07:27:04 2:06 oracleprod
oracle 25754 2.5 1.0 8640 6388  - A  08:10:03 1:03 oracleprod
oracle 41616 4.5 1.0 8312 6052  - A  07:00:59 4:57 oracleprod
```

Using egrep to Identify Top CPU Consumers

Yet another approach uses the extended **grep** command **egrep** to display the top CPU consumers. In the output below, you see a root process called **kproc** using 88.3 percent of the CPU:

```
root> ps augxww|egrep "RSS| "|head
```

```
USER      PID %CPU %MEM   SZ  RSS TTY STAT STIME   TIME COMMAND
root      516 88.3  0.0   16    4  - A      Nov 21 194932:05 kproc
oracle  41616  4.4  1.0 8312 6052  - A    07:00:59  4:57
oracle  20740  2.7  1.0 8140 5888  - A    08:52:32  0:02
oracle  17402  2.4  1.0 8296 6044  - A    07:27:04  2:06
oracle  25754  2.4  1.0 8640 6388  - A    08:10:03  1:03
oracle  13168  1.6  1.0 8196 5760  - A    05:33:06  3:15
oracle  20666  1.0  1.0 8304 6052  - A    08:15:19  0:22
oracle  14922  0.6  1.0 8300 5720  - A    01:01:46  2:57
oracle  44518  0.6  1.0 8080 5828  - A    08:47:47  0:02
```

Show Number of Active Oracle Dedicated Connection Users

Another common command is to use **ps** to count the number of dedicated UNIX connections that have been spawned by the Oracle listener. If you are not using the multithreaded server, this command will give you an accurate count of the number of Oracle connections on the UNIX server.

```
root> ps -ef|grep $ORACLE_SID|grep -v grep|grep -v ora_|wc -l

    121
```

The UNIX kill Command

As we noted in Chapter 1, there are times when it is necessary to kill all Oracle processes or a selected set of Oracle processes. You may want to kill all Oracle processes when the database is "locked" and you cannot enter server manager and gracefully stop the database.

When you are forced to terminate Oracle on a UNIX server, you have to perform the following steps:

1. Kill all Oracle processes associated with the ORACLE_SID.

2. Use the **ipcs -pmb** command to identify all held RAM memory segments, then use the **ipcrm -m** command to release the RAM memory from UNIX.

3. Use the **ipcs -sa** command to display held semaphores and then use the **ipcrm -s** command to release the held semaphores for the instance.

As we noted in Chapter 1, you can create a single command to terminate all Oracle processes associated with your hung database instance:

```
root> ps -ef|grep $ORACLE_SID| \
        grep -v grep|awk '{print $2}'|xargs -i kill -9 {}
```

You can then check for held memory using the **ipcs -pmb** command and remove the memory held by the database:

```
root> ipcs -pmb
IPC status from /dev/kmem as of Mon Sep 10 16:45:16 2001
T     ID      KEY         MODE        OWNER  GROUP  SEGSZ    CPID  LPID
Shared Memory:
m   24064 0x4cb0be18  --rw-r-----  oracle    dba 28975104   1836 23847
m       1 0x4e040002  --rw-rw-rw-    root   root    31008    572   572
m       2 0x411ca945  --rw-rw-rw-    root   root     8192    572   584
m    4611 0x0c6629c9  --rw-r-----    root   root  7216716   1346 23981
m       4 0x06347849  --rw-rw-rw-    root   root    77384   1346  1361
```

Here you see that the only RAM memory segment owned by Oracle is ID=24064. The following command will release this memory segment:

```
root> ipcrm -m 24064
```

Killing Stubborn UNIX Processes

There are times when a UNIX process cannot be killed, even with the powerful **kill -9** command. In these cases, a special trick is required to force the UNIX task to terminate. If you have a situation where a process continues to display with the **ps** command, even after you have issued a **kill -9** command against the process, you can use this trick.

The stubborn process can be killed by piping the null device (/dev/null) to the ttyname as a part of the kill command. The following command is indispensable when killing stubborn UNIX tasks:

```
root> cat /dev/null > /dev/ttyname kill -9 pid#
```

Displaying Kernel Values in UNIX

UNIX has a wealth of kernel parameters that are very important to the Oracle professional. The setting for memory, semaphores, and other kernel tuning parameters can have a huge impact on the performance of the Oracle server. We will begin with a general overview of the commands used to display kernel values in each major dialect of UNIX.

Displaying Server Values in HP-UX

The HP-UX dialect of UNIX will have different commands depending on the version of HP-UX that you are running. In all versions of HP-UX, the **lsdev** command will display the names of all of the devices on your UNIX server.

```
root> lsdev
      Character      Block       Driver        Class
            0          -1        cn            pseudo
            3          -1        mm            pseudo
           16          -1        ptym          ptym
           17          -1        ptys          ptys
           27          -1        dmem          pseudo
           28          -1        diag0         diag
           46          -1        netdiag1      unknown
           52          -1        lan2          lan
```

In HP-UX version 11, the command is different. Here we display all kernel parameters for an HP-UX version 11 server:

```
root> kmtune

Parameter               Value
=======================================================================
NSTRBLKSCHED            2
NSTREVENT               50
NSTRPUSH                16
NSTRSCHED               0
STRCTLSZ                1024
STRMSGSZ                65535
acctresume              4
acctsuspend             2
aio_listio_max          256
aio_max_ops             2048
aio_physmem_pct         10
aio_prio_delta_max      20
bufcache_hash_locks     128
bufpages                (NBUF*2)
chanq_hash_locks        256
create_fastlinks        0
dbc_max_pct             50
dbc_min_pct             5
default_disk_ir         0
desfree                 0
dnlc_hash_locks         64
dontdump                0
dskless_node            0
dst                     1
initmodmax              50
io_ports_hash_locks     64
iomemsize               40000
lotsfree                0
max_async_ports         50
max_fcp_reqs            512
max_mem_window          0
max_thread_proc         64
maxdsiz                 0x04000000
maxdsiz_64bit           0x0000000040000000
maxfiles                60
maxfiles_lim            1024
maxqueuetime            0
maxssiz                 0x00800000
maxssiz_64bit           0x00800000
maxswapchunks           512
maxtsiz                 0x04000000
```

```
maxtsiz_64bit          0x0000000040000000
maxuprc                (NPROC-130)
maxusers               350
maxvgs                 10
mesg                   1
minfree                0
modstrmax              500
msgmap                 (2+MSGTQL)
msgmax                 8192
msgmnb                 16384
msgmni                 50
msgseg                 2048
msgssz                 8
msgtql                 40
nbuf                   0
ncallout               (16+NPROC)
ncdnode                150
nclist                 (100+16*MAXUSERS)
ncsize                 (NINODE+VX_NCSIZE)
ndilbuffers            30
netisr_priority        -1
netmemmax              0
nfile                  (90*(NPROC+16+MAXUSERS)/10+32+2*(NPTY+NSTRPTY+NSTRTEL))
nflocks                500
nhtbl_scale            0
public_shlibs          1
region_hash_locks      128
remote_nfs_swap        0
rtsched_numpri         32
scroll_lines           100
scsi_maxphys           1048576
sema                   1
semaem                 16384
semmap                 (SEMMNI+2)
semmni                 200
semmns                 800
semmnu                 30
semume                 10
semvmx                 32767
sendfile_max           0
shmem                  1
shmmax                 1073741824
shmmni                 500
shmseg                 300
st_ats_enabled         1
vx_ninode              0
vx_noifree             0
vxfs_max_ra_kbytes     1024
vxfs_ra_per_disk       1024
```

The **kmtune** command can be refined with the **grep** command to only display desired classes of values. For example, here you add the **grep** command to only display shared memory variables:

```
root> kmtune|grep -i shm

shmem            1
shmmax           1073741824
shmmni           500
shmseg           300
```

Displaying Server Kernel Values in AIX UNIX

The basic command to display server values in AIX is the **lsdev -C** command. This command will display all of the attached components including disk, memory, CPUs, buses, and other hardware components:

```
root> lsdev -C

sys0        Available 00-00           System Object
sysplanar0  Available 00-00           System Planar
pci0        Available 00-fef00000     PCI Bus
pci1        Available 00-fed00000     PCI Bus
isa0        Available 10-58           ISA Bus
sa0         Available 01-S1           Standard I/O Serial Port
sa1         Available 01-S2           Standard I/O Serial Port
siokma0     Available 01-K1           Keyboard/Mouse Adapter
fda0        Available 01-D1           Standard I/O Diskette Adapter
scsi0       Available 10-60           Wide SCSI I/O Controller
pci2        Defined   20-78           PCI Bus
sioka0      Available 01-K1-00        Keyboard Adapter
sioma0      Available 01-K1-01        Mouse Adapter
hdisk0      Available 10-60-00-0,0    16 Bit SCSI Disk Drive
hdisk1      Available 10-60-00-1,0    16 Bit SCSI Disk Drive
lvdd        Available                 LVM Device Driver
mem0        Available 00-00           Memory
proc0       Available 00-00           Processor
proc1       Available 00-01           Processor
proc2       Available 00-02           Processor
proc3       Available 00-03           Processor
L2cache0    Available 00-00           L2 Cache
pmc0        Available 00-00           Power Management Controller
tty0        Available 01-S1-00-00     Asynchronous Terminal
rootvg      Defined                   Volume group
inet0       Available                 Internet Network Extension
en2         Defined                   Standard Ethernet Network
et0         Defined                   IEEE 802.3 Ethernet Network
```

```
lo0         Available                       Loopback Network Interface
pty0        Available                       Asynchronous Pseudo-Terminal
gxme0       Defined                         Graphics Data Transfer Assist
rcm0        Defined                         Rendering Context Manager
aio0        Available                       Asynchronous I/O
ssa0        Available 10-70                 IBM SSA 160 SerialRAID Adapter
ssa1        Available 20-60                 IBM SSA 160 SerialRAID Adapter
ssar        Defined                         SSA Adapter Router
pdisk0      Available 10-70-3070-09-P SSA160 Physical Disk Drive
pdisk1      Available 10-70-34D0-12-P SSA160 Physical Disk Drive
hdisk2      Available 10-70-L               SSA Logical Disk Drive
hdisk3      Available 10-70-L               SSA Logical Disk Drive
pdisk8      Available 20-60-34D0-13-P SSA160 Physical Disk Drive
pdisk9      Available 20-60-34D0-15-P SSA160 Physical Disk Drive
hdisk10     Available 20-60-L               SSA Logical Disk Drive
hdisk11     Available 20-60-L               SSA Logical Disk Drive
enclosure0  Available 00-00-3070            SSA Enclosure
enclosure1  Available 00-00-34D0            SSA Enclosure
loglv03     Defined                         Logical volume
lv04        Defined                         Logical volume
loglv04     Defined                         Logical volume
scsi1       Available 20-68                 Wide SCSI I/O Controller
rmt0        Available 20-68-00-4,0          Differential SCSI DLT Tape Drive
rmt1        Available 20-68-00-5,0          Differential SCSI DLT Tape Drive
lus         Available                       Legato SCSI User Interface Release
```

To see the base values for the server in AIX, you can enter the **lsattr -El sys0** command. This is useful for displaying UNIX kernel variables that are used by Oracle such as **maxuproc** and **maxbuf**.

root> **lsattr -El sys0**

```
keylock     normal      State of system keylock at boot time
maxbuf      20          Maximum number of pages in block I/O BUFFER CACHE
maxmbuf     0           Maximum Kbytes of real memory allowed for MBUFS
maxuproc    200         Maximum number of PROCESSES allowed per user
autorestart false       Automatically REBOOT system after a crash
iostat      true        Continuously maintain DISK I/O history
realmem     3137536     Amount of usable physical memory in Kbytes
conslogin   enable      System Console Login
fwversion   IBM,L99071 Firmware version and revision levels
maxpout     0           HIGH water mark for pending write I/Os per file
minpout     0           LOW water mark for pending write I/Os per file
fullcore    false       Enable full CORE dump
rtasversion 1           Open Firmware RTAS version
modelname   IBM,9076-WCN  Machine name
systemid    IBM,010013864 Hardware system identifier
```

Next, let's look at UNIX command to display CPU information on your Oracle server.

Displaying the Number of CPU Processors in UNIX

You need to have special commands for each dialect of UNIX to display CPU information. Knowing the number of CPUs is very important to the Oracle DBA because it shows the number of parallel query processes that can be concurrently executing on the UNIX server. Table 2-2 shows the common commands for each major dialect.

Now let's take a close look at the commands for each dialect.

Display the Number of CPUs in HP-UX

In HP-UX, the **ioscan** command is used to display the number of processors:

```
root> ioscan -C processor | grep processor | wc -l
16
```

Display Number of CPUs in Solaris

In Sun Solaris, the **prsinfo** command can be used to count the number of CPUs on the processor:

```
root> psrinfo -v|grep "Status of processor"|wc -l
     2
```

For details about the Solaris CPUs, the **-v** (verbose) option can be used with the **prsinfo** command:

```
root> psrinfo -v
```

```
Status of processor 0 as of: 12/13/00 14:47:41
  Processor has been on-line since 11/05/00 13:26:42.
  The sparcv9 processor operates at 450 MHz,
       and has a sparcv9 floating point processor.
Status of processor 2 as of: 12/13/00 14:47:41
  Processor has been on-line since 11/05/00 13:26:43.
  The sparcv9 processor operates at 450 MHz,
       and has a sparcv9 floating point processor.
```

Display Number of CPUs in Linux

To see the number of CPUs on a Linux server, you can **cat** the /proc/cpuinfo file. In the following example, you can see that your Linux server has four CPUs:

```
root> cat /proc/cpuinfo|grep processor|wc -l
     4
```

UNIX Dialect	Command to Display the Number of CPUs
Linux	cat /proc/cpuinfo|grep processor|wc -l
Solaris	psrinfo -v|grep "Status of processor"|wc -l
AIX	lsdev -C|grep Process|wc -l
HP-UX	ioscan -C processor | grep processor | wc -l

TABLE 2-2. *UNIX Commands to Display the Number of CPUs*

Display CPUs in AIX

The **lsdev** command can be used to see the number of CPUs on an IBM AIX server. Here you see that this AIX server has four CPUs:

```
root> lsdev -C|grep Process|wc -l
      4
```

Using nice and priocntl to Change UNIX Execution Priority

While CPU shortages generally require the addition of more processors on the server, there are some short-term things that you can do to keep running until the new processors arrive. Within the server, all tasks are queued to the CPUs according to their dispatching priority, and the dispatching priority is commonly referred to as the *nice value* for the task. Those tasks with a low nice value are scheduled ahead of other tasks in the CPU queue, while those tasks with a high nice value are serviced later.

In emergency situations where you cannot immediately get more CPUs, you can assign a very low dispatching priority to the Oracle background process, causing them to get CPU cycles ahead of other tasks on the server. This will ensure that Oracle gets all of the CPU that it requires, but it will slow down any external tasks that are accessing the Oracle database. To do this, the system administrator can alter the CPU dispatching priority of tasks with the UNIX **nice** or **priocntl** command. The UNIX **nice** command is used to change dispatching priorities, but these numeric ranges vary by operating system. In general, the lower the nice value, the higher the priority.

Displaying the Nice Values

In UNIX, you can use the **ps -elf** command to see each task and its dispatching priority. In the example below, the NI column shows the existing dispatching priority for the task. Note that there are special nice values—SY (system) and RT (real time)—and these have the highest dispatching priority.

```
root> ps -elf|more
```

F	S	UID	PID	PPID	C	PRI	NI	...	SZ	...	STIME	TTY	TIME	CMD
19	T	root	0	0	0	0	SY	...	0	...	Dec 21	?	0:00	sched
8	S	root	1	0	0	41	20	...	98	...	Dec 21	?	0:00	init -
19	S	root	2	0	0	0	SY	...	0	...	Dec 21	?	0:00	pageout
19	S	root	3	0	1	0	SY	...	0	...	Dec 21	?	22:13	fsflush
8	S	root	182	1	0	41	20	...	217	...	Dec 21	?	0:00	usr/lib
8	S	qmaill	173	161	0	41	20	...	207	...	Dec 21	?	0:00	splog
8	S	root	45	1	0	48	20	...	159	...	Dec 21	?	0:00	devfs
8	S	root	47	1	0	49	20	...	284	...	Dec 21	?	0:00	devf
8	S	root	139	1	0	46	20	...	425	...	Dec 21	?	0:00	syslod
8	S	root	126	1	0	77	20	...	247	...	Dec 21	?	0:00	inetd
8	S	root	1600	1	0	0	RT	...	268	...	Dec 22	?	0:00	xntpd

Changing Nice Values

Again, you need to note that there are huge dialect differences when using the **nice** command. In Linux, you can use **nice** to change the dispatching priority, but in Solaris you must use the **priocntl** command. You must have root authority to change the dispatching priority, and you will need to consult with your system administrator before changing CPU dispatching priorities.

Now that you have an understanding of the processors on an Oracle database server, let's turn our attention to monitoring the RAM memory consumption on your Oracle server.

Memory Management Commands in UNIX

There are numerous tools in UNIX that allow the display and management of RAM memory. These commands fall into two areas:

- Display the amount of RAM on the server
- Display the held RAM memory segments on the server

Let's take a look at each type of command.

Displaying the Total RAM on the UNIX Server

The following commands can be used to see how much RAM memory exists on a server, but they do not show how much RAM is in use. We will be covering those commands in a later section.

In Table 2-3 you see that each dialect of UNIX has very different commands for displaying the amount of total RAM on the UNIX server.

Let's take a closer look at the RAM memory commands on each dialect of UNIX.

Display RAM Memory Size on Tru64 UNIX

In Tru64 UNIX, you need to use the **uerf** command to display RAM memory. Here you issue the **uerf** command with the **-i mem** argument and you can see that you have 3 gigabytes of RAM on this server:

```
root> uerf -r 300 | grep -i mem
3064M
```

NOTE
This command does not work on all versions of Tru64 UNIX. Use this instead—it works on versions 4.0x and 5.x: **/bin/vmstat -P | grep -i mem**.

Display RAM Memory Size on Solaris

The **prtconf** Solaris UNIX command can be used on all Solaris servers to quickly see the amount of available RAM memory:

```
root> prtconf|grep -i mem
```

Display RAM Memory Size on AIX

In the IBM AIX dialect of UNIX, there is a two-step command to display the amount of available RAM memory. You start with the **lsdev** command to show all devices that are attached to the UNIX server. The **lsdev** command produces a large listing of

Dialect of UNIX	RAM Memory Display Command
Tru64 UNIX	uerf -r 300	grep -i mem
Solaris	prtconf|grep -i mem
AIX	lsdev -C|grep mem
Linux	free
HP-UX	swapinfo -tm

TABLE 2-3. *UNIX RAM Memory Display Commands*

all devices, but you can pipe the output from **lsdev** to the **grep** command to refine the display to only show the name of the device that has the RAM memory:

```
root> lsdev -C|grep mem

mem0        Available 00-00            Memory
```

Here you see that mem0 is the name of the memory device on this AIX server. Now you can issue the **lsattr -El** command (passing **mem0** as an argument) to see the amount of memory on the server. In the following example, you can see that this server has 2 gigabytes of RAM memory attached to the mem0 device:

```
root> lsattr -El mem0

size     2048 Total amount of physical memory in Mbytes  False
goodsize 2048 Amount of usable physical memory in Mbytes False
```

Display RAM Size in Linux
In Linux the **free** command can be used to quickly display the amount of RAM memory on the server:

```
root> free
                total       used       free     shared    buffers     cached
Mem:          3728668     504688    3223980      41316     430072      29440
-/+ buffers/cache:         45176    3683492
Swap:          265032        608     264424
```

Next, let's look at how to view the actual usage of RAM memory segments on a UNIX server.

Display RAM Memory in HP-UX
In HP-UX, you use the **swapinfo -tm** command to display the amount of RAM. Here you see that this server has 8 gigabytes of RAM:

```
root> swapinfo -tm
8096
```

Show RAM Swap Usage in HP-UX
The HP-UX dialect of UNIX, you can also use the **swapinfo** command to display the swap usage for a server. In this case, you see the swap disk in the dev column, with 1 gigabyte of swap allocated to the /dev/fs0/lv9 logical volume:

```
root> swapinfo -tam
```

```
              Mb      Mb      Mb   PCT  START/      Mb
TYPE       AVAIL    USED    FREE  USED  LIMIT RESERVE  PRI  NAME
dev         1024      25     999   2%      0       -    1  /dev/fs0/lv9
reserve        -     999    -999
memory      3966    3547     419  89%
total       4990    4571     419  92%      -       0    -
```

Viewing Allocated RAM Memory Segments in UNIX

To see all allocated memory segments on your server, enter the **ipcs** (interprocess control system) command. The **ipcs** command shows all held memory segments on the server, and those owned by the **oracle** user represent the allocated memory for the Oracle System Global Area (SGA).

```
root> ipcs -pmb
IPC status from <running system> as of Mon Sep 10 13:56:17 EDT 2001
T       ID      KEY         MODE         OWNER    GROUP  SEGSZ     CPID
Shared Memory:
m      2400    0xeb595560 --rw-r-----   oracle    dba    281051136 15130
m       601    0x65421b9c --rw-r-----   oracle    dba    142311424 15161
m       702    0xe2fb1874 --rw-r-----   oracle    dba    460357632 15185
m       703    0x77601328 --rw-r-----   oracle    dba    255885312 15231
```

Here you see all of the UNIX RAM memory segments that are associated with each Oracle SGA on the Oracle server. We also see the size of each memory segment and this can give us a clue about which segment is associated with each SGA.

To see the specific memory segments, you can enter SQL*Plus as SYSDBA and issue the **oradebug ipc** command:

```
oracle> sqlplus /nologin

SQL*Plus: Release 8.1.7.0.0 - Production on Mon Sep 10 14:00:02 2001
(c) Copyright 2000 Oracle Corporation.  All rights reserved.

SQL> connect system/manager as sysdba;
Connected.

SQL> oradebug ipc
Information written to trace file.
```

Next, you go to the udump directory where you **cat** the trace file to see the details about the RAM memory segment for this database. In the listing you see the shared memory ID (Shmid) number 703, indicating that 703 is the RAM region associated with this database instance:

```
cheops*testsid-/u01/app/oracle/admin/testsid/bdump
>udump

cheops*testsid-/u01/app/oracle/admin/testsid/udump
>ls -alt|head

total 3212
drwxr-xr-x   2 oracle   dba       4096 Sep 10 14:01 .
-rw-r-----   1 oracle   dba      17721 Sep 10 14:01 testsid_ora_17727.trc
-rw-r-----   1 oracle   dba      17820 Sep 10 14:00 testsid_ora_17690.trc
-rw-r-----   1 oracle   dba        919 Sep  9 01:03 testsid_ora_15231.trc

cheops*testsid-/u01/app/oracle/admin/testsid/udump
>cat testsid_ora_17727.trc

Dump file /u01/app/oracle/admin/testsid/udump/testsid_ora_17727.trc
Oracle8i Enterprise Edition Release 8.1.7.0.0 - 64bit Production
With the Partitioning option
JServer Release 8.1.7.0.0 - 64bit Production
ORACLE_HOME = /u01/app/oracle/product/8.1.7_64
System name:    SunOS
Node name:      cheops
Release:        5.8
Version:        Generic_108528-03
Machine:        sun4u
Instance name: testsid
Redo thread mounted by this instance: 1
Oracle process number: 0
17727
Dump of unix-generic skgm context
areaflags           00000037
realmflags          0000000f
mapsize             00002000
protectsize         00002000
lcmsize             00002000
seglen              00002000
largestsize  0000040000000000
smallestsize 0000000000400000
stacklimit   ffffffff7f87e2ef
stackdir                  -1
mode                     640
magic              acc01ade
Handle:            101e319c0 `/u01/app/oracle/product/8.1.7_64testsid'
Dump of unix-generic realm handle
/u01/app/oracle/product/8.1.7_64testsid', flags = 00000000
 Area #0 `Fixed Size' containing Subareas 0-0
  Total size 0000000000018ebc Minimum Subarea size 00000000
```

```
    Area   Subarea    Shmid       Stable Addr      Actual Addr
       0       0       703 0000000380000000 0000000380000000
                                 Subarea size      Segment size
                                 000000000001a000 000000000f408000
Area #1 `Variable Size' containing Subareas 1-1
  Total size 000000000d774000 Minimum Subarea size 00100000
    Area   Subarea    Shmid       Stable Addr      Actual Addr
       1       1       703 000000038001a000 000000038001a000
                                 Subarea size      Segment size
                                 000000000d800000 000000000f408000
Area #2 `Database Buffers' containing Subareas 3-3
  Total size 00000000007d0000 Minimum Subarea size 00004000
    Area   Subarea    Shmid       Stable Addr      Actual Addr
       2       3       703 000000038eb2e000 000000038eb2e000
                                 Subarea size      Segment size
                                 00000000007d0000 000000000f408000
Area #3 `Redo Buffers' containing Subareas 4-4
  Total size 0000000000104000 Minimum Subarea size 00000000
    Area   Subarea    Shmid       Stable Addr      Actual Addr
       3       4       703 000000038f2fe000 000000038f2fe000
                                 Subarea size      Segment size
                                 0000000000104000 000000000f408000
Area #4 `Lock Manager' containing Subareas 5-5
  Total size 0000000000004000 Minimum Subarea size 00000000
    Area   Subarea    Shmid       Stable Addr      Actual Addr
       4       5       703 000000038f402000 000000038f402000
                                 Subarea size      Segment size
                                 0000000000004000 000000000f408000
Area #5 `Java' containing Subareas 2-2
  Total size 0000000001313000 Minimum Subarea size 00000000
    Area   Subarea    Shmid       Stable Addr      Actual Addr
       5       2       703 000000038d81a000 000000038d81a000
                                 Subarea size      Segment size
                                 0000000001314000 000000000f408000
Area #6 `skgm overhead' containing Subareas 6-6
  Total size 0000000000002000 Minimum Subarea size 00000000
    Area   Subarea    Shmid       Stable Addr      Actual Addr
       6       6       703 000000038f406000 000000038f406000
                                 Subarea size      Segment size
                                 0000000000002000 000000000f408000
Dump of Solaris-specific skgm context
sharedmmu 00000001
shareddec         0
Maximum processes:              = 2000
Number of semaphores per set:   = 62
Semaphores key overhead per set: = 4
User Semaphores per set:        = 58
Number of semaphore sets:       = 35
Semaphore identifiers:          = 35
Semaphore List=
589929
```

```
------------- system semaphore information -------------
IPC status from <running system> as of Mon Sep 10 14:01:29 EDT 2001
T        ID       KEY          MODE       OWNER   GROUP   CREATOR   CGROUP
  Semaphores:
s     6488064    0xd75025fc  --ra-r-----   oracle   dba    oracle     dba
s     1507329    0xd75025fd  --ra-r-----   oracle   dba    oracle     dba
s     1507330    0xd75025fe  --ra-r-----   oracle   dba    oracle     dba
s     1507331    0xd75025ff  --ra-r-----   oracle   dba    oracle     dba
s     1507332    0xd7502600  --ra-r-----   oracle   dba    oracle     dba
s     1507333    0xd7502601  --ra-r-----   oracle   dba    oracle     dba
s     1507334    0xd7502602  --ra-r-----   oracle   dba    oracle     dba
s     1507335    0xd7502603  --ra-r-----   oracle   dba    oracle     dba
s     1507336    0xd7502604  --ra-r-----   oracle   dba    oracle     dba
s     1507337    0xd7502605  --ra-r-----   oracle   dba    oracle     dba
s     1507338    0xd7502606  --ra-r-----   oracle   dba    oracle     dba
s     1507339    0xd7502607  --ra-r-----   oracle   dba    oracle     dba
s     1507340    0xd7502608  --ra-r-----   oracle   dba    oracle     dba
s     1507341    0xd7502609  --ra-r-----   oracle   dba    oracle     dba
```

TIP
When Oracle crashes, sometimes there are memory segments that are held by the server and must be manually deallocated. In the example below, you can remove the SGA memory for this instance. Remember, you only manually remove UNIX memory when Oracle has abnormally terminated.

```
root> ipcrm -m 703
```

Viewing RAM Swap Paging in UNIX

Note that in a later section we show you how to use the **glance** utility to display RAM swap activity.

RAM Paging in AIX

The **lsps -a** command is used in the IBM AIX UNIX dialect to display the swap usage for a server:

 `root> lsps -a`

```
Page Space   Physical Volume   Volume Group   Size    %Used  Active  Auto
paging00     hdisk3            maxvg          40MB      0       no     no
hd6          hdisk0            rootvg         2048MB    3       yes    yes
```

Making Oracle RAM Non-Swappable in HP-UX and Solaris

In several dialects of UNIX (for example HP-UX and Solaris), it is possible to "pin" the SGA on the UNIX server so that it will never become eligible for a page out. This marking of the RAM region as non-swappable tells UNIX never to page out the region and ensures that it always stays in real RAM memory, never going to the swap disk. Note that you cannot do this on IBM AIX. The pinning is done by setting the following **init.ora** parameters.

```
lock_sga=true  --  init.ora parm for hp/ux UNIX
USE_ISM=true -- Sun Solaris "Intimate Shared Memory" init.ora parm
```

Please note that in Oracle8i (release 8.1.5 and greater) for Solaris, the **USE_ISM** parameter becomes a hidden parameter and defaults to True. This means that the SGA will always be non-swappable in Solaris.

Let's begin by looking at how memory is configured for a database server and explore how to manage memory on a large server.

UNIX Server Memory Settings

The first step when tuning server memory is to review the kernel settings that relate to available memory. The kernel settings for memory usage (that is, **SHMMAX**, **SHMMNI**, **db_max_pct**) are critical to effective Oracle performance, and you should double-check all of your kernel parameters to ensure that the server memory is properly configured.

You also must verify the configuration of the swap disk. As you may know, the swap disk is a special system disk that is reserved to accept memory frames that are paged out from physical RAM. Most servers recommend that the size of the swap disk be set to double the amount of physical RAM.

Very Large Memory and Oracle

It is important to note that some servers are not capable of addressing "high memory." The high-memory boundary is a physical constraint that is determined by the bit size of the application, and the only way to utilize above-the-line memory is to use special OS techniques. For example, in all 32-bit versions of Oracle, all memory over 1.7 gigabytes cannot be addressed regardless of the amount of RAM on the server. This can cause a very perplexing problem, since the database server will experience page in operations, while **top** and **glance** utilities report that there is excess memory on the server. In short, the sum of all SGA memory for all of the Oracle instances on the server cannot exceed 1.7 gigabytes. For some UNIX environments, such as Solaris, there are special patches that can be applied on a 32-bit server to allow the DBA to create SGA regions in excess of 2 gigabytes.

If you cannot upgrade to 64-bit Oracle and you want to address memory above the line, operating system techniques can be used. For example, in HP-UX, special patches can be applied to allow Oracle regions to run above 1.7 gigabytes. HP calls this technique "memory windows," and it uses a **SHARED_MAGIC** executable to route application to above-the-line memory regions.

Bear in mind that all 32-bit applications are required to run in low memory. For example, Oracle applications are currently 32 bit and will not be able to address high memory above the 1.7 gigabyte limit. Fortunately, all versions of 64-bit Oracle are capable of addressing high memory. However, you must ensure that your Oracle Database and any other applications are capable of addressing all of the available memory. In the following example, you see a clear case of RAM overload, even though the CPU appears to be 99 percent idle:

TO_CHAR(START_DA	RUNQUE_WAITS	PAGE_IN	SYSTEM_CPU	USER_CPU	IDLE_CPU
06/02/2000 05:01	2	85	1	0	99
06/02/2000 13:47	2	193	0	0	99
06/03/2000 05:04	0	114	2	3	95
06/03/2000 22:31	1	216	0	1	99
06/04/2000 05:02	0	146	1	1	99
06/04/2000 22:34	1	71	1	8	90
06/05/2000 06:57	1	213	0	0	99
06/05/2000 07:25	1	113	0	0	99
06/05/2000 07:35	1	72	0	0	99
06/05/2000 11:06	1	238	0	1	99

Making Oracle SGA RAM Memory Non-swappable

Just like with CPU shortages, the best remedy to a RAM problem is to add additional RAM to the server. However, there are some short-term techniques that can be used to prevent the Oracle SGA memory from paging. On some operating systems, it is possible to use a memory-fencing technique to ensure that the Oracle SGA is never paged out to the swap disk.

Memory Fencing with the lock_sga Initialization Parameter   The **init.ora** parameter **lock_sga** will lock the entire SGA into physical RAM memory, making it ineligible for swapping. The **lock_sga** parameter does not work for Windows NT or AIX, and the setting for **lock_sga** will be ignored. For AIX 4.3.3 and above, you can set the **SHM_PIN** parameter to keep the SGA in RAM; you can get details about this from your AIX documentation.

Solaris Memory Fencing   In Sun Solaris, you can set the **use_ism** parameter to invoke intimate shared memory for the Oracle SGA. In releases of Oracle prior to Oracle8i, you can set the **init.ora** parameter **use_ism=true**. The init.ora parameter

use_ism was rendered obsolete in 8.1.3, and in Oracle8i **use_ism** becomes a hidden parameter that defaults to True. Memory page locking is implemented in Solaris by setting some bits in the memory page's page structure. The page out, which runs if free memory gets low, checks the status of the page's lock fields. If the field is nonzero, the page is considered locked in memory and thus not marked as a candidate for freeing.

CAUTION
*There is a bug associated with **use_ism** on some versions of Solaris. For details, see MetaLink for Note:1057644.6, Note:69863.1, Note:1055268.6, Doc ID 77604.1, Note:48764.1, and Note:1054590.6.*

You can access MetaLink at: http://metalink.oracle.com/home.html
Next, let's look at semaphore management in UNIX.

Semaphore Management in UNIX

A semaphore is a term used for a signal flag used by the Navy to communicate between ships. In some dialects of UNIX, semaphores are used by Oracle to serialize internal Oracle processes and guarantee that one thing happens before another thing. Oracle uses semaphores in HP-UX and Solaris to synchronize shadow processes and background processes. However, AIX UNIX does not use semaphores, and a post/wait driver is used instead to serialize tasks.

The number of semaphores for an Oracle database is normally equal to the value of the **processes** initialization parameter. For example, a database where **processes=200** would need to have 200 UNIX semaphores allocated for the Oracle database.

When allocating semaphores in UNIX, it is critical that your UNIX kernel parameter **semmns** be set to at least double the high-water mark of processes for every database instance on your server. If you fail to allocate enough semaphores by setting **semmns** too low, your Oracle database will fail at startup time with the message:

```
ORA-7279: spcre: semget error, unable to get first semaphore set
```

Let's talk about setting the **semmns** kernel parameter. To make changes in kernel shared memory or semaphore parameters, you need to perform the following steps:

1. Shut down any running Oracle instances.

2. Locate the kernel configuration file for your OS.

3. Make the necessary changes using the system utilities or the vi editor.

Today, most dialects of UNIX have specialized system administration utilities to perform kernel management (see Table 2-4).

System Default Values for Semaphores

The number of UNIX semaphores is determined by the value of the **semmns** UNIX kernel parameter.

Viewing Semaphores in HP-UX Version 11

In HP-UX version 11, the command to display kernel parameters is **kmtune**, and you can **grep** to see the semaphore settings:

```
root> kmtune|grep sem

sema            1
semaem          16384
semmap          (SEMMNI+2)
semmni          200
semmns          800
semmnu          30
semume          10
semvmx          32767
```

Counting Used Semaphores

The **ipcs** UNIX command has a **-sa** option that can be used to display semaphores. The total number of semaphores is determined by summing the NSEMS column in the **ipcs** display. In the example that follows, you see that there are four semaphores held by the **root** user and 475 semaphores held by the **oracle** user in three database instances:

```
root> ipcs -as|grep oracle
IPC status from /dev/kmem as of Mon Sep 10 17:25:21 2001
T  ID     KEY         MODE        OWNER  GROUP   CREATOR   CGROUP NSEMS
s  15 0x00000000 --ra-r-----  oracle  dba     oracle      dba   400
```

Determine What Oracle Database Has a Semaphore Set

As we have noted, when an Oracle database hangs, you may have leftover background processes, held RAM memory segments, and held semaphore sets. When you have multiple instances on a UNIX server and need to release a semaphore set for an Oracle database, you must first determine which semaphore set belongs to your crippled instance.

UNIX Dialect	Utility Name
HP-UX	SAM
SCO	SYSADMSH
AIX	SMIT
Solaris	ADMINTOOL

TABLE 2-4. *UNIX Kernel Management Tools*

Unfortunately, you cannot tell with the **ipcs -sa** command which semaphore set belongs to each Oracle database. Here is the Oracle procedure for determining the semaphore set number for an individual Oracle database so that you can remove the semaphores with the **ipcs** command:

```
root> svrmgrl

Oracle Server Manager Release 2.3.2.0.0 - Production

Copyright (c) Oracle Corporation 1994, 1995. All rights reserved.

Oracle7 Server Release 7.3.2.3.0 - Production Release
With the distributed and replication options
PL/SQL Release 2.3.2.3.0 - Production

SVRMGR> connect internal
Connected.
SVRMGR> oradebug ipc
------------- Shared memory --------------
Seg Id      Address    Size
24064       c1739000   28975104
Total: # of segments = 1, size = 28975104
------------- Semaphores ----------------
Total number of semaphores = 400
Number of semaphores per set = 400
Number of semaphore sets = 1
Semaphore identifiers:
```

In Oracle8i and beyond, you can use SQL*Plus to perform the same function:

```
root> sqlplus /nologin

SQL*Plus: Release 3.3.2.0.0 - Production on Mon Sep 10 17:27:04 2001
```

```
Copyright (c) Oracle Corporation 1979, 1994.  All rights reserved.

SQL> connect system/manager as sysdba;
Connected.
```

Since you cannot get the semaphore set number for the crippled database, you must determine the semaphore set using the process of elimination. You issue the above commands for each live database on the server, and the unclaimed semaphore set will belong to the crippled instance.

Once identified, you can use the following procedure for removing the semaphore set.

Removing a Semaphore Set for Oracle

Start by issuing the **ipcs -sb** command to display details of the semaphore set:

```
root> ipcs -sb|grep oracle
s       67 0x00000000 --ra-r-----     oracle       dba     400
s      223 0x00000000 --ra-r-----     oracle       dba     400
s      334 0x00000000 --ra-r-----     oracle       dba     300
```

Now you can remove the semaphores from the locked-up database. In this example, we'll assume that set 223 is the one for the crippled database:

```
root> ipcrm -s 223
```

Now you can confirm that the semaphores are deleted:

```
root> ipcs -sb|grep oracle

s       67 0x00000000 --ra-r-----     oracle       dba     400
s      334 0x00000000 --ra-r-----     oracle       dba     300
```

Next, let's take a look at how you can examine UNIX system log messages.

Displaying System Log Messages

In UNIX, a system failure will often precipitate an Oracle crash. Any hardware associated with disk, CPU, or RAM may cause an Oracle database crash, and the UNIX system logs can be used to identify the initial cause of the Oracle failure.

The following commands are used to display the UNIX error logs. We need to note that you should regularly check the UNIX logs, even if there is no Oracle failure. These commands can also be useful for detecting transient disk I/O problems, memory failures, and so on.

Show Server Log on HP-UX

In HP-UX you have a file in the /var/adm directory called syslog to hold all UNIX system messages. In the command that follows, you search the syslog for any lines that contain the word "error":

```
root> grep -i error /var/adm/syslog/syslog.log|more

May  1 20:30:08 sprihp01 syslog: NetWorker media: (warning)
dev/rmt/c5t6d0BESTn reading: I/O error
```

Show Server Log on AIX

In the IBM AIX operating system, you use the **errpt** command to display the contents of the system log:

```
root> errpt -a|more
------------------------------------------------------------------------
LABEL:          CORE_DUMP
IDENTIFIER:     C60BB505

Date/Time:      Tue May  9 10:34:47
Sequence Number: 24908
Machine Id:     000138644C00
Node Id:        sp2k6n03
Class:          S
Type:           PERM
Resource Name:  SYSPROC
```

Again, checking the UNIX system logs should be a regular activity for the Oracle DBA. Next, let's take a look at how UNIX can be monitored for performance problems.

UNIX Server Monitoring Commands

UNIX provides a wealth of commands that help the Oracle DBA understand what is happening on the server. We will begin with a discussion of the most popular commands and utilities for monitoring UNIX, including **top**, **svmon**, **glance**, and **vmstat**. In Chapter 3, we will discuss how to use the output from these utilities to determine your overall server performance.

Using the UNIX top Utility

The **top** utility is used to show CPU consumption, RAM memory consumption, and the **top** sessions on a UNIX server. The **top** utility is invoked by entering the **top** command from the UNIX prompt. The output from **top** is displayed in three sections.

The top Load Averages

At the very beginning of the **top** output, you see a series of three numbers. These are the called load average metrics. The *load average* is an arbitrary number that describes the load on the system. The first load average value is the immediate load for the past minute. The next value represents the load average from five minutes ago. The third value is the load average from 15 minutes ago. Whenever the load average rises above 1, you can assume that the processors are fully burdened and you should immediately run **vmstat** to check the run queue values.

Here you start with information on the server load average. The load average is an arbitrary number that describes the load on the server. In general, a number less than 1 is ideal, and here you see three load average values.

The load average display shows the load averages for the past minute, the past five minutes, and the past ten minutes. A low load average is ideal, and the load average should stay below zero. Whenever the value exceeds 1 there may be a CPU overload problem.

```
System: penguin                              Mon Sep 10 17:35:13
001
Load averages: 0.52, 0.38, 0.34
213 processes: 211 sleeping, 2 running
```

The top CPU Summary

The first output from **top** shows the load on each processor and the current **top** sessions in terms of CPU utilization. **top** gives details on each CPU on the server, and you can immediately see from the listing that follows that this server has six CPUs, numbered 0–5:

```
root> top
```

```
Cpu states:
CPU   LOAD   USER    NICE    SYS    IDLE   BLOCK   SWAIT   INTR    SSYS
 0    0.63   10.9%   0.0%    4.0%   85.1%  0.0%    0.0%    0.0%    0.0%
 1    0.40   27.4%   0.0%    7.4%   65.3%  0.0%    0.0%    0.0%    0.0%
---   ----   -  -   -  -   -  -   -----
avg   0.52   19.1%   0.0%    5.7%   75.3%  0.0%    0.0%    0.0%    0.0%

Memory: 100428K (25608K) real, 107920K (30120K) virtual, 328948K free
```

top Sessions

Now let's look at the second section from the **top** command. The second section of **top** output details the current **top** sessions in terms of CPU utilization, as follows:

```
System: core-prod                         Mon Dec 15 08:19:56 2001
Load averages: 0.06, 0.08, 0.03
3172 processes: 3138 sleeping, 34 running
Cpu states:
CPU   LOAD   USER   NICE    SYS    IDLE  BLOCK  SWAIT   INTR   SSYS
 0    0.11   0.0%   0.0%   0.0%  100.0%  0.0%   0.0%   0.0%   0.0%
 1    0.02   0.0%   0.0%   0.0%  100.0%  0.0%   0.0%   0.0%   0.0%
 2    0.02   0.0%   0.0%   0.0%  100.0%  0.0%   0.0%   0.0%   0.0%
 3    0.03   0.0%   0.0%   0.0%  100.0%  0.0%   0.0%   0.0%   0.0%
 4    0.00   0.0%   0.0%   0.0%  100.0%  0.0%   0.0%   0.0%   0.0%
 5    0.01   0.0%   0.0%   0.0%  100.0%  0.0%   0.0%   0.0%   0.0%
---   ----  -----  -----  -----  -----  -----  -----  -----  -----
avg   0.03   0.0%   0.0%   0.0%  100.0%  0.0%   0.0%   0.0%   0.0%

Memory: 736056K (417860K) real, 733560K (422192K) virtual, 1101512K free  Page#
1/54

CPU TTY    PID USERNAME PRI NI   SIZE    RES STATE    TIME %WCPU  %CPU COMMAND
 3   ?   16664 oracle   154 20 20304K 1892K sleep    15:32 2.21  2.21 oracleTE
 5   ?      36 root     152 20    0K    0K  run      57:52 1.65  1.65 vxfsd
 2   ?     477 root     154 20   32K   80K  sleep   160:55 0.71  0.71 syncer
 3   ?   14963 oracle   154 20 4448K 2780K sleep     4:39 0.32  0.32 oraweb
 0   ?   15980 oracle   154 20 4704K 3020K sleep     4:41 0.31  0.31 oraweb
 0 pts/tb 21355 root    158 20  536K  184K sleep     0:00 0.77  0.30 sh
```

In this section of the **top** output, you see the process ID (PID), username, the dispatching priority (PRI), the nice value (NI), the size of each task's memory (SIZE), the state, the execution time, and the percentage of CPU being used by each process.

While **top** has many columns of information, there are only a few columns that are of interest to you as the Oracle DBA:

■ **Load averages**   These are the load averages for the entire server. Values greater than 1 may indicate an overload problem on the server.

■ **CPU**   The first section of the **top** output shows a load summary for each CPU. The CPU column in the detailed listing shows which CPU is servicing each individual task.

■ **LOAD**   The LOAD column shows the load on each of the CPUs.

■ **NI**   The NI (nice) value is the dispatching priority of the task, and refers to the rate that the task receives services from the CPUs.

■ **IDLE**   This shows the percentage of time that each CPU has been idle.

Next, let's take a look at using the **svmon** utility in the IBM AIX operating system.

Using svmon on IBM AIX

The **svmon** utility can be used in the HP-UX and AIX environments to display server values. Here is an example listing from **svmon**:

 root> **svmon**

```
                 size       inuse       free       pin     virtual
memory        1048566     1023178       4976     55113      251293
pg space       524288       10871

                 work        pers       clnt
pin            55116           0          0
in use        250952      772224          2
```

Here is a list of the column definitions for the above output:

- **size** The number of real memory frames (size of real memory)

- **inuse** The number of frames containing pages

- **pin** Number of frames containing pinned pages in use

The **svmon -p** command can also be used to display characteristics for a specific process ID (PID):

root> **svmon -P 26060**

```
-----------------------------------------------------------------

   Pid Command      Inuse      Pin   Pgsp  Virtual    64-bit     Mthrd
 26060 pr            6871     1607   1022     6001         N         N

  Vsid  Esid Type Description         Inuse    Pin Pgsp Virtual Addr
 24029     d work shared library text  3992      0   22    2779  0..65535
     0     0 work kernel seg           2509   1606  926    2897  0..32767


5475..65535
 105e4         2 work process private   188      1   48     230  0..273 :

5298..65535
 285ea     f work shared library data    92      0   26      95  0..919
 185e6     1 pers code,/dev/lvs001:301    81      0    -       -  0..149
 6c59b     - pers /dev/lvs001:92402        6      0    -       -  0..9
 744fd     - pers /dev/lvs001:763909       3      0    -       -  0..9
 7c5ff     - pers /dev/lvs001:1327130      0      0    -       -  0..29
```

The sar Utility in UNIX

The **sar** utility is short for *system activity reporter*. This system activity reporter is quite popular in HP-UX systems, and is now becoming available for AIX and Solaris dialects of UNIX. **sar** has much of the same functionality as the **vmstat** utility, but provides additional details.

There are four main ways to invoke **sar**, each producing a different output display as shown in Table 2-5.

NOTE
*Each dialect of UNIX has different display formats for the **sar** utility. For example, some of the argument flags in Solaris are not available on HP-UX. Please check your UNIX-specific documentation for details on your UNIX server.*

The output from **sar** reports usually shows a time-based snapshot of activity. This is true for all reports that you'll see in this section. When you issue the **sar** command, you pass two numeric arguments. The first represents the time interval between samples, and the second represents the number of samples to take, as in this example:

```
sar -u 10 5
```

The **sar** command in this example is requesting five samples taken at 10 second intervals.

sar -u: The CPU Report

The **sar -u** command is very useful for seeing the overall CPU consumption over time. In the example that follows, you execute **sar -u** to see the state of the CPU.

sar Command Arguments	UNIX Display Output
sar -b	Monitor UNIX buffer activity
sar -u	Monitor CPU usage
sar -w	RAM memory switching and swapping activity
sar -d	Monitor disk usage

TABLE 2-5. *Arguments for the UNIX sar Command*

CPU time can be allocated into four sections: user mode, system mode, waiting on I/O, and idle.

```
root> sar -u 2 5

HP-UX corp-hp1 B.11.00 U 9000/800     12/25/00

07:18:44    %usr    %sys    %wio    %idle
07:18:46       0       0       1       99
07:18:48       0       0       1       99
07:18:50       4       0      13       83
07:18:52       2       1       7       90
07:18:54       0       0       3       98

Average        1       0       5       93
```

sar -w: The Memory Switching and Swapping Activity Report

The **sar -w** command is especially useful if you suspect that your database server is experiencing a memory shortage. The following example shows the swapping activity report that you get from **sar**:

```
root> sar -w 5 5

HP-UX corp-hp1 B.11.00 U 9000/800     12/25/00

07:19:33 swpin/s bswin/s swpot/s bswot/s pswch/s
07:19:38    0.00     0.0    0.00     0.0     261
07:19:43    0.00     0.0    0.00     0.0     231
07:19:48    0.00     0.0    0.00     0.0     326
07:19:53    0.00     0.0    0.00     0.0     403
07:19:58    0.00     0.0    0.00     0.0     264

Average     0.00     0.0    0.00     0.0     297
```

The column descriptions for **sar -w** are as follows:

- **swpin/s** Number of process swap-ins per second

- **swpot/s** Number of process swap-outs per second

- **bswin/s** Number of 512-byte swap-ins per second

- **bswot/s** Number of 512-byte swap-outs per second

- **pswch/s** Number of process context switches per second

sar -b: The Buffer Activity Report

The **sar -b** command causes **sar** to report buffer activity, which equates to disk I/O activity and is especially useful if you suspect that your database is I/O bound. The report shows real disk I/O, and the interaction with the UNIX Journal File System (JFS) buffer. For example, here you see a sample of **sar** output over a five-second interval:

```
>sar -b 1 5

HP-UX corp-hp1 B.11.00 U 9000/800     12/25/00

07:20:40 bread/s lread/s %rcache bwrit/s lwrit/s %wcache pread/s pwrit/s
07:20:41       0      72     100       6       7      14       0       0
07:20:42       0       3     100       3       3       0       0       0
07:20:43       0       3     100       0       9     100       0       0
07:20:44       0      26     100       6      12      50       0       0
07:20:45       0      19     100       3      15      80       0       0

Average        0      25     100       4       9      61       0       0
```

In the output shown here, you see the following data columns:

- **bread/s**   Number of physical reads from disk per second.

- **lread/s**   Number of reads per second from the UNIX JFS buffer cache.

- **%rcache**   Buffer cache hit ratio (for the UNIX JFS buffer cache) for read requests.

- **bwrit/s**   Number of physical writes to disk per second. This gives the DBA an indication of the overall write activity on the server.

- **lwrit/s**   Number of writes per second to the UNIX JFS buffer cache.

- **%wcache**   Buffer cache hit ratio (for the UNIX JFS buffer cache) for write requests.

- **pread/s**   Number of reads per second from disk. This is an excellent measure of the load on the I/O subsystem.

- **pwrit/s**   Number of writes per second to disk.

The **sar -b** command is often used in reactive tuning when you want to correlate what is happening inside Oracle with what is happening on the database server. Now let's turn our attention to the UNIX **sadc** utility.

Using the UNIX sadc Utility

The **sadc** utility is short for System Activity Report Package. The **sadc** utility is a popular package that can be used inside **cron** to schedule collections of server statistics.

The **sadc** utility is designed for use by the UNIX system administrator, and all **sadc** reports must be run as **root** and provide detailed server information.

The sacd sa1 Report

One of the most popular **sadc** reports is **sa1**. Here is a Bourne shell script that is commonly submitted as the **root** user to capture server details:

```
#! /usr/bin/sh
# @(#) $Revision: 72.3 $
#       sa1.sh

DATE=`date +%d`
ENDIR=/usr/lbin/sa
DFILE=/var/adm/sa/sa$DATE
cd $ENDIR
if [ $# = 0 ]
then
        exec $ENDIR/sadc 1 1 $DFILE
else
        exec $ENDIR/sadc $* $DFILE
fi
```

Using the glance Utility

Another popular utility for UNIX is the **glance** utility. The **glance** utility originated on HP-UX systems, but it is now becoming available for other UNIX dialects, including Solaris and AIX. The **glance** screens can be driven either by clicking function keys or by a command driver. Figure 2-6 shows the basic letter commands for **glance**.

You start the **glance** utility by entering the **glance** command from the UNIX prompt. The **glance** utility provides a graphical display of UNIX server performance (see Figure 2-7). Note at the bottom of the screen that you have various function keys to display additional details. We will start with the initial display screen and then move on to address each major **glance** function.

The glance Process Summary Screen

The first screen in **glance** displays the current CPU, memory, disk, and swap consumption, and also reports on the **top** processes. The top of the **glance** screen

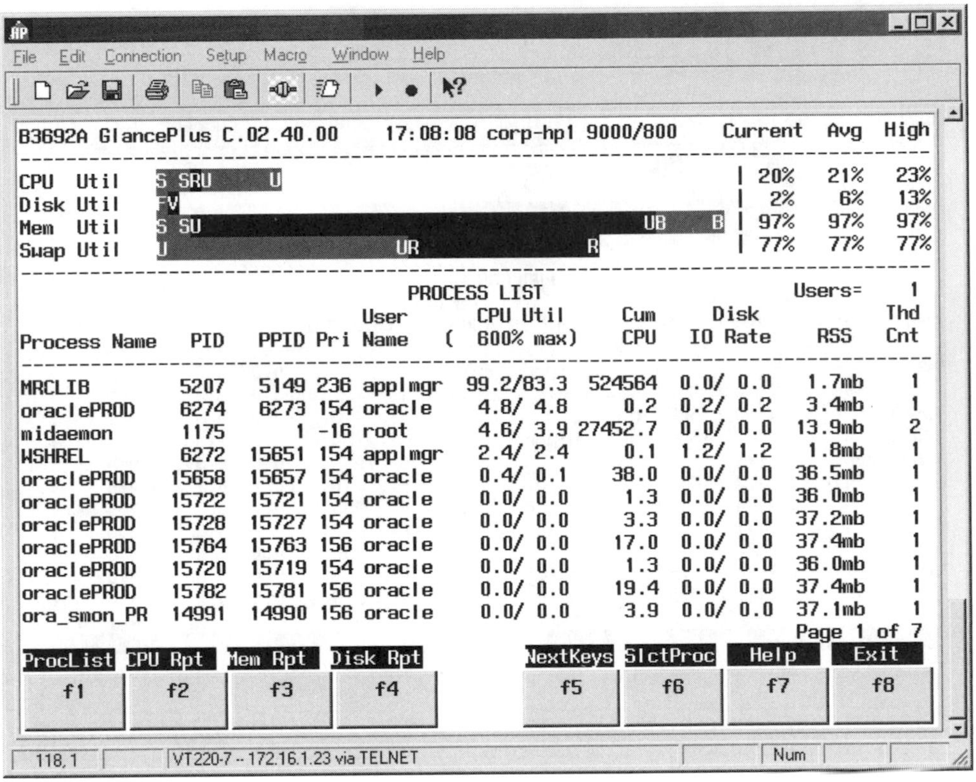

```
┌─────────────────────────────────────────────────────────────────────────┐
│ ₩P                                                              _□×        │
│ File  Edit  Connection  Setup  Macro  Window  Help                        │
│ ║ ☐ ☞ ⊟ ⧉ │ ⬚ ⬚ │ ⬛ ⬚ │ ▶ ● │ ▸?                                         │
│ ┌─────────────────────────────────────────────────────────────────────┐▲│
│ │ B3692A GlancePlus C.02.40.00    17:08:08 corp-hp1 9000/800  Current Avg High │
│ │                                                                       │ │
│ │ CPU  Util  S SRU    U                        │ 20%  21%  23%          │ │
│ │ Disk Util  FV                                │  2%   6%  13%          │ │
│ │ Mem  Util  S SU                      UB    B │ 97%  97%  97%          │ │
│ │ Swap Util  U             UR            R     │ 77%  77%  77%          │ │
│ │ ─────────────────────────────────────────────────────────────────────│ │
│ │                        PROCESS LIST                    Users=     1   │ │
│ │                         User   CPU Util   Cum    Disk            Thd  │ │
│ │ Process Name   PID   PPID Pri Name  ( 600% max)  CPU   IO Rate   RSS  Cnt │ │
│ │ ─────────────────────────────────────────────────────────────────────│ │
│ │ MRCLIB        5207   5149 236 applmgr 99.2/83.3 524564 0.0/ 0.0  1.7mb   1 │ │
│ │ oraclePROD    6274   6273 154 oracle   4.8/ 4.8    0.2 0.2/ 0.2  3.4mb   1 │ │
│ │ midaemon      1175      1 -16 root     4.6/ 3.9 27452.7 0.0/ 0.0 13.9mb  2 │ │
│ │ WSHREL        6272  15651 154 applmgr  2.4/ 2.4    0.1 1.2/ 1.2  1.8mb   1 │ │
│ │ oraclePROD   15658  15657 154 oracle   0.4/ 0.1   38.0 0.0/ 0.0 36.5mb   1 │ │
│ │ oraclePROD   15722  15721 154 oracle   0.0/ 0.0    1.3 0.0/ 0.0 36.0mb   1 │ │
│ │ oraclePROD   15728  15727 154 oracle   0.0/ 0.0    3.3 0.0/ 0.0 37.2mb   1 │ │
│ │ oraclePROD   15764  15763 156 oracle   0.0/ 0.0   17.0 0.0/ 0.0 37.4mb   1 │ │
│ │ oraclePROD   15720  15719 154 oracle   0.0/ 0.0    1.3 0.0/ 0.0 36.0mb   1 │ │
│ │ oraclePROD   15782  15781 156 oracle   0.0/ 0.0   19.4 0.0/ 0.0 37.1mb   1 │ │
│ │ ora_smon_PR  14991  14990 156 oracle   0.0/ 0.0    3.9 0.0/ 0.0 37.1mb   1 │ │
│ │                                                         Page 1 of 7   │ │
│ │ ─────────────────────────────────────────────────────────────────────│ │
│ │ ProcList CPU Rpt Mem Rpt Disk Rpt      NextKeys SlctProc Help   Exit   │ │
│ │   f1     f2      f3      f4               f5      f6      f7     f8     │ │
│ └─────────────────────────────────────────────────────────────────────▼┘ │
│ [ 118,1 ]    [ VT220-7 -- 172.16.1.23 via TELNET ]          [ Num ]       │
└─────────────────────────────────────────────────────────────────────────┘
```

FIGURE 2-6.   *The **glance** command summary screen*

shows stacked histograms for CPU, disk, memory, and swap. Within each histogram you can see two portions, the system (s) and user (U) values.

The default **glance** screen is the process screen. Underneath the histograms, you see a list of all of the **top** processes on our Oracle server. These **glance** screens are from an Oracle applications system, and you see the **top** processes. Here you see multiple tasks of **f45runw**, which is the driving task for Oracle SQL*Forms. The tasks on the process screen are displayed in the order of current CPU consumption, and you also see data on cumulative CPU consumption (Cum CPU) and the disk I/O rate. In this example, you see high activity for the Oracle checkpoint background process (**ora_ckpt_PR**).

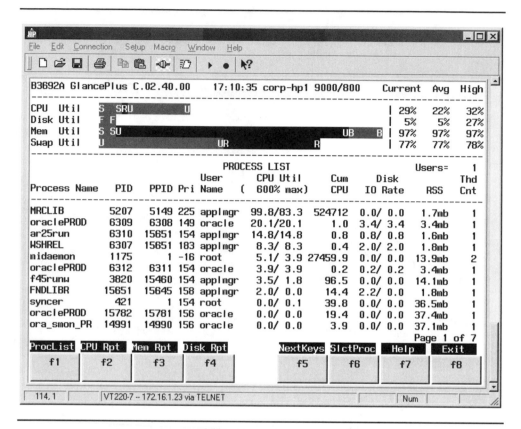

FIGURE 2-7. *The **glance** utility screen*

The glance CPU Screen

The **glance** CPU screen shows CPU consumption for the major UNIX system calls. These columns sum to 100 percent and allow you to view the totals for the CPU components (see Figure 2-8). The major CPU components include:

- **user()** Shows total usage for tasks in user execution mode

- **nice()** Sequences UNIX tasks for the run queue

- **interrupts()** Shows activity for the task interrupted to perform a UNIX system call

- **Idle()** Shows the amount of the CPU in idle state

In Figure 2-8, you can see that your server is 90 percent idle.

The glance Memory Screen

The memory screen in **glance** shows total RAM memory usage on your UNIX server (see Figure 2-9). The important rows in this display are the Page In row and the KB Paged In row.

As we noted earlier in this chapter, RAM page in operations are highly undesirable, and this screen shows a clear shortage of RAM on this server. In this case, we know that this server has a 32-bit Oracle system running on a 64-bit server, and 32-bit Oracle does not address SGA sizes in excess of 1.2 gigabytes. Hence, you see competition for RAM memory and significant RAM memory paging. By the way, this server should be upgraded to 64-bit Oracle where UNIX will be able to address high memory.

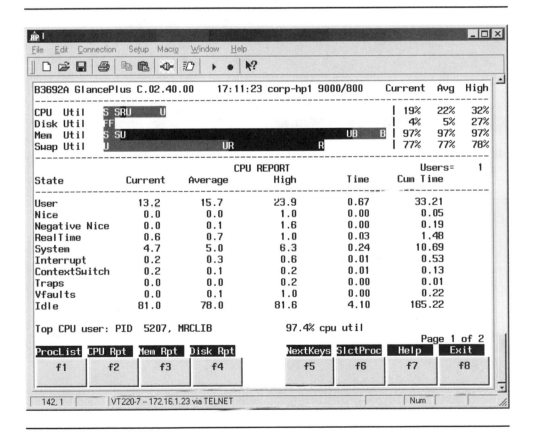

FIGURE 2-8. *The glance CPU screen*

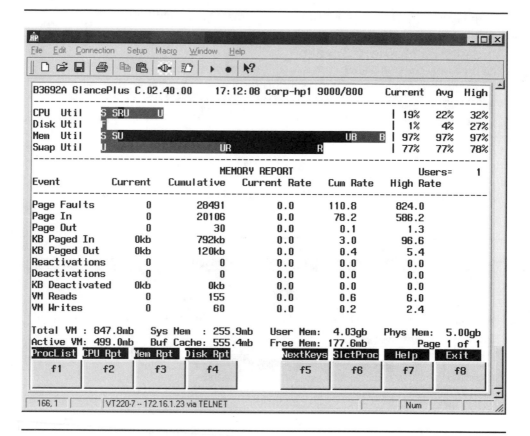

FIGURE 2-9. *The **glance** memory screen*

The glance Disk Screen
The F4 key invokes the **glance** disk display, shown in Figure 2-10. This screen shows both the logical and physical disk reads. A logical disk read is a read request, while a physical read is a logical read request that was forced to perform a disk read because the data block did not exist in the UNIX JFS data buffer. Here you see that UNIX has made 1,662 logical requests, which resulted in 157 physical disk reads. This gives the UNIX JFS a buffer cache hit ratio of 94 percent.

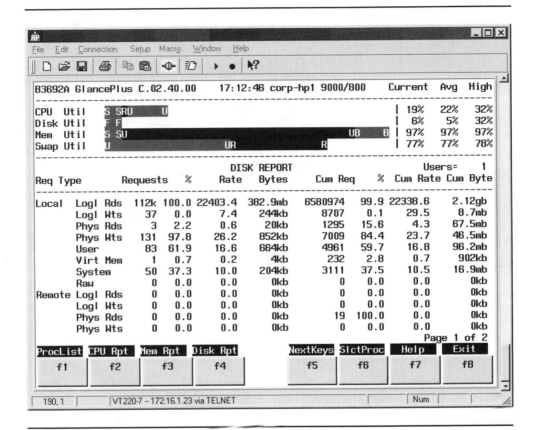

FIGURE 2-10. *The **glance** disk screen*

In Chapter 8, we will go into great detail on using **glance** for monitoring disk activity.

The glance Global Waits Screen

The global waits screen shows all major UNIX wait events as a percentage of total waits on the server. In Figure 2-11, you see waits on semaphores, pipes, and sleep operations.

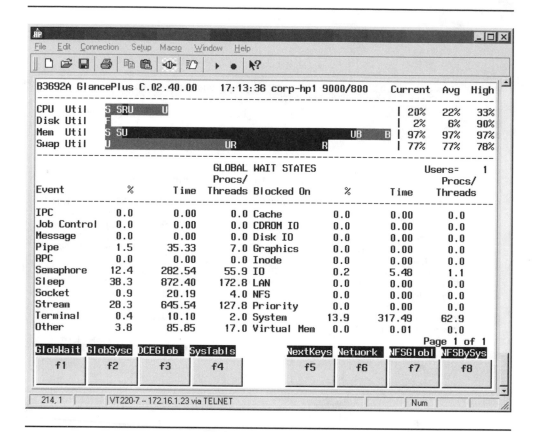

FIGURE 2-11. *The **glance** global wait state screen*

The glance Global System Calls Screen

This **glance** screen, shown in Figure 2-12, shows all system calls for the major UNIX system calls that we discussed earlier in this chapter. Here you see the summaries for **fork()**, **read()**, **write()**, **open()**, and **close()** system calls.

On this screen we see a system call signature that is typical of Oracle databases. The **read()** and **write()** system calls are consuming well over 90 percent of the server. This signature is often quite different for Oracle app server, where the majority of work is computational rather than I/O related.

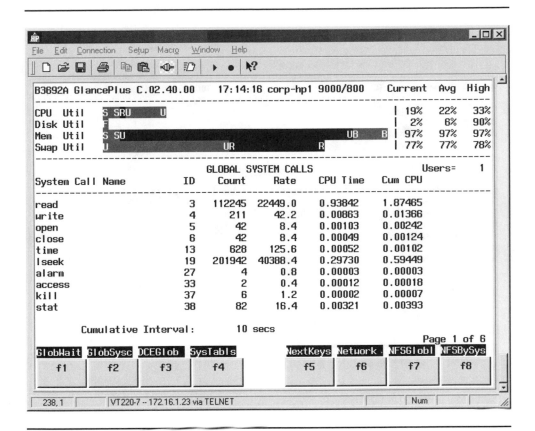

FIGURE 2-12.   *The **glance** global system calls screen*

The glance System Table Screen

This screen displays the system table for the UNIX server. Unlike Oracle tables, UNIX system tables are in-memory structures that allow UNIX to govern internal operations. In Figure 2-13 you see a typical signature for an Oracle database with the majority of activity in the file table.

The glance Swap Screen

The **glance** swap screen is very important for monitoring the usage of RAM on the UNIX server. Here you see all of the defined swap disk space, the size of the swap

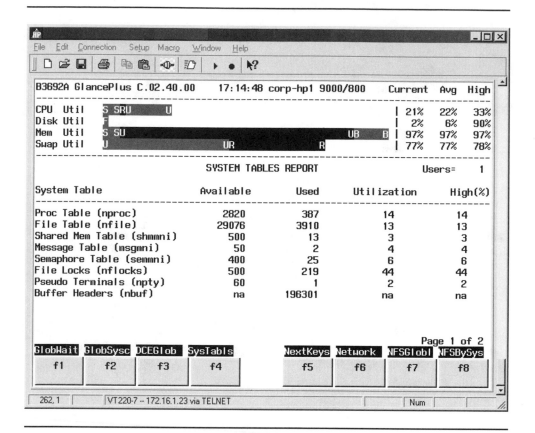

FIGURE 2-13.   *The **glance** system tables screen*

disk area, and the amount of swap that has been used. This screen is very important when monitoring your UNIX server for RAM overloads (see Figure 2-14).

Next, let's look at the most popular monitoring command, **vmstat**, and see how **vmstat** can quickly show UNIX server performance.

Overview of the vmstat Utility

The **vmstat** utility is the most common UNIX monitoring utility, and it is found in the majority of UNIX dialects (note that **vmstat** is called **osview** on the IRIX dialect of UNIX). The **vmstat** utility displays various server values over a given time interval.

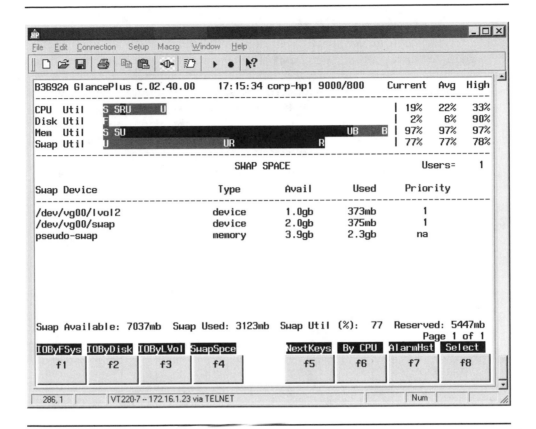

FIGURE 2-14.   *The **glance** swap screen*

The **vmstat** utility is invoked from the UNIX prompt, and it has several numeric parameters. The first numeric argument to **vmstat** represents the time interval (expressed in seconds) between server samples. The second argument specifies the number of samples to be reported. In the example that follows, **vmstat** is executed to take five samples at two-second intervals:

```
root> vmstat 2 5
```

Almost all UNIX servers have some version of **vmstat**. Before we look at the details for this powerful utility, let's explore the differences that you are likely to see.

Dialect Differences in vmstat

Because each hardware vendor writes its own **vmstat** utility, there are significant differences in **vmstat** output. The **vmstat** output is different depending on the dialect of UNIX, but each dialect contains the important server metrics.

Because vendors have written their own versions of the **vmstat** utility, it can be useful to consult the online UNIX documentation to see the display differences. In UNIX, you can see your documentation by invoking the man pages. The term *man* is short for manual, and you can see the documentation for your particular implementation of **vmstat** by entering **man vmstat** from your UNIX prompt.

The following is a sample of **vmstat** output for the four most popular dialects of UNIX. In each example, the important metrics appear in bold.

vmstat for Solaris

In the Sun Solaris operating environment, the output from **vmstat** will appear like this:

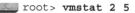 root> **vmstat 2 5**

```
procs       memory          page        disk           faults       cpu
r  b  w   swap    free    re   mf  pi  po …  s6  --  --   in   sy   cs  us sy id
0  0  0  2949744  988800  0    4   0   0  …  0   0   0   148  200   41  0  0 99
0  0  0  2874808  938960  27  247  0   1  …  0   0   0   196  434   64  1  2 98
0  0  0  2874808  938960  0    0   0   0  …  0   0   0   134   55   32  0  0 100
0  0  0  2874808  938960  0    0   0   0  …  0   0   0   143  114   39  0  0 100
0  0  0  2874808  938960  0    0   0   0  …  0   0   0   151   86   38  0  0 100
```

vmstat for Linux

In the Linux operating environment, the output from **vmstat** will appear like this:

root> **vmstat 2 5**

```
 procs                        memory  swap    io    system       cpu
r  b  w  swpd   free   buff   cache   si … bi  bo   in   cs  us sy  id
1  0  0   140  90372  726988  26228   0  …  0   0   14    7  0  0   4
0  0  0   140  90372  726988  26228   0  …  0   2  103   11  0  0 100
0  0  0   140  90372  726988  26228   0  …  0   5  106   10  0  0 100
0  0  0   140  90372  726988  26228   0  …  0   0  101   11  0  0 100
0  0  0   140  90372  726988  26228   0  …  0   0  102   11  0  0 100
```

vmstat for AIX

In the IBM AIX operating environment, the output from **vmstat** will appear like this:

root> **vmstat 2 5**

kthr		memory				page				faults			cpu			
r	b	avm	fre	re	pi	po	fr	sr	cy	in	sy	cs	us	sy	id	wa
7	5	220214	141	0	0	0	42	53	0	1724	12381	2206	19	46	28	7
9	5	220933	195	0	0	1	216	290	0	1952	46118	2712	27	55	13	5
13	5	220646	452	0	0	1	33	54	0	2130	86185	3014	30	59	8	3
6	5	220228	672	0	0	0	0	0	0	1929	25068	2485	25	49	16	10

vmstat for HP-UX

In the Hewlett Packard HP-UX operating environment, the output from **vmstat** will appear like this:

```
root> vmstat 2 5
r  b  w   avm     free   re  at  pi po ...    in    sy     cs   us sy  id
1  0  0  70635  472855  10   5   2  0  ...  2024  2859   398    4  1  96
1  0  0  74985  472819   9   0   1  0  ...  1864  1820   322    0  0 100
0  0  0  83056  472819   2   0   0  0  ...  1846  1684   302    0  0 100
0  0  0  81390  472819   0   0   0  0  ...  1847  1571   288    0  0 100
0  0  0  78788  472819   0   0   0  0  ...  1852  1608   291    0  0 100
```

Now that you have seen the different display options for each dialect of **vmstat**, let's take a look at the data items in **vmstat** and understand the common values that you can capture in STATSPACK tables.

What to Look for in vmstat Output

As you can see, each dialect of **vmstat** reports different information about the current status of the server. Despite these dialect differences, there are only a small number of metrics that are important for server monitoring. These metrics include:

- **r (run queue)**   The run queue value shows the number of tasks executing and waiting for CPU resources. When this number exceeds the number of CPUs on the server, a CPU bottleneck exists, and some tasks are waiting for execution.

- **pi (page in)**   A page in operation occurs when the server is experiencing a shortage of RAM memory. While all virtual memory server will page out to the swap disk, page in operations show that the server has exceeded the available RAM storage. Any nonzero value for **pi** indicates excessive activity as RAM memory contents are read in from the swap disk.

- **us (user CPU)**   This is the amount of CPU that is servicing user tasks.

- **sy (system CPU)**   This is the percentage of CPU being used to service system tasks.

- **id (idle)**   This is the percentage of CPU that is idle.

- **wa (wait, IBM AIX only)**   This shows the percentage of CPU that is waiting on external operations such as disk I/O.

Note that all of the CPU metrics are expressed as percentages. Hence, all of the CPU values (**us + sy + id + wa**) will always sum to 100. Now that you have a high-level understanding of the important **vmstat** data, let's look into some methods for using **vmstat** to identify server problems.

Identifying CPU Bottlenecks with vmstat

Waiting CPU resources can be shown in UNIX **vmstat** command output as the second column under the kthr (kernel thread state change) heading. Tasks may be placed in the wait queue (**b**) if they are waiting on a resource, while other tasks appear in the run queue (**r**) column. As you see in Figure 2-15, server tasks are queued for execution by the server.

In short, the server is experiencing a CPU bottleneck when **r** is greater than the number of CPUs on the server.

Remember that you need to know the number of CPUs on your server because the **vmstat** run queue value must never exceed the number of CPUs. A run queue value of 32 is perfectly acceptable for a 36-CPU server, while a value of 32 would be a serious problem for a 24-CPU server.

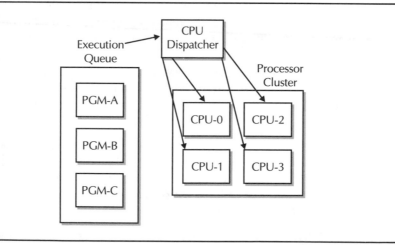

FIGURE 2-15.   *Tasks queuing for service by the CPUs*

In the example that follows, you run the **vmstat** utility. For these purposes, we are interested in the first two columns: the run queue, **r**, and the kthr wait **b** column. You can see that there is an average of about eight new tasks entering the run queue every five seconds (the **r** column), while there are five other tasks that are waiting on resources (the **b** column). Also, a nonzero value in the **b** column may indicate a bottleneck.

root> **vmstat 5 5**

```
kthr     memory              page                  faults        cpu
-----  -----------  ------------------------  ------------  -----------
 r  b    avm    fre  re  pi  po  fr   sr  cy   in    sy   cs  us sy id wa
 7  5  220214   141   0   0   0  42   53   0  1724 12381 2206 19 46 28  7
 9  5  220933   195   0   0   1 216  290   0  1952 46118 2712 27 55 13  5
13  5  220646   452   0   0   1  33   54   0  2130 86185 3014 30 59  8  3
 6  5  220228   672   0   0   0   0    0   0  1929 25068 2485 25 49 16 10
```

The rule for identifying a server with CPU resource problems is quite simple. Whenever the value of the run queue **r** column exceeds the number of CPUs on the server, tasks are forced to wait for execution. There are several solutions to managing CPU overload, and these alternatives are presented in their order of desirability:

1. Add more processors (CPUs) to the server.

2. Load balance the system tasks by rescheduling large batch tasks to execute during off-peak hours.

3. Adjust the dispatching priorities (nice values) of existing tasks.

To understand how dispatching priorities work, you must remember that incoming tasks are placed in the execution queue according to their nice value (see Figure 2-16. Here you can see that tasks with a low nice value are scheduled for execution above those tasks with a higher nice value.

Now that you can see when the CPUs are overloaded, let's look into **vmstat** further and see how you can tell when the CPUs are running at full capacity.

Identifying High CPU Usage with vmstat

You can easily detect when you are experiencing a busy CPU on the Oracle database server. Whenever the **us** (user) column plus the **sy** (system) column times approach 100 percent, the CPUs are operating at full capacity.

Please note that it is not uncommon to see the CPU approach 100 percent even when the server is not overwhelmed with work. This is because the UNIX internal

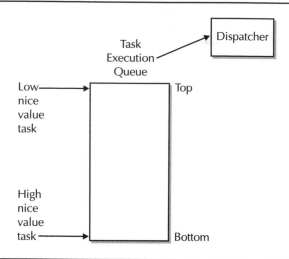

FIGURE 2-16. *Tasks queued for execution according to their nice value*

dispatchers will always attempt to keep the CPUs as busy as possible. This maximizes task throughput, but it can be misleading for a neophyte.

Remember, it is not a cause for concern when the user + system CPU values approach 100 percent. This just means that the CPUs are working to their full potential. The only metric that identifies a CPU bottleneck is when the run queue **r** value exceeds the number of CPUs on the server.

```
root> vmstat 5 1
```

```
kthr     memory            page                faults       cpu
----- ----------- ------------------------ ------------ -----------
 r  b   avm    fre  re  pi  po  fr   sr  cy  in   sy  cs  us sy id wa
 0  0 217485   386   0   0   0   4   14   0 202  300 210  20 75  3  2
```

Please note that in Chapter 9 we will describe a detailed method for capturing **vmstat** information inside STATSPACK extension tables. The approach of capturing server information along with Oracle information provides the Oracle DBA with a complete picture of the operation of the system.

The UNIX Watch Command

One common method for watching UNIX server load is to monitor the load average for the server. The load average is an arbitrary number that shows overall resource consumption of the server. Most load average displays have three values for the load average. The load average display shows the load averages for the past minute, the past five minutes, and the past ten minutes. A low load average is ideal, and the load average should stay below zero. Whenever the value exceeds 1 there may be a CPU overload problem.

 root> **w**

```
  5:54pm  up 2 days, 22:45,  29 users,  load average: 0.08, 0.14, 0.22
User      tty          login@ idle  JCPU   PCPU   what
root      ttyp1        7:11pm 25:47                tee -a /u01/home/crup
triha     ttyp2        4:48pm   20      3      3   runmenu50 pamenu
lpayne    ttyp3        5:29pm   24                 runmenu50 pamenu
burleson  ttyp5        5:50pm                      -sh
tteply    ttyp6        5:05pm   10      1      1   runmenu50 pamenu
kjoslin   ttyp7        1:29pm   30     38     38   runmenu50 pamenu
jperry    ttyp8        6:48am    1     51     51   runmenu50 pamenu
kharstad  ttype        3:38pm  2:16                -sh
cmconway  ttyqc       11:53am   17      5      5   runmenu50 pamenu
jhahn     ttyr7        1:43pm   10      2      2   runmenu50 pamenu
tbailey   ttyrb       12:12pm  1:38      4      4   runmenu50 pamenu
```

Now, let's conclude this chapter with a review of the main concepts and tools.

Conclusion

This chapter has been designed to give you a high-level conceptual overview of UNIX server management for Oracle. In this chapter, we have emphasized the following points:

- The **ps** command is very useful for displaying and managing Oracle tasks.

- The **kill** command can be used to delete Oracle processes.

- UNIX provides a host of commands to view RAM memory usage in UNIX. The **ipcs** command can be used to view held RAM memory segments, and the **ipcrm** command can be used to remove memory segments after an Oracle database crash.

- On many dialects of UNIX, the server uses semaphores to the serialization of Oracle work. UNIX commands can be used to check and remove semaphores after an Oracle database crash.

■ UNIX possesses specific commands to display the number of CPU and the amount of memory on the server.

■ There are several common UNIX utilities for displaying server performance, including **watch**, **top**, **glance**, and **sar**.

Next, let's take a look at capturing UNIX server statistics. The next chapter will present a method for using **vmstat** for monitoring in UNIX and show you how to create special STATSPACK extension tables to store your server statistics.

CHAPTER
3

Capturing UNIX
Server Statistics
with STATSPACK

racking the performance of the UNIX server is critical for the Oracle DBA because no amount of Oracle tuning is going to solve a server-related performance problem. Of course, SQL statements can be tuned to reduce server load, but you always need to pay careful attention to the performance of your Oracle server.

When tuning a UNIX Oracle server, you must always remember the goal of fully loading the CPUs and RAM on the server. Unused processing and RAM power can never be reclaimed, and with the significant depreciation of the value of most servers, maximizing the utilization is a noble goal. On any server that is dedicated to an Oracle database, you want to dedicate as much hardware resources to Oracle as possible without causing a server-related slowdown.

This chapter will cover the following topics:

- UNIX monitoring goals

- Extending STATSPACK to capture server statistics

- Reporting on server statistics

Let's begin with a brief review of the goals of UNIX server monitoring.

UNIX Monitoring Goals

The monitoring of the UNIX environment involves monitoring disk, RAM, CPU, and network components. For this book, we consider server monitoring to be limited to CPU and RAM memory monitoring. We have divided the total UNIX monitoring tasks into three general areas:

- **Server monitoring**   Monitoring CPU and RAM memory

- **Disk monitoring**   Monitoring the I/O subsystem (see Chapter 4)

- **Network monitoring**   Protocol and packet monitoring (see Chapter 5)

Let's begin with an overview of UNIX CPU monitoring goals.

UNIX CPU Monitoring

CPU consumption on an Oracle server is a simple matter because the server manages all CPU transactions automatically. All servers are configured to use CPU cycles on an as-needed basis, and the Oracle database will use CPU resources freely. The internal machine code will manage the assignment of processors to active tasks and ensure that the maximum amount of processing power is applied to each task.

CPU shortages are evidenced in cases where the CPU run queue is greater than the number of CPUs, as shown in Figure 3-1. In these cases, the only solutions are to increase the number of CPUs on the processor or reduce the CPU demands on Oracle. You can decrease CPU demands on Oracle by turning off Oracle Parallel Query, replacing the standard Oracle listener with the multithreaded server (MTS), and other actions that would reduce the processing demands on the hardware.

Tasks are serviced in UNIX according to their internal dispatching priority. Important tasks such as the UNIX operating system tasks will always have a more favorable dispatching priority because the UNIX system tasks drive the operating system.

CPU overload is usually evidenced by high values in the **vmstat** run queue column. Whenever the run queue value exceeds the number of CPUs of the server, some task may be waiting for service. When you see a CPU overload, you have several alternatives:

- **Add additional processors** This is usually the best solution, because an Oracle server that is overloading the CPU will always run faster with additional processors.

- **Reduce server load** If the CPU overload is not constant, task load balancing may be the solution. For example, it is not uncommon to see a server overloaded during peak work hours, and then return to 80 percent idle in the evenings. In these cases, batch tasks can be rescheduled to execute when there are more idle CPU resources available.

- **Alter task dispatching priorities** Most all UNIX operating systems allow the **root** user to change the dispatching priority for tasks. As a general rule, the online database background tasks are given more priority (a smaller priority value), while less critical batch processes are placed with less

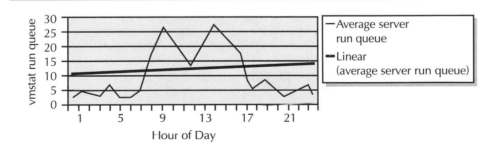

FIGURE 3-1. *CPU overload on an Oracle server with 12 CPUs*

priority (a higher priority value). However, altering the default dispatching priorities is not a good long-term solution, and it should only be undertaken in emergency situations.

Upgrading an Entire Server

On mission-critical databases where speed is a primary concern, adding additional processors may not be the best solution. Oracle tuning professionals will sometimes recommend upgrading to a faster server architecture. Many of the new 64-bit CPU processors will handle Oracle transactions an order of magnitude faster than their 32-bit predecessors. For example, in the IBM AIX environment, the IBM SP2 processors run on 32 bits. IBM's next generation of processors utilize a 64-bit technology, and these systems can process information far faster than their 32-bit ancestors. The new IBM Blackbird and Regatta servers will often double the overall processing speed of an Oracle database.

When making recommendations for upgrades of entire servers, many Oracle tuning professionals use the analogy of the performance of a 16-bit PC compared to the performance of 32-bit PC. In general, moving to faster CPU architecture can greatly improve the speed of Oracle applications, and many vendors such as IBM will allow you to actually load your production system onto one of the new processors for speed benchmarks prior to purchasing the new servers.

Adding Additional CPU Processors

Most symmetric multiprocessor (SMP) architectures for Oracle databases servers are expandable, and additional processors can be added at any time. Once added, the processor architecture will immediately make the new CPUs available to the Oracle database.

The problem with adding additional processors is the high cost, which can often outweigh the cost of a whole new server. Adding additional processors to an existing server can commonly cost over $100,000, and most managers require a detailed cost-benefit analysis when making the decision to buy more CPUs. Essentially, the cost-benefit analysis compares the lost productivity of the end users (due to the response time latency) with the additional costs of the processors.

Another problem with justifying additional processors is the sporadic nature of CPU overloads. Oracle database servers often experience "transient" overloads, and there will be times when the processors are heavily burdened and other times when the processors are not at full utilization. Before recommending a processor upgrade, most Oracle tuning professionals will perform a load-balancing analysis to ensure that any batch-oriented tasks are presented to the server at non-peak hours.

Load Balancing of Server Tasks

When CPU overload is experienced, the DBA will generally see periods during the day when the run queue gets quite long and other periods at night when the processors are mostly idle (see Figure 3-2). A common question asked by a system administrator is, "The CPU is 40 percent idle for 16 hours a day, so why should we add more processors?"

However, there are times when it makes sense to add more processors, even if the processors are idle during off-peak times. For example, if you are working in an online environment, the only response time that matters is the time between 7:00 A.M. and 8:00 P.M. when your online users are active. The fact that the server is largely idle during the middle of the night has no bearing on the decision to upgrade with additional CPUs.

Once you identify the times when the CPU activity is excessive, you need to go to STATSPACK and examine the activity at the times of the overload. Once you have identified the times when the processors are overloaded, you must then see if it is possible to reschedule batch tasks to run at off-peak hours. On an Oracle database server, tasks may be scheduled in many ways:

- The **dbms_job** utility

- The UNIX **cron** utility

- A TP monitor such as Tuxedo

- Oracle Concurrent Manager (for Oracle Applications)

- SAPGUI if you are running SAP

Regardless of the method of scheduling Oracle tasks, the idea is to find large batch tasks that can be scheduled during peak processing times. Your task is to find a large regularly scheduled SQL task that runs during these times.

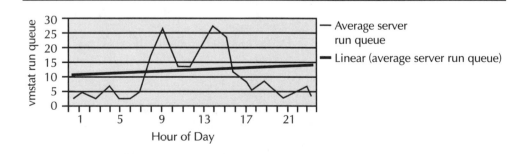

FIGURE 3-2. *Average Oracle server run queue values before task load balancing*

STATSPACK Solutions for Finding High-Impact Tasks   Within STATSPACK, you can examine the stats$sql_summary table, looking for SQL statements that are executed during the peak hours. The high-impact tasks will generally be associated with SQL statements that have a high value for *rows processed*. Here is an easy STATSPACK table query to find the SQL:

rpt_top_sql.sql

```
set lines 80;
set pages 999;
set heading off;

select
   to_char(snap_time,'yyyy-mm-dd hh24'),
   substr(sql_text,1,50)
from
   stats$sql_summary a,
   stats$snapshot     sn
where
   a.snap_id = sn.snap_id
and
   to_char(snap_time,'hh24') = 10
or
   to_char(snap_time,'hh24') = 15
order by
   rows_processed desc;
```

Here is a sample of the output from this report, showing the beginning of all SQL statements, ordered in descending order of rows_processed. This tells the DBA which SQL statements are causing the most I/O resources.

```
Yr.  Mo dy Hr SQL_TEXT
------------ --------------------------------------------------
2000-09-20 10 begin :retCode := toc_maint . toc_insert_entry ( :
2000-09-20 10 begin :retCode := toc_maint . toc_insert_entry ( :
2000-09-20 15 INSERT INTO TOC_ENTRY ( ISBN,TOC_SEQ_NBR,VISUAL_PA
2000-09-20 15 INSERT INTO TOC_ENTRY ( ISBN,TOC_SEQ_NBR,VISUAL_PA
2000-09-20 15 SELECT PAGE_SEQ_NBR   FROM PAGE  WHERE (ISBN = :b1
2000-09-20 15 SELECT PAGE_SEQ_NBR   FROM PAGE  WHERE (ISBN = :b1
2000-09-21 10 select 'ALTER ' || substr(object_type,1,20) || ' '
2000-09-21 10 DECLARE job BINARY_INTEGER := :job; next_date DATE
2000-09-21 10 DECLARE job BINARY_INTEGER := :job; next_date DATE
2000-09-21 10 DECLARE job BINARY_INTEGER := :job; next_date DATE
2000-09-20 15 SELECT IMAGE_BLOB   FROM PAGE_IMAGE  WHERE (ISBN =
2000-09-20 15 SELECT IMAGE_BLOB   FROM PAGE_IMAGE  WHERE (ISBN =
```

```
2000-09-20 15 begin pageimages_curs . page_get_image ( :myisbn:i
2000-09-20 15 SELECT IMAGE_BLOB   FROM PAGE_IMAGE  WHERE (ISBN =
2000-09-20 15 BEGIN sys.dbms_ijob.remove(:job); END;
2000-09-20 15 begin pageimages_curs . page_get_image ( :myisbn:i
2000-09-20 15 BEGIN sys.dbms_ijob.remove(:job); END;
```

If you are diligent, you can locate the online or batch SQL tasks that are overwhelming the server. Once you reschedule the offending tasks to run during off-peak hours, your average run queue for the server falls below the number of CPUs, as shown in Figure 3-3.

Of course, load balancing Oracle tasks is often not as trivial is it might appear. The Oracle DBA generally has no control over when members of the end-user community submit batch-oriented work against the Oracle database. Unless you are using scheduling tools such as Oracle's Concurrent Manager, the end users are free to submit large resource-intensive reports against Oracle any time they feel like it. In shops where end users generate ad hoc SQL statements, there are three Oracle features that can govern end-user query resources:

■ The dbms_resource_manager PL/SQL package can be used to govern end-user resources. In the example that follows, dbms_resource_manager is called to assign CPU, SQL plan, and parallel query options for the ADHOC_Group of end users:

```
SQL> execute dbms_resource_manager.update_plan_directive(
        plan => 'SINGLE_LEVEL_PLAN',
        group_or_subplan => 'ADHOC_Group',
        new_comment => 'ADHOC day users sessions at level 1',
        new_cpu_p1 => 10,
        new_parallel_degree_limit_p1 => 0);
```

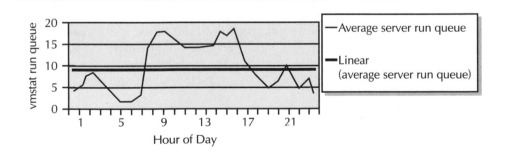

FIGURE 3-3. *Average Oracle server run queue values after task load balancing*

■ Oracle Applications systems have a profile feature to restrict ad hoc queries. For ad hoc users, their Oracle user ID is associated with a group, and the group is linked to a profile that governs the amount of server resources the end users are allowed to use.

■ SQL*Plus profiles are for end users who execute queries from SQL*Plus. The product_user_profile table can be used to restrict access.

Hence, it is up to the Oracle professional to become a detective, and hunt through the library cache in order to see when high-resource statements are being added to the Oracle system.

The stats$sql_summary table is one STATSPACK table that has a great deal of information to help you find offending SQL statements. SQL statements within the stats$sql_summary table can be sorted according to a number of resource utilization metrics, including rows processed, buffer gets, disk reads, and executions.

Even though Oracle developers write most SQL, it is still the duty of the Oracle DBA to monitor the behavior of the SQL within the system in order to determine those SQL statements that are creating excessive load upon the server processor. The Oracle DBA must also load balance those intensive SQL statements by requiring the end users to submit them during less active times.

Monitoring RAM Memory Consumption

In the UNIX environment, RAM memory is automatically managed by the operating system. In systems with virtual memory, a special disk called *swap* is used to hold chunks of RAM that cannot fit within the available RAM on the server. In this fashion, a virtual memory server can allow tasks to allocate memory above the RAM capacity on the server. As the server is used, the operating system will move some memory pages out to the swap disk in case the server exceeds its physical capacity. This is called a page out operation. Remember, page out operations occur even when the database server has not exceeded the RAM capacity.

RAM memory shortages are evidenced by page in operations. Page in operations cause Oracle slowdowns because tasks must wait until their memory region is moved back into RAM from the swap disk. The remedy for memory overload is to add more memory or to reduce the demands on memory by reducing sort_area_size, implementing the multithreaded server, or reducing the values for shared_pool or db_block_buffers.

As we briefly noted in Chapter 1, there are several remedies for overloaded RAM memory:

■ **Add RAM**   Add additional RAM to the server.

■ **Reduce Oracle RAM**   Reduce the size of the SGA regions by down-sizing the shared pool or data block buffers.

■ **Implement the multithreaded server**   Implementing the MTS will reduce RAM demands by shifting RAM demand from individual Program Global Areas (PGS) into a shared large_pool inside the Oracle SGA.

■ **Tune SQL**   You can often tune expensive SQL statements to reduce the demands on the server.

Next, let's move on and take a look at how to build an easy UNIX server monitor by extending the Oracle STATSPACK tables.

Capturing Server Performance Data Inside STATSPACK

Now that you have seen that **vmstat** can provide useful information about the status of the Oracle database server, how can you create a mechanism for monitoring these **vmstat** statistics? As we noted in our discussion of **vmstat**, system-level resource contention is transient and fleeting, and it is often very easy to miss a bottleneck unless you are constantly vigilant. For this reason, you need to create an extension to the STATSPACK tables that will constantly poll the hardware and collect any data relating to resource contention.

The concept behind this extension is to execute the **vmstat** utility and capture the performance information within an Oracle table called stats$vmstat.

While this technique works very well for monitoring the Oracle database server, these operating system statistics can also be used to monitor the other computers in your system. These include the application servers (web servers) and the Oracle database server. We will show you how to collect **vmstat** statistics on a remote server later in this chapter.

A Script to Capture vmstat Information

It is a simple matter to create an Oracle table to store this information and use a script to populate the table. Creating the automated **vmstat** monitor begins by creating an Oracle table to contain the **vmstat** output:

cr_vmstat_tab.sql

```
connect perfstat/perfstat;

drop table stats$vmstat;
create table stats$vmstat
(
     start_date          date,
     duration            number,
     server_name         varchar2(20),
```

```
    runque_waits           number,
    page_in                number,
    page_out               number,
    user_cpu               number,
    system_cpu             number,
    idle_cpu               number,
    wait_cpu               number
)
tablespace perfstat
storage (initial    10m
        next        1m
        pctincrease 0)
;
```

Now that you have defined an Oracle table to capture the **vmstat** information, you need to write a UNIX script that will execute **vmstat**, capture the **vmstat** output, and place it into the Oracle table.

The main script to collect the **vmstat** information is a Korn shell script called get_vmstat.ksh. As we noted earlier, each dialect of UNIX displays **vmstat** information in different columns, so you need slightly different scripts for each type of UNIX.

The idea is to write a script that continually runs the **vmstat** utility and then directs the results into your Oracle table, as shown in Figure 3-4.

The script shows the **vmstat** capture utility script for the Linux operating system. The scripts at the Oracle Press web site contain complete code for a **vmstat** script for all of the major UNIX dialects. Go to http://www.oraclepressbooks.com/ to get the code.

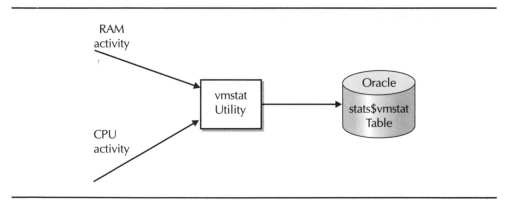

FIGURE 3-4. *Capturing vmstat output into a STATSPACK extension table*

Note that you must change this script in several places to make it work for you:

■ You must set the ORACLE_HOME to your directory:

```
ORACLE_HOME=/usr/app/oracle/admin/product/8/1/6
```

■ You must set your ORACLE_SID in the **sqlplus** command:

```
$ORACLE_HOME/bin/sqlplus -s perfstat/perfstat@testsys1<<EOF
```

■ You can change the duration of samples by resetting the SAMPLE_TIME UNIX variable:

```
SAMPLE_TIME=300
```

get_vmstat.ksh (Linux version)

```
#!/bin/ksh

# This is the Linux version

ORACLE_HOME=/usr/app/oracle/admin/product/8/1/6
export ORACLE_HOME

PATH=$ORACLE_HOME/bin:$PATH
export PATH
SERVER_NAME=`uname -a|awk '{print $2}'`
typeset -u SERVER_NAME
export SERVER_NAME

# sample every five minutes (300 seconds) . . . .
SAMPLE_TIME=300

while true
do
   vmstat ${SAMPLE_TIME} 2 > /tmp/msg$$


# run vmstat and direct the output into the Oracle table . . .
cat /tmp/msg$$|sed 1,3d | awk  '{ printf("%s %s %s %s %s %s\n", $1, $8, $9,
14, $15, $16) }' | while read RUNQUE PAGE_IN PAGE_OUT USER_CPU SYSTEM_CPU
DLE_CPU
   do
```

```
$ORACLE_HOME/bin/sqlplus -s perfstat/perfstat@testsys1<<EOF
insert into perfstat.stats\$vmstat
                        values (
                          sysdate,
                          $SAMPLE_TIME,
                          '$SERVER_NAME',
                          $RUNQUE,
                          $PAGE_IN,
                          $PAGE_OUT,
                          $USER_CPU,
                          $SYSTEM_CPU,
                          $IDLE_CPU,
                          0
                                );
        EXIT
EOF
    done
done

rm /tmp/msg$$
```

Because of the differences in implementations of **vmstat**, the first task is to identify the columns of the **vmstat** output that contain the information you want to capture. Once you know the columns that you want to capture, you can add these columns to the **vmstat** script to put the output into your table.

Dialect	Run Queue column	Page In column	Page Out column	User column	System column	Idle column	Wait column
HP-UX	1	8	9	16	17	18	NA
AIX	1	6	7	14	15	16	17
Solaris	1	8	9	20	21	22	NA
Linux	1	8	9	14	15	16	NA

Using this table, you can adjust the capture script according to your operating system. You customize the script by changing the line in the script that reads the **vmstat** output and places it into the stats$vmstat table. Here is a summary of the UNIX dialect changes to this line.

HP-UX vmstat Columns

```
cat /tmp/msg$$|sed 1,3d |\
  awk  '{ printf("%s %s %s %s %s %s\n", $1, $8, $9, $16, $17, $18) }'  |\
  while read RUNQUE PAGE_IN PAGE_OUT USER_CPU SYSTEM_CPU IDLE_CPU
```

IBM AIX vmstat Columns

```
cat /tmp/msg$$|sed 1,3d |\
  awk  '{ printf("%s %s %s %s %s %s\n", $1, $6, $7, $14, $15, $16, $17) }'  |\
  while read RUNQUE PAGE_IN PAGE_OUT USER_CPU SYSTEM_CPU IDLE_CPU WAIT_CPU
```

Sun Solaris vmstat Columns

```
cat /tmp/msg$$|sed 1,3d |\
  awk  '{ printf("%s %s %s %s %s %s\n", $1, $8, $9, $20, $21, $22) }'  |\
  while read RUNQUE PAGE_IN PAGE_OUT USER_CPU SYSTEM_CPU IDLE_CPU
```

Linux vmstat columns

```
cat /tmp/msg$$|sed 1,3d |\
  awk  '{ printf("%s %s %s %s %s %s\n", $1, $8, $9, $14, $15, $16) }'  |\
  while read RUNQUE PAGE_IN PAGE_OUT USER_CPU SYSTEM_CPU IDLE_CPU
```

Internals of the vmstat Capture Script

It is important to understand how the get_vmstat.ksh script functions, so let's examine the steps in this script:

1. It executes the **vmstat** utility for the specified elapsed-time interval (SAMPLE_TIME=300).

2. The output of **vmstat** is directed into the /tmp directory.

3. The output is then parsed using the **awk** utility, and the values are inserted into the mon_vmstats table.

Once started, the get_vmstat.ksh script will run continually and capture the **vmstat** information into your stats$vmstat table. This script is an example of a UNIX daemon process. A daemon process is a continuously-running UNIX process, and this daemon will run continually to sample the server status. However, the script may be terminated if your server is rebooted, so it is a good idea to place a **crontab** entry to make sure that the get_vmstat script is always running. Below is a script called run_vmstat.ksh that will ensure that the **vmstat** utility is always running on your server.

Note that you must make the following changes to this script:

■ Set the file location variable **vmstat** to the directory that contains your get_vmstat.ksh script:

```
vmstat=`echo ~oracle/vmstat`
```

■ Create a small file in your UNIX file directory ($vmstat) called mysid. This file will contain one line and specify the name of your ORACLE_SID:

```
ORACLE_SID=`cat ${vmstat}/mysid`
```

run_vmstat.ksh

```
#!/bin/ksh

# First, we must set the environment . . . .
vmstat=`echo ~oracle/vmstat`
export vmstat
ORACLE_SID=`cat ${vmstat}/mysid`
export ORACLE_SID

ORACLE_HOME=`cat /etc/oratab|grep $ORACLE_SID:|cut -f2 -d':'`
export ORACLE_HOME
PATH=$ORACLE_HOME/bin:$PATH
export PATH

#---------------------------------------
# If it is not running, then start it . . .
#---------------------------------------
check_stat=`ps -ef|grep get_vmstat|grep -v grep|wc -l`;
oracle_num=`expr $check_stat`
if [ $oracle_num -le 0 ]
 then nohup $vmstat/get_vmstat_linux.ksh > /dev/null 2>&1 &
fi
```

The run_vmstat.ksh script can be scheduled to run hourly on the server. As you can see by examining the code, this script checks to see if the get_vmstat.ksh script is executing. If it is not executing, the script resubmits it for execution. In practice, the get_vmstat.ksh script will not abort, but if the server is shut down and restarted, the script will need to be restarted.

Here is an example of the UNIX **crontab** file. For those not familiar with **cron**, it is a UNIX scheduling facility that allows tasks to be submitted at specific times. Note that it schedules the run_vmstat.ksh script every hour, and runs a **vmstat** exception report every day at 7:00 A.M.

```
00 * * * * /home/vmstat/run_vmstat.ksh > /home/vmstat/r.lst

00 7 * * * /home/vmstat/run_vmstat_alert.ksh prodb1 > /home/vmstat/v.lst
```

Now that you see how to monitor the Oracle database server, let's examine how you can use this technique to report on other Oracle-related servers. This technique is very handy for reporting on Oracle web servers and application servers.

Reporting vmstat Information on Other Oracle Servers

To get a complete picture of the performance of your total Oracle system, you must also monitor the behavior of all of the servers that communicate with Oracle. For example, many Oracle environments have other servers:

- **Oracle Applications**   In Oracle Applications products, you generally have separate application servers communicating with the database server.

- **SAP with Oracle**   In SAP, you have separate application servers that communicate with Oracle.

- **Real Application Clusters (Oracle Parallel Server)**   With RAC, you have multiple Oracle database servers, all sharing the same database.

- **Oracle Web Applications**   When using Oracle databases on the Web, you have separate web servers that direct the communications into the database.

This technique in get_vmstat.ksh can easily be extended to measure the performance of other servers in your Oracle environment. Note that the stats$vmstat table has a column to store the server name. Since you can separate **vmstat** metrics by server, you simply need to create a remote **vmstat** script that will capture the performance of the other servers and send the data to a central database. Because only the database server contains an Oracle database, the **vmstat** data will be sent to the database from the remote server using database links. Any server that has a Net8 client can be used to capture **vmstat** information.

If you take a close look at the get_vmstat script from above, you see that this script can be executed on a remote server. The script will send the **vmstat** data to the server that contains your Oracle database using a database link. Note where the script enters SQL*Plus using **sqlplus perfstat/perfstat@prod**.

By collecting the data remotely, you can capture a complete picture of the performance of all of the components of the Oracle environment, not just the database server. This is important in cases where you need to track slow performance of ecommerce systems. Using this **vmstat** information, you can go back to the time of the slowdown and see which web servers may have been overloaded and also examine the load on the database server.

Now that you understand how to capture server statistics into Oracle tables, you are ready to see how you can use this valuable information to ensure that your server is not the cause of Oracle performance problems. In the next section, we will look at some of the specific causes of server resource shortages and see techniques that can be used to reduce demands on the CPU and RAM. We will also explore some prewritten scripts that will automatically alert you to exceptional server conditions.

Reporting on UNIX Server Statistics

Once the data is captured in the stats$vmstat table, there is a wealth of reports that can be generated. Because all of the server statistics exist inside a single Oracle table, it is quite easy to write SQL*Plus queries to extract the data.

The **vmstat** data can be used to generate all types of interesting reports. There are four classes of **vmstat** reports:

- **Exception reports** These reports show the time period where predefined thresholds are exceeded.

- **Daily trend reports** These reports are often run and used with Excel spreadsheets to produce trending graphs.

- **Hourly trend reports** These reports show the average utilization, averaged by the hour of the day. These reports are very useful for showing peak usage periods in a production environment.

- **Long-term predictive reports** These reports generate a long-term trend line for performance. The data from these reports is often used with a linear regression to predict when additional RAM memory or CPU power is required for the server.

Let's now examine the script that can be used to generate these server reports and see how this information can help you tune your Oracle database.

Server Exception Reports

The SQL script vmstat_alert.sql can quickly give a complete exception report on all of the servers in your Oracle environment. This report will display times when the CPU and RAM memory exceed your predefined thresholds:

```
set lines 80;
set pages 999;
set feedback off;
set verify off;

column my_date heading 'date        hour' format a20
column c2       heading runq    format 999
column c3       heading pg_in   format 999
column c4       heading pg_ot   format 999
column c5       heading usr     format 999
column c6       heading sys     format 999
column c7       heading idl     format 999
column c8       heading wt      format 999


ttitle 'run queue > 2|May indicate an overloaded CPU|When runqueue exceeds
the number of CPUs| on the server, tasks are waiting for service.';


select
 server_name,
 to_char(start_date,'YY/MM/DD    HH24') my_date,
 avg(runque_waits)        c2,
 avg(page_in)             c3,
 avg(page_out)            c4,
 avg(user_cpu)            c5,
 avg(system_cpu)          c6,
 avg(idle_cpu)            c7
from
perfstat.stats$vmstat
WHERE
runque_waits > 2
and start_date > sysdate-&&1
group by
 server_name,
 to_char(start_date,'YY/MM/DD    HH24')
ORDER BY
 server_name,
 to_char(start_date,'YY/MM/DD    HH24')
;

ttitle 'page_in > 1|
May indicate overloaded memory|
Whenever Unix performs a page-in, the RAM memory |
 on the server has been exhausted and swap pages are being used.';


select
```

```
 server_name,
 to_char(start_date,'YY/MM/DD     HH24') my_date,
 avg(runque_waits)         c2,
 avg(page_in)              c3,
 avg(page_out)             c4,
 avg(user_cpu)             c5,
 avg(system_cpu)           c6,
 avg(idle_cpu)             c7
from
perfstat.stats$vmstat
WHERE
page_in > 1
and start_date > sysdate-&&1
group by
 server_name,
 to_char(start_date,'YY/MM/DD     HH24')
ORDER BY
 server_name,
 to_char(start_date,'YY/MM/DD     HH24')
;

ttitle 'user+system CPU > 70%|
Indicates periods with a fully-loaded CPU subs-system.|
Periods of 100% utilization are only a |
 concern when runqueue values exceeds the number of CPs on the server.';


select
 server_name,
 to_char(start_date,'YY/MM/DD     HH24') my_date,
 avg(runque_waits)         c2,
 avg(page_in)              c3,
 avg(page_out)             c4,
 avg(user_cpu)             c5,
 avg(system_cpu)           c6,
 avg(idle_cpu)             c7
from
perfstat.stats$vmstat
WHERE
(user_cpu + system_cpu) > 70
and start_date > sysdate-&&1
group by
 server_name,
 to_char(start_date,'YY/MM/DD     HH24')
ORDER BY
 server_name,
 to_char(start_date,'YY/MM/DD     HH24')
;
```

The standard **vmstat** alert report is used to alert the Oracle DBA and system administrator to out-of-bounds conditions on each Oracle server. These conditions include:

- **CPU waits > 40%**   (AIX version only) This may indicate I/O-based contention. The solution is to spread files across more disks or add buffer memory.

- **Runqueue > xxx**   (Where xxx is the number of CPUs on the server, 2 in this example) This indicates an overloaded CPU. The solution is to add additional processors to the server.

- **Page_in > 2**   Page in operations indicate overloaded memory. The solution is to reduce the size of the Oracle SGA, PGA, or add additional RAM memory to the server.

- **User CPU + System CPU > 90%**   This indicates periods where the CPU is highly utilized.

While the SQL here is self-explanatory, let's look at a sample report and see how it will help your system administrator monitor the server's behavior:

```
SQL> @vmstat_alert 7

Wed Dec 20                                                        page    1
                              run queue > 2
                        May indicate an overloaded CPU.
                When runqueue exceeds the number of CPUs
                 on the server, tasks are waiting for service.


SERVER_NAME        date          hour       runq pg_in pg_ot  usr  sys  idl
---------------    --------------------      ---- ----- ----- ---- ---- ----
AD-01              00/12/13      17             3     0     0   87    5    8

Wed Dec 20                                                        page    1
                              page_in > 1
                       May indicate overloaded memory.
                Whenever Unix performs a page-in, the RAM memory
          on the server has been exhausted and swap pages are being used.

SERVER_NAME        date          hour       runq pg_in pg_ot  usr  sys  idl
---------------    --------------------      ---- ----- ----- ---- ---- ----
AD-01              00/12/13      16             0     5     0    1    1   98
AD-01              00/12/14      09             0     5     0   10    2   88
AD-01              00/12/15      16             0     6     0    0    0  100
```

```
AD-01            00/12/19    20          0   29    2    1    2   98
PROD1DB          00/12/13    14          0    3   43    4    4   93
PROD1DB          00/12/19    07          0    2    0    1    3   96
PROD1DB          00/12/19    11          0    3    0    1    3   96
PROD1DB          00/12/19    12          0    6    0    1    3   96
PROD1DB          00/12/19    16          0    3    0    1    3   96
PROD1DB          00/12/19    17          0   47   68    5    5   91
```

Wed Dec 20   page   1
                         user+system > 70%
            Indicates periods with a fully-loaded CPU sub-system.
                  Periods of 100% utilization are only a
            concern when runqueue values exceeds the number of CPUs on the server.

SERVER_NAME	date	hour	runq	pg_in	pg_ot	usr	sys	idl
AD-01	00/12/13	14	0	0	2	75	2	22
AD-01	00/12/13	17	3	0	0	87	5	8
AD-01	00/12/15	15	0	0	0	50	29	22
AD-01	00/12/15	16	0	0	0	48	33	20
AD-01	00/12/19	07	0	0	0	77	4	19
AD-01	00/12/19	10	0	0	0	70	5	24
AD-01	00/12/19	11	1	0	0	60	17	24
PROD1	00/12/19	12	0	0	1	52	30	18
PROD1	00/12/19	13	0	0	0	39	59	2
PROD1	00/12/19	14	0	0	0	39	55	6
PROD1	00/12/19	15	1	0	0	57	23	20

You may notice that this exception report gives the hourly average for the **vmstat** information. If you look at the get_vmstat.ksh script, you will see that the data is captured in intervals of every 300 elapsed seconds (five-minute intervals). Hence, if you see an hour where your server is undergoing stress, you can modify your script to show the **vmstat** changes every five minutes. You can also run this report in conjunction with other STATSPACK reports to identify what tasks may have precipitated the server problem. The stats$sql_summary table is especially useful for this purpose.

Daily vmstat Trend Reports

One of the jobs of the Oracle tuning expert is to monitor the database and the server for regular trends. This is not just an exercise in searching for trends because every database will exhibit regular patterns of CPU and memory consumption.

Using the stats$vmstat table, it is very easy to write a query that will aggregate the CPU and memory. Below is a sample SQL script that aggregates server values:

```
connect perfstat/perfstat;
set pages 9999;

set feedback off;
set verify off;

column my_date heading 'date' format a20
column c2        heading runq    format 999
column c3        heading pg_in   format 999
column c4        heading pg_ot   format 999
column c5        heading usr     format 999
column c6        heading sys     format 999
column c7        heading idl     format 999
column c8        heading wt      format 999


select
 to_char(start_date,'day') my_date,
-- avg(runque_waits)        c2
-- avg(page_in)             c3,
-- avg(page_out)            c4,
avg(user_cpu + system_cpu)              c5,
-- avg(system_cpu)          c6,
-- avg(idle_cpu)            c7,
avg(wait_cpu)            c8
from
   stats$vmstat
group  BY
 to_char(start_date,'day')
order by
 to_char(start_date,'day')
;
```

Here you can see that you can easily get any of the **vmstat** values aggregated by day. In the output below you see the average user and wait CPU times for each day of the week:

```
SQL> @rpt_vmstat_dy
Connected.

date                  usr   wt
-------------------- ---- ----
friday                  8    0
monday                 10    0
saturday                1    0
```

```
sunday                     1      0
thursday                   6      0
tuesday                   15      0
wednesday                 11      0
```

This data can be extracted into MS-Excel and quickly plotted for graphical reference, as shown in Figure 3-5. Please note that my book *Oracle High-Performance Tuning with STATSPACK* covers a method of plotting STATSPACK data in MS-Excel.

Hourly vmstat Trend Reports

You can use the same techniques to average **vmstat** information by the hour of the day. An average by hour of the day can provide very valuable information regarding times when the server is experiencing stress:

```
connect perfstat/perfstat;
set pages 9999;

set feedback off;
set verify off;

column my_date heading 'date' format a20
column c2        heading runq   format 999
column c3        heading pg_in  format 999
column c4        heading pg_ot  format 999
column c5        heading cpu    format 999
column c6        heading sys    format 999
column c7        heading idl    format 999
column c8        heading wt     format 999


select
 to_char(start_date,'day')  my_date,
-- avg(runque_waits)        c2
-- avg(page_in)             c3,
-- avg(page_out)            c4,
avg(user_cpu + system_cpu)          c5,
-- avg(system_cpu)          c6,
-- avg(idle_cpu)            c7,
avg(wait_cpu)            c8
from
   stats$vmstat
group  BY
 to_char(start_date,'day')
order by
 to_char(start_date,'day')
;
```

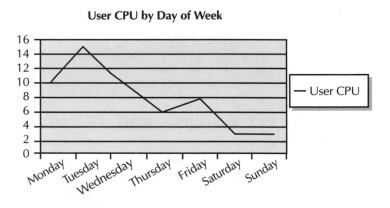

User CPU by Day of Week

FIGURE 3-5.   *A daily report of vmstat metrics*

Here you see the output from this script. You get the average run queue and user + system CPU values and wait CPU values, aggregated by hour of the day:

```
SQL> @rpt_vmstat_hr
Connected.


date                 runq  cpu   wt
-------------------- ---- ---- ----
00                      0    4    0
01                      0    .    U
02                      0    3    0
03                      0    1    0
04                      0    1    0
05                      0    1    0
06                      0    1    0
07                      0    1    0
08                      0    1    0
09                      0    1    0
10                      0    1    0
11                      0    1    0
12                      0   11    0
13                      0   21    0
14                      0   23    0
15                      0   20    0
16                      0   15    0
17                      0   20    0
18                      0   12    0
19                      0   10    0
```

```
20                      0    5    0
21                      0    1    0
22                      0    1    0
23                      0    1    0
```

This hourly information can also be extracted into MS-Excel for graphical plotting charts that show trends that may not be evident from a raw observation.

Long-Term Server Analysis and Trending

You can also use the data from stats$vmstat to gather information for long-term trend analysis, as shown in Figure 3-6. The nature of the **vmstat** tables allows the DBA to extract an ongoing average and then chart the data in MS-Excel. This Excel chart can also be enhanced to add a linear regression that can be used to predict future usage.

This long-term trend analysis is very useful for IT managers who must plan for additional server resources. For these managers, knowing the rate at which CPU and memory are being consumed on the server is critical, since there is often a lag time of several weeks between ordering and installing new hardware resources. If you want more detail on using STATSPACK information for management planning, please see my book *Oracle High-Performance Tuning with STATSPACK* (Oracle Press, 2001).

Daily Server Alert Report

As we have repeatedly noted, the Oracle DBA is very interested in monitoring conditions on the Oracle database servers and web servers. This script is generally

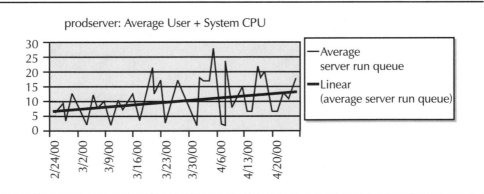

FIGURE 3-6. *A long-term hardware resource predictive report*

run daily to report on exceptional conditions within any server in the Oracle environment. The data is collected in five-minute intervals and reported with hourly averages. When the DBAs find an out-of-bounds server condition, they can run detailed reports that display the data in five-minute intervals.

run_vmstat.ksh

This is the driver script that submits the vmstat_alert report and e-mails the output to the appropriate staff members.

```ksh
#!/bin/ksh

# First, we must set the environment . . . .
ORACLE_SID=$1
export ORACLE_SID
ORACLE_HOME=`cat /var/opt/oracle/oratab|grep
ORACLE_SID:|cut -f2 -d':'`
export ORACLE_HOME
PATH=$ORACLE_HOME/bin:$PATH
export PATH


sqlplus /<<!
spool /tmp/vmstat_$1.ls
@vmstat_alert
spool off;
exit;
!

# Mail the report
check_stat=`cat /tmp/vmstat_$1.lst|wc -l`;
oracle_num=`expr $check_stat`
if [ $oracle_num -gt 3 ]
  then
    cat /tmp/vmstat_$1.lst|mailx -s "vmstat alert" \
    don@remote-dba.net \
    terry@wildcreek.com
fi
```

vmstat_alert.sql

This report provides information on the server conditions that may contribute to poor performance.

This report gathers the following server information.

Run queue waits   When the run queue exceeds the number of CPUs, the server is experiencing CPU bottlenecks:

```
Fri Dec 29                                                      page    1
                           run queue > 2
                    May indicate an overloaded CPU


SERVER_NAME          date          hour      runq pg_in pg_ot  usr  sys  idl
----------------     --------------------    ---- ----- ----- ---- ---- ----
BAD-01               00/12/22       13          6     0     0   62    7   32
BAD-01               00/12/22       15          3     0     0   82   18    0
BAD-01               00/12/22       17          3     0     0   76   16    8
BAD-01               00/12/27       11          3     0     0   77    5   20
```

RAM Swapping   When page in operations exist, the maximum RAM capacity of the server has been exceeded:

```
Fri Dec 29                                                      page    1
                           page_in > 1
                    May indicate overloaded memory


SERVER_NAME          date          hour      runq pg_in pg_ot  usr  sys  idl
----------------     --------------------    ---- ----- ----- ---- ---- ----
AD-01                00/12/22       14          0    19     0    1    1   97
AD-01                00/12/26       11          0    32     0    0    0   99
AD-01                00/12/28       17          0     5     0    0    1   99
JANETDB              00/12/22       13          0     3     0    1    3   96
JANETDB              00/12/22       14          0    27     1    6   17   77
JANETDB              00/12/22       15          0     3     0    1    3   96
JANETDB              00/12/22       16          0     7     0    3    9   88
JANETDB              00/12/22       17          0    10     0    4   10   86
JANETDB              00/12/22       18          0     2     1    1    3   96
JANETDB              00/12/23       09          0     2     0    1    3   96
JANETDB              00/12/24       03          0     4     0    1    3   96
JANETDB              00/12/26       10          0     3     0    1    3   96
JANETDB              00/12/26       11          0     2    21    8   17   75
JANETDB              00/12/26       12          0    10    10   13   27   60
JANETDB              00/12/27       09          0    10     0    1    3   96
JANETDB              00/12/27       10          0     5     0    1    3   96
JANETDB              00/12/27       11          0     6     0    1    3   95
JANETDB              00/12/28       03          0     2     0    1    3   96
JANETDB              00/12/28       11          0     2     0    1    3   95
JANETDB              00/12/28       21          0     3     1    2    4   95
```

High CPU   The DBA is often interested in times when the database CPU utilization is greater than 95 percent.

Fri Dec 29   page   1
                              user+system > 70%
                          Indicates an overloaded CPU

SERVER_NAME	date	hour	runq	pg_in	pg_ot	usr	sys	idl
AD-01	00/12/22	08	2	0	0	69	3	28
AD-01	00/12/22	13	12	0	0	89	11	1
AD-01	00/12/22	15	0	0	0	63	29	8
AD-01	00/12/22	17	1	0	0	53	27	20
AD-01	00/12/26	12	1	0	0	77	4	19
AD-01	00/12/27	11	3	0	0	86	6	9

Now let's wrap up this chapter with a review of the major points.

Conclusion

The focus of this chapter has been on the use of Oracle extension tables to monitor the performance of the Oracle UNIX server. The main points of this chapter include:

- The UNIX **vmstat** utility provides a wealth of information about the ongoing performance of the database server.

- The **vmstat** run queue value (**r**) can indicate a CPU shortage whenever the run queue exceeds the number of CPUs on the server.

- The **vmstat** page in values (**pi**) can indicate a RAM memory shortage.

- You can easily define the STATSPACK extension table to hold historical server information and use a UNIX shell script to periodically collect server performance information.

- The UNIX server information can be used to generate alert reports and long-term trend reports.

Now that you have an understanding of the methods for extending STATSPACK to monitor your database server, you are ready to look at the Oracle network environment. Distributed Oracle databases have become commonplace, and the time required to transfer information over the network can have a huge impact on the overall performance of the Oracle database application.

CHAPTER
4

Disk Management
in UNIX

his chapter deals with the single most important component of Oracle tuning: the time required to fetch data blocks from disk. Because I/O bottlenecks are the greatest source of response time problems in any Oracle database, the Oracle DBA must constantly be alert for I/O-related slowdowns. Every time that Oracle has to visit the disk to retrieve a database block, time is wasted and Oracle must wait for the I/O to complete.

The purpose of this chapter is to show how to minimize the amount of I/O in your Oracle database. In a data warehouse you can't minimize your I/O, but you always want to make sure that I/O is as efficient as possible.

This chapter covers the following topics:

- Basic UNIX disk management commands

- Monitoring UNIX mount points

- Configuring Oracle tablespaces and datafiles

- Mapping Oracle datafiles to UNIX

- Oracle tuning factors that affect disk I/O

- Oracle internals and disk I/O

- Mapping Oracle disk architectures

- STATSPACK reports for Oracle datafiles

- Extending STATSPACK for disk I/O data

- Viewing I/O signatures with STATSPACK

Here we will deal exclusively with I/O at the Oracle level, and how the Oracle DBA can identify patterns within the I/O subsystem and load balance their database for optimal performance.

NOTE
You are encouraged to run these prepared STATSPACK scripts against your database. It is only after you get insight into the I/O patterns within your database that you will be able to properly load balance your I/O subsystem.

We must emphasize that there are many techniques that can be performed within Oracle to reduce the amount of I/O, and stress that the primary motive for all Oracle tuning is to reduce I/O on the disks.

Basic UNIX Disk Management Commands

Within UNIX there is a mapping hierarchy of files. At the lowest level of the hierarchy you see the discrete datafiles, such as the files that comprise the Oracle database. These files are located within a UNIX mount point. A mount point is an area of logical storage that has no direct relationship to the physical disks.

Each UNIX mount point can be made up of one or many logical volumes (sometimes known as volume groups). The UNIX system administrator (SA) allocates chunks of physical partitions to the logical volumes. At the lowest level, chunks of a disk are separated into physical partitions.

In sum, the hierarchy can be defined as follows:

- A disk consists of physical partitions.

- A logical volume consists of physical partitions.

- A mount point consists of a file system built on the logical volume.

Viewing Physical Volumes

There are several differences when displaying physical volumes, each depending on your dialect of UNIX. The physical volume display generally corresponds directly to disk spindles, but sometimes the internals of the disk devices are hidden by mapping software at the disk level. For example, EMC disk arrays often have hidden mappings that cannot be seen with standard UNIX commands.

In HP-UX you can use the **pvdisplay** command is to display physical volumes, while in AIX the **lspv** command is invoked.

Viewing UNIX Volume Groups

Now you need to inspect the mapping between a physical partition and a UNIX volume group. The following commands can be used to pair volume groups with UNIX mount points in Solaris and AIX:

```
root> lsvg -o

vgpvg116
vgpvg153
vgpvg624
```

For details on a specific volume group, you can use the **lsvg -l** command, passing the volume group name as a parameter:

```
root> lsvg -l appvg01

appvg01:
LV NAME                 TYPE      LPs    PPs   PVs   LV STATE      MOUNT POINT
loglv00                 jfslog    1      1     1     open/syncd    N/A
lv01                    jfs       123    123   1     open/syncd    /u01
lv17                    jfs       62     62    1     open/syncd    /legato
```

Now let's use the **xargs** UNIX command to directly display the volume groups. The **xargs** UNIX command is used to pass the complete output of the first command (**lsvg -o** in this case) one at a time to the **lsvg -l** command. This is equivalent to running **lsvg -o**, gathering the logical volume name and issuing the **lsvg -l** command for each logical volume.

```
root> lsvg -o|xargs lsvg -l

appvg16:
LV NAME                 TYPE      LPs    PPs   PVs   LV STATE      MOUNT POINT
loglv15                 jfslog    1      1     1     open/syncd    N/A
lv16                    jfs       489    489   1     open/syncd    /u16
appvg15:
LV NAME                 TYPE      LPs    PPs   PVs   LV STATE      MOUNT POINT
loglv14                 jfslog    1      1     1     open/syncd    N/A
lv15                    jfs       489    489   1     open/syncd    /u15
```

Now that you understand UNIX volume groups, let's take a closer look at displaying UNIX mount points.

Display UNIX Mount Points

A UNIX *mount point* is the UNIX location of disk storage. There are two main commands to display base file systems: **bdf** and **df**.

As the Oracle DBA, you should know the mapping between your physical disks, logical volumes, and mount points. If you do not know this mapping, the detection of a hot disk will not be helpful since you will be unable to trace the hot disk to an Oracle datafile.

The best way to start a file placement strategy is to create a transparent disk architecture whereby the DBA can correlate the datafile name to a specific Oracle table or index. Let's explore how you create this type of architecture.

Let's start with HP-UX. The **bdf** command is used with HP-UX to display a file system:

```
root> bdf

Filesystem          kbytes      used    avail %used Mounted on
/dev/vg00/lvol3     143360    140317     2868   98% /
/dev/vg00/lvol1      83733     28295    47064   38% /stand
/dev/vg00/lvol8    1597440    642544   895482   42% /var
/dev/vg00/lvol7     999424    503351   465097   52% /usr
/dev/vg05/u08      6291456   5445579   794737   87% /u08
/dev/vg05/u07      2621440   1048595   174643   42% /u07
/dev/vg05/u06     12582912   6520474  5888678   53% /u06
/dev/vg05/u05      8388608   6450888  1877206   77% /u05
/dev/vg04/u04     71675904  45483648 25987920   64% /u04
/dev/vg03/u03     35545088  29105880  6339604   82% /u03
/dev/vg02/u02     35545088  33483744  2045828   94% /u02
/dev/vg01/u01     17772544   8259264  9364928   47% /u01
/dev/vg00/lvol14     65536      8053    53992   13% /tmp
/dev/vg00/lvol16    630784    581669    46143   93% /opt
/dev/vg00/lvol15     61440     44001    16355   73% /home
```

On AIX and Solaris, the **df** command is the primary command to display mount points:

```
root> df -k
Filesystem    1024-blocks      Free %Used    Iused %Iused Mounted on
/dev/hd4            32768     11636   65%     2017    13% /
/dev/hd2           802816     15920   99%    26308    14% /usr
/dev/hd9var         49152     28316   43%      567     5% /var
/dev/hd3            32768     14420   56%      285     4% /tmp
/dev/hd1           131072     20484   85%     5611    18% /home
/dev/lv01         2015232    843328   59%     5750     2% /u01
/dev/lv02         2015232    247172   88%      916     1% /u02
/dev/lv03         4521984    944420   80%      199     1% /u03
/dev/lv04         4505600   1646880   64%       53     1% /u04
```

In HP-UX version 11, the **df -k** command can be used, but the output is different in HP-UX than AIX and Solaris:

```
root> df -k
/home            (/dev/vg00/lvol5       )  :    60356 total allocated Kb
                                                16355 free allocated Kb
                                                44001 used allocated Kb
                                                   72 % allocation used
```

```
/opt              (/dev/vg00/lvol6      ) :   627811 total allocated Kb
                                              46140 free allocated Kb
                                             581671 used allocated Kb
                                                 92 % allocation used
/tmp              (/dev/vg00/lvol4      ) :    62052 total allocated Kb
                                              53872 free allocated Kb
                                               8180 used allocated Kb
                                                 13 % allocation used
/u01              (/dev/vg01/u01        ) : 17624192 total allocated Kb
                                            9364928 free allocated Kb
                                            8259264 used allocated Kb
                                                 46 % allocation used
/u02              (/dev/vg02/u02        ) : 35529552 total allocated Kb
                                            2047288 free allocated Kb
                                           33482264 used allocated Kb
                                                 94 % allocation used
/u03              (/dev/vg03/u03        ) : 35445484 total allocated Kb
                                            6339604 free allocated Kb
                                           29105880 used allocated Kb
                                                 82 % allocation used
/u04              (/dev/vg04/u04        ) : 71471568 total allocated Kb
                                           25987920 free allocated Kb
                                           45483648 used allocated Kb
                                                 63 % allocation used
```

Show Mount Points for a Disk in AIX

You can use the list physical volume command **lspv** to display disk mount points in IBM AIX. Here you restrict the **lspv** command to display the mount points that map to disk hdisk16:

```
root> lspv -l hdisk16

hdisk16:
LV NAME               LPs    PPs    DISTRIBUTION          MOUNT POINT
Loglv53               1      1      00..01..00..00..00    N/A
Lv75                  175    175    00..207..108..60..00  /u01
```

Next, let's see how automated scripts can be used to monitor UNIX file systems.

Setting Your UNIX Oracle Environment for Dialect Differences

When you write UNIX scripts that remotely access servers with different dialects of UNIX, you must be able to issue the appropriate command based on the current

UNIX dialect. For example, if you are on HP-UX you need to use the **bdf** command, and if you are on Solaris you need to use the **df -k** command.

The following is a script that will set a UNIX variable to your OS dialect. This script sets the **$dialect_df** UNIX environment variable to the proper syntax depending upon the dialect if UNIX. If you work in an environment where you change frequently between UNIX dialects, you can execute the **$dialect_df** command to execute the appropriate command.

```
#***************************************************************
# Set-up the dialect changes for HP-UX and AIX (df -k) vs (bdf)
#***************************************************************
os=`uname -a|awk '{ print $1 }'`
if [ $os = "OSF1" ]
then
    alias df="df -k"
fi
if [ $os = "AIX" ]
then
    alias df="df -k"
fi
if [ $os = "IRIX64" ]
then
    alias df="df -k"
fi
if [ $os = "HP-UX" ]
then
    alias df="bdf"
fi
```

Monitoring File System Free Space in UNIX

We have some very important scripts for monitoring UNIX file free space in Chapter 12, but this is a good time to see how simple commands can be written to monitor the free space within any UNIX mount point.

One of the most important jobs of the Oracle DBA in a UNIX environment is ensuring that none of the UNIX file systems becomes full. When you create tablespaces with the **autoextend** option, you move the monitoring from Oracle to UNIX. Whenever tablespaces are allowed to grow within the UNIX mount point, you must be always vigilant to make sure that the file system does not become full.

When a UNIX file system for an Oracle datafile cannot extend, your entire database will hang, waiting for room to extend. Given the importance of this monitoring, most Oracle DBAs in UNIX write scripts to monitor all of their file systems or preallocate space for datafiles to ensure that they will not autoextend beyond the space for a file system.

Let's take a look at how this works.

Display All Filesystems

We will start by issuing a **df -k** command to get a listing of all UNIX mount points. Note that the mount point display command is different depending on the dialect of UNIX you are using:

- **Solaris**   Use the **df –k** command

- **AIX**   Use the **df –k** command

- **HP-UX**   Use the **bdf** command

- **Linux**   Use the **df –m** command

This example file system display is from the Solaris dialect of UNIX:

```
root> df -k
Filesystem           kbytes     used    avail capacity  Mounted on
/dev/dsk/c0t0d0s0    4032504   104381 3887798     3%    /
/dev/dsk/c0t0d0s4    4032504   992890 2999289    25%    /usr
/proc                      0        0       0     0%    /proc
fd                         0        0       0     0%    /dev/fd
mnttab                     0        0       0     0%    /etc/mnttab
/dev/dsk/c0t0d0s3    4032504   657034 3335145    17%    /var
swap                 4095176        8 4095168     1%    /var/run
swap                 4095192       24 4095168     1%    /tmp
/dev/dsk/c0t0d0s5    1984564   195871 1729157    11%    /opt
/dev/dsk/c0t0d0s7   14843673  1619568 13075669   12%    /helpdesk
/dev/oradg/u02vol   12582912  8717924 3744252    70%    /u02
/dev/oradg/u01vol    8796160  5562586 3132548    64%    /u01
/dev/oradg/u04vol   10035200  1247888 8519534    13%    /u04
/dev/oradg/u03vol   12582912  2524060 9744542    21%    /u03
/dev/dsk/c0t0d0s6    1984564   931591  993437    49%    /export/home
/vol/c0t/orcl901_3    270364   270364       0   100%    /cdrom/orcl901_3
```

Here you see the following display columns:

1. File system name

2. Kilobytes in the file system

3. Kilobytes used in the file system

4. Kilobytes available in the file system

5. File system capacity

6. Mount point associated with the file system

Your goal is to filter this output to see the available space for the Oracle file systems. You also see rows in this server that are not associated with Oracle files.

Display Oracle File Systems

Your next step is to eliminate all file systems except the Oracle file systems. In this system, you are using the Oracle Optimal Flexible Architecture (OFA), and all Oracle file systems begin with /u0. Hence, you can use the UNIX **grep** utility to eliminate all lines except for those containing the string /u0:

```
root> df -k|grep /u0
/dev/vx/dsk/oradg/u02vol 12582912 8717924 3744252     70%    /u02
/dev/vx/dsk/oradg/u01vol 8796160 5563610 3131556      64%    /u01
/dev/vx/dsk/oradg/u04vol 10035200 1247888 8519534     13%    /u04
/dev/vx/dsk/oradg/u03vol 12582912 2524060 9744542     21%    /u03
```

Extract the Available Space for Each File System

Now that you have the Oracle file systems, you can use the UNIX **awk** utility to extract the fourth column, which is the available space in the file system:

```
root> df -k|grep /u0|awk '{ print $4 }'
3744252
3132546
8519534
9744542
```

Create the Script to Check Space in All File Systems

Now that you see the command, you can place this command inside a loop to evaluate the free space for each file system. Note that your command is placed inside the Korn shell for loop, and the command is enclosed in back-ticks (the key immediately above the TAB key).

check_filesystem_size.ksh

```
#!/bin/ksh

for i in `df -k|grep /u0|awk '{ print $4 }'`
do
   # Convert the file size to a numeric value
   filesize=`expr i`

   # If any filesystem has less than 100k, issue an alert
   if [ $filesize  -lt 100 ]
   then
      mailx -s "Oracle filesystem $i has less than 100k free."\
         don@burleson.cc\
```

```
        oracle_dba@my.company.com
    fi
done
```

This simple script will check every file system on the server and e-mail you as soon as any file system has less than 100K of free space.

Scheduling the File Alert

We generally place this type of script in a crontab file, and execute it every three minutes as shown in this UNIX crontab entry:

```
#*************************************************************
# This is the every 5 min. trace file alert report for the DBAs
#*************************************************************
1,3,5,7,9,11,13,15,17,19,21,23,25,27,29,31,33,35,37,39,41,43,45,
47,49,51,53,5,57,59 * * * * /home/oracle/check_filesystem_size.ksh >
dev/null >&1
```

Next, let's take a look at how you can optimize Oracle tablespaces and UNIX datafiles.

Configuring Oracle Tablespaces and UNIX Datafiles

Since different application processes have different I/O patterns, hot disks may appear on different disks at different times during each day. The goal of disk load balancing is to eliminate disk I/O bottlenecks, but it is important to remember that these bottlenecks are transient in nature. Since Oracle transactions happen very quickly, a disk may experience an I/O bottleneck for a very short period, and this short-duration bottleneck may repeat itself thousands of times each day. However, many Oracle administrators make the mistake of summarizing I/O by the hour, and the disk will appear not to have bottlenecks since the I/O spikes will have disappeared in the hourly average, as shown in Figure 4-1.

To get the most accurate results, you should collect I/O statistics at frequent intervals—preferably no more than ten minutes between samples—over a representative time period, such as a week. Because individual application processes have different I/O patterns, bottlenecks may appear on different disks at various times during each day. And because Oracle transactions happen very quickly, a disk may experience an I/O bottleneck for a very short period, but a short-duration bottleneck may nonetheless repeat itself thousands of times each day. If you make the mistake of summarizing I/O by the hour, as many DBAs do, you won't see these bottlenecks because the I/O spikes will not be evident in the hourly average.

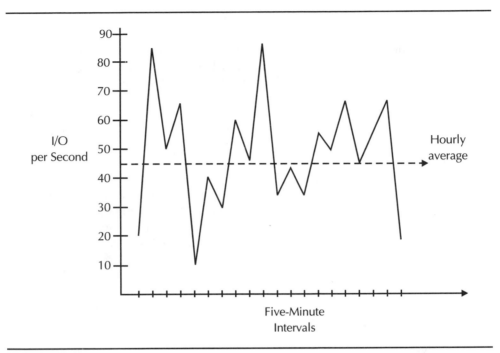

FIGURE 4-1. *Short disk I/O spikes can be lost with long measurement intervals*

The point is simple: in order to accurately identify and correct disk I/O bottlenecks, you must measure in minor duration, preferably no more than ten minutes between samples. We will discuss this technique in Chapter 8 where we will show how to extend STATSPACK to capture disk **iostat** information.

The goal of load balancing is to distribute the files across disks so as to achieve a single static optimal I/O throughput. Moving Oracle datafiles to other disks is not a trivial operation, and Oracle must be stopped before the file can be moved to another disk. However, the good news is that once the I/O subsystem is balanced, the files will not need to be moved unless new processes change the I/O pattern for the disks.

The goal is to find the optimal file placement where overall load balance is achieved for all of the many variations of disk access. Load balancing is essentially the identification of hot disks, and the movement of datafiles to less-used cool disks. As such, disk load balancing is an iterative process since it is possible that relocating a datafile may relieve contention for one process, only to cause I/O contention for an unrelated process. Also, for databases placed on a small number of disks, it is possible that I/O contention cannot be avoided. Consider a 30GB database spread across disks with 20 competing processes for data. On average, ten processes would be queued waiting for I/O from each of the two disks. Clearly, these types of systems will always experience I/O contention.

Within Oracle in any UNIX environment, you have a hierarchical relationship between entities. Each physical disk has many UNIX mount points, each mount point has many Oracle datafiles, and each datafile may have many Oracle tables, as shown in Figure 4-2.

After using data collected by **iostat** to identify a hot disk, you would use data collected by the Oracle utilities to identify which mount point and file contain the table causing the excessive I/O activity.

Identifying the hot disk is only the beginning of the quest. You must then see what mount point on the disk is causing the problem, which datafile on the mount point, and finally, what Oracle table is causing the excessive I/O. Only with this approach can the Oracle administrator fully understand how to perform disk load balancing. With that in mind, let's look at the first method for collecting Oracle I/O statistics. We will then move on to look at collecting UNIX I/O statistics.

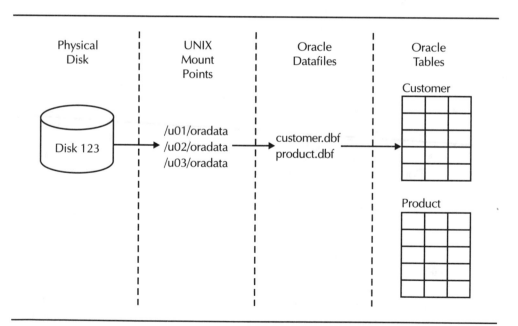

FIGURE 4-2. *The hierarchy of Oracle file structures on UNIX*

Oracle Tuning Factors that Influence Disk I/O

As you know, one of the primary goals of all Oracle tuning activities is to reduce disk I/O. We will be discussing these techniques throughout this book, but we need to mention them here so you will understand how the instance parameters can affect disk I/O. There are three areas where the settings for Oracle have a direct impact on the amount of disk I/O. The settings for the Oracle instance (**init.ora**) impact disk I/O, the settings for Oracle objects (tables and indexes) affect disk I/O, and the execution plans for Oracle SQL also have a direct impact on disk I/O.

Oracle Instance

There are several database instance parameters that have a direct impact on lowering physical disk I/O:

- **Large db_block_size**   The block size of the database has a dramatic effect on the amount of disk I/O. As a general rule, the larger the block size, the less the disk I/O.

- **Large db_block_buffers**   The greater the number of data buffers, the smaller the chance that Oracle will need to perform disk I/O.

- **Multiple database writers (DBWR) processes**   Multiple database writer background processes allow for more efficient writing to the datafiles.

- **Large sort_area_size**   The greater the **sort_area_size** in RAM, the less disk sorting will take place in the TEMP tablespace.

- **Large online redo logs**   The larger the online redo logs, the less frequent the log switches.

Oracle Objects

Inside the database, settings for table and indexes can reduce physical disk I/O:

- **Low pctused**   The smaller the value of **pctused**, the less I/O will occur on subsequent SQL inserts.

- **Low pctfree**   If **pctfree** is set to allow all rows to expand without fragmenting, the less disk I/O will occur on subsequent SQL selects.

- **Reorganizing tables to cluster rows with indexes**   If tables are placed in the same physical order as the most frequently used index, disk I/O will drop dramatically.

Oracle SQL

Within SQL statements, there are many techniques to reduce physical disk I/O:

- **Preventing unnecessary full table scans using indexes or hints**   This is the most important way to reduce disk I/O because many SQL queries can use indexes to reduce disk I/O.

- **Using bitmapped indexes**   The use of bitmapped indexes will reduce full table scans on tables with low-cardinality columns, thereby reducing disk I/O.

- **Applying SQL hints**   Many hints make SQL run faster and with less disk I/O. For example, the USE_HASH hint will reduce disk I/O by performing joins within SGA memory, reducing calls for database blocks.

Now that we have reviewed some of the things you can do within Oracle to reduce disk I/O, let's take a close look at the nature of disk I/O and examine the internal workings of the disk I/O subsystem.

Oracle Internals and Disk I/O

From an Oracle perspective, most databases can be characterized as either online transaction processing (OLTP) systems or decision support systems (DSS) systems. The patterns of I/O vary greatly between a data warehouse and decision support type of application, and one that processes online transactions. While OLTP may appear random, upon closer inspection, you will see clear areas of impact to the Oracle database and understand methods to alleviate I/O contention.

The db_file_multiblock_read_count and Disk I/O

Oracle has an **init.ora** parameter that controls the rate for which blocks are read when long contiguous data blocks are requested. The **db_block_size** parameters can have a dramatic impact on system performance. In addition, there is an important relationship between **db_block_size** and the **db_file_multiblock_read_count** parameter. At the physical level in UNIX, Oracle always reads in a minimum of 64K blocks.

Therefore, the values of **db_file_multiblock_read_count** and **db_block_size** should be set so that their product is 64K. For example:

8K blocks	**db_block_size** = 8,192	**db_file_multiblock_read_count** = 8
16K blocks	**db_block_size** = 16,384	**db_file_multiblock_read_count** = 4

Again, the **db_file_multiblock_read_count** is most beneficial for systems that perform frequent full table scans, such as data warehouses.

The Database Writer Process and Disk I/O

You may remember that earlier in this chapter we stated that the database writer (DBWR) background processes are responsible for writing dirty data blocks into disk.

For highly active databases, the database writer is a very important Oracle function since the DBWR processes govern the rate at which changed blocks are written to disk. Let's begin with a brief overview of the functions of the DBWR and see how it writes data blocks to disk.

When Oracle detects that a data block in the buffer cache has been changed, the data block is marked as dirty. Once marked as dirty, the block is queued for a database writer process, which writes the block back to the disk. The DBWR background processes have two responsibilities:

■ Scanning the buffer cache, looking for dirty buffers to write

■ Writing the dirty buffers to the disk

It is important to note that every operating system has implemented disk I/O very differently. Hence, the internal process of writing data blocks is specific to the operating system.

Tuning the database writer processes is also important. Within the Oracle data buffer, read-only data blocks can age-out of the buffer, but dirty blocks must be retained in the data buffer until the database writer has copied the block to disk.

Oracle offers two **init.ora** parameters for implementing multiple database writers:

■ **dbwr_io_slaves** This is a method whereby a master database writer process spawns additional slave processes to handle the database writes. This option is also used on database servers where asynchronous I/O is not supported. Some UNIX server systems (such as Solaris and AIX) support asynchronous I/O. If your platform does *not* support asynchronous I/O, you can simulate the asynchronous I/O by defining I/O slave processes.

■ **db_writer_processes** Starting with Oracle 8.0.5, Oracle8 supports true multiple DBWR processes, with no master/slave relationships. This parameter requires that the database server support asynchronous I/O.

Remember, you should only implement multiple database writers when you have a clear indication of writing backlogs. Implementing **db_io_slaves** or **db_writer_processes** comes at a cost in server resources. The multiple writer processes and I/O slaves are intended for large databases with high I/O throughput, and you should only implement multiple database writers if your system requires the additional I/O throughput.

In addition, there are several other **init.ora** parameters that affect the behavior of the DBWR processes:

- **db_block_lru_latches**   This is the number of LRU latches for database blocks. You cannot set **db_writer_process** to a value that is greater than **db_block_lru_latches**.

- **log_checkpoint_interval**   This controls the number of checkpoints issued by the DBWR process. Frequent checkpoints make recovery time faster, but it may also cause excessive DBWR activity during high-volume update tasks. The minimum value for **log_checkpoint_interval** should be set to a value larger than the largest redo log file.

- **log_checkpoint_timeout**   This should be set to zero.

NOTE
*Multiple **db_writer_process** and multiple **dbwr_io_slaves** are mutually exclusive. If both are set, the **dbwr_io_slaves** parameter will take precedence.*

Now that you understand how the DBWR processes work, let's see where you can go to find information about their performance.

Monitoring the Database Writers with STATSPACK
You can begin your journey by looking at the stats$sysstat table. There are numerous statistics that STATSPACK keeps in this table that provide information about the DBWR behavior.

```
sql> select distinct name from stats$sysstat where name like 'DBWR%'
NAME
----------------------------------------------------------------
DBWR Flush object call found no dirty buffers
DBWR Flush object cross instance calls
DBWR buffers scanned
DBWR checkpoint buffers written
DBWR checkpoint write requests
DBWR checkpoints
DBWR cross instance writes
DBWR free buffers found
DBWR incr. ckpt. write requests
DBWR lru scans
```

```
DBWR make free requests
DBWR revisited being-written buffer
DBWR skip hot writes
DBWR summed scan depth
DBWR timeouts
DBWR transaction table writes
DBWR undo block writes
```

Most of these values are of no interest, but a few of them are quite useful. Let's look at the functions of some of the useful values:

- **DBWR checkpoints**   This is the number of checkpoint messages that were sent to the DBWR from Oracle. During checkpoint processing, the log writer hands over to the DBWR a list of modified blocks that are to be written to disk.

- **DBWR buffers scanned**   This is the number of buffers looked at when scanning for dirty buffers to write to the database. This count includes all inspected buffers, including both dirty and clean buffers.

- **Summed dirty queue length**   This is the sum of the queue length after every write request has completed.

- **Write requests**   This is the total number of write requests that were made by Oracle to the database writers.

The main task is determining if the default configuration for the database writers is sufficient for your database. The *summed dirty queue length* and *write requests* are the two metrics in STATSPACK that are useful for measuring the efficiency of the DBWR background processes.

By dividing the summed dirty queue length by the number of write requests, you can get the average length of the queue following the completion of the write.

The following STATSPACK query will measure the dirty queue length for the time period between each snapshot. Any value above 100 indicates a shortage of DBWR processes.

rpt_dbwr_alert.sql

```
-- Written by Donald K. Burleson   1/25/01

set pages 999;

column c1 heading "Write request length" format 9,999.99
column c2 heading "Write Requests"       format 999,999
column c3 heading "DBWR checkpoints"      format 999,999
column mydate heading 'Yr.  Mo Dy  Hr.'  format a16
```

```
select distinct
   to_char(snap_time,'yyyy-mm-dd HH24')  mydate,
   a.value/b.value                       c1,
   b.value                               c2,
   c.value                               c3
from
   stats$sysstat   a,
   stats$sysstat   b,
   stats$sysstat   c,
   stats$snapshot sn
where
   sn.snap_id = a.snap_id
and
   sn.snap_id = b.snap_id
and
   sn.snap_id = c.snap_id
and
   a.name = 'summed dirty queue length'
and
   b.name = 'write requests'
and
   c.name = 'DBWR checkpoints'
and
   a.value > 0
and
   b.value > 0
and
   a.value/b.value > 3
;
```

Here is the output from this report. Here you see that the average queue length is quite small, ranging from 2 to 5. According to Oracle, you should only become concerned if the average queue length after writes is more than 50 blocks.

Yr. Mo Dy Hr.	Write request length	Write Requests	DBWR checkpoints
2000-12-25 01	4.71	20,103	44,016
2000-12-25 02	4.62	20,520	44,260
2000-12-25 03	4.51	21,023	45,235
2000-12-25 04	4.31	22,002	47,198
2000-12-25 05	4.13	22,948	49,134
2000-12-25 06	3.96	23,902	51,055
2000-12-25 07	3.81	24,867	52,991
2000-12-25 08	3.67	25,808	54,913
2000-12-25 09	3.54	26,731	56,797
2000-12-25 10	3.42	27,667	58,673

```
2000-12-25 11                   3.31        28,618        60,622
2000-12-25 12                   3.20        29,580        62,544
2000-12-25 13                   3.10        30,524        64,489
2000-12-25 14                   3.01        31,492        66,418
2001-01-01 01                   4.70        13,492        31,992
2001-01-01 02                   4.37        14,481        34,007
2001-01-01 03                   4.09        15,486        36,032
```

You can easily extend the STATSPACK report to report on the average values, aggregated by hour of the day and day of the week. This will help the DBA identify trends in database write activity. The following is an example of the STATSPACK script that averages the queue length values by hour of the day:

rpt_dbwr_hr.sql

```
set pages 999;

column c1 heading "Write request length" format 9,999.99
column c2 heading "Write Requests"        format 999,999
column c3 heading "DBWR checkpoints"      format 999,999

select distinct
   to_char(snap_time,'HH24')              mydate,
   avg(a.value/b.value)                   c1
from
   stats$sysstat   a,
   stats$sysstat   b,
   stats$snapshot sn
where
   sn.snap_id = a.snap_id
and
   sn.snap_id = b.snap_id
and
   a.name = 'summed dirty queue length'
and
   b.name = 'write requests'
and
   a.value > 0
and
   b.value > 0
group by
   to_char(snap_time,'HH24')
;
```

Here is the output from this script. You can now easily take this output and plot a graphical representation on the data from an Excel spreadsheet.

```
                   Hr.  Write request length
    ----------------  --------------------
    00                              1.11
    01                              2.60
    02                              2.51
    03                              2.43
    04                              1.99
    05                              1.91
    06                              1.84
    07                              1.55
    08                               .96
    09                               .98
    10                               .80
    11                               .75
    12                               .76
    13                               .74
    14                               .74
    15                               .71
    16                               .61
    17                               .99
    18                               .97
    19                               .93
    20                               .86
    21                               .89
    22                               .86
    23                               .95
```

Here you see that the DBWR is busiest in the early morning hours between midnight and 8:00 A.M. This is because this database does its batch updates during this processing window.

You can slightly alter the above script and aggregate the average queue length, summarized by the day of the week. Here, you take the averages and group them by day:

rpt_dbwr_dy.sql

```
Set pages 999;


column c1 heading "Write request length" format 9,999.99
column c2 heading "Write Requests"        format 999,999
column c3 heading "DBWR checkpoints"      format 999,999
column mydate heading 'Day of Week'

select distinct
   to_char(snap_time,'day')                   mydate,
   avg(a.value/b.value)                          c1
from
   stats$sysstat  a,
```

```
       stats$sysstat  b,
       stats$snapshot sn
where
   sn.snap_id = a.snap_id
and
   sn.snap_id = b.snap_id
and
   a.name = 'summed dirty queue length'
and
   b.name = 'write requests'
and
   a.value > 0
and
   b.value > 0
group by
   to_char(snap_time,'day')
;
```

Here is the output. Again, it is simple to create a graph from this output.

```
Day of week        Write request length
---------------    --------------------
friday                              .18
monday                             2.31
saturday                            .02
sunday                             1.96
thursday                           1.53
tuesday                             .43
wednesday                           .10
```

Figure 4-3 shows the graph. Here, you see that the overall efficiency of the database writer is fine, but the peak write times are on Monday, Wednesday, and Sunday.

In summary, the database writer processes will work fine for most Oracle databases without modification. However, when you detect that the summed dirty queue length is too high, you can look at increasing the number of database writer processes.

Next, let's examine Oracle file organization techniques.

Oracle File Organization Techniques

Regardless of whether or not you use RAID, it is very important for the Oracle DBA to identify all high-volume and high-activity tables and move them into isolated tablespaces. By keeping the high-volume tables in a separate tablespace, the Oracle administrator can manipulate the datafiles in the tablespace to minimize I/O contention on the disk, as shown in Figure 4-4.

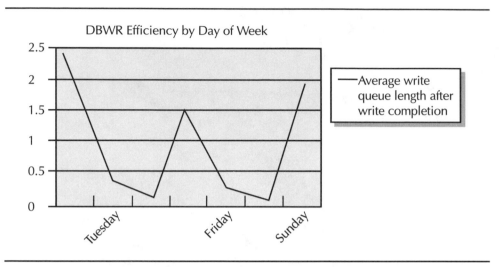

FIGURE 4-3. *Average queue length after write completion by day of week*

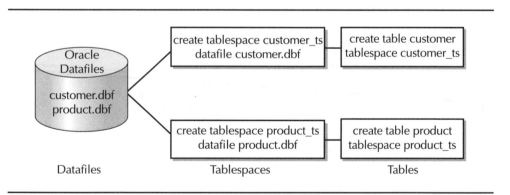

FIGURE 4-4. *Segregating Oracle tables into separate tablespaces*

Without segregation, some tablespaces may have hundreds of tables and indexes, and it is impossible to tell which objects are experiencing the high I/O. The stats$filestatxs table will provide details about read and write I/O at the file level, but it is often difficult to tell the tables that are causing the high I/O because a file may contain many objects.

With segregation, the DBA can generate STATSPACK file I/O reports from the stats$filestatxs table that show all read and write I/O for the datafile. If the Oracle datafile maps to only one table, you can easily see the total I/O for the table. Later in this chapter you will see a STATSPACK script called rpt_io_pct.sql that serves this purpose.

Because of the high-speed transaction-oriented nature of most Oracle applications, you generally see high activity in specific areas within each tablespace. While this chapter describes the basics of I/O load balancing for Oracle datafiles and tablespaces, the settings for the individual tables will also have a profound influence on the performance of the entire database. We will look at disk I/O within Oracle and examine these areas:

- Transient disk hot spots
- Disk I/O patterns within highly active tables

Transient Disk Hot Spots

In any Oracle database it is not uncommon to see sporadic hot spots appear on disks as the I/O signature changes. As you know, Oracle offers a wealth of data buffering tools that are designed to keep Oracle data blocks within RAM and prevent I/O. These techniques include table caching and separate data buffers. However, unless you have your database fully cached in the data buffers, you will always experience I/O activity.

I/O Patterns Within High-Update Tables

There is a special case of disk I/O that occurs when a transaction table experiences high-volume **insert** and **update** operations. For example, consider an order processing system with 3,000 data entry operators constantly slamming orders into a large order table. Let's further assume that at any given time, there are 200 transactions inserting into this table. As you will see, a close inspection of the datafiles will reveal several important characteristics within tables that have high-volume inserts:

- Roving hot spots on disk
- The sparse table phenomenon

Roving Hot Spots on Disk

To understand roving hot spots on disk we will give a simple example. Let's assume that your database has a table named transaction that has 200 data entry operators constantly adding rows. The transaction table is defined with 200 freelists, and the table is gathering free blocks by raising the high-water mark for the Oracle table.

As you know, freelists are the mechanism used by Oracle tables to allow them to accept concurrent insert and delete activity. You should always define an Oracle tables' freelists to a value equal to the high-water mark of concurrent inserts into that table.

This example assumes that there are not any free blocks on the freelists for the table, such as the case where the APPEND hint is used with the **insert** statements. Since you know that Oracle bumps the high-water mark for a table in increments of five blocks, your 200 concurrent inserts would generate intensive SQL **insert** activity that is isolated to a set of 1,000 blocks within the table.

Because each of the **insert** transactions must request a separate free block from the transaction table to insert their new transactions, Oracle will grab free blocks (five at a time) from sequential free space in the tablespace. These free blocks are likely to be contiguous blocks on the disk. Since these contiguous blocks are likely to reside on the same disk cylinder, it is likely that this disk would experience I/O contention at the end of the table.

As your data entry operators continue to hand key entries into the transaction table, you see the hot spot moving along the disk as new cylinders are accesses by the table (see Figure 4-5).

As you can see, the hot spot will travel through the tablespaces as Oracle blocks become full and the Oracle tables expand. So long as all of the SQL **insert** statements add blocks into a new data block, the hot spot will travel cleanly across the disks.

However, what happens after a transaction purge job is run? When older transactions are deleted from the table, blocks become free and are added to one of the 100 freelists for the table. As the freelists are loaded with newly empty blocks from the purge job, the hot spot will travel backward in the table, returning to the area of the table where the purge job removed the rows, as shown in Figure 4-6.

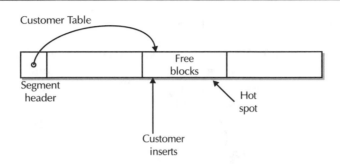

FIGURE 4-5. *The roving hot spot within a transaction table*

Oracle tablespaces that contain high-volume tables often experience the "roving hot spot" phenomenon. This is especially true for tables where rows are inserted and deleted on a date-time basis, such as a fact table with an Oracle data warehouse.

You see this type of time-based entry into many Oracle tables. For example, orders for goods are inserted in a time-based sequence, data warehouses load their data in a time sequence, and most every online system adds and purges rows based on a time sequence.

So, given that these roving hot spots will appear, what can you do to manage the activity? The trick to managing roving hot spots is to ensure that the free blocks always reside on adjacent cylinders. When Oracle data blocks are re-added to the

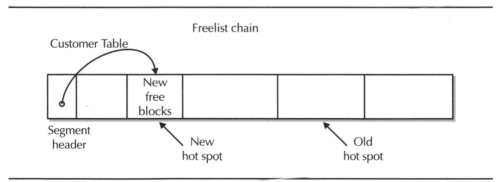

FIGURE 4-6. *The hot spot travels back in the table*

freelists, you cannot guarantee that they will be close together on the disk, and this condition can create a "disk thrashing" situation. Disk thrashing occurs when free blocks are located on widely distant cylinders on the disk (see Figure 4-7). As your 200 tasks compete for free blocks, the read-write heads thrash back and forth attempting to meet the needs of each transaction. The time required for a disk's read-write head to move between cylinders is called *seek delay*, and seek delay is the single most time-consuming factor in disk access.

There are several techniques that can be used to remedy this problem:

- **Segregate objects** Identify all tables with high insert activity and segregate then into a separate tablespace.

- **Use fresh data blocks** Ensure that all new inserts go onto new data blocks at the end of the table by using the APPEND hint in all **insert** statements.

- **Reorganize tables** Reorganize the table after purge jobs are run to reclaim the freed blocks onto the end of the table.

In addition to roving hot spots, these highly active Oracle tables will also manifest themselves as sparse tables.

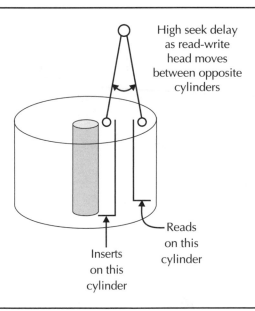

FIGURE 4-7. *High seek delay on a disk*

The Sparse Table Phenomenon

Sparse tables generally occur when a highly active table is defined with many freelists, and the table has heavy **insert** and **delete** activity. In a sparse table, the table will appear to have thousands of free blocks, yet the table will continue to extend, and the table will behave as if Oracle does not have any free data blocks. A sparse table in a data warehouse can consume a huge amount of unnecessary storage, consuming many gigabytes of new storage while the table appears to have lots of free space. Remember, when you have multiple freelists, the freelists are independent and Oracle cannot share freelist blocks. An **insert** task will only attach to one freelist, and it is only able to use free blocks that are attached to that freelist.

The cause of a sparse table is a lack of balance between **insert** and **delete** activity. In this example, you have three freelists defined for the table, and each freelist gets new blocks in five-block chunks as the table expands. Next, a single job is run to remove the blocks, as shown in Figure 4-8.

As you can see, only one of the three freelists is populated with the free blocks! The other two freelists remain empty, and must request blocks by increasing the high-water mark for the table. This causes the table to extend, even though it may be largely empty. Extension occurs because each freelist is unaware of the contents of other freelists inside the segment header.

The remedy, of course, is to parallelize the purge job into three simultaneous **delete** tasks. By parallelizing the purge, all three freelists are evenly populated with newly empty blocks, as shown in Figure 4-9.

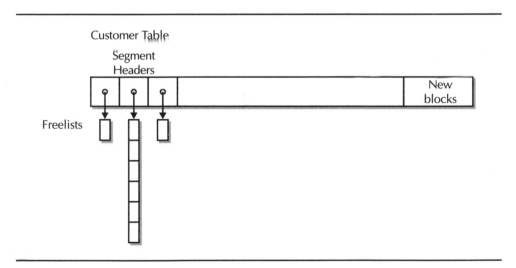

FIGURE 4-8. *Unbalanced freelists*

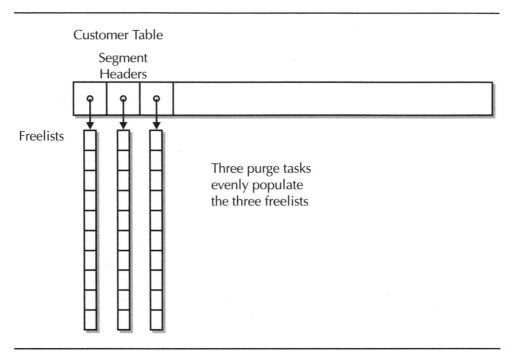

FIGURE 4-9. *Parallelizing a purge for a table with multiple freelists*

Of course, you must set the number of freelists to the number of simultaneous **insert** or **update** operations, so you cannot reduce the number of freelists without introducing segment header contention.

So, what can you do to identify sparse tables? The query that follows selects tables that contain multiple freelists, with more than one extent, where there is excessive free space.

To find tables with excessive free blocks on a freelist, you must compute the amount of data used within the table. First, you calculate the average row length (**avg_row_len**) in the data dictionary view and the number of rows (**num_rows**) by performing a table **analyze** (such as **analyze table xxx estimate statistics**). When you multiply the number of rows in the table by the average row length, you approximate the actual consumed size of the data within the table. You then compare this value with the actual number of allocated bytes in the table.

The idea is that a sparse table will have far more allocated space than consumed space because a single freelist contains a disproportional number of free blocks. The following is a script called sparse.sql that generates this report:

sparse.sql

```
column c1   heading "Tablespace";
column c2   heading "Owner";
column c3   heading "Table";
column c4   heading "Bytes M" format 9,999;
column c5   heading "Extents" format 999;
column c7   heading "Empty M" format 9,999;
column c6   heading "Blocks M" format 9,999;
column c8   heading "NEXT M" format 999;
column c9   heading "Row space M" format 9,999;
column c10  heading "Pct Full" format .99;

select
        substr(dt.table_name,1,10) c3,
        ds.extents c5,
        ds.bytes/1048576 c4,
        dt.next_extent/1048576 c8,
        (dt.empty_blocks*4096)/1048576 c7,
        (avg_row_len*num_rows)/1048576 c9,
        (ds.blocks*4096)/1048576 c6,
        (avg_row_len*num_rows)/(ds.blocks*4096) c10
from    sys.dba_segments ds,
        sys.dba_tables    dt
where   ds.tablespace_name = dt.tablespace_name
  and   ds.owner = dt.owner
  and   ds.segment_name = dt.table_name
and dt.freelists > 1
and ds.extents > 1
and dt.owner not in ('SYO','SYSTEM')
and (avg_row_len*num_rows)/1048576 > 50
and ds.bytes/1048576 > 20
order by c10;
```

Here is the output from sparse.sql. This will identify tables that have lots of free space within their existing extents. If any of these tables extend before using up their free blocks, you can assume that the table has a freelist imbalance. The remedy for this imbalance is to reorganize the table.

Table	Extents	Bytes M	NEXT M	Empty M	Row space M	Blocks M	Pct Full
TST03	65	1,241	20	14	118	1,241	.10
LIKE	3	148	49	24	76	148	.52
VBRK	2	124	4	0	69	124	.56
STXL	35	1,775	40	7	1,021	1,775	.57
VBAK	5	234	49	0	136	234	.58
KOCLU	27	1,889	49	27	1,144	1,889	.61

VBUP	2	866	49	0	570	866	.66
VBUK	2	147	28	0	103	147	.70
VBAP	46	4,314	50	0	3,034	4,314	.70
NASTY	3	137	10	2	97	137	.71
VBPA	5	582	32	0	426	582	.73
LIME	7	2,350	49	0	1,735	2,350	.74
VBRP	45	2,675	49	0	2,029	2,675	.76
WFPRC	30	123	10	7	95	123	.77
VLPMA	16	575	25	23	444	575	.77
EXCDOC	18	432	20	13	337	432	.78
VRPMA	24	700	20	7	549	700	.78
VBEP	4	2,134	49	49	1,698	2,134	.80

Now that you understand the general nature of I/O activity in an Oracle database, let's look at some global solutions for placing Oracle datafiles onto your disk devices.

Mapping Oracle Disk Architectures

Today's disk devices are normally delivered as complete I/O subsystems, with their own memory cache, channels, disk adapters, and SCSI adapters. Understanding the architecture requires mapping the number of ports, the size of the disk cache, the number of disk adapters, and the mapping of I/O channels between the disks and the disk cache. Figure 4-10 shows a sample of a disk architecture map for a disk array.

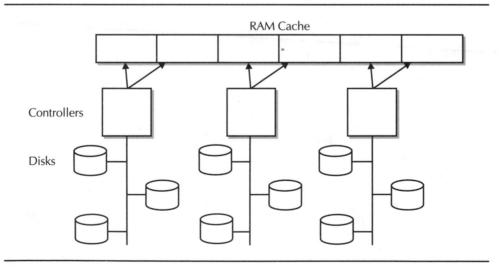

FIGURE 4-10. *A sample architecture of a disk array*

Developing this type of disk map is very important to load balancing within Oracle because there are many possible bottlenecks within the disk array subsystem that can cause slowdowns. In addition to monitoring for disk waits, you also need to monitor for SCSI contention, channel contention, and contention between the disk adapters. Fortunately, many of the major disk vendors (EMC, IBM) provide their own proprietary disk utilities (such as NaviStar, Open Symmetrics Manager) to perform these disk monitor functions.

The Multiple RAM Buffer Issue

You are also seeing disk arrays being delivered with a separate RAM cache for the disk arrays, as shown in Figure 4-11. These RAM caches can be many gigabytes in size and contain special software tools for performing asynchronous writes and minimizing disk I/O.

The Oracle DBA needs to consider the RAM cache on the disk array, because it changes the basic nature of disk I/O. As you know, when Oracle cannot find a data block in one of the data buffers in the SGA, Oracle will issue a physical read request to the disk array. This physical read request is received by the disk array, and the disk RAM cache is checked for the desired block. If the desired block is in the RAM cache, the disk array will return the block to Oracle without making a physical disk I/O.

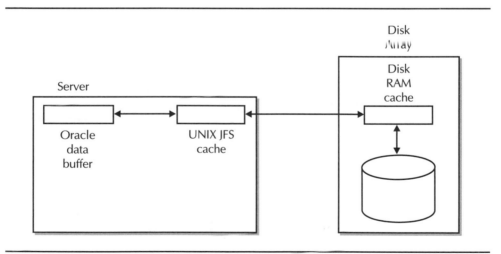

FIGURE 4-11. *Multiple RAM caches with an Oracle database*

The fact that Oracle physical requests may not match actual read requests is a very important point, because it can lead to misleading statistics. For example, the stats$filestatxs table shows the number of reads and writes to files. If you are using a disk array such as EMC, these I/O statistics will not correspond to the actual disk reads and writes. The only conclusive way to check "real" disk I/O is to compare the physical I/O as measured on the disk array with Oracle's read and write statistics. In many cases, the disks are performing less than half the I/O reported by Oracle, and this discrepancy is due to the caching of data blocks on the disk array RAM memory.

Next, let's look at file striping and see how it can be used to load balance the I/O subsystem.

File Striping with Oracle

File striping is the process of splitting a tablespace into small datafiles and placing these datafiles across many disks. With the introduction of RAID (redundant arrays of inexpensive disks), you also have the option of block-interleaf striping (RAID 1), which places each data block in the tablespace on a separate disk.

Other methods of Oracle file striping involve taking a large tablespace and splitting it into many Oracle datafiles. These files may then be spread across many disks to reduce I/O bottlenecks, as shown in Figure 4-12.

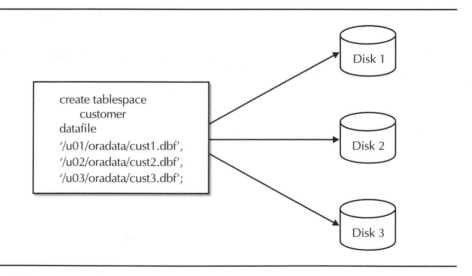

FIGURE 4-12. *Striping a tablespace across multiple disks*

However, manual file striping has become obsolete because of the large size of disks. In 1990, a 20GB database would probably have been composed of 20 physical disks, each within 1GB of storage. With many disks in a database, the Oracle DBA could improve throughput by manually striping the busiest tablespaces across many disks.

Commercials disks are getting larger every year, and it is very difficult to find small disk devices that contain less than 36GB of storage. Just ten years ago, the IBM 3380 disk was considered huge at 1GB of storage. Today, the smallest disks available are 18GB. The larger disks mean that there are fewer disk spindles, and fewer opportunities for manual file striping. Since it is often not possible to isolate Oracle tablespaces on separate disks without wasting a huge amount of disk space, the Oracle administrator must balance active with inactive tablespaces across their disks.

NOTE
There is a new feature in Oracle8i called "single table clusters." By using a cluster, the keys are grouped in the same physical block—reducing I/O and speeding data retrieval by key.

Using RAID with Oracle

As you may know, there are more than six different types (called *levels*) of RAID architectures, and each has its own relative advantages and disadvantages. For the purposes of an Oracle database, many of the RAID schemes do not possess the high performance required for an Oracle database, and are omitted from this discussion.

Please note that RAID 5 is not considered for databases that perform write activity since the processing overhead for updates makes it too slow for most Oracle applications. The following are the most commonly used RAID architectures for Oracle databases:

■ **Raid 0** RAID 0 is commonly referred to as block-level striping. This is an excellent method for performing load balancing of the Oracle database on the disk devices, but it does nothing for high availability since none of the data is duplicated. Unlike manual datafile striping, where the Oracle professional divides an Oracle tablespace into small datafiles, with RAID 0, the Oracle datafile is automatically striped one block at a time across all of the disk devices. In this fashion, every datafile has pieces residing on each disk, and the disk I/O load will become very well balanced. Note that a disk failure in RAID 0 results in the loss of the datafiles storage on this device. A good recommendation is to only put temporary tables on this that can be easily recovered in the case of a disk failure.

- **RAID 1**   RAID 1 is commonly called disk mirroring. Since the disks are replicated, RAID 1 may involve double or triple mirroring. The RAID 1 architecture is designed such that a disk failure will cause the I/O subsystem to switch to one of the replicated disks with no service interruption. RAID 1 is used when high availability is critical, and with triple mirroring, the mean time to failure (MTTF) for an Oracle database is measured in decades. (Note that disk controller errors may cause RAID 1 failures, although the disks remain healthy.)

- **RAID 0+1**   Raid 0+1 is the combination of block-level striping and disk mirroring. The advent of RAID 0+1 has made Oracle-level striping obsolete since RAID 0+1 stripes at the block level, dealing out the table blocks, one block per disk, across each disk device. RAID 0+1 is also a far better striping alternative since it distributes the load evenly across all of the disk devices, and the load will rise and fall evenly across all of the disks. This relieves the Oracle administrator of the burden of manually striping Oracle tables across disks and provides a far greater level of granularity than Oracle striping, because adjacent data blocks within the same table are on different disks.

- **RAID 5**   Some of the newer hardware-based Raid 5 storage does extremely well in performance in data warehouses. RAID 5 is a good approach for Oracle data warehouses where the load speeds are not important and where the majority of the system I/O is read-only activity.

Note that the use of RAID does not guarantee against catastrophic disk failure. Oracle specifically recommends that all production databases be run in **archivelog** mode regardless of the RAID architecture, and that periodic Oracle backups should be performed. Remember that there are many components to I/O subsystems—including controllers, channels, disk adapters, and SCSI adapters—and a failure of any of these components could cause unrecoverable disk failures of your database. RAID should only be used as an additional level of insurance, and not as a complete recovery method.

Using Oracle with Raw Devices

Because of the high amount of I/O that many Oracle systems experience, many Oracle DBAs consider the use of "raw" devices. A raw device is defined as a disk that bypasses the I/O overhead created by the Journal File System (JFS) in UNIX. The reduction in overhead can improve throughput, but only in cases where I/O is already the bottleneck for the Oracle database. Furthermore, raw devices require a tremendous amount of manual work for both the Oracle administrator and the system administrator. Oracle recommends that raw devices should only be considered when the Oracle database is I/O bound. However, for these types of Oracle databases, raw devices can dramatically improve overall performance. If the database is not I/O bound, switching to raw devices will have no impact on performance.

It is worth mentioning here the feature in Oracle 8.1.7 called directIO supported on some of the platforms. Veritas also has a product called QuickIO. These options give Oracle near RAW performance without the additional overhead in managing RAW devices.

In many UNIX environments such as AIX, raw devices are called virtual storage devices (VSDs). These VSDs are created from disk physical partitions (PPs), such that a single VSD can contain pieces from several physical disks. It is the job of the system administrator to create a pool of VSDs for the Oracle administrator. The Oracle administrator can then take these VSDs and combine them into Oracle datafiles. This creates a situation where an Oracle datafile may be made from several VSDs. This many-to-many relationship between Oracle datafiles and VSDs makes Oracle administration more challenging.

In summary, raw devices for Oracle databases can provide improved I/O throughput only for databases that are already I/O bound.

However, this performance gain comes at the expense of increased administrative overhead for the Oracle administrator. You also know that raw devices will only improve the performance of Oracle databases whose Oracle subsystem is clearly I/O bound. For systems that are not I/O bound, moving to raw devices will not result in any performance gains.

The UNIX **iostat** utility is great for showing those physical disks that have bottlenecks. Since you know the tablespace and table for each hot datafile, you can intelligently move the hot datafiles to a less active disk. Let's begin by exploring the nature of disk load balancing for Oracle.

Load Balancing Disks with Oracle Databases

With terabyte-sized and Web-enabled Oracle8 databases becoming more commonplace, the task of disk load balancing has never been more critical. These huge databases are too massive to be cached in an Oracle data buffer, yet these databases often serve thousands of users who expect instant response times. The most important thing that the DBA can do to minimize disk I/O is to balance the load on the disks.

By placing datafiles strategically on the physical disks, you can minimize the likelihood of any one disk becoming stalled while handling simultaneous I/O requests. This section provides a strategy for collecting I/O information into Oracle tables and generating reports to deliver maximum guidance in the load-balancing process for multiple physical disk systems. The purpose of collecting I/O statistics is to provide data for load balancing. Load balancing involves moving datafiles on the physical disks such that no single disk becomes stalled waiting for simultaneous I/O requests.

STATSPACK Reports for Oracle Datafiles

To perform I/O load balancing, you need to get information about the amount of I/O for an Oracle datafile, relative to the total I/O from the database. Remember, a hot file is not necessarily causing a disk bottleneck. The goal of the STATSPACK technique that follows is to alert the Oracle DBA to those datafiles that are taking a disproportionate amount of I/O relative to other files in the database.

The script you use for this purpose is called rpt_hot_files.sql, and this script is also incorporated into your generalized DBA alert script, statspack_alert.sql.

Let's take a look at how this rpt_hot_files.sql script works. The idea is to compare the overall I/O between snapshots (hourly in this case) to the total I/O for the database, as shown in Figure 4-13.

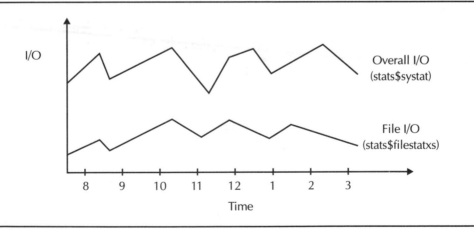

FIGURE 4-13. *Elapsed time I/O comparison*

To get the data you need, you rely on two STATSPACK tables:

- **stats$sysstat** The stats$sysstat table contains two important metrics. These are used to compute the total read I/O and write I/O for the entire database:

    - Total physical reads (**statistic#=40**)

    - Total physical writes (**statistic#=44**)

- **stats$filestatxs** The stats$filestatxs table contains detailed read I/O and write I/O, totaled by datafile name.

You then compare the system-wide total for read and write I/O with the individual I/O for each Oracle datafile. This allows you to quickly generate an alert report to tell you which files are having the most I/O activity. If you were judicious in placing important tables and indexes into separate tablespaces and datafiles, this report will tell you exactly which database objects are the most active.

Note that you can adjust the thresholds for the rpt_hot_files.sql script. You can set the threshold to 25 percent, 50 percent, or 75 percent, reporting on any files that exceed this threshold percentage of total read and write I/O.

This is a very important script and appears in the generic statspack_alert.sql script. It is critical that the DBA become aware whenever an Oracle datafile is consuming a disproportionate amount of disk I/O. The script that follows is somewhat complex, but it is worth your time to carefully examine it to understand the query. Let's examine the main steps of this SQL statement:

1. You select the individual I/O from stats$filestatxs and compare the value for each file to the total I/O as reported in stats$systat.

2. The WHERE clause determines when a file will be reported. You have the option of adjusting the reporting threshold by commenting out one of the three choices—25 percent, 50 percent, or 75 percent—of the total I/O.

rpt_hot_files.sql

```
set pages 9999;
set feedback off;
set verify off;

column mydate heading 'Yr. Mo Dy  Hr.' format a16
column file_name format a35
```

```
column reads   format 99,999,999
column pct_of_tot   format 999


--prompt
--prompt
--prompt ************************************************************
--prompt  This will identify any single file whose read I/O
--prompt  is more than 25% of the total read I/O of the database.
--prompt
--prompt  The "hot" file should be examined, and the hot table/index
--prompt  should be identified using STATSPACK.
--prompt
--prompt  - The busy file should be placed on a disk device with
--prompt     "less busy" files to minimize read delay and channel
--prompt     contention.
--prompt
--prompt  - If small file has a hot small table, place the table
--prompt     in the KEEP pool
--prompt
--prompt  - If the file has a large-table full-table scan, place
--prompt     the table in the RECYCLE pool and turn on parallel query
--prompt     for the table.
--prompt ************************************************************
--prompt
--prompt


select
   to_char(snap_time,'yyyy-mm-dd HH24')   mydate,
   new.filename                           file_name,
   new.phyrds-old.phyrds                  reads,
   ((new.phyrds-old.phyrds)/
   (
   select
      (newreads.value-oldreads.value) reads
   from
      perfstat.stats$sysstat oldreads,
      perfstat.stats$sysstat newreads,
      perfstat.stats$snapshot    sn1
   where
      sn.snap_id = sn1.snap_id
   and
      newreads.snap_id = sn.snap_id
   and
      oldreads.snap_id = sn.snap_id-1
```

```
       and
         oldreads.statistic# = 40
       and
         newreads.statistic# = 40
       and
         (newreads.value-oldreads.value) > 0
       ))*100 pct_of_tot
from
   perfstat.stats$filestatxs old,
   perfstat.stats$filestatxs new,
   perfstat.stats$snapshot    sn
where
   snap_time > sysdate-&1
and
   new.snap_id = sn.snap_id
and
   old.snap_id = sn.snap_id-1
and
   new.filename = old.filename
and
   -- *********************************************************
   -- Low I/O values are misleading, so we filter for high I/O
   -- *********************************************************
   new.phyrds-old.phyrds > 100
and
-- *********************************************************
-- The following will allow you to choose a threshold
-- *********************************************************
 (new.phyrds-old.phyrds)*4>   -- This is 25% of total
-- (new.phyrds-old.phyrds)*2>     This is 50% of total
   (new.phyrds-old.phyrds)*1.25> -- This is 75% of total
-- *********************************************************
-- This subquery computes the sum of all I/O during the snapshot period
-- *********************************************************
(
select
   (newreads.value-oldreads.value) reads
from
   perfstat.stats$sysstat oldreads,
   perfstat.stats$sysstat newreads,
   perfstat.stats$snapshot    sn1
where
   sn.snap_id = sn1.snap_id
and
   newreads.snap_id = sn.snap_id
and
```

```
   oldreads.snap_id = sn.snap_id-1
and
  oldreads.statistic# = 40
and
  newreads.statistic# = 40
and
  (newreads.value-oldreads.value) > 0
)
;


--prompt
--prompt
--prompt ************************************************************
--prompt  This will identify any single file whose write I/O
--prompt  is more than 25% of the total write I/O of the database.
--prompt
--prompt  The "hot" file should be examined, and the hot table/index
--prompt  should be identified using STATSPACK.
--prompt
--prompt  - The busy file should be placed on a disk device with
--prompt    "less busy" files to minimize write delay and channel
--prompt    channel contention.
--prompt
--prompt  - If small file has a hot small table, place the table
--prompt    in the KEEP pool
--prompt
--prompt ************************************************************
--prompt




select
   to_char(snap_time,'yyyy-mm-dd HH24')  mydate,
   new.filename                          file_name,
   new.phywrts-old.phywrts               writes,
   ((new.phywrts-old.phywrts)/
   (
   select
      (newwrites.value-oldwrites.value) writes
   from
      perfstat.stats$sysstat    oldwrites,
      perfstat.stats$sysstat    newwrites,
      perfstat.stats$snapshot   sn1
   where
```

```
      sn.snap_id = sn1.snap_id
   and
      newwrites.snap_id = sn.snap_id
   and
      oldwrites.snap_id = sn.snap_id-1
   and
     oldwrites.statistic# = 44
   and
     newwrites.statistic# = 44
   and
     (newwrites.value-oldwrites.value) > 0
   ))*100 pct_of_tot
from
   perfstat.stats$filestatxs old,
   perfstat.stats$filestatxs new,
   perfstat.stats$snapshot    sn
where
   snap_time > sysdate-&1
and
   new.snap_id = sn.snap_id
and
   old.snap_id = sn.snap_id-1
and
   new.filename = old.filename
and
   -- ********************************************************
   -- Low I/O values are misleading, so we only take high values
   -- ********************************************************
   new.phywrts-old.phywrts > 100
and
-- ********************************************************
-- Here you can choose a threshold value
-- ********************************************************
 (new.phyrds-old.phywrts)*4>  -- This is 25% of total
-- (new.phyrds-old.phywrts)*2> -- This is 50% of total
-- (new.phyrds-old.phywrts)*1.25> -- This is 75% of total
-- ********************************************************
-- This subquery computes the sum of all I/O during the snapshot period
-- ********************************************************
(
select
   (newwrites.value-oldwrites.value) writes
from
   perfstat.stats$sysstat    oldwrites,
   perfstat.stats$sysstat    newwrites,
```

```
  perfstat.stats$snapshot  sn1
where
  sn.snap_id = sn1.snap_id
and
  newwrites.snap_id = sn.snap_id
and
  oldwrites.snap_id = sn.snap_id-1
and
 oldwrites.statistic# = 44
and
 newwrites.statistic# = 44
and
 (newwrites.value-oldwrites.value) > 0
)
;
```

It is highly recommended that the DBA run this STATSPACK report daily so the DBA can constantly monitor for hot datafiles. The following is a sample of the output from this script. Note how it identifies hot files on an hourly basis.

```
***********************************************************
This will identify any single file whose read I/O
is more than 50% of the total read I/O of the database.
***********************************************************


Yr. Mo Dy  Hr. FILE_NAME                                 READS PCT_OF_TOT
--------------- ---------------------------------- ----------- ----------
2000-12-14 14    /u02/oradata/prodb1/bookd01.dbf          354         62
2000-12-14 15    /u02/oradata/prodb1/bookd01.dbf          123         63
2000-12-14 16    /u02/oradata/prodb1/bookd01.dbf          132         66
2000-12-14 20    /u02/oradata/prodb1/bookd01.dbf          124         65
2000-12-15 15    /u02/oradata/prodb1/bookd01.dbf          126         72
2001-01-05 09    /u02/oradata/prodb1/system01.dbf         180         63
2001-01-06 14    /u03/oradata/prodb1/perfstat.dbf         752        100
2001-01-06 15    /u02/oradata/prodb1/bookd01.dbf          968         69


***********************************************************
This will identify any single file whose write I/O
is more than 50% of the total write I/O of the database.
***********************************************************
```

```
Yr. Mo Dy  Hr. FILE_NAME                                    WRITES PCT_OF_TOT
---------------  ------------------------------------- ---------- ----------
2000-12-18 21     /u02/oradata/prodb1/bookd01.dbf           2654        58
2000-12-29 15     /u02/oradata/prodb1/bookd01.dbf           1095        49
```

Now that you have examined how to identify hot files, let's take a look at other useful STATSPACK reports that can tell you about disk activity.

Detailed Disk and File I/O with STATSPACK

Statistics that are captured in the stats$filestatxs table will show details of read and write activity at the file level. However, STATSPACK does not show I/O at the mount point or disk level, and it is up to the Oracle administrator to know the mapping of files to mount points and mount points to disks. On the other hand, statistics that are captured at the UNIX level will show read and write I/O only at the physical disk level. Again, it is up to the Oracle administrator to know all of the mount points and datafiles that reside on each physical disk. If you segregate tables and indexes into separate tablespaces, you know the objects that reside in each file, and you can tell which tables and indexes are experiencing the high I/O.

NOTE
For users of disk arrays products such as EMC and Net App, you may need third-party products to view I/O statistics. These products include Precise*SQL, or DBView from EMC.

Rather than running the off-the-shelf utilities that generate a printed report for a single time period, you can modify the utilities to collect the I/O data over five-minute intervals and store the results in Oracle database tables for easy access and report generation:

- **File statistics**   The stats$filestatxs table contains the I/O data collected by STATSPACK. The I/O data includes the actual number of physical reads and writes, the number of block reads and writes, and the time required to perform each operation.

- **Disk statistics**   The next section will explore extending STATSPACK to capture external disk I/O with the UNIX **iostat** utility and place the data in a STATSPACK extension table called stats$iostat. The stats$iostat table also includes read and write times corresponding to specific dates, but at the disk level. It collects information from the **iostat** utility, using the script **get_iostat.ksh**.

To provide a cross-reference between the filestat and iostat tables, you added the vol_grp (volume/group) table, which links mount points to physical disks. You need to populate this table manually, based on how your disks are partitioned into mount points. The design of the vol_grp, filestat, and iostat tables lets you aggregate, or average, I/O data over time and summarize it by disk, mount point, tablespace, or datafile.

A STATSPACK Report on Specific I/O Activity

If the DBA is prudent in segregating Oracle objects into distinct tablespaces and datafiles, STATSPACK can be used to create extremely useful reports that show individual I/O or selected datafiles or groups of related datafiles.

The script that follows accepts a filename "mask" that can be used to report on selected groups of related datafiles. For example, if you have named your customer-related datafiles customer.dbf, custhistory.dbf, and custorders.dbf, the following script can be run to report on all datafile names that contain the string "cust". In this example, you execute the script with the filename mask to see the I/O history for these datafiles.

rpt_file_io.sql

```
set pages 9999;

column snapdate format a16
column filename format a40
column mydate heading 'Yr. Mo Dy  Hr.' format a16

select
   to_char(snap_time,'yyyy-mm-dd') mydate,
--   old.filename,
   sum(new.phyrds-old.phyrds)   phy_rds,
   sum(new.phywrts-old.phywrts) phy_wrts
from
   perfstat.stats$filestatxs old,
   perfstat.stats$filestatxs new,
   perfstat.stats$snapshot    sn
where
   new.snap_id = sn.snap_id
and
   old.filename = new.filename
and
   old.snap_id = sn.snap_id-1
and
```

```
    (new.phyrds-old.phyrds) > 0
and
    old.filename like '%&1%'
group by
    to_char(snap_time,'yyyy-mm-dd'),
    old.filename
;
```

Here is the output from this script, showing total read and write I/O per day for your cust datafiles:

2000-12-12	833	2770
2000-12-13	6	9
2000-12-14	2	80
2000-12-15	2	26
2000-12-16	2	4
2000-12-17	2	3
2000-12-18	7	226
2000-12-19	87	556
2000-12-20	141	640
2000-12-21	26	452
2000-12-22	45	368
2000-12-23	10	115
2000-12-24	3	14
2000-12-25	5	54
2000-12-26	169	509
2000-12-27	14	101
2000-12-28	25	316
2000-12-29	13	120
2000-12-30	7	158
2000-12-31	2	129
2001-01-01	4	264
2001-01-02	57	756
2001-01-03	56	317
2001-01-04	1110	123
2001-01-05	1075	386
2001-01-06	20	293
2001-01-07	1	6
2001-01-08	955	1774
2001-01-09	247	1145
2001-01-10	538	1724
2001-01-11	387	1169
2001-01-12	1017	1964
2001-01-13	115	397
2001-01-14	89	443

```
2001-01-15                22          125
2001-01-16              1267         1667
2001-01-17               646         2082
2001-01-18               588         2359
2001-01-19                46          296
```

Once gathered, this data can be graphed (see Figure 4-14) to see the detailed activity of the tables and indexes within these datafiles.

Often, the graphical representation of the data is more useful, because the unique I/O signature of the data becomes obvious.

Next, let's examine some STATSPACK tools that can be used to identify potential disk bottlenecks.

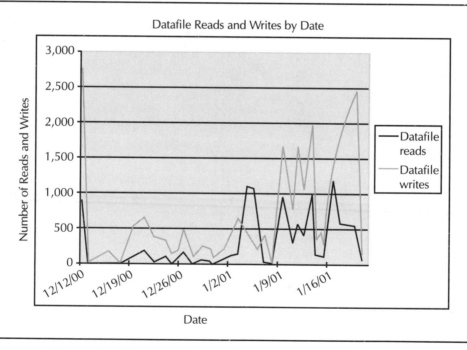

FIGURE 4-14. *File I/O for a selected subset of Oracle datafiles*

A STATSPACK Script to Identify Hot Datafiles

The first step in balancing the load on disks is to find out where they're out of balance by identifying possible bottlenecks. Start by identifying hot disks—those with a disproportionate amount of activity. For example, if one disk in a ten-disk system were experiencing 50 percent of the I/O, measured as the number of reads, writes, or both, you would consider the disk to be hot.

Detecting I/O-Related Slowdowns in AIX

If you are using the IBM AIX operating system, it is easy to detect when a database server may be experiencing I/O slowdowns. An I/O bound database server is usually evidenced by a high value in the **wa** (wait) column of the UNIX **vmstat** utility. For example, in the following output you see that 45 percent of the CPU time is being used waiting for database I/O:

```
Prompt> vmstat 5 1

kthr      memory              page                   faults         cpu
----- -----------  ------------------------  ------------ -----------
 r  b   avm    fre  re  pi  po  fr   sr  cy   in   sy  cs us sy id wa
 0  0 217485   386   0   0   0   4   14   0  202  300 210 14 19 22 45
```

The Approach to Locating Hot Disks

For other operating environments, you should be concerned whenever you see a backlog of I/O tasks waiting to access data on a single disk. For other operating systems, the **iostat** utility can be used to detect I/O issues.

Once you've identified the hot disks, look closely to find out which files and tables on the disks experience most of the activity, so you can move them to less-active disks as needed. The actual process of identifying hot files and disks involves running data collection utilities, such as STATSPACK and the UNIX **iostat** utility, and then using the collected I/O data to pinpoint the sources of excessive I/O measurements.

Here are the cardinal rules for disk I/O:

■ There is a difference between a busy disk and a disk that is waiting for I/O to complete. In Chapter 8 we will explore the UNIX **iostat** utility and show how you can identify busy disks.

■ If you are using RAID such as RAID 0+1, the Oracle data blocks will be spread randomly across all of the disks, and load will rise and fall in a uniform fashion.

■ Senior Oracle DBAs often prefer not to implement RAID striping so that they have more control over the disk I/O subsystem.

■ Many disk arrays such as EMC provide sophisticated disk monitoring tools such as Open Symmetrics Manager and Navistar. These tools report on more than simple disk waits, and highlight contention for disks, channels, and disk adapters.

Now that you understand the basic principles behind locating hot disks, you are ready to look at how you can locate unobtrusive disk trends by aggregating disk I/O by hour of the day and day of the week.

Viewing I/O Signatures with STATSPACK

You will find that your database will develop distinctive I/O signatures. The I/O signature for an OLTP database will be very different than that of a data warehouse, and you can use these I/O signatures to determine regular times when the disk I/O subsystem is overloaded. When you aggregate disk information by day of the week and hour of the day, you can see some very interesting patterns.

NOTE
When developing I/O signatures for your database, it is important to begin at the global level and drill down for successive detail. For example, after running the global reports, you will find spikes in your database I/O during specific times. Your next step should be to isolate these I/O spikes to specific Oracle database files by closer inspection of the STATSPACK data, and running the rpt_io_pct.sql script to report on specific datafiles.

Let's begin by taking a look at a STATSPACK script to average disk read and write activity by the day of the week:

rpt_avg_io_dy.sql

```
set pages 9999;

column reads  format 999,999,999
column writes format 999,999,999

select
   to_char(snap_time,'day'),
   avg(newreads.value-oldreads.value) reads,
   avg(newwrites.value-oldwrites.value) writes
from
   perfstat.stats$sysstat oldreads,
   perfstat.stats$sysstat newreads,
   perfstat.stats$sysstat oldwrites,
   perfstat.stats$sysstat newwrites,
   perfstat.stats$snapshot    sn
where
   newreads.snap_id = sn.snap_id
and
   newwrites.snap_id = sn.snap_id
and
   oldreads.snap_id = sn.snap_id-1
and
   oldwrites.snap_id = sn.snap_id-1
and
  oldreads.statistic# = 40
and
  newreads.statistic# = 40
and
  oldwrites.statistic# = 41
and
  newwrites.statistic# = 41
having
   avg(newreads.value-oldreads.value) > 0
and
   avg(newwrites.value-oldwrites.value) > 0
group by
   to_char(snap_time,'day')
;
```

The output from the script will take a running average by the day of the week and display the output as follows:

```
TO_CHAR(S        READS        WRITES
---------     ------------  ------------
friday           72          2,093
monday          221          8,896
saturday        211          5,869
sunday          160          5,056
thursday        338          7,232
tuesday         603         11,765
wednesday       316          7,781
```

This output can then be pasted into an Excel spreadsheet, resequenced, and displayed using the Excel Chart Wizard. In Figure 4-15, you see the I/O signature for an Oracle database. Note that this signature clearly shows peak write activity on Mondays, Tuesdays, and Wednesdays. From this signature, the Oracle DBA knows that this database is loaded during the first part of each week.

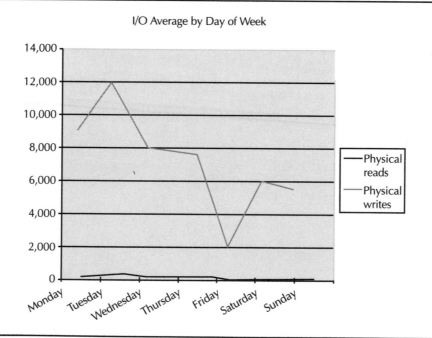

FIGURE 4-15. *Average I/O signature by day of the week*

Now, let's see how easy it is to change this report to aggregate the data by the hour of the day. The following script is identical to the aggregate averages by day of the week except that the date format string has been changed from 'day' to 'HH24':

rpt_avg_io_hr.sql

```
set pages 9999;

column reads  format 999,999,999
column writes format 999,999,999

select
   to_char(snap_time,'HH24'),
   avg(newreads.value-oldreads.value) reads,
   avg(newwrites.value-oldwrites.value) writes
from
   perfstat.stats$sysstat oldreads,
   perfstat.stats$sysstat newreads,
   perfstat.stats$sysstat oldwrites,
   perfstat.stats$sysstat newwrites,
   perfstat.stats$snapshot   sn
where
   newreads.snap_id = sn.snap_id
and
   newwrites.snap_id = sn.snap_id
and
   oldreads.snap_id = sn.snap_id-1
and
   oldwrites.snap_id = sn.snap_id-1
and
  oldreads.statistic# = 40
and
  newreads.statistic# = 40
and
  oldwrites.statistic# = 41
and
  newwrites.statistic# = 41
having
   avg(newreads.value-oldreads.value) > 0
and
   avg(newwrites.value-oldwrites.value) > 0
group by
   to_char(snap_time,'HH24')
;
```

Now when you execute this script you see the read and write averages displayed by the hour of the day. Again, you can paste this output into a spreadsheet and create a graphical representation, thereby getting a visual picture of the I/O signature:

TO	READS	WRITES
00	250	6,103
02	180	4,701
03	174	4,580
04	195	5,832
05	191	5,109
06	171	4,669
07	221	4,727
08	354	5,353
09	264	9,531
10	258	7,994
11	249	7,397
12	364	8,499
13	341	7,902
14	326	8,288
15	305	10,891
16	279	9,019
17	692	17,291
18	592	10,444
19	448	9,911
20	385	8,247
21	395	11,405
22	366	9,182
23	271	7,308

The graph in Figure 4-16 is a graphical representation of the I/O signature of physical reads by hour of the day. Here you see a clear daily trend where the read activity increases throughout the afternoon and a high peak of read activity every day at 6:00 P.M. This information can be extremely valuable to the Oracle DBA. In this example, the DBA could encourage the end-user community to direct their processing to periods before 5:00 P.M.

You can also plot the physical write activity in a graph, as shown in Figure 4-17. In this case, you see a gradual pattern of increasing writes to the database, peaking in the late afternoon. This pattern would be confirmed by an increase in the number of archived redo logs generated later in the day.

Now that you understand how to plot UNIX disk statistics, let's wrap up this chapter with a review of the major topics.

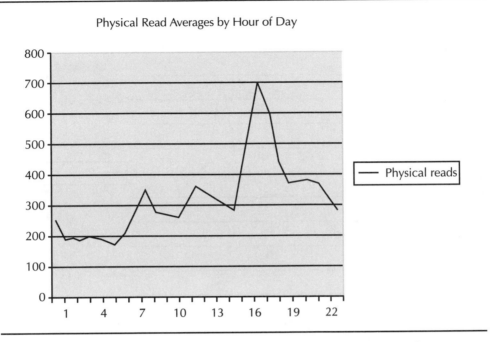

Physical Read Averages by Hour of Day

FIGURE 4-16. *Oracle physical read activity averages by hour of the day*

Conclusion

This chapter has been concerned with managing and monitoring UNIX files for Oracle databases. We have covered an immense amount of material in this chapter, and you should now see the importance of disk load balancing and how to use STATSPACK to monitor the behavior of the disk I/O subsystem. Remember, disk I/O is the single largest component of Oracle performance. The major points of this chapter include:

■ UNIX partitions disks into logical volumes, which are then assigned to mount points. You can use the **bdf** and **df -k** commands to view the file system.

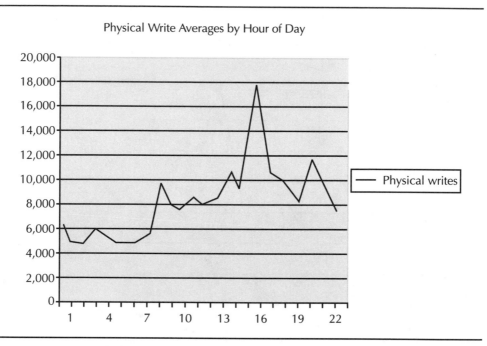

FIGURE 4-17. *Oracle physical write activity averages by hour of the day*

- The DBA should clearly understand the mapping from the Oracle datafiles to UNIX mount points, and the mount points to the disks.

- The UNIX **iostat** utility is very useful for observing I/O at the disk level. Special STATSPACK extension table can be defined to capture **iostat** information for time-series analysis.

- There are several Oracle initialization parameters that effect disk I/O. The most important are **db_block_size** (**db_xk_block_size** in Oracle9i), **db_block_buffers** (**db_cache_size** on Oracle9i), **sort_area_size** and **optimizer_mode**.

- The parameters for Oracle tables and indexes have an effect on disk I/O. A low value for PCTUSED will reduce disk I/O at insert time.

■ For tables that are accessed exclusively by a single index, resequencing the table rows in the same order as the index can reduce disk I/O by several orders of magnitude.

■ In SQL tuning, removing large-table full-table scans will reduce disk I/O and improve performance.

■ The introduction of function-based indexes and bitmap indexes has greatly reduced disk I/O for certain Oracle SQL queries.

■ Very large tables should be segregated into separate tablespaces.

■ Tables with multiple freelists often require periodic reorganization to coalesce the freelist chains.

■ RAID 0+1 is very effective for removing disk hot spots. RAID 5 should never be used for OLTP databases and is for read-only applications.

■ Raw devices improve I/O throughput by bypassing the UNIX buffer cache. However, moving to raw devices will only improve performance if disk I/O is your bottleneck.

Now that we have covered disks in UNIX, we are ready to begin exploring UNIX network administration. The next chapter will discuss how UNIX network traffic can affect the performance of Oracle and show you some tools for improving performance across a distributed Oracle network.

CHAPTER
5

Network Management
in UNIX for Oracle

ith UNIX being the dominant platform for Oracle databases, we must spend some time discussing how distributed Oracle databases communicate.

This chapter will cover the following topics in UNIX network management:

- Network traffic in a UNIX environment
- Oracle networking and UNIX
- TNS and UNIX
- Optimizing Net8 configuration
- Monitoring network performance with STATSPACK

As we noted in Chapter 1, the performance of any Oracle UNIX server can be affected by external issues with disk, CPU, RAM, and the network. Let's begin with an overview of network issues with UNIX.

Network Tuning in a UNIX Environment

Tuning a network is a very long, painstaking process of gathering statistics and analyzing them. Unfortunately, there are no quick or simple answers that will solve all network performance issues. Basically, you will have to generate a sniffer trace and check for utilization statistics, retransmissions, and delta times.

Remember, some network problems can exist outside of the Oracle server (client connection, LAN, or switch). The procedures in this chapter focus on the UNIX server and can help provide evidence if the problem is beyond the UNIX server.

Note that while it is easy to extend STATSPACK to monitor disk I/O information, it is extremely difficult to extend STATSPACK to capture network traffic information. Network information varies widely between systems, and it is almost impossible to capture meaningful disk I/O information into STATSPACK extension tables.

The most basic tool used by network administrators is the UNIX **netstat** utility. Unfortunately, **netstat** is implemented differently by all of the UNIX vendors, and the output from **netstat** looks very different depending on the operating system that you are using. Let's take a brief tour of **netstat** and see how it can be used by the Oracle DBA to monitor network activity.

Using the UNIX netstat Utility

netstat is a generic UNIX utility that displays the contents of various network-related structures in various formats. These formats are determined by the options passed to the **netstat** command.

Though it is very good at telling the DBA what is happening on the network at the current time, **netstat** does not give a good trending capability or periodic snapshot functionality. Most network administrators purchase a specialized third-party tool for long-term network monitoring. Let's look at some of the differences in **netstat** and see some of the network information that **netstat** provides about the current state of the network.

netstat on Solaris

On a Sun Solaris server, the **netstat** utility provides information about all network traffic touching the server:

```
root> netstat

TCP: IPv4
    Local Address    Remote Address      Swind Send-Q Rwind Recv-Q  State
    --------------   --------------------  -----  ------ -----  ------  -------
    sting.32773      ting.1521            32768      0 32768      0 ESTABLISHED
    sting.1521       ting.32773           32768      0 32768      0 ESTABLISHED
    sting.32774      ting.1521            32768      0 32768      0 ESTABLISHED
    sting.1521       ting.32774           32768      0 32768      0 ESTABLISHED
    sting.32775      ting.1521            32768      0 32768      0 ESTABLISHED
    sting.1521       ting.32775           32768      0 32768      0 ESTABLISHED
    sting.1521       az.janet.com.32777   24820      0 24820      0 ESTABLISHED
    sting.1521       rumpy.jan.com.34601  24820      0 24820      0 ESTABLISHED
    sting.22         onsrv1.jan.com.1120  31856      0 24616      0 ESTABLISHED
    sting.1521       rumpy.jan.com.35460  24820      0 24820      0 ESTABLISHED

Active UNIX domain sockets
Address     Type          Vnode       Conn    Local Addr       Remote Addr
300021bda88 stream-ord 30002225e70 00000000 /var/tmp/.oracle/s#255.1
300021bdc30 stream-ord 300021f02c0 00000000 /var/tmp/.oracle/sextproc_key
300021bddd8 stream-ord 300021f0848 00000000 /var/tmp/.oracle/s#252.1
```

netstat for Linux

In Linux, you can see that the output from **netstat** is quite different from Solaris:

```
Proto Recv-Q Send-Q Local Address       Foreign Address          State
tcp       0      0 donsrv1.rov:netbios-ssn intranet.janet.com:1351 ESTABLISHED
tcp       0      0 donsrv1.janet.com:1120 sting.janet.com:ssh      TIME_WAIT
tcp       0     40 donsrv1.janet.com:ssh  hpop3-146.gloryroa:1096  ESTABLISHED
tcp       0      0 donsrv1.rov:netbios-ssn 192.168.1.105:1025       ESTABLISHED
```

```
tcp     0     0 donsrv1.janet.com:6010  donsrv1.janet.com:1104   CLOSE_WAIT
tcp     0     0 donsrv1.janet.com:6010  donsrv1.janet.com:1103   CLOSE_WAIT
tcp     0     0 donsrv1.janet.com:1023  grumpy.janet.com:ssh     ESTABLISHED
tcp     0     0 donsrv1.janet.com:ssh   exodus-rtr-2.arsdi:2195  ESTABLISHED
tcp     0     0 donsrv1.rov:netbios-ssn 192.168.1.107:1025       ESTABLISHED
tcp     0     0 donsrv1.rov:netbios-ssn 192.168.1.126:1030       ESTABLISHED
Active UNIX domain sockets (w/o servers)
Proto RefCnt Flags       Type       State       I-Node Path
unix  1      [ ]         STREAM     CONNECTED   741    @0000002a
unix  1      [ ]         STREAM     CONNECTED   745    @0000002b
unix  0      [ ]         STREAM     CONNECTED   182    @0000001a
unix  1      [ ]         STREAM     CONNECTED   763    @00000030
unix  8      [ ]         DGRAM                  397    /dev/log
unix  0      [ ]         DGRAM                  234471
unix  0      [ ]         DGRAM                  234252
unix  0      [ ]         DGRAM                  843
unix  1      [ ]         STREAM     CONNECTED   764    /tmp/.X11-unix/X0
unix  1      [ ]         STREAM     CONNECTED   746    /tmp/.font-unix/fs-1
unix  1      [ ]         STREAM     CONNECTED   748    /tmp/.X11-unix/X0
unix  0      [ ]         DGRAM                  654
unix  0      [ ]         DGRAM                  589
unix  0      [ ]         DGRAM                  560
unix  0      [ ]         DGRAM                  419
[oracle@donsrv1 oracle]$ netstat -sp tcp
Ip:
    15753092 total packets received
    1 with invalid headers
    0 forwarded
    0 incoming packets discarded
    99397 incoming packets delivered
    20325485 requests sent out
Icmp:
    1041 ICMP messages received
    37 input ICMP message failed.
    ICMP input histogram:
        destination unreachable: 972
        timeout in transit: 31
        echo requests: 27
        echo replies: 11
    490 ICMP messages sent
    0 ICMP messages failed
    ICMP output histogram:
        destination unreachable: 463
        echo replies: 27
Tcp:
    131 active connections openings
    0 passive connection openings
    14 failed connection attempts
    0 connection resets received
```

```
    6 connections established
    15652680 segments received
    20276668 segments send out
    6933 segments retransmited
    2 bad segments received.
    25 resets sent
Udp:
    97289 packets received
    11 packets to unknown port received.
    3 packet receive errors
    48279 packets sent
TcpExt:
    9 packets pruned from receive queue because of socket buffer overrun
        unix  0      [ ]        DGRAM                   407
```

Hopefully, this brief description of the **netstat** utility will give you an appreciation for the scope and complexity of network tuning.

In practice, an experienced UNIX network administrator will have specialized utilities such as UNIX *sniffers*, which will monitor and tune network traffic. The network administrator can monitor various connections on the LAN and, working together, the problem can be resolved. It would be very unusual for a DBA to run a network sniffer to locate a problem.

Next, let's have a brief overview of UNIX for Oracle distributed connections.

Oracle Networking and UNIX

While the Oracle Transparent Network Substrate (TNS) keeps the underlying UNIX layer hidden from Oracle, it is still quite important to fully understand the interaction between Oracle networking and UNIX.

When a client process communicates with a UNIX Oracle server, Oracle goes through several layers of abstraction to establish the connection (see Figure 5-1).

Here you see that the client code calls Net8, and Net8 calls the Net8 protocol adapter. The protocol adapter in turn passes the information to the UNIX interface, which creates the connection.

To understand this abstraction, let's take a simple example. Let's assume that you issue the following distributed request to a remote Oracle UNIX database:

```
select
    count(*)
from
    emp@new_york;
```

Let's follow each step of the process.

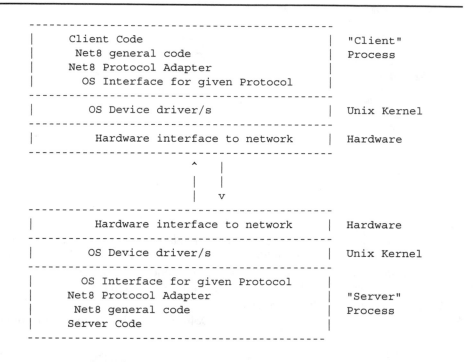

```
-------------------------------------------------
|          Client Code                          |   "Client"
|             Net8 general code                 |   Process
|          Net8 Protocol Adapter                |
|             OS Interface for given Protocol   |
-------------------------------------------------
|          OS Device driver/s                   |   Unix Kernel
-------------------------------------------------
|          Hardware interface to network        |   Hardware
-------------------------------------------------
                       ^   |
                       |   |
                       |   v
-------------------------------------------------
|          Hardware interface to network        |   Hardware
-------------------------------------------------
|          OS Device driver/s                   |   Unix Kernel
-------------------------------------------------
|             OS Interface for given Protocol   |
|          Net8 Protocol Adapter                |   "Server"
|             Net8 general code                 |   Process
|          Server Code                          |
-------------------------------------------------
```

FIGURE 5-1. *Oracle networking and UNIX*

Preparing to Connect to a Remote Server

The first step in the process is for Oracle to go to the database link. In the case of this query, you are looking at the new_york database link. A review of this link from the **dba_db_links** view shows you the information contained in the link:

```
SQL> select * from dba_db_links where db_link = 'NEW_YORK';
OWNER
-----------------------------
DB_LINK
-------------------------------------------------------------------
USERNAME
-----------------------------
HOST
-------------------------------------------------------------------
CREATED
---------
READMAN
```

```
NEW_YORK
MASTER
(DESCRIPTION =
        (ADDRESS =
         (COMMUNITY = TCP)
         (PROTOCOL = TCP)
         (HOST = nyserv1)
         (PORT = 1521)
        )
        (CONNECT_DATA = (SID = prodcust)
        (SERVER = DEDICATED))
     )
01-AUG-01
```

Here you see that the database link contains almost all of the information you need to connect to the remote server. You have:

- The remote server hostname (nyserv1)

- The network protocol (TCP/IP)

- The listening port on the remote server (1521)

- The name of the remote Oracle database (prodcust)

- The remote Oracle user ID (master)

- The remote user ID password (hidden from display)

The only thing remaining is the translation of the UNIX hostname into an IP address. In UNIX, a file called /etc/hosts is used to look up the IP address using the hostname. Here is an example of a /etc/hosts file:

```
root> cat /etc/hosts
127.0.0.1     localhost
192.144.12.205  marvin   marvin.ibm.com loghost pr4oddb-01
192.121.13.206  nyserv1  nyserv1.ibm.com loghost pr4oddb-01
192.144.1.200   blake    blake.ibm.com loghost pr4oddb-01
```

Here you see that UNIX will look up the IP address in /etc/hosts and resolve the hostname to 192.121.13.206.

Once Oracle has built the connect string for the remote server, the information is passed to UNIX, which establishes the connection to the remote server. The Oracle listener process is attached to port 1521 on the remote server, and this listener process receives the connection request and spawns a UNIX process ID (PID) on behalf on the incoming connection. After the process is created, the listener attaches the request to Oracle.

Checking Net8 Adapters in UNIX

UNIX has an adapter command that can be used to display all network adapters that are linked with your Oracle listener in UNIX. To see how this command works, go to your $ORACLE_HOME/bin directory and issue the UNIX command **adapters tnslsnr**:

```
root> cd $ORACLE_HOME/bin

root> adapters tnslsnr

Net Protocol Adapters linked with tnslsnr are:
BEQ Protocol Adapter
IPC Protocol Adapter
TCP/IP Protocol Adapter
RAW Protocol Adapter

Net Naming Adapters linked with tnslsnr are:
Oracle TNS Naming Adapter
Oracle Naming Adapter
```

This listing will show you the direct linking between Oracle Net8 software and the UNIX protocol adapters.

Now that you have the general idea about remote connectivity in UNIX, let's take a closer look at the internal mechanism of Oracle's Transparent Network Substrate.

TNS and UNIX for Oracle

With Oracle databases shared across geographical areas, it is very important for the Oracle professional to recognize the importance of network communications on the performance of their databases. As you may know, Oracle provides for distributed communications between databases by using its Transparent Network Substrate (TNS).

The TNS is a distributed protocol that allows for transparent database communications between remote systems. The TNS acts as an insulator between Oracle's logical request for data and the physical communications between the distributed servers. Because of this insulation between the Oracle logical data request and the internal workings of the network, much of the network performance tuning is in the hands of the network administrator. In other words, the Oracle administrator has very little direct control over the network configuration settings that can affect the overall performance of their database (see Figure 5-2).

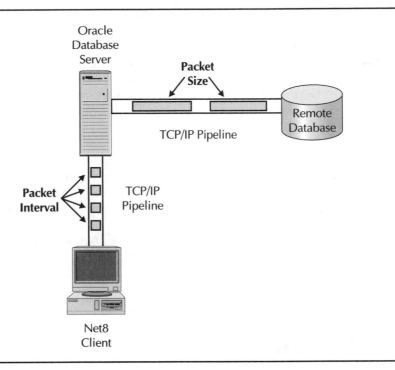

FIGURE 5-2. *Tuning the Oracle network*

However, there are some important settings that can be used to improve the performance of distributed transactions. This section will explore the **init.ora** parameters that relate to distributed communications, and also examine some of the TCP parameters such as **tcp.nodelay**, which can be used to change the basic packet-shipping mechanisms within the Oracle database.

We will investigate different parameters within the sqlnet.ora, tnsnames.ora, and protocol.ora files, which can be used to change the size and configuration of the TCP packets. These tools often have a profound impact on the behavior of the underlying network transport layer and improve throughput of all Oracle transactions.

A common misconception about Net8 is that you can tune the Oracle network parameters to realize performance gains across a network. With a few minor exceptions, all network traffic is outside the scope of Oracle and cannot be tuned from within the Oracle environment. Net8 is simply a layer in the OSI model and it resides above the network-specific protocol stack. In other words, virtually all network tuning is external to the Oracle environment. When a remote data request is initialized, Net8 will get the data for the packet and hand it over to the protocol stack for transmission. The protocol stack will then create a packet with this data and send it over the network. Because Net8 simply passes data to the protocol stack, there is very little Net8 can do to improve performance.

However, the DBA can control the size and frequency of the network packets. The Oracle DBA has a wealth of tools that can change the packet size, and frequency that packets are sent over the network. For a simple example, the refresh interval for a snapshot can be changed to ship larger amounts over the network at a less frequent interval.

To understand how the Oracle DBA can configure Oracle for better network performance, we must first start with a brief overview of a distributed Oracle database. We will then explore the internals of Oracle Transparent Network Substrate (TNS), and look at the tools that network administrators use to tune network traffic.

In each of these sections, we will discuss the tuning options that are available to help the DBA manage and tune distributed Oracle communications. Let's begin by looking at the configuration parameters that affect network performance.

Managing Net8 in a UNIX Environment

The Oracle UNIX administrator has access to the listener control utility to manage the Oracle listeners for each UNIX server. You can always see the listener process from UNIX by issuing the UNIX **ps** command, and using **grep** to grab the PID. Note the use of the **grep -v grep** command to exclude the process line with your **grep** command:

```
root> ps -ef|grep list|grep -v grep
   oracle 14202     1  0   Oct 28 ?        0:00
u01/app/oracle/product/8.1.7_64/bin/tnslsnr callout_listener –inherit
```

In emergencies, you can use the UNIX **kill** command to destroy the listener process, but Oracle recommends that you always try the **lsnrctl stop** command before killing the listener.

Managing the UNIX Oracle Listener

Oracle provides the listener control utility to allow the UNIX DBA to manage the listeners on their Oracle UNIX server. To see all of the options, you can enter the **lsnrctl help** command at the UNIX prompt:

```
oracle> lsnrctl help

LSNRCTL for Solaris: Version 8.1.7.0.0 - Production on 31-OCT-2001 19:54:57

(c) Copyright 1998 Oracle Corporation.  All rights reserved.

The following operations are available
An asterisk (*) denotes a modifier or extended command:

start              stop              status
services           version           reload
save_config        trace             spawn
dbsnmp_start       dbsnmp_stop       dbsnmp_status
change_password    quit              exit
set*               show*
```

You can extend the listener help facility to get details on any command by adding the required command. For example, here you get the help for the **lsnrctl help trace** command:

```
oracle> lsnrctl help trace

LSNRCTL for Solaris: Version 8.1.7.0.0 - Production on 31-OCT-2001 19:56:45

(c) Copyright 1998 Oracle Corporation.  All rights reserved.

trace OFF | USER | ADMIN | SUPPORT [<listener_name>]
 set tracing to the specified level
```

This online facility should give you all the information you need to maintain the listener in UNIX.

Starting and Stopping the Listener

It is very easy to start and stop the listener on a UNIX server. You simply enter the **lsnrctl start** or **lsnrctl stop** command. Each of these commands provides descriptive information about the current status.

```
oracle> lsnrctl start

LSNRCTL for Solaris: Version 8.1.7.0.0 - Production on 31-OCT-2001 19:31:46

(c) Copyright 1998 Oracle Corporation.  All rights reserved.

Starting /u01/app/oracle/product/8.1.7_64/bin/tnslsnr: please wait...

TNSLSNR for Solaris: Version 8.1.7.0.0 - Production
System parameter file is /var/opt/oracle/listener.ora
Log messages written to
```

```
u01/app/oracle/product/8.1.7_64/network/log/listener.log
Listening on: (DESCRIPTION=(ADDRESS=(PROTOCOL=tcp)(HOST=sting)(PORT=1521)))

Connecting to (ADDRESS=(PROTOCOL=tcp)(PORT=1521)(HOST=sting.rovia.com))
STATUS of the LISTENER
------------------------
Alias                    LISTENER
Version                  TNSLSNR for Solaris: Version 8.1.7.0.0 -
roduction
Start Date               31-OCT-2001 19:31:47
Uptime                   0 days 0 hr. 0 min. 0 sec
Trace Level              off
Security                 OFF
SNMP                     OFF
Listener Parameter File  /var/opt/oracle/listener.ora
Listener Log File
u01/app/oracle/product/8.1.7_64/network/log/listener.log
Services Summary...
   testar                has 1 service handler(s)
   testm1                has 1 service handler(s)
   testm2                has 1 service handler(s)
The command completed successfully
```

Note that the **lsnrctl start** command shows the location of the all-important listener.log file.

To stop the listener in a UNIX environment, simply enter the **lsnrctl stop** command. Remember, if you are using dedicated connections to Oracle, it is safe to briefly stop and restart the listener. This is because existing UNIX connections continue to be maintained if the listener is stopped, and the only problem would be that new connections must wait until you restart the listener to connect to Oracle.

```
oracle> lsnrctl stop

LSNRCTL for Solaris: Version 8.1.7.0.0 - Production on 31-OCT-2001 19:31:39

(c) Copyright 1998 Oracle Corporation.  All rights reserved.

Connecting to (ADDRESS=(PROTOCOL=tcp)(PORT=1521)(HOST=sting.rovia.com))
The command completed successfully
```

While this listener is running, you can issue the **lsnrctl stat** command to see the existing status of the listener process:

```
oracle> lsnrctl stat

LSNRCTL for Solaris: Version 8.1.7.0.0 - Production on 31-OCT-2001 19:34:16

(c) Copyright 1998 Oracle Corporation.  All rights reserved.
```

```
Connecting to (ADDRESS=(PROTOCOL=tcp)(PORT=1521)(HOST=sting.rovia.com))
STATUS of the LISTENER
----------------------
Alias                  LISTENER
Version                TNSLSNR for Solaris: Version 8.1.7.0.0 -
roduction
Start Date             31-OCT-2001 19:31:47
Uptime                 0 days 0 hr. 2 min. 29 sec
Trace Level            off
Security               OFF
SNMP                   OFF
Listener Parameter File   /var/opt/oracle/listener.ora
Listener Log File
u01/app/oracle/product/8.1.7_64/network/log/listener.log
Services Summary...
  testm1               has 5 service handler(s)
  testm2               has 5 service handler(s)
  testar               has 1 service handler(s)
  testm1               has 1 service handler(s)
  testm1               has 5 service handler(s)
  testm2               has 1 service handler(s)
  testm2               has 5 service handler(s)
The command completed successfully
```

Debugging UNIX Net8 Problems

As we mentioned, the listener.log is the all-important file when diagnosing networking problems in an Oracle environment. You can easily see the location of the listener.log file by issuing the **lsnrctl stat** command at the UNIX prompt, but in most cases the listener.log is located in the $ORACLE_HOME/network/log directory in UNIX.

Because the listener.log file contains all successful connection messages, the file can get quite large. Hence, the UNIX DBA can use the **grep** command to filter out only those messages that relate to Net8 connection errors:

```
oracle> grep -i error $ORACLE_HOME/network/log/listener.log |more
Error listening on:
ADDRESS=(PROTOCOL=tcp)(PORT=1521)(HOST=sting.rovia.com))
 TNS-12560: TNS:protocol adapter error
   Solaris Error: 125: Address already in use
```

You can also use the UNIX **tail** command to display the last 50 lines of the listener.log file, to only see the most recent messages:

```
root> tail -50 listener.log
31-OCT-2001 17:19:16 * (CONNECT_DATA=(SID=testarsd)(CID=(USER=adamf))) *
ADDRESS=(PROTOCOL=tcp)(HOST=192.168.1.205)(PORT=56468)) * establish *
```

```
estarsd * 0
31-OCT-2001 17:19:57 *
CONNECT_DATA=(SID=testc2)(CID=(PROGRAM=)(HOST=donald.rovia.com)(USER=sean)))
 (ADDRESS=(PROTOCOL=tcp)(HOST=192.168.1.208)(PORT=4602)) * establish *
estc2 * 0
31-OCT-2001 17:20:00 * (CONNECT_DATA=(SID=testarsd)(CID=(USER=sean))) *
ADDRESS=(PROTOCOL=tcp)(HOST=192.168.1.205)(PORT=56469)) * establish *
estarsd * 0
31-OCT-2001 17:20:02 *
CONNECT_DATA=(SID=testarsd)(CID=(PROGRAM=)(HOST=grumpy)(USER=nsadmin))) *
ADDRESS=(PROTOCOL=tcp)(HOST=192.168.1.223)(PORT=47993)) * establish *
estarsd * 0
31-OCT-2001 17:20:02 * service_update * testc1 * 0
31-OCT-2001 17:20:15 * service_update * testc2 * 0
31-OCT-2001 17:20:58 *
CONNECT_DATA=(SID=testc1)(CID=(PROGRAM=)(HOST=donald.rovia.com)(USER=adamf))
 * (ADDRESS=(PROTOCOL=tcp)(HOST=192.168.1.208)(PORT=4605)) * establish *
estc1 * 0
31-OCT-2001 17:21:00 * (CONNECT_DATA=(SID=testarsd)(CID=(USER=adamf))) *
ADDRESS=(PROTOCOL=tcp)(HOST=192.168.1.205)(PORT=56477)) * establish *
estarsd * 0
31-OCT-2001 17:21:39 *
CONNECT_DATA=(SID=testc2)(CID=(PROGRAM=)(HOST=donald.rovia.com)(USER=adamf))
 * (ADDRESS=(PROTOCOL=tcp)(HOST=192.168.1.208)(PORT=4608)) * establish *
estc2 * 0
31-OCT-2001 17:21:41 * (CONNECT_DATA=(SID=testarsd)(CID=(USER=adamf))) *
ADDRESS=(PROTOCOL=tcp)(HOST=192.168.1.205)(PORT=56480)) * establish *
estarsd * 0
```

Optimizing Oracle Net8 Configuration

There are several tuning parameters that will affect the performance of Net8 connections between servers. However, you must always remember that the tuning of the network is outside the scope of Oracle, and the services of a qualified network administrator should be used. The following parameter files contain settings that affect the size and frequency of packet shipping across the network:

■ sqlnet.ora server file

   automatic_ipc

■ sqlnet.ora client file

   break_poll_skip

■ tnsnames.ora file

   SDU, TDU

- listener.ora file

    SDU TDU

- protocol.ora file

    tcp.nodelay

Remember, these are the only tuning parameters that will affect the performance of the Oracle Net8 layer. Let's discuss these parameters and see how they can be adjusted to improve Net8 throughput.

The tcp.nodelay Parameter in protocol.ora

By default, Net8 waits before transmitting a request until the buffer is filled up. This can mean on some occasions that a request is not sent immediately to its destination. Most often, this behavior occurs when large amounts of data are streamed from one end to another, and Net8 waits until the buffer is full before transmitting the packet. To remedy this problem, you can add a protocol.ora file and specify **tcp.nodelay** to stop delays in the buffer flushing process.

For all TCP/IP implementations, the protocol.ora file can be specified to indicate no data buffering. This parameter can be used on both the client and the server. The statement in protocol.ora is:

```
tcp.nodelay = yes
```

By specifying this parameter, TCP buffering is skipped and every request is sent immediately. In some cases, setting this parameter can cause network slowdowns. The network traffic can increase due to the smaller (and more frequent) network packets being transmitted between the client and the server.

Oracle recommends that **tcp.nodelay** should only be used if TCP timeouts are encountered. However, in conditions of high-volume traffic between database servers, setting **tcp.nodelay** can make a huge improvement in performance.

The automatic_ipc parameter of sqlnet.ora

The **automatic_ipc** parameter speeds local connections to a database because it bypasses the network layer. If **automatic_ipc=on**, Net8 will first check to see if a local database with the same alias definition exists. If so, the connection will be translated to a local IPC connection and will therefore bypass the network layers. This is, of course, only useful on database servers and is a completely useless feature on Net8 clients.

On the database server, the **automatic_ipc** parameter should only be used in cases where a Net8 connection must be made to the local database. If no local database connections are needed or required, put this parameter to **off**, and all Net8 clients should have this setting to improve performance.

SDU and TDU parameters in tnsnames.ora

The **SDU** and **TDU** parameters are placed in the tnsnames.ora and listener.ora files. **SDU** is the session data unit, and specifies the size of the packets to send over the network. Ideally, this size should not surpass the size of the MTU (maximum transmission unit). This MTU value is fixed and depends on the actual network implementation used. Oracle recommends that **SDU** should be set to MTU.

NOTE
*Prior to release 7.3.3, both **SDU** and **TDU** were fixed at 2K and couldn't be changed.*

The TDU (transport data unit) is the default packet size used within Net8 to group data together. Ideally, the **TDU** parameter should be a multiple of the **SDU** parameter. The default values for **SDU** and **TDU** are 2,048, and the maximum value is 32,767 bytes.

The following guidelines apply for **SDU** and **TDU**:

- On fast network connections (T1 or T3 lines), you should set **SDU** and **TDU** equal to the MTU for your network. On standard Ethernet networks, the default MTU size is set to 1,514 bytes. On standard token ring networks, the default MTU size is 4,202.

- The **SDU** should never be set greater than **TDU** because you will waste network resources by shipping wasted space in each packet.

- If your users are connecting via modem lines, you may want to set **SDU** and **TDU** to smaller values because of the frequent resends that occur over modem lines.

- If the multi-threaded server (MTS) is used, you must also set the **mts_dispatchers** with the proper MTU **TDU** configuration.

Here is an example of these parameters on a token ring network with an MTU of 4,202:

listener.ora

```
SID_LIST_LISTENER =
    (SID_LIST =
        (SID_DESC =
            (SDU = 4202)
            (TDU = 4202)
            (SID_NAME = ORCL)
```

```
                    (GLOBAL_DBNAME = ORCL.WORLD)
               )
          )
```

tnsnames.ora

```
ORCL.WORLD =
    (DESCRIPTION =
        (SDU=4202)
        (TDU=4202)
        (ADDRESS =
            (PROTOCOL = TCP)
            (HOST = fu.bar)
            (PORT = 1521)
        )
        (CONNECT_DATA = (SID = ORCL))
    )
```

Again, you must remember that the **SDU** and **TDU** settings are a direct function
of the connection speed between the hosts. If you have a fast T1 line, set
SDU=TDU=MTU. For slower modem lines, you need to experiment with smaller
values of **SDU** and **TDU**.

If you are using Oracle8i, the database will automatically register instances in
the listener.ora file unless you take one of the following actions:

- Implement the multi-threaded server (MTS) and define the **mts_dispatchers**
  in your init.ora file:

```
MTS_DISPATCHERS=" (DESCRIPTION=(SDU=8192)(TDU=8192)\
ADDRESS=(PARTIAL=TRUE)(PROTOCOL=TCP)(HOST=supsund3)))\

(DISPATCHERS=1)"
```

- Use **service_name=global_dbname** in the Connect_Data section of the
  tnsnames.ora file, where global_dbname is configured in listener.ora. Note
  that this setting will disable the use of transparent application failover (TAF),
  which is not supported using **global_dbname**. For details, see "Configuring
  Transparent Application Failover" in the Net8 Administrator's Guide.

- Do not use automatic service registration. To do this, you must set the
  init.ora parameter **local_listener** to use a different TCP port than the one
  defined in your listener.ora file.

Next, let's look at the **queuesize** parameter and see how it affects network
performance.

The queuesize Parameter in listener.ora

The undocumented **queuesize** parameter determines the number of requests the listener can store while working to establish a connection. This parameter is only used for very high-volume databases, where the listener is spawning thousands of connections per hour. The size of the **queuesize** parameter should be equal to the number of expected simultaneous connections. Here is an example of this parameter in the listener.ora file:

```
LISTENER =
  (ADDRESS_LIST =
      (ADDRESS =
        (PROTOCOL = TCP)
        (HOST = marvin)
        (PORT = 1521)
        (QUEUESIZE = 32)
      )
  )
```

The disadvantage of this parameter is that it uses more memory and resources because it is preallocating resources for anticipated connect requests. If you have high-volume connections into a dedicated listener, you may want to implement the multi-threaded server (MTS) and use prespawned Oracle connections. Also, note that there are some restrictions of the MTS queue size, and some versions of UNIX do not allow queues greater than five.

The break_poll_skip Parameter of sqlnet.ora

This value specifies the number of packets to skip before checking for a user break. This is a client-only sqlnet.ora parameter and affects the amount of CPU consumed on the Net8 client.

The general rules for **break_poll_skip** are as follows:

■ The higher the **break_poll_skip** value, the less frequent CTRL-C checking, and the less CPU overhead used.

■ The lower the **break_poll_skip** value, the more frequent CTRL-C checking, and the more CPU overhead used.

The default value for **break_poll_skip** is 4. Remember, this parameter is only useful on a Net8 client sqlnet.ora file, and only functions on servers that support in-band breaks.

The disable_oob Parameter of sqlnet.ora

Out-of-band break checks can be disabled by adding this parameter to the sqlnet.ora file. If for some specific reason the checks should not be performed, set this parameter to **on**. By default, Net8 assumes **off** for this parameter and will perform out-of-band checks.

When **disable_oob=on**, Oracle's use of urgent data messages is disabled. The negative impact of using this parameter is the usage of the interrupt key. When you use **disable_oob**, you lose the break functionality of the interrupt key such as CTRL-C. A break is a function in Net8 that allows a user of an application to interrupt or stop a transaction before it is complete, returning both the client and the server to a state from which they can continue.

The epc_disabled Environment Variable

Starting in Oracle 7.3.2, Oracle Server Tracing (**otrace**) is enabled by default. A practical implication of this is that every connection and every request sent over Net8 is logged in the Oracle trace files process.dat and regid.dat. After long-term use of the database, these trace files can become enormous, slowing down the connection time dramatically.

The solution is to implement a **crontab** job to periodically remove the trace files or to disable the **otrace** facility. It is highly recommended that the DBA disable the **otrace** facility unless they require it for session tracing. Here are the steps:

1. Shut down the databases and listeners.

2. Remove the *.dat files from your $ORACLE_HOME/otrace/admin directory.

3. Re-create the dat files with the UNIX **touch** command.

4. Specify **'epc_disabled=TRUE'** in the runtime environment of the UNIX Oracle .profile, .login, or .cshrc login file. This will disable the **otrace** facility.

5. Modify the listener.ora file to specify **epc_disabled=TRUE** in the **sid_desc** for each database.

6. Restart the database and listeners.

7. Run the **otrccref** command from $ORACLE_HOME/bin.

Other Oracle Features that Affect Network Behavior

Now that we have covered the basic Oracle parameters that govern network traffic, let's look at some techniques in the Oracle environment that can be used to manage network activity. In general, there are several options:

- Using array fetches
- Using the multi-threaded server (MTS)
- Using connection pooling
- Using ODBC
- Using Oracle replication

Using Array Fetches to Improve Network Throughput

In databases that are using PL/SQL stored procedures and functions or a language such as C that supports array fetches, you can reduce Oracle network calls by using bulk array fetches. For example, instead of fetching one row at a time from a cursor, it is more efficient to fetch ten rows with a single network round trip.

Many Oracle tools such as SQL*Plus, SQL*Forms, and the language precompilers allow for the use of the **arraysize** parameter. The **arraysize** parameter allows multiple rows to be returned in a single database access. This has the effect on the network of making fewer TCP/IP packets, each with more data inside each packet. This technique can often greatly aid the performance of long-running client/ server tasks.

Oracle8i also offers enhanced bulk fetching through the Oracle Call Interface (OCI). The programming aspects of array fetching are beyond the scope of this text, but you can get more information on array fetch techniques in the Oracle-supplied documentation and on Oracle's MetaLink web site.

Using the Multi-threaded Server

When your database server experiences a large volume of incoming connections, the overhead of spawning a dedicated process to service each request can cause measurable overhead on the server. This is because the default listener process "bequeaths" the incoming connection, creating a process ID (PID) on the Oracle server and directing this process to establish the connection to Oracle.

To reduce this overhead, the MTS can be implemented to allow new connections to attach to prespawned shadow processes. Note that Oracle does not recommend using the MTS unless you average more than 300 connections on the server.

The basic premise of the MTS is that Oracle creates dispatcher processes, each with a set of pre-established connections into the Oracle database. Each dispatcher owns a set of prespawned connections into the database. By pre-establishing the connections to Oracle, server resources are minimized, and RAM storage is also minimized because each session will not allocate a personal **sort_area_size** in the Program Global Area (PGA). Instead, all dispatchers share the same User Global Area (UGA), thereby reducing memory demands on the database server.

One of the problems with the dedicated listener is that each incoming transaction is spawned by the listener as a separate operating system task. With the MTS, all communications to a database are handled through a single dispatcher instead of separate UNIX process IDs on each database. If you have constant connection loads of 300 users or more, using the MTS translates into faster performance for most online tasks. The only real downside to using the MTS is that the DBA cannot directly observe Oracle connections using the UNIX **ps-ef | grep oracle** command.

However, be aware that the MTS is not a panacea, especially at times when you want to invoke a dedicated process for your program. For Pro*C programs and I/O-intensive SQL*Forms applications, or any batch processes that have little idle time, you may derive better performance using a dedicated listener process. For shops that segregate tasks into online and batch modes, the DBA sometimes creates separate listeners—one with the MTS and another for dedicated connections.

In general, the MTS offers benefits such as reduced memory use, fewer processes per user, and automatic load balancing. However, the DBA must be careful to set the proper number of dispatcher processes and the proper number of servers within each dispatcher. Also, because the MTS uses the **shared_pool** for process sorting, the DBA will also see increased demands on the **shared_pool**.

Connections using the MTS will place the UGA inside the Oracle SGA. To hold the UGA storage for MTS connections, Oracle has provided the **large_pool** init.ora parameter. The large pool is an area of the SGA similar to the shared pool, but with restrictions on its usage such that only certain types and sizes of memory can be allocated in this pool. When using the MTS, Oracle recommends that the **large_pool** be set to a value greater than the default of 614,000 bytes.

Inside Oracle, the **v$queue** and **v$dispatcher** system views will indicate if the number of MTS dispatchers is too low. Even though the number of dispatchers is specified in the init.ora file, you can change it online in SQL*DBA with the **ALTER SYSTEM** command:

```
SVRMGRL> ALTER SYSTEM SET MTS_DISPATCHERS = 'TCPIP,4';
```

If you encounter problems with the MTS, you can quickly regress to dedicated servers by issuing an **ALTER SYSTEM** command. The following command turns off the MTS by setting the number of MTS servers to zero:

```
SVRMGRL> ALTER SYSTEM SET MTS_SERVERS=0;
```

The DBA must be careful when bouncing the database and listener. In some cases, the instance must be bounced if the listener is stopped, or it will restart in dedicated mode. Whenever an instance is to be bounced, stop the listener, shut down the instance, restart the listener, and start up the instance. The listener reads the MTS parameters only if it is running before startup of the instance. Therefore, bouncing the listener will disable the MTS. To implement the MTS, you need to add the following init.ora parameters:

```
# ---------------------
# Multi-threaded Server parameters
# ---------------------
local_listener="(address_list=
   (address=(protocol=tcp)(host=sting.janet.com)(port=1521))
   )"
MTS_MAX_DISPATCHERS=5
MTS_MAX_SERVERS=20
MTS_DISPATCHERS="(ADDRESS=
   (PROTOCOL=tcp)(HOST=sting.janet.com))(DISPATCHERS=3)
   "
service_names=testb1
```

Monitoring the MTS with the lsnrctl Command

If you are using the MTS in UNIX, you can issue the **lsnrctl services** command at the UNIX prompt to see the status of every dispatcher that you have defined:

```
oracle> lsnrctl services

LSNRCTL for Solaris: Version 8.1.7.0.0 - Production on 31-OCT-2001 19:35:24

(c) Copyright 1998 Oracle Corporation.  All rights reserved.

Connecting to (ADDRESS=(PROTOCOL=tcp)(PORT=1521)(HOST=sting.rovia.com))
Services Summary...
  testc1               has 5 service handler(s)
    DISPATCHER established:0 refused:0 current:0 max:1022 state:ready
      D003 <machine: sting, pid: 14280>
```

```
      (ADDRESS=(PROTOCOL=ipc)(KEY=#14280.1))
  testc2                 has 5 service handler(s)
    DISPATCHER established:0 refused:0 current:0 max:1022 state:ready
      D003 <machine: sting, pid: 14352>
      (ADDRESS=(PROTOCOL=ipc)(KEY=#14352.1))
  testarsd               has 1 service handler(s)
    DEDICATED SERVER established:0 refused:0
      LOCAL SERVER
  testc1                 has 1 service handler(s)
    DEDICATED SERVER established:0 refused:0
      LOCAL SERVER
  testc1                 has 5 service handler(s)
    DISPATCHER established:0 refused:0 current:0 max:1022 state:ready
      D002 <machine: sting, pid: 14278>
      (ADDRESS=(PROTOCOL=tcp)(HOST=sting)(PORT=43208))
    DISPATCHER established:0 refused:0 current:0 max:1022 state:ready
      D001 <machine: sting, pid: 14276>
      (ADDRESS=(PROTOCOL=tcp)(HOST=sting)(PORT=43207))
    DISPATCHER established:0 refused:0 current:0 max:1022 state:ready
      D000 <machine: sting, pid: 14274>
      (ADDRESS=(PROTOCOL=tcp)(HOST=sting)(PORT=43205))
    DEDICATED SERVER established:0 refused:0
      LOCAL SERVER
  testc2                 has 1 service handler(s)
    DEDICATED SERVER established:0 refused:0
      LOCAL SERVER
  testc2                 has 5 service handler(s)
    DISPATCHER established:0 refused:0 current:0 max:1022 state:ready
      D002 <machine: sting, pid: 14350>
      (ADDRESS=(PROTOCOL=tcp)(HOST=sting)(PORT=43215))
    DISPATCHER established:0 refused:0 current:0 max:1022 state:ready
      D001 <machine: sting, pid: 14348>
      (ADDRESS=(PROTOCOL=tcp)(HOST=sting)(PORT=43214))
    DISPATCHER established:0 refused:0 current:0 max:1022 state:ready
      D000 <machine: sting, pid: 14342>
      (ADDRESS=(PROTOCOL=tcp)(HOST=sting)(PORT=43212))
    DEDICATED SERVER established:0 refused:0
      LOCAL SERVER
The command completed successfully
```

Here you see, for every dispatcher, the high-water mark of connections, the current connections, the total connections, and the number of refused connections. This command can be very useful for debugging the MTS when connection problems occur.

Now that you see how the MTS can relieve stress on the server, let's look at the connection pooling features of Oracle8i.

Connection Pooling and Network Performance

Connection pooling is a resource utilization feature that enables you to reduce the number of physical network connections to an MTS dispatcher. This reduction is achieved by sharing or pooling a set of connections among the client processes. Connection pooling effectively allows Oracle to maximize the number of physical network connections to the multi-threaded server. Connection pooling is achieved by sharing or pooling a dispatcher's set of connections among multiple client processes (see Figure 5-3).

Connection pooling reuses physical connections and makes them available for incoming clients, while still maintaining a logical session with the previous idle connection. By using a timeout mechanism to temporarily release transport connections that have been idle for a specified period, connection pooling will "suspend" a previous connection and reuse the physical connection. When the idle client has more work to do, the physical connection is reestablished with the dispatcher.

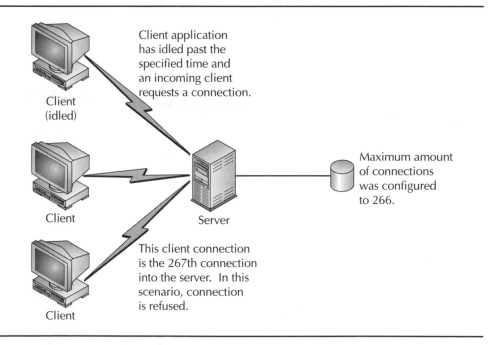

FIGURE 5-3. *Multi-threaded server connections*

By default, connection pooling is disabled on both incoming and outgoing network connections. To enable connection pooling, you must alter the **mts_dispatchers** parameter in the init.ora file. In the following example, you enable the Net8 connection pooling feature by adding the **POOL** argument to the **mts_dispatchers** parameter:

```
MTS_DISPATCHERS = "(PROTOCOL=TCP)(DISPATCHERS=3)(POOL=3)"
```

If a number is specified, connection pooling is enabled for both incoming and outgoing network connections and the number specified is the timeout in ticks for both incoming and outgoing network connections.

```
MTS_DISPATCHERS = "(PROTOCOL=TCP)(DISPATCHERS=3)(POOL=ON)"
```

If **ON**, **YES**, **TRUE**, or **BOTH** is specified, connection pooling is enabled for both incoming and outgoing network connections, and the default timeout (set by Net8) will be used for both incoming and outgoing network connections.

```
MTS_DISPATCHERS = "(PROTOCOL=TCP)(DISPATCHERS=3)(POOL=IN)"
```

If **IN** is specified, connection pooling is enabled for incoming network connections and the default timeout (set by Net8) will be used for incoming network connections.

```
MTS_DISPATCHERS = "(PROTOCOL=TCP)(DISPATCHERS=3)(POOL=OUT)"
```

If **OUT** is specified, connection pooling is enabled for outgoing network connections and the default timeout (set by Net8) will be used for outgoing network connections.

In practice, connection pooling is rarely used except in cases where the database server is overwhelmed with incoming Net8 requests.

ODBC and Network Performance

The Open Database Connectivity (ODBC) product was initially developed by Microsoft as a generic database driver. Its architecture has now been generalized and many different vendors are offering open database connectivity products that are based on ODBC. ODBC consists of more than 50 functions that are invoked from an application using a call-level API. The ODBC API does not communicate with a database directly. Instead, it serves as a link between the application and a generic interface routine. The interface routine, in turn, communicates with the database drivers via a Service Provider Interface (SPI).

ODBC has become popular with database vendors such as Oracle, and Oracle is creating new ODBC drivers that will allow ODBC to be used as a gateway into their database products. Essentially, ODBC serves as the "traffic cop" for all data within the client/server system. When a client requests a service from a database, ODBC receives the request and manages the connection to the target database. ODBC manages all of the database drivers, checking the status information as it arrives from the database drivers.

It is noteworthy that the database drivers should be able to handle more than just SQL. Many databases have a native API that requires ODBC to map the request into a library of functions. An example would be a SQL Server driver that maps ODBC functions to database library function calls. Databases without a native API (in other words, non-SQL databases) can also be used with ODBC, but they go through a much greater transformation than the native API calls.

Database connectivity using ODBC has a high amount of overhead in many Oracle applications. The inherent flexibility of ODBC means that the connection process to Oracle is not as efficient as a native API call to the database. Most companies that experience ODBC-related performance problems will abandon ODBC and replace it with a native communications tool such as the Oracle Call Interface (OCI). In sum, ODBC is great for ad hoc database queries from MS Windows, but it is too slow for most production applications. Now let's turn our attention to Oracle replication and see how the replication parameters can affect Oracle performance.

Tuning with Oracle Replication

Oracle replication was first introduced as a method to allow Oracle tables to reside on widely separated servers. Replication was a godsend for companies that needed to have synchronized databases across the globe. Of course, it is still far faster to process a table on a local host than it is to process a remote table across the Net8 distributed communication lines.

Several factors influence the decision about replicating Oracle tables. The foremost considerations are the size of the replicated table and the volatility of the tables, as shown in Figure 5-4. Large, highly active tables with many updates, deletes, and inserts will require a lot of system resources to replicate and keep synchronized with the master table. Smaller, less active tables would be ideal candidates for replication, since the creation and maintenance of the replicated table would not consume a high amount of system resources.

Oracle's advanced replication facility is relatively mature, and Oracle now supports multimaster replication whereby many sites can accept new rows and propagate them to the other snapshots.

From a performance perspective, you need to be concerned about how often the snapshots are refreshed. You can refresh the replicated table in full, you can re-create the snapshot at will, you can choose periodic refreshes of the snapshot, and you can use database triggers to propagate changes from a master table to the snapshot table. Although the choice of technique depends upon the individual application, some general rules apply.

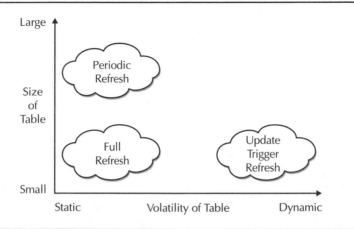

FIGURE 5-4. *The replication alternatives based on size and volatility*

Tiny Static Tables

If a replicated table is small and relatively static, it is usually easier to drop and re-create the snapshot than to use Oracle's **REFRESH COMPLETE** option. A crontab file can be set up to invoke the drop and re-creation at a predetermined time each day, completely refreshing the entire table.

Another popular alternative to the snapshot is using Oracle's distributed SQL to create a replicated table directly on the slave database. In the following example, the New York database creates a local table called emp_nc, which contains New York employee information from the master employee table at corporate headquarters:

```
CREATE TABLE emp_nc
AS SELECT
    emp_nbr,
    emp_name,
    emp_phone,
    emp_hire_date
FROM
    emp@hq
WHERE
    department = 'NC';
```

For highly static table that seldom changes, you can also specify refreshes to run quarterly. The following example refreshes a table completely on the first Tuesday of each quarter:

```
CREATE SNAPSHOT
    cust_snap1
```

```
REFRESH COMPLETE
    START WITH SYSDATE
    NEXT NEXT_DAY(ADD_MONTHS(trunc(sysdate,'Q'),3),'TUESDAY')
AS
SELECT
    cust_nbr, cust_name
FROM
    customer@hq
WHERE
    department = 'NC';
```

Large Dynamic Tables

Very large replicated tables will consume too much time if you drop and re-create
the snapshot or if you use the **REFRESH COMPLETE** option. For static tables, a
snapshot log would not contain very many changes—you could direct Oracle to
propagate the changes to the replicated table at frequent intervals. Let's take a look
at the different refresh intervals that can be specified for a snapshot:

```
CREATE SNAPSHOT
    cust_snap1
REFRESH FAST
    START WITH SYSDATE
    NEXT SYSDATE+7
AS
SELECT
    cust_nbr, cust_name
FROM
    customer@hq
WHERE
    department = 'NC';
```

Now that we have covered the parameters and techniques that affect network
performance, let's look at how you can use STATSPACK to see the network activity.

Monitoring Network Performance from Oracle STATSPACK

From STATSPACK, you can query the stats$system_event table to see the amount of
time Oracle has waited for network packets. As you recall, there are several system
events that can show you network activity:

```
SQL> select distinct event from stats$system_event
  2  where event like 'SQL%';

EVENT
```

```
-------------------------------------------------------------
SQL*Net break/reset to client
SQL*Net message from client
SQL*Net message from dblink
SQL*Net message to client
SQL*Net message to dblink
SQL*Net more data from client
SQL*Net more data to client
```

From this STATSPACK table, you can select all of the significant events, the number of waits, and the average wait time in seconds. Remember, most networks such as TCP/IP send an acknowledgement when a packet has been received, as shown in Figure 5-5.

The rpt_event.sql script that follows can be run to see all Oracle system events that were captured in the STATSPACK stats$system_event table.

rpt_event.sql

```
set pages 999;

column mydate       heading 'Yr. Mo Dy Hr'     format a13;
column event                                   format a30;
column waits                                   format 999,999;
column secs_waited                             format 999,999,999;
column avg_wait_secs                           format 99,999;

select
   to_char(snap_time,'yyyy-mm-dd HH24')               mydate,
   e.event,
   e.total_waits - nvl(b.total_waits,0)          waits,
   ((e.time_waited - nvl(b.time_waited,0))/100) /
   nvl((e.total_waits - nvl(b.total_waits,0)),.01)  avg_wait_secs
from
   stats$system_event b,
   stats$system_event e,
   stats$snapshot      sn
where
   e.snap_id = sn.snap_id
and
   b.snap_id = e.snap_id-1
and
   b.event = e.event
and
   e.event like 'SQL*Net%'
and
   e.total_waits - b.total_waits  > 100
and
   e.time_waited - b.time_waited > 100
;
```

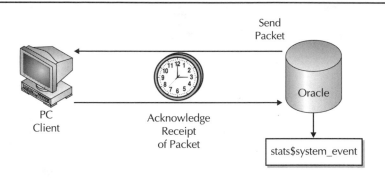

FIGURE 5-5. *Tracking network latency by timing between send and acknowledgement*

Here is a sample of the output from this report, showing the events and the wait times for each event. This is a great report for showing specific times when the network is overloaded with packet traffic.

Yr. Mo Dy Hr EVENT	WAITS	AVG_WAIT_SECS
2000-09-20 15 SQL*Net message from client	1,277	1
2000-09-20 16 SQL*Net message from client	133	64
2000-09-20 18 SQL*Net message from client	325	1
2000-09-20 19 SQL*Net message from client	410	0
2000-09-20 20 SQL*Net message from client	438	22
2000-09-20 22 SQL*Net message from client	306	8
2000-09-21 10 SQL*Net message from client	253	4
2000-09-21 12 SQL*Net message from client	208	0
2000-09-21 13 SQL*Net message from client	230	6
2000-09-21 14 SQL*Net message from client	311	6
2000-09-21 17 SQL*Net message from client	269	21
2000-09-21 18 SQL*Net message from client	222	29
2000-09-21 19 SQL*Net message from client	362	22
2000-09-22 11 SQL*Net message from client	111	32
2000-09-22 15 SQL*Net message from client	353	10
2000-09-22 20 SQL*Net message from client	184	18
2000-09-22 22 SQL*Net message from client	642	104
2000-09-23 11 SQL*Net message from client	125	22
2000-09-23 12 SQL*Net message from client	329	11
2000-09-23 13 SQL*Net message from client	329	172
2000-09-23 14 SQL*Net message from client	310	4
2000-09-23 15 SQL*Net message from client	501	17
2000-09-23 16 SQL*Net message from client	197	49
2000-09-23 19 SQL*Net message from client	214	20
2000-09-24 16 SQL*Net message from client	343	251

These STATSPACK reports can often give the DBA an idea about potential network problems because Oracle captures the number of seconds that have been waited for each distributed event. Of course, Oracle can identify a latency problem, but you need to go out to the network to find the exact cause of the network problem.

Conclusion

This chapter describes the main characteristics of tuning Net8 transactions in a UNIX environment. The main points of this chapter include the following:

- There are very few controls over network communication for Oracle.

- The **tcp.nodelay** parameter can be used to adjust packet sizes across the network

- The **SDU** and **TDU** parameters provide some control over the internal network behavior.

Now that you understand the tools you have to change Oracle packet characteristics and how to use STATSPACK to identify potential network problems, let's move on and take a look at managing session information in a UNIX environment.

PART
II

The Interaction
Between Oracle and
the UNIX Server

CHAPTER
6

Oracle Interfaces
with the UNIX Server

his chapter is concerned with the interface layer between the Oracle and the UNIX operating system. As you know, Oracle interacts with the I/O subsystem to read and write from disk, and Oracle also interfaces with the RAM memory and CPU on the database server.

While only a process dump can directly display the interactions between Oracle and the server, Oracle provides several tools, including background process dumps, to show you the nature of these interactions between Oracle and UNIX. The topics in this chapter will include:

- The interaction between the Oracle background processes and CPU consumption

- The interaction between Oracle and the RAM memory regions, including PGA and SGA memory

- The interaction between Oracle and the disk devices

We already covered the main tools for monitoring CPU and memory consumption in Chapter 2. This chapter takes the basic concepts from Chapter 2 and expands on some Oracle-centric techniques that you can use for observing the interaction between Oracle and the UNIX OS.

The Oracle Background Processes in UNIX

An important consideration when using Oracle with UNIX is that the interaction between UNIX and Oracle is automatic and largely beyond the control of the Oracle DBA. For example, UNIX is designed to allow any Oracle process to use any available CPU, and the assignment of UNIX processes to CPUs is automatic and uncontrollable. Table 6-1 shows some of the options available to the Oracle DBA when tuning the interface between Oracle and UNIX.

Let's begin with an overview of the Oracle background processes and see how you can measure the interaction of the background processes and Oracle server resources.

As Oracle has evolved, the number and complexity of the background processes have increased. For our discussion, we have separated the Oracle background processes into the main background process and the processes that are optional. We will limit our discussion to those background processes that are the most important for understanding the interaction between Oracle and UNIX.

UNIX Component	DBA Consumption Control
RAM	init.ora parameters
	Alter session commands
	Alter system commands
	Add additional RAM memory
CPU	Add additional CPUs to server
Disk	init.ora parameters, such as **db_file_multiblock_read_count**
	Data buffer adjustment
Network	Parameters in the sqlnet.ora file
	Parameters in the protocol.ora file

TABLE 6-1.   *UNIX Components and Oracle Adjustments*

Displaying CPU and RAM for Oracle UNIX Processes

The UNIX **ps -eo** command can be used to display details about the resource consumption for any Oracle process on the database server. This command displays the RAM memory consumption (**vsz**) and the percentage CPU (**pcpu**), so the **ps –eo** command is especially useful for quickly identifying Oracle processes in UNIX that are consuming a disproportional amount of machine resources.

Here you see this UNIX command executed on a UNIX server. Note that the **sort +3** directs UNIX to sort in order of percentage CPU (the fourth column, since UNIX numbers columns from zero). The tail command displays only the top CPU consumers among all of the Oracle UNIX processes.

```
root> ps -eo pid,user,vsz,pcpu,nice|grep ora|sort +3|tail

  PID   USER   VSZ    %CPU NI
15042   oracle 291464   3.1 20
15044   oracle 291432   4.0 20
15046   oracle 291576   6.5 20
20186   oracle 490632   8.2 20
20556   oracle 519224   9.4 20
20778   oracle 488152  19.3 20
20848   oracle 516792  20.1 20
```

In the listing we see the following information displayed:

- **vsz** (virtual memory size) This displays the total amount of RAM memory that has been used by the process.

- **pcpu** (percentage of CPU) This displays the current CPU consumption for the Oracle task as a percentage of all other tasks on the CPU.

- **nice** (dispatching priority) In UNIX systems where the DBA has altered the nice values for the Oracle background processes, you can see the relative dispatching priority for each UNIX task.

Once we know the PID for the processes with the highest RAM memory and CPU consumption, we can use the **ps –ef** command to display details about the UNIX process.

The Main Oracle Background Processes

Regardless of the version of Oracle and the options installed, you always see the mainstay background processes. These include pmon, smon, dbwr, lgwr, and arch. These background processes will exist regardless of the version of Oracle of the OS environment (see Figure 6-1).

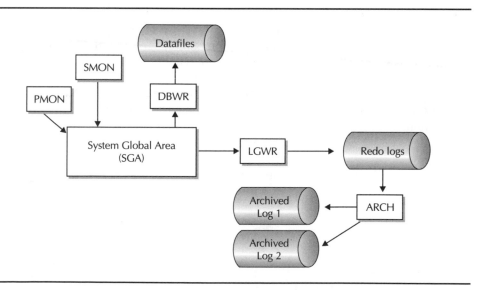

FIGURE 6-1. *The main Oracle background processes*

The System Monitor Background Process (SMON)
The SMON background process performs all system monitoring functions on the Oracle database. The SMON process performs a "warm start" each time Oracle is restarted, ensuring that any in-flight transactions at the time of the last shutdown are recovered. For example, if Oracle crashed hard with a power failure, the SMON process is attached at startup time and detects any uncompleted work, using the rollback segments to recover the transactions. In addition, SMON performs periodic cleanup of temporary segments that are no longer needed, and also performs tablespace operations, coalescing contiguous free extents into larger extents.

In UNIX, the SMON process will always be executing. You can tell when SMON is performing a coalesce operation because the CPU usage for the process will increase.

The Process Monitor Background Process (PMON)
The PMON background process is responsible for interfacing with the rollback segments to rollback any abnormally terminated transactions. Just like SMON, the PMON process is always executing in UNIX, but it remains largely idle except when recovering aborted transactions. Later in this chapter we will show you how to dump the PMON process and see details about its interaction with UNIX.

The Log Writer Background Process (LGWR)
The LGWR background process is the first in a series on redo log processes that writes the contents of the redo log buffer to the online redo log files. It writes to the online redo log files in batches and the entries always contain the most up-to-date status of the database. In UNIX, the LGWR process will perform the writes from the RAM **log_buffer** to the online redo log file even if your database is not in ARCHIVELOG mode.

The Database Writer Background Process (DBWR)
The DBWR background process is responsible for managing the interaction between the Oracle RAM data buffers (and the dictionary cache) and the physical disks. The DBWR process performs batch writes of the changed blocks back to the datafiles.

In UNIX, the DBWR process is asynchronous. This means that a database write does not always result in an immediate physical I/O by the DBWR. Rather, the DBWR process may wait until a set of "dirty" blocks have accumulated in the data buffers, and then write out the entire set of blocks in a single operation.

When using a sophisticated back-end storage system such as hardware raid storage devices with large caches, the nature of database writes becomes even more complex. Often, these boxes will defer writes to the physical disks in order to optimize I/O throughput. To do this, the disk box will send an immediate acknowledgement back to the DBWR process that the I/O has been completed, when in reality the data block resides in RAM storage in the disk cache. This complex interaction often leads to finger-pointing between the disk vendor and Oracle whenever a bug causes a disk write to fail.

The Archiver Background Process (ARCH)

The ARCH background process is invoked when your database is running in ARCHIVELOG mode. If you are archiving your redo logs, the redo logs are touched by several background processes. First, the LGWR process copies the **log_buffer** contents to the online redo log files, and then the ARCH process copies the online redo log files to the archived redo log file system on UNIX. The ARCH process commonly offloads the most recent online redo log file whenever a log switch operation occurs in Oracle. You can observe a log switch in the Oracle alert log, and the online redo logs should be sized such that you do not experience a log switch more than once every 15 minutes.

In UNIX, the ARCH process is I/O intensive and you can use **top**, **glance**, or **watch** to observe the ARCH process writing the data blocks to the archived redo log file.

Parallel Query Background Process (Pnnn)

The Oracle parallel query slave processes are used whenever Oracle invokes a parallel full-table scan. Oracle partitions the target table and then fires off a UNIX process for each table partition. When not in use, the parallel query processes disappear from UNIX. Since most Oracle databases that perform parallel query are doing full-table scans against very large tables, the Oracle DBA can watch the parallel query slaves appear in the UNIX environment. For example, if you are doing a query with parallel degree five, you can use the UNIX **ps** command to watch Oracle direct UNIX to create six parallel query slaves, with names like **ora_p000_prodsid** through **ora_p005_prodsid.**

There are two init.ora parameters that affect parallel query slaves. If the **parallel_min_servers** parameter is set, Oracle keeps this number of query slaves around at all times.

The extra parallel query process is the parallel query coordinator, and this UNIX process will remain alive until all of the factotum processes have completed their subtable scans. Once all of the data has been retrieved, you can sometimes observe Oracle invoke a disk sort in the TEMP tablespace. Whenever a parallel large-table full-table scan contains an **order by** or a **group by** on a large result set, the Oracle parallel query coordinator will pass the unsorted result set to Oracle, where the Oracle DBA can watch the creation of temporary segments in the TEMP tablespace to sort the result set.

The Recoverer Background Process (RECO)

RECO is a background process for distributed transactions. The RECO process manager two-phase commits to track and resolve doubtful transactions.

In UNIX, the RECO process awakens whenever a single transaction spans two geographical locations. For example, the following transaction requires a two-phase commit:

```
Update     -- Local update transaction
   emp
set
   sal = sal * 1.1
where
   dept = 30;

update    -- Remote update transaction
   emp@new_york
set
   sal = sal * 1.1
where
   dept = 40;
```

In this case, the RECO process will ensure that both the remote update and the local update complete or roll back as a single unit.

You will see the RECO process running whenever the distributed option of Oracle is installed, but the RECO process will only show activity when remote updates are being executed as part of a two-phase commit.

Oracle Snapshot Background Process (SNP)

The Oracle snapshot processes are an integral part of Oracle advanced replication and Oracle materialized views. The SNP processes are used to refresh replicated and preaggregated data. The SNP processes will awaken when signaled by the implementation **dbms_job** routine. Snapshots and materialized views are scheduled for periodic refreshes with the **dbms_job** package, and the SNP process will awaken whenever a request is made to refresh a snapshot or materialized view.

Now that you understand the functions of the major Oracle background processes and how the background processes interact with UNIX, let's do a brief review of the tools you can use to watch CPU consumption for the Oracle background processes.

Monitoring Oracle CPU Consumption in UNIX

As we noted in Chapter 2, most Oracle DBAs use the **glance**, **watch**, or **top** utility to monitor CPU consumption on their Oracle server. Since this text is targeted at UNIX DBAs, it is important to understand that there is a difference between how the background processes/threads are implemented on UNIX and NT. On UNIX, a separate operating system process is created to run each of the background functions listed earlier. On NT, they are run as different threads within the same process.

As a quick review from earlier chapters, any of the following **ps** commands can be used to display the top CPU consumers from UNIX:

```
root> ps auxgw|sort +2|tail

USER        PID %CPU %MEM   SZ   RSS  TTY STAT    STIME  TIME COMMAND
oracle    14922  0.6  1.0 8300 5720    - A    01:01:46  2:57 oracleprod
oracle    22424  0.6  1.0 8328 6076    - A    07:48:43  0:21 oracleprod
oracle    44518  0.8  1.0 8080 5828    - A    08:47:47  0:02 oracleprod
oracle    20666  1.0  1.0 8304 6052    - A    08:15:19  0:22 oracleprod
oracle    13168  1.6  1.0 8196 5760    - A    05:33:06  3:15 oracleprod
oracle    17402  2.5  1.0 8296 6044    - A    07:27:04  2:06 oracleprod
oracle    25754  2.5  1.0 8640 6388    - A    08:10:03  1:03 oracleprod
oracle    41616  4.5  1.0 8312 6052    - A    07:00:59  4:57 oracleprod
```

Yet another approach uses the **egrep** command to display the top CPU consumers. In the following example you see an Oracle process called from SQL*Forms using 18.9 percent of the CPU:

```
root> ps augxww|egrep "RSS| "|head

USER        PID %CPU %MEM   SZ   RSS  TTY STAT    STIME   TIME COMMAND
oracle      516 18.9  0.0   16     4   - A    Nov 21 194932:05 runform45
oracle    41616  4.4  1.0 8312 6052    - A    07:00:59   4:57
oracle    20740  2.7  1.0 8140 5888    - A    08:52:32   0:02
oracle    17402  2.4  1.0 8296 6044    - A    07:27:04   2:06
oracle    25754  2.4  1.0 8640 6388    - A    08:10:03   1:03
oracle    13168  1.6  1.0 8196 5760    - A    05:33:06   3:15
oracle    20666  1.0  1.0 8304 6052    - A    08:15:19   0:22
oracle    14922  0.6  1.0 8300 5720    - A    01:01:46   2:57
oracle    44518  0.6  1.0 8080 5828    - A    08:47:47   0:02
```

Here is another more sophisticated permutation of the **ps** command to display the top 20 CPU consumers in UNIX. Note that in this command you eliminate the Oracle background processes by using **grep** to only find LOCAL processes. Then you sort on column 2 (actually the third column because UNIX starts numbering columns from 0) to sort the result set in descending order of CPU consumption:

```
root> ps -ef|grep LOCAL|cut -c1-15,42-79|sort -rn +2 | head -20

    oracle 27825    3:45 oraclePROD (DESCRIPTION=(LOCAL=
    oracle 25856    2:49 oraclePROD (DESCRIPTION=(LOCAL=
    oracle 28018    1:00 oraclePROD (DESCRIPTION=(LOCAL=
    oracle 27787    0:90 oraclePROD (DESCRIPTION=(LOCAL=
    oracle 27750    0:83 oraclePROD (DESCRIPTION=(LOCAL=
    oracle 27447    0:71 oraclePROD (DESCRIPTION=(LOCAL=
    oracle 26519    0:63 oraclePROD (DESCRIPTION=(LOCAL=
```

```
oracle 25896    0:51 oraclePROD (DESCRIPTION=(LOCAL=
oracle 25894    0:50 oraclePROD (DESCRIPTION=(LOCAL=
oracle 25892    0:41 oraclePROD (DESCRIPTION=(LOCAL=
oracle 25890    0:40 oraclePROD (DESCRIPTION=(LOCAL=
oracle 25888    0:39 oraclePROD (DESCRIPTION=(LOCAL=
oracle 25886    0:11 oraclePROD (DESCRIPTION=(LOCAL=
oracle 25884    0:11 oraclePROD (DESCRIPTION=(LOCAL=
oracle 25882    0:11 oraclePROD (DESCRIPTION=(LOCAL=
oracle 25880    0:10 oraclePROD (DESCRIPTION=(LOCAL=
oracle 25878    0:02 oraclePROD (DESCRIPTION=(LOCAL=
oracle 25876    0:02 oraclePROD (DESCRIPTION=(LOCAL=
```

Many Oracle DBAs use the **glance**, **watch**, **sar**, or **top** UNIX utility to monitor the behavior of Oracle processes in UNIX. Please see Chapter 2 for details on using these tools in your UNIX environment.

Oracle Interaction with the UNIX Server CPUs

In UNIX, Oracle utilizes as many CPUs as are available on the database server. This is completely transparent to the Oracle DBA since the UNIX task dispatcher manages this interaction according to the **nice** values of the background processes.

Here is a simple Solaris UNIX command to show the percentage of CPU consumption for a specific Oracle background process. Here you use the Solaris command **ps -o pcpu** to display the percentage CPU consumption for all processes on the server, and the **sort** command to display the highest CPU consumers. The list is sorted in ascending order with the highest CPU consumer last in the output.

```
root> ps -eo pid,user,vsz,pcpu,nice|sort +3|tail

  PID    USER    VSZ %CPU NI
    0    root      0  0.0 SY
    2    root      0  0.0 SY
  416    root   8024  0.1 20
  706    root  12320  0.1 20
 9109  oracle   1808  0.1 20
10085  oracle   1808  0.1 20
10086    root   1880  0.1 20
10087  oracle   5472  0.1 20
    3    root      0  0.4 SY
```

Note that Solaris UNIX does not provide a facility for assigning specific processes to specific CPUs. However, there are some dialects of UNIX that allow the Oracle DBA to preassign the Oracle background processes to specific CPUs. This technique is most commonly undertaken when a large server shares many applications, of which Oracle is just one. In these cases, you want to partition the application such that Oracle does not consume a disproportional amount of CPU cycles.

Partitioning CPUs in Tru64 UNIX

While many dialects of UNIX offer no control over the assignment of processes to CPUs, Compaq Tru64 UNIX has several ways to segregate Oracle onto isolated CPUs:

- **Hard partitioning** This is done at the hardware level.

- **Processor sets** This technique allows the capability with a number of their servers to define groups of processors, called processor sets or **psets**.

To force a process to run on a specific **pset**, you have two options:

- Precede the execution of all Unix-level commands with the Compaq UNIX **runon** command.

- Assign the UNIX PID to a CPU with the Compaq UNIX **pset_assign_pid** command.

To perform the CPU partitioning, the following shell script can be created and placed in the UNIX Oracle .profile file:

assign_pset.ksh

```
#!/bin/ksh
#-------------------------------------------------------------------------
#
# This script will capture the processor set currently used by a process,
# and then validate   the processor set number.
# If it's incorrect, it will reassign the given
# process to the proper processor set.
#
#  This script is used when you want to limit applications/users to certain
#  processors,
#  such as having more processors on the server than licensed for a product.
#
# Arguments
#     -m <A|C>       A to check All processes or C for Current process,
#                    such as called from $HOME/.profile.
#
# Maintenance History
# Date          Init   Description
# -----------   -----  ----------------------------------------------
# 08/31/2001    dch    Created.
#-------------------------------------------------------------------------

MODE="C"
THISFILE=$(basename $0)
```

```
#\
# Define variables for reassigning processes.  Currently processors 0-3 are
# for Application1 (and the default).
# Processors 4-7 are for Application2 and -15 are for Oracle.
#/
ORA_USER_GROUP="oracle,orausr1,orausr2,orausr3"
ORA_PSET_NUM=$(pset_info |tail -17|grep "^ 15"|awk '{print $4}')

APP1_USER_GROUP="app1usr1,app1usr2,app1usr3"
APP1_PSET_NUM=$(pset_info |tail -17|grep "^ 0"|awk '{print $4}')

APP2_USER_GROUP="app2usr1,app2usr2,app2usr3"
APP2_PSET_NUM=$(pset_info |tail -17|grep "^ 4"|awk '{print $4}')

#--------------------------------------------------------------------------
function USAGE
{
        echo "$THISFILE -m <A|C>"
        exit -1
}

#--------------------------------------------------------------------------
function CHECK_PSETS
{
        if [ $IN_PSET != $1 ]; then
           echo "Changing process $IN_USER PID $IN_PID from CPU group \
             $IN_PSET to $1..."
           pset_assign_pid $1 $IN_PID
        fi
}

#--------------------------------------------------------------------------
function DUMP_USERS
{
#\
# If in interactive mode (only setting the current PID), pass the PID as an
rgument to
# "ps".
#/
        if [ "$MODE" = "C" ]; then
           PID_LIST="-p $$"
        else
           PID_LIST=""
        fi

#\
# Dump processes so that their pset (processor set) can be verified.
#/
        ps -eo pset,pid,user,command "$PID_LIST" | grep -v PSET | \
        while read IN_PSET IN_PID IN_USER IN_COMMAND
        do
           if $(echo "${ORA_USER_GROUP}" | grep -w "$IN_USER" >/dev/null);
hen
                CHECK_PSETS $ORA_PSET_NUM
              elif $(echo "${APP1_USER_GROUP}" | \
               grep -w "$IN_USER" /dev/null); then
                 CHECK_PSETS $APP1_PSET_NUM
              elif $(echo "${APP2_USER_GROUP}" | \
```

```
            grep -w "$IN_USER" /dev/null); then
                CHECK_PSETS $APP2_PSET_NUM
            fi
        done
}

#-------------------------------------------------------------------------
while getopts ":m:" OPT
do
    case $OPT in
        m ) typeset -u OPTARG=$OPTARG
            case "$OPTARG" in
                A | C) MODE="$OPTARG";;
                *    ) USAGE;;
            esac;;
        \?) USAGE;;
        * ) USAGE;;
    esac
done

DUMP_USERS
```

Once the CPU is assigned to a processor set, you can trace CPU consumption for specific UNIX processes using the **ps** command. Fortunately, the Compaq UNIX **ps** command has a number of options that prove vital in this area. The base command:

```
ps -eo pid,user,pset,psr,command
```

gives the Unix PID, username, processor group number, processor number, and command information on all processes running on the box with output similar to the following:

```
PID USER       PSET   PSR COMMAND
  0 root          0    ~0 [kernel idle]
  1 root          0     1 /sbin/init -a
  3 root          0     0 /sbin/kloadsrv
  5 root          0     2 /sbin/hotswapd
 87 root          0     1 /sbin/update
 90 oracle        3     9 ora_pmon_ORCL
 91 oracle        3     9 ora_lgwr_ORCL
 92 oracle        3    13 ora_dbw0_ORCL
 93 oracle        3    13 ora_ckpt_ORCL
 94 oracle        3    15 ora_reco_ORCL
 95 oracle        3    14 ora_smon_ORCL
100 oracle        3     8 oracleORCL (LOCAL=NO)
```

The **ps** command can be expanded to only include Oracle processes as follows:

```
ps -eo pid,user,pset,psr,command -u oracle
```

You can also add sorting options, to see values by processor group number or processor number:

```
root> ps -eo pid,user,pset,psr,command | sort -k 3n -k 2
```

The following aliases were created to more easily display the relevant information:

```
alias all_ps="ps -eo pid,user,pset,psr,command | sort -k 3n -k 4n -k 2"
alias ora_ps="ps -eo pid,user,pset,psr,command -u oracle | sort -k 3n -k n"
```

For additional details on this procedure, please see the February 2002 issue of *Oracle Internals*, "Limiting Oracle to a Set Number of Processors," by David Herring, the DBA for Acxiom Corporation.

Next, let's look at how to see CPU consumption details by getting a background process dump.

Getting a Background Process Dump from Oracle

You can get a dump of important Oracle background processes and see the detailed interaction with UNIX. Let's use the PMON process as an example and see how to generate and read a process dump.

Oracle has delivered a hidden tool within the server manager (SQL*Plus in Oracle8 and beyond), that allows you to view specific internal Oracle structures and the UNIX system calls. The following procedure provides a process dump for the Oracle database and shows all statistics for any Oracle background process.

You start by issuing the **oradebug setorapid** command to process 2. In this example, process number 2 is the Oracle process monitor (PMON):

```
SQL> connect system/mnager as sysdba;
SQL> oradebug setorapid 2
Unix process pid: 25159, image: ora_pmon_test
```

Next, you issue the **oradebug procstat** command to generate the statistics:

```
SQL> connect system/manager as sysdba;
SQL> oradebug procstat
Statement processed.
```

Now you can use the **oradebug TRACEFILE_NAME** command to see the location of your trace file:

```
SQL> oradebug TRACEFILE_NAME
/app/oracle/admin/orcl/bdump/pmon_25159.trc
```

Now you have the name of your trace file from the PMON process. The following is the listing from this trace file. As you can see, this provides detailed information regarding important PMON activities:

```
SQL> !cat /u01/app/oracle/admin/mysid1/bdump/mysid1_pmon_25159.trc
Dump file /u01/app/oracle/admin/mysid1/bdump/mysid1_pmon_25159.trc
Oracle8i Enterprise Edition Release 8.1.6.1.0 - 64bit Production
With the Partitioning option
JServer Release 8.1.6.1.0 - 64bit Production
ORACLE_HOME = /u01/app/oracle/product/8.1.6_64

ystem name:     SunOS
Node name:      burleson-01
Release:        5.8
Version:        Generic_108528-03
Machine:        sun4u
Instance name: mysid1
Redo thread mounted by this instance: 1
Oracle process number: 2
Unix process pid: 25159, image: oracle@burleson-01 (PMON)

*** 2001-07-04 12:13:25.042
*** SESSION ID:(1.1) 2001-07-04 12:13:24.979
----- Dump of Process Statistics -----
User level CPU time = 121
System call CPU time = 47
Other system trap CPU time = 0
Text page fault sleep time = 0
Data page fault sleep time = 0
Kernel page fault sleep time = 0
User lock wait sleep time = 0
All other sleep time = 562367527
Wait-cpu (latency) time = 0
Minor page faults = 0
Major page faults = 346
Swaps = 0
Input blocks = 251
Output blocks = 0
Messages sent = 0
Messages received = 0
Signals received = 1827660
Voluntary context switches = 1828280
Involuntary context switches = 58531459
System calls = 141934171
Chars read and written = 28650
Process heap size = 1425416
Process stack size = 565248
```

Let's take a closer look at these interaction statistics. In the process statistics section, you see the amount of time that PMON spent in USER versus SYSTEM CPU time. As you may know, USER CPU time is incurred on behalf of specific UNIX processes, while SYSTEM CPU time is incurred when performing a system-wide service.

You also see details about the context switches between UNIX and Oracle, as well as details about RAM memory usage and other internal details about the interaction between PMON and UNIX. These detailed statistics can be very useful in cases where you suspect inappropriate behavior within a background process and you need to see details about the interaction between the background process and UNIX.

Now that you see how to inspect the Oracle interaction with the UNIX processors, let's take a look at the interaction between Oracle and RAM memory on the UNIX server.

Oracle and RAM Usage

The interaction between Oracle and the RAM memory regions is largely transparent to the DBA. At startup time, Oracle issues the UNIX **malloc()** command to allocate the RAM memory region for the System Global Area (SGA). Also, Oracle will allocate individual Program Global Areas (PGA) for all dedicated connections to the UNIX Oracle server.

You can easily see the held memory segments in UNIX by issuing the UNIX **ipcs** command:

```
root> ipcs -pmb
IPC status from /dev/kmem as of Mon Sep 10 16:45:16 2001
T     ID     KEY         MODE        OWNER  GROUP  SEGSZ     CPID  LPID
Shared Memory:
m  24064 0x4cb0be18 --rw-r----- oracle    dba 28975104  1836 23847
m      1 0x4e040002 --rw-rw-rw-   root   root    31008   572   572
m      2 0x411ca945 --rw-rw-rw-   root   root     8192   572   584
m   4611 0x0c6629c9 --rw-r-----   root   root  7216716  1346 23981
m      4 0x06347849 --rw-rw-rw-   root   root    77384  1346  1361
```

At the Oracle level, you can also see the details about the SGA component sizes by viewing the Oracle alert log or by issuing the **show sga** command:

```
SQL> connect system/manager as sysdba;
SQL> show sga

Total System Global Area    4830836 bytes
Fixed Size                    46596 bytes
Variable Size               3948656 bytes
Database Buffers             819200 bytes
Redo Buffers                  16384 bytes
```

We reviewed in Chapter 2 how you can measure overall RAM memory behavior for Oracle in UNIX, but there is still additional information that can be gathered.

On UNIX, the background processes attach to shared memory, one of the standard interprocess communication methods on UNIX. On NT, this is not necessary, as the Oracle threads all share the same virtual address space anyway.

Here is a version of the UNIX **ps** command that allows the display of the relative RAM memory consumption of an Oracle background process. Note that it uses the **-o vsz** command to get the RAM virtual memory size, and the UNIX **sort** command to display the top RAM consumer processes. In this listing, the last entry is the highest RAM consumer.

```
root> ps -eo pid,user,vsz,pcpu,nice|grep ora|sort +3|tail

  PID    USER   VSZ    %CPU NI
15042    oracle 291464  0.0 20
15044    oracle 291432  0.0 20
15046    oracle 291576  0.0 20
20186    oracle 490632  0.0 20
20556    oracle 519224  0.0 20
20778    oracle 488152  0.0 20
20848    oracle 516792  0.0 20
```

One of the major concerns about RAM memory management for Oracle is the amount of RAM paging. We deliberately oversimplified demand paging in Chapter 2 for illustration purposes, and we are now ready to take a closer look at how RAM paging works in UNIX.

Understanding UNIX RAM Memory Paging

As we noted in Chapter 2, most Oracle DBAs rely on the **pi** column in **vmstat** to signal when the server is swapping RAM memory. However, there is more to the story.

There are times when the **pi** column will be non-zero, even though there is no real RAM swapping. To illustrate this, let's take a simple example. Suppose that you invoke a 20 megabyte Oracle executable program, such as a Pro*C program. You don't need to load all 20MB of the executable into RAM all at once. Rather, you just want to load those pieces of the executable code that require immediate execution. Hence, UNIX will load memory frames as necessary and rely on the principle of spatial locality to minimize the number of pages in your RAM working set.

To manage the memory segments, the UNIX kernel builds a memory map of the entire program when it starts. Included in this map is a note on whether the storage is in memory or on swap disk.

As the program starts, it begins accessing some of its pages that have never been loaded into RAM memory. You may see **vmstat** page ins when a large number of programs are starting and allocating their RAM memory.

During normal operation, you may see various points in time when paging in happens a lot, and this is not always a cause for concern. Remember, a UNIX process may page in when the UNIX program is starting or is accessing parts of its code it has not used before.

Paging out (the **po** column in **vmstat**) happens frequently as UNIX prepares for the possibility of a page in. With UNIX virtual memory you are always anticipating running out of RAM memory, and a page out is a method for being ready for a subsequent page in. Also, as UNIX processes end they call the **free()** system call to free the RAM pages so they can be used by new processes.

Internals of RAM Memory Paging

So if RAM paging in **pi** may be acceptable and paging out **po** may be acceptable, how do you tell when the RAM on a server is overstressed and swapping? One answer is to correlate the UNIX scan rate with page in operations. When an Oracle server begins to run low on RAM memory, the page-stealing daemon process awakens and UNIX begins to treat the RAM memory as a sharable resource, moving memory frames to the swap disk with paging operations.

The page-stealing daemon operates in two modes. When RAM memory shortages are not critical, the daemon will steal small chunks of least recently used RAM memory from a program. As RAM resource demands continue to increase, the page-stealing daemon escalates and begins to page out entire programs' RAM regions. In short, you cannot always tell if the page in operations that you see are normal housekeeping or a serious memory shortage unless you correlate the activity of the page-stealing daemon with the page in output.

To aid in this, the **vmstat** utility gives the **sr** column to designate the memory page scan rate. If you see the scan rate rising steadily, you will have hit the page-stealing daemon's first threshold, indicating that entire programs' RAM memory regions are being paged out to the swap disk. Next, you will begin to see high page in numbers as the entire process in paged back into RAM memory (see Figure 6-2).

Carefully review the list that follows from HP-UX **vmstat**. The scan rate is the far right column, and here you see the value of **sr** rising steadily as the page-stealing daemon prepares for a page in. As the **sr** value peaks, you see the page in operation (**pi**) as the real RAM memory on the Oracle server is exceeded.

```
root> vmstat 2
         procs            memory              page
    r    b    w     avm    free   re   at   pi   po   fr   de   sr
    3    0    0   144020   12778   17    9    0   14   29    0    3
    3    0    0   144020   12737   15    0    1   34    4    0    8
    3    0    0   144020   12360    9    0    1   46    2    0   13
    1    0    0   142084   12360    5    0    3   17    0    0   21
    1    0    0   142084   12360    3    0    8    0    0    0    8
```

1	0	0	140900	12360	1	0	10	0	0	0	0
1	0	0	140900	12360	0	0	9	0	0	0	0
1	0	0	140900	12204	0	0	3	0	0	0	0
1	0	0	137654	12204	0	0	0	0	0	0	0

As we have already noted, you can also use the **glance** utility to see details about memory consumption (see Figure 6-3).

In sum, an Oracle DBA must always be vigilant in their monitoring for RAM memory paging. Next, let's look at the techniques for pinning the Oracle RAM memory inside the UNIX server.

SGA Memory Pinning

In HP-UX and Solaris, it is possible to "pin" the SGA so that it will never experience a page in. This method is also known as *memory fencing* or *memory pinning*, depending on the UNIX vendor. Essentially, memory pinning marks the Oracle SGA as being non-swappable, and the memory region always resides at the most recently used area of the RAM heap. Only that memory above and beyond the Oracle SGA is eligible for paging. On a dedicated Oracle UNIX server, this technique essentially prioritizes the Oracle SGA, telling UNIX to page in only the RAM memory associated with individual connections to Oracle (PGA memory), and not the Oracle SGA region (see Figure 6-4).

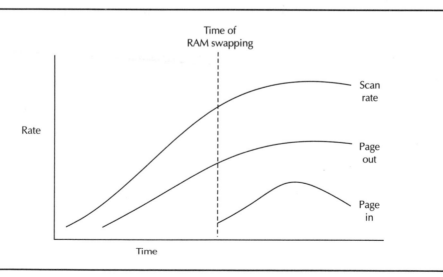

FIGURE 6-2. *Interaction between scan rate, page out, and page in*

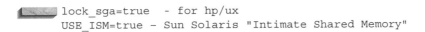

FIGURE 6-3. *The glance screen for memory*

Please note that not all dialects of UNIX support RAM memory fencing, and you cannot do RAM memory fencing on IBM AIX, Linux, and other dialects of UNIX.

In Solaris and HP-UX, the pinning is done by setting the following init.ora parameters:

```
lock_sga=true  - for hp/ux
USE_ISM=true - Sun Solaris "Intimate Shared Memory"
```

NOTE
*In Oracle 8.1.5 and beyond, **USE_ISM** is a hidden parameter and defaults to True.*

RAM Page Fencing for Oracle

As you know, in a shared memory environment such as UNIX, a virtual memory operating system will allow for the referencing of RAM memory beyond the physical

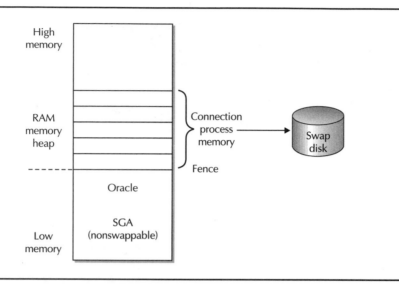

FIGURE 6-4. *Memory fencing for Oracle*

limit of RAM. When the physical RAM is exceeded, UNIX will swap the contents of RAM memory to the swap disk and give the RAM memory to another task. This swapping is done in UNIX based upon a least recently used algorithm.

To see if your server is experiencing a shortage of RAM, you can view memory swapping on UNIX by starting the **vmstat** command, and looking at the page in (**pi**) column. Whenever **pi** is non-zero, memory paging is occurring and Oracle may run very slowly.

Of course, it is important to the DBA that the SGA memory never swaps out to disk. When a memory swap occurs, the swapped task will cease processing for the duration of the swap, until the memory pages are read back into RAM. This can mean significant slowdowns for Oracle.

The solution for the Oracle DBA is page fencing. By marking the SGA as ineligible for swapping, the operating system will ensure that the SGA always stays in RAM memory. Today, page fencing is available for Solaris and HP-UX. Unfortunately, it is completely undocumented, and the init.ora parameters are buried deep in the release notes. In any case, the following sections show the details on how to do RAM memory fencing in AIX and HP-UX.

RAM Fencing in IBM AIX

The **lock_sga** init.ora parameter will lock the entire SGA into physical RAM memory, making it ineligible for swapping. The **lock_sga** parameter does not work for Windows

NT or AIX, and the setting for **lock_sga** will be ignored. For AIX 4.3.3 and above, you can set the **SHM_PIN** parameter to keep the SGA in RAM. For details, see your AIX documentation.

RAM Memory Fencing in HP-UX

In HP-UX, the **LOCK_SGA=true** init.ora parameter is used. In addition, the following steps must be completed:

Log on as **root**:

```
%su root
```

Create the file /etc/privgroup:

```
$vi /etc/privgroup
```

Add the following line to the file:

```
dba MLOCK
```

Note: The group **dba** is assuming the **oracle** owner's ID is part of the **dba** group. As **root**, run the following command:

```
$/etc/setprivgrp -f /etc/privgroup
```

RAM Memory Fencing in Sun Solaris

On Solaris, you can use Intimate Shared Memory (ISM), which will effectively lock the SGA into non-swappable RAM memory. You need to set it up at the OS level (contact Sun Microsystems for details), and at the Oracle level you can use the **USE_ISM=true** init.ora parameter. In releases of Oracle prior to Oracle8i, you can set the init.ora parameter **USE_ISM=true**. The **USE_ISM** init.ora parameter was made obsolete in 8.1.3, and in Oracle8i the **use_ism** becomes a hidden parameter that defaults to True. Memory page locking is implemented in Solaris by setting some bits in the memory page's page structure.

Now that you see the interface details between UNIX and Oracle, let's move on and look at how Oracle interacts with the disk I/O subsystem.

Oracle Interaction with the UNIX Disk I/O Subsystem

We have already covered the use of STATSPACK and the UNIX **iostat** utility to see disk reads and writes from Oracle, but we are now ready to take a closer look at the interaction between Oracle and the UNIX disk subsystem.

Remember, the tools we presented in Chapter 4 give you techniques for monitoring disk I/O over time, but you still need details about I/O waits and other internal UNIX events that are associated with disk I/O.

Once a background process issues an I/O request, it manifests itself in UNIX as an I/O object. To UNIX, an I/O object represents a byte stream, and UNIX is not aware that it is reading a database file. Within UNIX, various operations are defined on the byte stream:

- **read()**   Read to the UNIX stream

- **write()**   Write to the UNIX stream

- **close()**   Close the UNIX stream

While these I/O details are well hidden inside the bowels of Oracle, there are some techniques you can use to see I/O details.

Checking for Oracle File Wait Conditions

As you know, Oracle provides clues about datafiles that are experiencing a disproportional amount of I/O activity. This information is critical when load balancing the I/O subsystem for any Oracle database. As a review, you can compare I/O values for individual datafiles in the stats$filestatxs table with the system-wide I/O values in the stats$sysstat table to identify any datafiles that experience a disproportional amount of I/O activity. Oracle also records wait statistics that track the **wait_count** for all datafiles in the **V$** views and also inside STATSPACK.

The basic information for this information is in the **v$waitstat** view, but STATSPACK users now have the ability to store file wait information and create reports that display waiting files. The following script can be run to detect those files that have more than 800 wait events per hour:

rpt_iowait.sql

```
break on snapdate skip 2

column snapdate format a16
column filename format a40

select
   to_char(snap_time,'yyyy-mm-dd HH24') snapdate,
   old.filename,
   new.wait_count-old.wait_count waits
from
   perfstat.stats$filestatxs old,
   perfstat.stats$filestatxs new,
```

```
   perfstat.stats$snapshot    sn
where
   snap_time > sysdate-&1
and
   new.wait_count-old.wait_count > 800
and
   new.snap_id = sn.snap_id
and
   old.filename = new.filename
and
   old.snap_id = sn.snap_id-1
and
   new.wait_count-old.wait_count > 0
;
```

Here is a sample listing from this script. This is a valuable tool for the Oracle professional to see when their database is experiencing excessive wait conditions:

```
************************************************************
When there is high I/O waits, disk bottlenecks may exist
Run iostats to find the hot disk and shuffle files to
remove the contention
************************************************************
```

```
SNAPDATE              FILENAME                                 WAITS
----------------      ----------------------------------   ----------

2001-01-28 23         /u03/oradata/PROD/applnysd01.dhf          169
                      /u04/oradata/PROD/applsysx01.dbf          722
                      /u03/oradata/PROD/rbs01.dbf              3016


2001-01-30 16         /u03/oradata/PROD/mrpd01.dbf              402


2001-01-31 23         /u03/oradata/PROD/applsysd01.dbf          319
                      /u04/oradata/PROD/applsysx01.dbf          402
```

As you see, most of the details about disk I/O are hidden from view, but Oracle does provide details about those times when UNIX could not complete an immediate I/O.

Let's wrap up this chapter and review the main points and concepts surrounding Oracle's interaction with UNIX.

Conclusion

This chapter has been concerned with looking at the detailed interaction between UNIX and the Oracle database. The main points of this chapter included:

- The UNIX **top** and **glance** utilities are the most common tools for viewing the interaction between Oracle and UNIX.

- You can use the UNIX **ps** command in a variety of ways to display Oracle processes according to their CPU consumption.

- The interaction layer between UNIX and Oracle is transparent.

- Internal details about CPU, memory, and disk I/O are often difficult to see in real time, and can only be revealed with a process dump.

- You can create a process dump on most of the Oracle background processes to see details about how the background processes communicate with UNIX.

- The Oracle RAM memory regions are allocated at startup time. Until Oracle9i, the Oracle SGA was static RAM memory that could not be changed dynamically.

- You can use the **ipcs** command to view held memory segments in UNIX and the **show sga** command in Oracle to view the SGA memory.

- In some dialects of UNIX, such as Solaris and HP-UX, it is possible to pin the SGA into RAM memory, making it ineligible for paging to the swap disk.

- Oracle disk I/O is largely transparent, but the **V$** views and STATSPACK provide methods for tracking UNIX I/O over time.

- You can run STATSPACK scripts to view UNIX disk I/O waits over time.

Next, let's move on and take an in-depth look at how to monitor Oracle activity at the session level and understand how UNIX session processes communicate with Oracle.

CHAPTER
7

Oracle Sessions
and UNIX

his chapter is designed to take a closer look at the interaction between Oracle and sessions within the Oracle instances on your server. Because there are two very different types of Oracle sessions, this chapter is divided into two parts, one for dedicated connections and another for connections using the multi-threaded server (MTS). This chapter covers the following topics:

- Monitoring UNIX dedicated connections to Oracle

- Monitoring UNIX multi-threaded server connections to Oracle

- Oracle9i and Dynamic RAM memory allocation

- Differences between Oracle8i and Oracle9i RAM management

Let's begin with a review of dedicated sessions in UNIX and see how you can watch them interact with Oracle.

Monitoring UNIX Dedicated Connections to Oracle

Oracle provides the **v$process** and **v$session** views within Oracle to get detailed information about Oracle sessions. Most importantly, you can see the UNIX process IDs for all executing processes on your database server. Remember, this technique only works when you are not using the Oracle dedicated listener, because invoking the Oracle multi-threaded server (MTS) causes Oracle connections to be funneled into prespawned shadow processes. In Oracle9i, dynamic connections are still permitted, but the PGA memory can be directly allocated and managed within Oracle.

The following script is extremely useful for showing all dedicated connections to Oracle. Please note that this script displays the UNIX process ID (PID) and also gives information about the executing program. It is also possible to enhance this script to show the actual SQL statement by joining into the **v$sql** view.

```
--**************************************************************
--    session.sql
--
--    © 2001 by Donald K. Burleson
--
--    No part of this SQL script may be copied. Sold or distributed
--    without the express consent of Donald K. Burleson
--**************************************************************
```

```
rem session.sql - displays all connected sessions
set echo off;
set termout on;
set linesize 80;
set pagesize 60;
set newpage 0;

select
   rpad(c.name||':',11)||rpad(' current logons='||
   (to_number(b.sessions_current)),20)||'cumulative logons='||
   rpad(substr(a.value,1,10),10)||'highwater mark='||
   b.sessions_highwater Information
from
   v$sysstat a,
   v$license b,
   v$database c
where
   a.name = 'logons cumulative'
;

ttitle "dbname Database|UNIX/Oracle Sessions";

set heading off;
select 'Sessions on database '||substr(name,1,8) from v$database;
set heading on;
select
      substr(a.spid,1,9)      pid,
      substr(b.sid,1,5)       sid,
      substr(b.serial#,1,5)   ser#,
      substr(b.machine,1,6)   box,
      substr(b.username,1,10) username,
      substr(b.osuser,1,8)    os_user,
      substr(b.program,1,30)  program
from
   v$session b,
   v$process a
where
   b.paddr = a.addr
and
   type='USER'
order by
   spid
;


ttitle off;
set heading off;
```

```
select 'To kill, enter SQLPLUS>  ALTER SYSTEM KILL SESSION',
''''||'SID, SER#'||''''||';' from dual;
spool off;
```

Here is a sample listing from running this script. Please note that it begins by displaying summaries of all current, cumulative, and the high-water mark for logons before displaying the details for each session:

```
SQL> @session

INFORMATION
----------------------------------------------------------------------------
PRODLIVE:  current logons=14  cumulative logons=166       highwater mark=14

                              UNIX/Oracle Sessions
                           Sessions on database PEMINE
Sat Oct 13                                                          page   1
                                dbname Database
                              UNIX/Oracle Sessions

PID       SID   SER#   BOX     USERNAME    OS_USER    PROGRAM
--------- ----- -----  ------  ----------  --------   -------------------------
1005      14    124    hawk    CASH        rhayes     runmenu50@hawk
1139      13    39     hawk    STAFF       clarson    runmenu50@hawk
1526      11    1550   hawk    BURLESON    burleson   sqlplus@hawk
1690      15    47     hawk    CASH        kjoslin    runmenu50@hawk
2482      16    263    hawk    STAFF       brobinso   runmenu50@hawk
2568      17    26     BELLEV  SCHED       Bellmont   F45RUN32.EXE
27180     9     228    hawk    PATIENT     daemon     sqlplus@hawk
29316     8     3238   hawk    CASH        jdutcher   runmenu50@hawk
29440     12    137    hawk    CASH        lchapman   runmenu50@hawk
3231      18    173    hawk    STAFF       jhahn      runmenu50@hawk
3241      19    39     BELLEV  SCHED       dplueger   F45RUN32.EXE
 273      20    11     BELLEV  SCHED       dplueger   R25SRV32.EXE

To kill, enter SQLPLUS>  ALTER SYSTEM KILL SESSION 'SID, SER#';
SQL>
```

Now, the first column of this output represents the UNIX process ID (PID) for each of the Oracle processes. The SID and SER in the second and third columns are also important because you need these values if you want to kill any Oracle session. The fourth column, labeled BOX, shows you the originating server for distributed requests. The fifth column is the Oracle user ID associated with the session, and the sixth column is the UNIX user who initiated the session.

If you want to move outside of Oracle and see details for the session at the UNIX level, you must correlate the Oracle PIS with the UNIX PID. To see details of these processes, you can write an Oracle script to filter the UNIX **ps** output to only include these processes:

ps_pid.ksh

```
#/bin/ksh
sqlplus cpi/oracle@prodlive<<!
set pages 999
set feedback off
set echo off
set heading off

spool /tmp/run_pid.ksh

select
    'ps -ef|grep '||spid||'grep -v grep'
from
    v\$process
where
    spid is not NULL
;

spool off;
!

# Execute the UNIX commands . . . .
chmod +x /tmp/*.ksh

/tmp/run_pid.ksh
```

Here is the output from this script. As you see, the SQL*Plus script builds the UNIX **ps** command for the Oracle PIDs and then executes the command:

```
root> /tmp/run_pid.ksh
    jjahn   3231  3129  0 08:12:17 ?           0:00 oraclePA
 bbeckero   2482  2377  0 07:59:26 ?           0:00 oraclePA
    scarf   2376   785  0 07:59:03 ttyp9       0:00 telnetd
  brobins   2377  2376  0 07:59:04 ttyp9       0:01 runmenu50 pamenu
    monte   1372     1  0 Sep 21  ?           5:58 /opt/hpnp/bin/hpnpd
    jmels   1886  1878  0 Sep 21  ttyp1       0:00 tee -a
```

This script allows you to see the start time for the UNIX connection and also see the cumulative CPU consumption for each task.

Now let's move on and take a look at how UNIX interacts with the Oracle multi-threaded server.

UNIX Interaction with the Multi-threaded Server

As you may know, the multi-threaded server (MTS) was developed in Oracle7 to provide an alternative to a dedicated server connection for Oracle processes. Instead of each connection spawning a UNIX PID and a UNIX RAM region for PGA memory, the MTS allows you to share prespawned Oracle connections. These prespawned connections share RAM memory by using the Oracle large pool. By sharing connections and RAM memory, Oracle connections can happen faster and with less overall resource consumption on the server. The MTS is sometimes used in Oracle Parallel Server (OPS) environments to give clients transparent failover capabilities when Net8 is set up for transparent application failover (TAF).

When using the MTS, Oracle allocates memory in a shared region called the User Global Area (UGA). If you have the **large_pool_size** defined in your init.ora file, the UGA memory will be allocated from the large pool. If you do not define a large pool, the UGA memory will be allocated from the Oracle shared pool. Oracle always recommends that you allocate a large pool if you are using the MTS.

Prerequisites for Using the MTS

In practice, the MTS is not for every Oracle application. In some cases, using the MTS will induce problems and cause the application to run slower than dedicated connections. There are several criteria that must be met when considering turning on the MTS:

- **High user volume**   Oracle only recommends using the MTS for databases that experience more than 300 concurrent connections, since the MTS does not always work well for low system loads.

- **High think time**   A database has a high think time when it spends more time manipulating data than retrieving data. The MTS is not appropriate if the database simply retrieves and reformats data. Using the MTS in this type of environment can cause performance degradation due to the overhead involved in switches and the amount of time that requests may wait in the queue before a shared server becomes available.

- **Small SQL result sets**   The MTS is designed to manage SQL queries that retrieve small result sets, such as a typical OLTP system. If SQL retrieves a very large result with thousands of rows, that session's MTS dispatcher can become overwhelmed with this single request. Unfortunately, when using the MTS, a "hog" on a dispatcher can adversely affect the response time of other sessions that are connected to that dispatcher.

You also need to note that the Oracle DBA has a great deal of control over the number and configuration of the MTS connections and the size of the large pool. Here is a quick summary of the MTX parameters that are defined in the init.ora file:

```
LARGE_POOL_SIZE=600000000

MTS_MAX_DISPATCHERS=5

MTS_MAX_SERVERS=50

MTS_SERVERS=5

MTS_DISPATCHERS="(ADDRESS=(PROTOCOL=tcp)(HOST=stool.com))(DISPATCHERS 3)"

MTS_DISPATCHERS="ipc, 1"
```

You have defined 600 megabytes for use by the large pool. The large pool is used as shared memory for MTS connections, primarily for sorting. Hence, the amount of the **large_pool** used by each MTS connection is directly related to the **sort_area_size** parameter.

Here you have defined that the MTS will start with three dispatcher processes and allocated dispatchers until five dispatcher processes exist.

mts.sql

```
--**************************************************************
--   mts.sql
--
--   © 2001 by Donald K. Burleson
--
--   No part of this SQL script may be copied. Sold or distributed
--   without the express consent of Donald K. Burleson
--**************************************************************
set pages 999;

spool mts.lst

column all_sess_mem format 999,999,999;
column sess_mem     format 999,999,999;
column username     format a10
column program      format a30

prompt *******************************************
prompt Total of all session RAM memory usage
prompt *******************************************
select
```

```
   sum(value) all_sess_mem
from
   v$sesstat    s,
   v$statname   n
where
   s.statistic# = n.statistic#
and
   n.name = 'session uga memory max';


prompt ******************************************
prompt Session memory detail
prompt ******************************************
select
   substr(b.username,1,10) username,
   substr(b.program,1,30)  program,
   value sess_mem
from
   v$session    b,
   v$sesstat    s,
   v$statname   n
where
   b.sid = s.sid
and
   s.statistic# = n.statistic#
and
   n.name = 'session uga memory'
and
   s.sid  in
      (select sid from v$session)
order by 3 desc
;

prompt ******************************************
prompt  Dispatcher Detail Usage
prompt ******************************************
prompt (If Time Busy > 50, then change MTS_MAX_DISPATCHERS in init.ora)
column "Time Busy" format 999,999.999
column busy        format 999,999,999
column idle        format 999,999,999

prompt ******************************************
prompt Time busy for each MTS dispatcher
prompt ******************************************
select
   name,
   status,
   idle,
```

```
   busy,
   (busy/(busy+idle))*100 "Time Busy"
from
   v$dispatcher;

prompt *******************************************
prompt Existing shared server processes
prompt *******************************************
select
   count(*) "Shared Server Processes"
from
   v$shared_server
where
   status = 'QUIT';


prompt *******************************************
prompt Average wait times for requests
prompt *******************************************
SELECT network      "Protocol",
      DECODE( SUM(totalq), 0, 'No Responses',
      SUM(wait)/SUM(totalq) || ' hundredths of seconds')
     "Average Wait Time per Response"
FROM
   v$queue      q,
   v$dispatcher d
WHERE
   q.type = 'DISPATCHER'
   AND
   q.paddr = d.paddr
GROUP BY network;


prompt *******************************************
prompt All average wait times for common requests
prompt *******************************************
select
   DECODE( totalq, 0, 'No Requests',
   wait/totalq || ' hundredths of seconds')
   "Average Wait Time Per Requests"
from
   v$queue
where
   type = 'COMMON';

prompt *******************************************
prompt All statistics from pq_sysstat
prompt *******************************************
```

```
select
   statistic,to_char(value) value
from
   sys.v_$pq_sysstat;


prompt *******************************************
prompt Percent busy for each MTS dispatcher
prompt *******************************************
select
   network
   "Protocol",to_char((sum(busy)/(sum(busy)+sum(idle))*100),'99.99999')
%Busy"
from
   v$dispatcher
group by
   network;


prompt *******************************************
prompt Dispatcher and queue details with average wait time
prompt *******************************************
select
   network "Protocol",
   decode(sum(totalq), 0, 'No Responses',
   to_char(sum(wait)/sum(totalq),'99.99999')||' hundreths of seconds')
   "AWT/Response"
from
   v$queue        q,
   v$dispatcher d
where
   q.type='DISPATCHER'
and
   q.paddr=d.paddr
group by
   network;


prompt *******************************************
prompt Sum of UGA Memory
prompt *******************************************
select
   s.type,
   s.server,
   s.status,
   sum(st.value)    uga_mem
from
   v$session    s,
   v$sesstat    st,
   v$statname   sn
```

```
where
   s.sid = st.sid
and
   st.statistic# = sn.statistic#
and
   sn.name = 'session uga memory'
group by
   type,
   server,
   status;

spool off;
```

This script combines a great deal of important information about the internals of the Oracle dispatchers and UGA memory. Here is a sample of the output from this script. Let's look at each section separately.

```
*********************************************
Total of all RAM session memory
*********************************************


ALL_SESS_MEM
------------
   5,588,088
```

Here you see the total for all session RAM memory within Oracle. This metric is especially useful when you need to know the total RAM memory demands of individual sessions in your Oracle instance.

This is the session UGA memory max statistic, and it is important to understand that this value is not the high-water mark for the database since startup time. Rather, it is the sum of all UGA memory that is currently being used at the time the query was executed.

```
*********************************************
Session memory detail
*********************************************


USERNAME   PROGRAM                            SESS_MEM
---------- ------------------------------- ------------
OPS$ORACLE sqlplus@diogenes (TNS V1-V3)        124,832
           oracle@diogenes (SMON)               63,984
           oracle@diogenes (RECO)               59,952
READER        ?  @donald.janet.com (TNS V       55,344
READER        ?  @donald.janet.com (TNS V       55,344
READER        ?  @donald.janet.com (TNS V       40,088
READER        ?  @donald.janet.com (TNS V       39,816
READER        ?  @donald.janet.com (TNS V       39,816
```

```
READER           ?  @donald.janet.com (TNS V        29,720
READER           ?  @donald.janet.com (TNS V        29,720
           oracle@diogenes (PMON)                    23,728
           oracle@diogenes (LGWR)                    23,728
           oracle@diogenes (CKPT)                    23,728
           oracle@diogenes (DBW0)                    21,936
```

The following is a sample output from the dispatcher usage section of the script:

```
DISPATCHER USAGE ...
(If Time Busy > 50, then change MTS_MAX_DISPATCHERS in init.ora)
*******************************************
Time busy for each MTS dispatcher
*******************************************

NAME STATUS                   IDLE          BUSY    Time Busy
---- ----------------  ------------  ------------  ------------
D000 WAIT                47,708,571           551         .001
D001 WAIT                47,708,153           960         .002
D002 WAIT                47,707,636         1,469         .003
D003 WAIT                47,708,990           105         .000


*******************************************
Existing shared server processes
*******************************************


Shared Server Processes
----------------------
                 6
```

This is a summary of the usage for the Oracle dispatcher processes. Here you see a summary of activity for each dispatcher and time busy for each dispatcher. You can also see the total number of shared server processes.

```
*******************************************
Average wait times for requests
*******************************************

Protocol
-----------------------------------------------------------
Average Wait Time per Response
-----------------------------------------------------------
(ADDRESS=(PROTOCOL=ipc)(KEY=#24326.1))
No Responses

(ADDRESS=(PROTOCOL=tcp)(HOST=diogenes)(PORT=59602))
.028715926624378535916338076461512086405 hundredths of seconds
```

```
(ADDRESS=(PROTOCOL=tcp)(HOST=diogenes)(PORT=59604))
.00603248259860788863109048723897911 8329 hundredths of seconds

(ADDRESS=(PROTOCOL=tcp)(HOST=diogenes)(PORT=59605))
.14535055266801334574093828729657958 6464 hundredths of seconds
```

Here you see the average latency for every dispatcher. This listing is good for
determining the load balancing and ensuring that the response time for each
dispatcher is acceptable.

```
*******************************************
All average wait times for common requests
*******************************************


Average Wait Time Per Requests
----------------------------------------------------------------------
.00725724020442930153321976149914 8211244 hundredths of seconds
```

Here you calculate the system-wide total for MTS requests response time. This
information is great when determining when additional dispatchers are required.

```
*******************************************
All statistics from v$pq_sysstat
*******************************************


STATISTIC                        VALUE
---------------------------       -------------------------------------
Servers Busy                     3
Servers Idle                     1
Servers Highwater                4
Server Sessions                  233
Servers Started                  0
Servers Shutdown                 0
Servers Cleaned Up               0
Queries Initiated                0
DML Initiated                    0
DFO Trees                        0
Sessions Active                  0
Local Msgs Sent                  2615
Distr Msgs Sent                  0
Local Msgs Recv'd                743
Distr Msgs Recv'd                0
```

The preceding listing shows details of all of the statistics in the **v$pq_sysstat**
structure. This listing can be useful when you need to monitor MTS totals.

```
************************************************
Percent busy for each MTS dispatcher
************************************************

Protocol                                              %Busy
--------------------------------------------------    ---------
 (ADDRESS=(PROTOCOL=ipc)(KEY=#24326.1))                .00022

(ADDRESS=(PROTOCOL=tcp)(HOST=diogenes)(PORT=59602))    .00115

(ADDRESS=(PROTOCOL=tcp)(HOST=diogenes)(PORT=59604))    .00201

(ADDRESS=(PROTOCOL=tcp)(HOST=diogenes)(PORT=59605))    .00308
```

The preceding report shows the relative load balancing for each MTS dispatcher. Since the assignments are supposed to be directed randomly to each dispatcher, the number for each dispatcher should be roughly the same.

```
************************************************
Dispatcher and queue details with average wait time
************************************************

Protocol
-----------------------------------------------------------------------
AWT/Response-----------------------------------------------------------
ADDRESS=(PROTOCOL=ipc)(KEY=#24326.1))                 No Responses

(ADDRESS=(PROTOCOL=tcp)(HOST=diogenes)(PORT=59602))    .02872 hund/secs

(ADDRESS=(PROTOCOL=tcp)(HOST=diogenes)(PORT=59604))    .00603 hund/secs

(ADDRESS=(PROTOCOL=tcp)(HOST=diogenes)(PORT=59605))    .14535 hund/secs
```

Here you see the average wait times for each dispatcher. Again, the loads to each dispatcher are balanced by Oracle, and there should not be significant differences between the average wait times, unless a specific task is hogging a dispatcher.

```
************************************************
Sum of UGA Memory
************************************************

TYPE        SERVER      STATUS      UGA_MEM
----------  ---------   --------    ----------
BACKGROUND  DEDICATED   ACTIVE         217056
USER        DEDICATED   ACTIVE         147968
USER        DEDICATED   INACTIVE        59440
USER        PSEUDO      INACTIVE      5126256
```

Here you see both background processes and MTS connections and the total amount of UGA memory used by these connections. It is important to note that Oracle will create new dispatcher processes as the load on the system increases, and this interaction with UNIX can be measured.

Of course, each new release of Oracle offers new techniques for managing RAM memory in Oracle. Starting in Oracle9i, you see a whole new approach to RAM memory management, and the RAM memory shifts from the UGA to the PGA region. Let's take a closer look at these new techniques.

Oracle9i Dynamic RAM and UNIX

Prior to Oracle9i, the Oracle DBA could only control UNIX memory for Oracle at database start time. Oracle provided several init.ora parameters to determine the RAM size of the SGA, and once the database was started, the SGA size and configuration could not be modified.

The movement of Oracle toward a 24x7 database has created the need for the Oracle DBA to adjust the size of the UNIX memory regions without stopping and restarting the database. More important, the dynamic SGA features of Oracle9i allow the DBA to monitor RAM memory usage within the SGA and adjust the SGA memory regions based on the existing demands on the Oracle database.

Oracle9i has also introduced a new RAM memory management technique whereby the DBA can preallocate all PGA memory, and allow Oracle to distribute the RAM memory to connections according to the sorting demands of the connections. This is a radical departure from traditional Oracle databases, and it has made the **sort_area_size** and other PGA parameters obsolete. Also, it is no longer necessary to issue **alter session** commands to change the **sort_area_size** for connections that require a large sort area.

Rather than allocate just the SGA, the Oracle9i DBA must fully allocate all of the RAM memory on the UNIX Oracle server, reserving 20 percent of the RAM memory for UNIX overhead (see Figure 7-1).

Total UNIX RAM memory

Fixed SGA region (sga_memory_max)	PGA memory region (pga_aggregate_target)	RAM reserved for UNIX OS tasks

20%

FIGURE 7-1. *Preallocation of SGA and PGA memory in Oracle*

Prior to Oracle9i, it was not uncommon for the Oracle DBA to have several copies of their init.ora parameter file, and then "bounce" the database daily to reconfigure the SGA for different processing modes. For example, the allocations of an SGA for online transaction processing (OLTP) is quite different than the processing mode for an Oracle data warehouse (see Figure 7-2).

Oracle recommends a different RAM memory configuration for OLTP databases and decision support applications (DSS) such as an Oracle data warehouse (Table 7-1). OLTP systems should allocate the majority of total UNIX RAM to the SGA, while data warehouse and DSS applications that are RAM memory intensive should allocate the majority of RAM for PGA connections.

Of course, if a single database operates in a dual modality, the Oracle DBA can run a script to dynamically change this memory allocation. For example, if a database runs in OLTP mode during the day and DSS mode at night, the DBA can run a script to steal RAM from the SGA and reallocate this RAM memory to the PGA region:

```
alter system set sga_memory_max = 3g;
alter system set pga_aggregate_target = 3g;
```

Starting in Oracle9i, Oracle has provided the ability to grow or shrink the following components of the SGA RAM memory:

- **Data buffer size**   alter system set db_cache_size=300m;

- **Shared pool size**   alter system set shared_pool_size=200m;

- **Total PGA RAM memory size**   alter system set pga_aggregate_target=2000m;

In UNIX, Oracle achieves the dynamic memory allocation by modifying the physical address space inside the UNIX memory region. This is done in UNIX by issuing **malloc()** and **free()** commands.

Processing Mode	SGA RAM	Total PGA RAM	UNIX RAM Overhead
OLTP	65%	15%	20%
Data warehouse and DSS	30%	50%	20%

TABLE 7-1.   *RAM Memory Changes Depending on Type of Application*

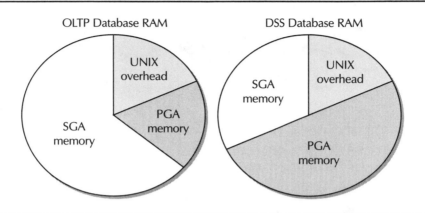

FIGURE 7-2. *Comparison of RAM for DSS and OLTP applications*

The new dynamic SGA features also allow the Oracle SGA to start small and grow on an as-needed basis. A new parameter called **sga_max_size** has been created to facilitate this process.

Oracle9i and UNIX Granules

Starting with Oracle9i, Oracle expanded the term *granule* to include a reserved region of RAM memory for SGA growth. A memory granule should not be confused with Oracle parallel query block range partition granules. Block range partition granules are used by OPQ to determine the block ranges for parallel query slaves, while a RAM memory granule is a unit of contiguous virtual memory allocation. If the current amount of SGA memory is less than the value of the **sga_max_size** init.ora parameter, Oracle is free to allocate more granules until the SGA size reaches the **sga_max_size** limit.

In Oracle9i, the DBA "reserves" granules for use by the dynamic SGA feature. When the DBA issues an **alter system** command to increase the size of a RAM memory region of the SGA, Oracle passes the command to a background process that allocates the RAM memory from the reserved space, adding the memory to the desired SGA component (see Figure 7-3).

NOTE
*At this time, Oracle9i does not support dynamic modification of the **large_pool_size** parameter or the **sga_max_size** parameter.*

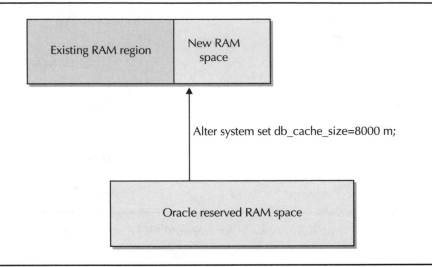

FIGURE 7-3. *Dynamic memory allocation*

The **v$process** view can be used to display the existing values for the new
Oracle9i parameters:

```
column name format 999,999,999,999

select
   name,
   value
from
   v$parameter
where
   name in
   (
   'sga_max_size',
   'shared_pool_size',
   'db_cache_size',
   'large_pool_size',
   'pga_aggregate_target'
   )
;

   NAME                      VALUE
   --------------------      -------------
   shared_pool_size          40,362,826
```

```
sga_max_size            5,392,635,193
large_pool_size             1,048,576
db_cache_size               4,194,304
pga_aggregate_target    2,403,628,363
```

This query gives you the current values of the dynamic memory parameters and allows the DBA to compare existing demands with current instance settings.

Changing Dynamic SGA and PGA Components

As we have noted, Oracle9i provides **alter system** commands to allow the DBA to change the configuration of the Oracle9i RAM memory. Before we look at using these features for automatic tuning, let's briefly review the main parameters and see how they operate. The following output is an example of a change that has been rejected by Oracle9i because there is insufficient UNIX memory to expand the selected pool:

```
SQL> alter system set shared_pool_size=64m;
alter system set shared_pool_size=64m
*
ERROR at line 1:
ORA-02097: parameter cannot be modified because specified value is invalid
ORA-04033: Insufficient memory to grow pool
```

In the case of the preceding example, the error was generated because the command would have exceeded the value of the **sga_max_size** parameter. In the example that follows, you expand the shared pool to 300 megabytes, and we can immediately confirm the change with the **show parameters** command:

```
SQL> connect system/manager as sysdba;
Connected.
SQL> alter system set shared_pool_size=300m;

System altered.

SQL> show parameter shared_pool

NAME                                 TYPE        VALUE
------------------------------------ ----------- -----------
shared_pool_reserved_size            big integer 1258291
shared_pool_size                     big integer 33554432
```

Now that you see how you can alter the individual SGA components, let's move on and take a look at how Oracle9i manages dynamic RAM memory in a UNIX environment.

Oracle9i PGA Memory Allocation for Dedicated Connections

When a dedicated connection is made to Oracle, an isolated memory region called the Program Global Area is allocated in UNIX RAM memory. The PGA consists of the following components:

- **Sort area**   This is the largest and most important area of the PGA.

- **Session information**   This small area contains the internal address for the connection to allow the connection to communicate with Oracle.

- **Cursor state**   This component of the PGA contains all re-entrant values for the executing connection.

- **Stack space**   This area contains miscellaneous control structures.

The largest component of a PGA is the sort area size, and Oracle allows you to dynamically change the sort area size at the session level:

```
alter session set sort_area_size=10m deferred;
```

When you issue this **alter session** command, you instruct UNIX to expand the sort area within the PGA at the time that the sort is required. To illustrate the deferred RAM memory allocation in UNIX, consider the diagram in Figure 7-4.

Here you see that Oracle interfaces with UNIX to issue the **malloc()** command to provide a RAM sort area. This RAM region is only allocated after the retrieval from the database has been completed, and the memory only exists for the duration that the sort is required. This technique reduces the RAM memory demands on the UNIX server and ensures that the RAM is only available when it is needed by Oracle.

Automatic RAM Memory Management in Oracle9i

As we have noted, a serious problem in Oracle8i was the requirement that all dedicated connections use a one-size-fits-all **sort_area_size**. Oracle9i now has the option of running automatic PGA memory management. Oracle has introduced a new init.ora parameter called **pga_aggregate_target**. When the **pga_aggregate_target** parameter is set and you are using dedicated Oracle connections, Oracle9i will ignore all of the PGA parameters in the init.ora file, including **sort_area_size** and **sort_area_retained_size**. Oracle recommends that the value of **pga_aggregate_target** be set to the amount of remaining memory (less a 20 percent overhead for other UNIX tasks) on the UNIX server after the instance has been started (see Figure 7-5).

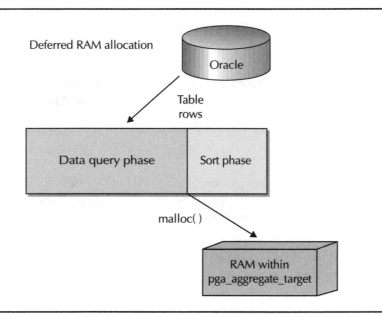

FIGURE 7-4. *Deferred UNIX RAM memory allocation for dedicated Oracle connections*

Once the **pga_aggregate_target** has been set, Oracle will automatically manage PGA memory allocation, based upon the individual needs of each Oracle connection. Oracle9i allows the **pga_aggregate_target** parameter to be modified at the instance level with the **alter system** command, thereby allowing the DBA to dynamically adjust the total RAM region available to Oracle9i.

Oracle9i also introduces a new parameter called **workarea_size_policy**. When this parameter is set to automatic, all Oracle connections will benefit from the shared PGA memory. When **workarea_size_policy** is set to manual, connections will allocate memory according to the values for the **sort_area_size** parameter.

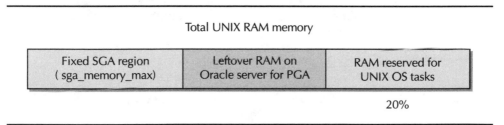

FIGURE 7-5. *Allocating the pga_aggregate_target for a UNIX server*

Under this automatic mode, Oracle tries to maximize the number of work areas that are using optimal memory and uses one-pass memory for the others.

New Oracle9i Views
for Automatic PGA RAM Memory Management

Oracle9i has introduced several new views and new columns in existing views to aid in viewing the internal allocation of RAM memory in Oracle9i. The following new **v$** views can be used to monitor RAM memory usage of dedicated Oracle9i connections:

- **v$process** Three new columns are added in Oracle9i for monitoring PGA memory usage. The new columns are called **pga_used_mem, pga_alloc_mem**, and **pga_max_mem**.

- **v$sysstat** There are many new statistics rows, including work area statistics for optimal, one-pass, and multi-pass.

- **v$pgastat** This new view shows internals of PGA memory usage for all background processes and dedicated connections.

- **v$sql_plan** This exciting new view contains execution plan information for all currently executing SQL. This is a tremendous tool for the performance tuning processional who must locate suboptimal SQL statements.

- **v$workarea** This new view provides detailed cumulative statistics on RAM memory usage for Oracle9i connections.

- **v$workarea_active** This new view shows internal RAM memory usage information for all currently executing SQL statements.

Let's take a closer look at these new Oracle9i features and scripts that allow you to see detailed RAM memory usage.

Using the Oracle9i v$sysstat View   The following query gives the total number and the percentage of time work areas were executed in these three modes since the database instance was started:

work_area.sql

```
select
    name                                profile,
    cnt,
    decode(total, 0, 0, round(cnt*100/total)) percentage
```

```
from
   (
      select
         name,
         value cnt,
         (sum(value) over ()) total
      from
         v$sysstat
      where
         name like 'workarea exec%'
   );
```

The output of this query might look like the following:

```
PROFILE                               CNT      PERCENTAGE
------------------------------------- -------- ----------
workarea executions - optimal            5395          95
workarea executions - onepass             284           5
workarea executions - multipass             0           0
```

The output of this query is used to tell the DBA when to dynamically adjust **pga_aggregate_target**. In general, the value of **pga_aggregate_target** should be increased when multi-pass executions is greater than zero, and reduced whenever the optimal executions is 100 percent.

Using the Oracle9i v$pgastat View   The **v$pgastat** view provides instance-level summary statistics on the PGA usage and the automatic memory manager. The following script provides excellent overall usage statistics for all Oracle9i connections:

check_pga.sql

```
column name   format a30
column value  format 999,999,999

select
   name,
   value
from
   v$pgastat
;
```

The output of this query might look like the following:

```
NAME                                                  VALUE
----------------------------------------------------- ----------
aggregate PGA auto target                       736,052,224
```

```
global memory bound                              21,200
total expected memory                           141,144
total PGA inuse                              22,234,736
total PGA allocated                          55,327,872
maximum PGA allocated                        23,970,624
total PGA used for auto workareas               262,144
maximum PGA used for auto workareas           7,333,032
total PGA used for manual workareas                   0
maximum PGA used for manual workareas                 0
estimated PGA memory for optimal                141,395
maximum PGA memory for optimal              500,123,520
estimated PGA memory for one-pass               534,144
maximum PGA memory for one-pass              52,123,520
```

In the preceding display from **v$pgastat**, you see the following statistics:

- **Aggregate PGA auto target**   This column gives the total amount of available memory for Oracle9i connections. As we have already noted, this value is derived from the value on the init.ora parameter **pga_aggregate_target**.

- **Global memory bound**   This statistic measures the maximum size of a work area, and Oracle recommends that whenever this statistic drops below 1 megabyte, you should increase the value of the **pga_aggregate_target** parameter.

- **Total PGA allocated**   This statistic displays the high-water mark of all PGA memory usage on the database. You should see this value approach the value of **pga_aggregate_target** as usage increases.

- **Total PGA used for auto workareas**   This statistic monitors RAM consumption for all connections that are running in automatic memory mode. Remember, not all internal processes are allowed by Oracle to use the automatic memory feature. For example, Java and PL/SQL will allocate RAM memory, and this will not be counted in this total PGA statistic. Hence, you can subtract value to the total PGA allocated to see the amount of memory used by connections and the RAM memory consumed by Java and PL/SQL.

- **Estimated PGA memory for optimal/one-pass**   This statistic estimates how much memory is required to execute all task connections RAM demands in optimal mode. Remember, when Oracle9i experiences a memory shortage, he will invoke the multi-pass operation to attempt to locate recently freed RAM memory. This statistic is critical for monitoring RAM consumption in Oracle9i, and most Oracle DBAs will increase **pga_aggregate_target** to this value.

Enhancements to the v$process View in Oracle9i   The **v$process** view has been enhanced with several new columns to show automatic PGA usage, including **pga_used_mem, pga_alloc_mem**, and **pga_max_mem**. Here is a query to display these values:

```
select
    program,
    pga_used_mem,
    pga_alloc_mem,
    pga_max_mem
from
    v$process;
```

The output of this query might look like the following:

```
PROGRAM                       PGA_USED_MEM PGA_ALLOC_MEM PGA_MAX_MEM
----------------------------- ------------ ------------- -----------
PSEUDO                                   0             0           0
oracle@janet (PMON)                 120463        234291      234291
oracle@janet (DBW0)                1307179       1817295     1817295
oracle@janet (LGWR)                4343655       4849203     4849203
oracle@janet (CKPT)                 194999        332583      332583
oracle@janet (SMON)                 179923        775311      775323
oracle@janet (RECO)                 129719        242803      242803
oracle@janet (TNS V1-V3)           1400543       1540627     1540915
oracle@janet (P000)                 299599        373791      635959
oracle@janet (P001)                 299599        373791      636007
oracle@janet (TNS V1-V3)           1400543       1540627     1540915
oracle@janet (TNS V1-V3)             22341       1716253     3625241
```

Here you see allocated, used, and maximum memory for all connections to Oracle. You can see the RAM demands of each of the background processes and you also have detailed information about individual connections.

Note that it is possible to join the **v$process** view with the **v$sql_plan** table to take a closer look at the RAM memory demands of specific connections.

Using the v$workarea Views in Oracle9i   Oracle also has two new views to show active work area space, the **v$sql_workarea** and the **v$sql_workarea_active** views. The **v$sql_workarea_active** view will display all of the work areas that are currently executing in the instance. Note that small sorts (under 65,535 bytes) are excluded from the view, but you can use the **v$sql_workarea_active** view to quickly monitor the size of all large active work areas.

```
select
    to_number(decode(SID, 65535, NULL, SID)) sid,
```

```
   operation_type              OPERATION,
   trunc(WORK_AREA_SIZE/1024)  WSIZE,
   trunc(EXPECTED_SIZE/1024)   ESIZE,
   trunc(ACTUAL_MEM_USED/1024) MEM,
   trunc(MAX_MEM_USED/1024)    "MAX MEM",
   number_passes               PASS
from
   v$sql_workarea_active
order by
   1,2;
```

Here is a sample listing from this script:

```
SID OPERATION                  WSIZE      ESIZE        MEM    MAX MEM PASS
--- --------------------     ------  ---------  ---------  --------- ----
 27 GROUP BY (SORT)              73         73         64         64    0
 44 HASH-JOIN                  3148       3147       2437       6342    1
 71 HASH-JOIN                 13241      19200      12884      34684    1
```

This output shows that session 44 is running a hash join whose work area is running in one-pass mode. This work area is currently using 2 megabytes of PGA memory and in the past has used up to 6.5 megabytes.

This view is very useful for viewing the current memory operations within Oracle. You can use the SID column to join into the **v$process** and **v$session** views for additional information about each task.

Viewing RAM Memory Usage for Specific SQL Statements

Oracle9i now has the ability to display RAM memory usage along with execution plan information. To get this information, you need to gather the address of the desired SQL statement from the **v$sql** view. For example, if you have a query that operates against the NEW_CUSTOMER table, you can run the following query to get the address:

```
select
   address
from
   v$sql
where
   sql_text like '%NEW_CUSTOMER';

88BB460C

1 row selected.
```

Now that you have the address, you can plug it into the following script to get the execution plan details and the PGA memory usage for the SQL statement:

plan_mem.sql

```
select
    operation,
    options,
    object_name                          name,
    trunc(bytes/1024/1024)               "input(MB)",
    trunc(last_memory_used/1024)         last_mem,
    trunc(estimated_optimal_size/1024)   opt_mem,
    trunc(estimated_onepass_size/1024)   onepass_mem,
    decode(optimal_executions, null, null,
            optimal_executions||'/'||onepass_executions||'/'||
            multipasses_exections)       "O/1/M"
from
    v$sql_plan      p,
    v$sql_workarea  w
where
    p.address=w.address(+)
and
    p.hash_value=w.hash_value(+)
and
    p.id=w.operation_id(+)
and
    p.address='88BB460C';
```

Here is the listing from this script. In addition to the execution plan, you also see details about RAM memory consumption for the hash join:

OPERATION	OPTIONS	NAME	input(MB)	LAST_MEM	OPT_MEM	ONEPASS_MEM	O/1/M
SELECT STATE							
SORT	GROUP BY		4582	8	16	16	26/0/0
HASH JOIN	SEMI		4582	5976	5194	2187	16/0/0
TABLE ACCESS	FULL	ORDERS	51				
TABLE ACCESS	FUL	LINEITEM	1000				

Here you see the details about the execution plan along with specific memory usage details. This is an exciting new advance in Oracle9i and gives the Oracle DBA the ability to have a very high level of detail about the internal execution of any SQL statement.

Moving Toward a Self-tuning Oracle9i Database

With these new dynamic SGA features in Oracle9i, we are moving toward an architecture where the Oracle DBA can monitor UNIX RAM memory usage and reconfigure the SGA and PGA regions according to existing usage patterns.

Oracle offers a degree of self-tuning capability with the new **pga_aggregate_target** parameter. By allowing Oracle9i to manage RAM memory demands according to the demands of each task, Oracle9i has been able to use sophisticated algorithms to improve the speed of RAM intensive tasks such as hash joins and large sorts.

However, the Oracle DBA is now able to dynamically deallocate RAM memory from one area and reallocate the RAM to another area of the SGA.

Changing RAM Configuration with UNIX Scripts

In a UNIX environment, it is very easy to schedule a task to change the RAM memory configuration when the processing needs change. For example, many Oracle databases operate in OLTP mode during normal work hours, and the database services memory-intensive batch reports at night.

As we have noted, an OLTP database should have a large value for **db_cache_size**. Conversely, memory-intensive batch tasks require additional RAM in the **pga_aggregate_target**.

The UNIX scripts that follows can be used to reconfigure the SGA between OLTP and DSS without stopping the instance. In this example, we assume that you have an isolated Oracle server with 8 gigabytes of RAM. We also assume that you reserve 20 percent of RAM for UNIX overhead, leaving a total of 6 gigabytes for Oracle and Oracle connections. These scripts are for HP-UX or Solaris, and accept the $ORACLE_SID as an argument.

The **dss_config.ksh** script will be run at 6:00 P.M. each evening to reconfigure Oracle for the memory-intensive batch tasks that run each night:

dss_config.ksh

```
#!/bin/ksh

# First, we must set the environment . . . .
ORACLE_SID=$1
export ORACLE_SID
ORACLE_HOME=`cat /etc/oratab|grep ^$ORACLE_SID:|cut -f2 -d':'`
#ORACLE_HOME=`cat /var/opt/oracle/oratab|grep ^$ORACLE_SID:|cut -f2 -d':'`
export ORACLE_HOME
PATH=$ORACLE_HOME/bin:$PATH
export PATH

$ORACLE_HOME/bin/sqlplus -s /nologin<<!
```

```
connect system/manager as sysdba;
alter system set db_cache_size=1500m;
alter system set shared_pool_size=500m;
alter system set pga_aggregate_target=4000m;
exit
!
```

The **oltp_config.ksh** script will be run at 6:00 A.M. each morning to reconfigure
Oracle for the OLTP usage during the day:

oltp_config.ksh

```
#!/bin/ksh

# First, we must set the environment . . . .
ORACLE_SID=$1
export ORACLE_SID
ORACLE_HOME=`cat /etc/oratab|grep ^$ORACLE_SID:|cut -f2 -d':'`
#ORACLE_HOME=`cat /var/opt/oracle/oratab|grep ^$ORACLE_SID:|cut -f2 -d':'`
export ORACLE_HOME
PATH=$ORACLE_HOME/bin:$PATH
export PATH

$ORACLE_HOME/bin/sqlplus -s /nologin<<!
connect system/manager as sysdba;

alter system set db_cache_size=4000m;
alter system set shared_pool_size=500m;
alter system set pga_aggregate_target=1500m;

exit
!
```

> **NOTE**
> *You can also use the **dbms_job** package to
> schedule these types of reconfiguration events.*

Now that you see a generic way to change the Oracle configuration, it should
be clear that you can develop a mechanism to constantly monitor the processing
demands on Oracle and issue the **alter system** commands according to existing
database demands.

Approaches to Self-tuning Oracle Databases

Until Oracle9i evolves into a complete self-tuning architecture, the Oracle DBA is
responsible for adjusting the RAM memory configuration according to the types of

connections. In general, you can use queries against the **v$** structures and STATSPACK to locate those times when Oracle connections change their processing characteristics. There are three types of approaches to automated tuning:

- **Normal scheduled reconfiguration**   A bimodal instance that performs OLTP and DSS during regular hours will benefit from a scheduled task to reconfigure the SGA and PGA.

- **Trend-based dynamic reconfiguration**   You can use STATSPACK to predict those times when the processing characteristics change and use the **dbms_job** package to fire ad hoc SGA and PGA changes.

- **Dynamic reconfiguration**   Just as Oracle9i dynamically redistributes RAM memory for tasks within the **pga_aggregate_target** region, the Oracle DBA can write scripts that steal RAM from an underutilized area and reallocate these RAM pages to another RAM area.

Rules for Changing Memory Sizes

There are three conditions that affect the decision to resize the Oracle RAM regions: one for the data buffer cache, another for the shared pool, and the third for PGA memory usage.

- **db_cache_size**   You may want to add RAM to the data buffer cache when the data buffer hit ratio falls below a predefined threshold.

- **shared_pool_size**   A high value for any of the library cache miss rations may signal the need to allocate more memory to the shared pool.

- **pga_aggregate_target**   When you see high values for multi-pass executions, you may want to increase the available PGA memory.

Let's take a close look at each of these conditions.

Adjusting the pga_aggregate_target Parameter   You may want to dynamically change the **pga_aggregate_target** parameter when any one of the following conditions is true:

- Whenever the value of the **v$sysstat** statistic "estimated PGA memory for one-pass" exceeds **pga_aggregate_target**, you want to increase **pga_aggregate_target**.

■ Whenever the value of the **v$sysstat** statistic "workarea executions –
multipass" is greater than 1 percent, the database may benefit from
additional RAM memory.

■ It is possible to over-allocate PGA memory, and you may consider reducing
the value of **pga_aggregate_target** whenever the value of the **v$sysstat** row
"workarea executions—optimal" consistently measures 100 percent.

Changing the shared_pool_size Parameter   We all know from Oracle8 that
Oracle offers several queries for determining when the Oracle shared pool is too
small. The library cache miss ratio tells the DBA whether to add space to the
shared pool, and it represents the ratio of the sum of library cache reloads to the
sum of pins.

In general, if the library cache ratio is over 1, you should consider adding to
the **shared_pool_size**. Library cache misses occur during the parsing and preparation
of the execution plans for SQL statements. The compilation of a SQL statement
consists of two phases: the parse phase and the execute phase. When the time
comes to parse a SQL statement, Oracle first checks to see if the parsed representation
of the statement already exists in the library cache. If not, Oracle will allocate
a shared SQL area within the library cache and then parse the SQL statement.
At execution time, Oracle checks to see if a parsed representation of the SQL
statement already exists in the library cache. If not, Oracle will reparse and execute
the statement.

The following STATSPACK script will compute the library cache miss ratio. Note
that the script sums all of the values for the individual components within the library
cache and provides an instance-wide view of the health of the library cache.

rpt_lib_miss.sql

```
set lines 80;
set pages 999;

column mydate heading 'Yr.  Mo Dy  Hr.' format a16
column c1 heading "execs"     format 9,999,999
column c2 heading "Cache Misses|While Executing"   format 9,999,999
column c3 heading "Library Cache|Miss Ratio"    format 999.99999

break on mydate skip 2;

select
   to_char(snap_time,'yyyy-mm-dd HH24')   mydate,
   sum(new.pins-old.pins)              c1,
```

```
        sum(new.reloads-old.reloads)             c2,
        sum(new.reloads-old.reloads)/
        sum(new.pins-old.pins)                    library_cache_miss_ratio
from
    stats$librarycache old,
    stats$librarycache new,
    stats$snapshot      sn
where
    new.snap_id = sn.snap_id
and
    old.snap_id = new.snap_id-1
and
    old.namespace = new.namespace
group by
    to_char(snap_time,'yyyy-mm-dd HH24')
;
```

Here is the output. This report can easily be customized to alert the DBA when
there are excessive executions or library cache misses.

| | | Cache Misses | |
Yr. Mo Dy Hr.	execs	While Executing	LIBRARY_CACHE_MISS_RATIO
2001-12-11 10	10,338	3	.00029
2001-12-12 10	182,477	134	.00073
2001-12-14 10	190,707	202	.00106
2001-12-16 10	2,803	11	.00392

Once this report identifies a time period where there may be a problem,
STATSPACK provides the ability to run detailed reports to show the behavior of
the objects within the library cache. In the preceding example, you see a clear
RAM shortage in the shared pool between 10:00 A.M. and 11:00 A.M. each day.
In this case, you could dynamically reconfigure the shared pool with additional
RAM memory from the **db_cache_size** during this period.

Adjusting the Data Buffer Cache Size   The following STATSPACK report
alerts the DBA to those times when the data buffer hit ratio falls below the preset
threshold. It is very useful for locating times when decision support type queries are
being run, since a large number of large-table full-table scans will make the data
buffer hit ratio drop. This script also reports on all three data buffers, including the
KEEP and RECYCLE pools, and it can be customized to report on individual pools.
Remember, the KEEP pool should always have enough data blocks to cache all table
rows, while the RECYCLE pool should get a very low buffer hit ratio, since it seldom
re-reads data blocks. If the data buffer hit ratio is less than 90 percent, you may want
to increase **db_cache_size** (**db_block_buffers** in Oracle8i and earlier).

```
*************************************************************
When the data buffer hit ratio falls below 90%, you
should consider adding to the db_cache_size parameter
*************************************************************
```

```
yr.  mo dy Hr.   Name     bhr
-------------- --------   -----
2001-01-27 09 DEFAULT      45
2001-01-28 09 RECYCLE      41
2001-01-29 10 DEFAULT      36
2001-01-30 09 DEFAULT      28
2001-02-02 10 DEFAULT      83
2001-02-02 09 RECYCLE      81
2001-02-03 10 DEFAULT      69
2001-02-03 09 DEFAULT      69
```

Here you will note those times when you might want to dynamically increase the value of the **db_cache_size** parameter. In the case of the preceding output, you could increase the **db_cache_size** each day between 8:00 A.M. and 10:00 A.M., stealing RAM memory from **pga_aggregate_target**.

Using the Oracle9i v$db_cache_advice View   Starting in Oracle9i, there is a new view that can predict the benefit of additional data buffers in the data buffer cache. This view shows the estimated miss rates for 20 potential buffer cache sizes, ranging from 10 percent of the current size to 200 percent of the current size.

This new feature is very similar to the Oracle7 utility to predict the benefit from adding additional data buffers. This utility used a view called **x$kcbrbh** to track buffer hits and the **x$kcbcbh** to track buffer misses.

Just like the Oracle7 model, you must preallocate the RAM memory for the data buffers in order to use this Oracle9i utility. The cache advice feature is enabled by setting the init.ora parameter **db_cache_advice** to the values of **on** or **ready**. These values can be set dynamically with the **alter system** command, so the DBA can turn on the predictive model while the database is running.

CAUTION
*When the DBA sets **dba_cache_advice=on**, Oracle will steal RAM pages from the shared pool, often with disastrous results to the library cache. For example, if the existing setting for **db_cache_size** is 500m, Oracle will steal a significant amount of RAM from the shared pool. To avoid this problem, the DBA should set **db_cache_advice=ready** in the init.ora file. When this is done, Oracle will preallocate the RAM memory at database startup time.*

Once the **db_cache_advice** is enabled and the database has run for a representative time period, the following query can be run to perform the prediction:

```
column size_for_estimate
    format 999,999,999,999
    heading 'Cache Size (m)'
column buffers_for_estimate
    format 999,999,999
    heading 'Buffers'
column estd_physical_read_factor
    format 999.90
    heading 'Estd Phys|Read Factor'
column estd_physical_reads
    format 999,999,999
    heading 'Estd Phys| Reads'

select
    size_for_estimate,
    buffers_for_estimate,
    estd_physical_read_factor,
    estd_physical_reads
from
    v$db_cache_advice
where
    name = 'DEFAULT'
and
    block_size  = (SELECT value FROM V$PARAMETER
                     WHERE name = 'db_block_size')
and
    advice_status = 'ON';
```

Here is the output from this script. Note that the range of values is from 10 percent of the current size up to double the current size.

Cache Size (MB)	Buffers	Estd Phys Read Factor	Estd Phys Reads	
30	3,802	18.70	192,317,943	◀——— 10% size
60	7,604	12.83	131,949,536	
91	11,406	7.38	75,865,861	
121	15,208	4.97	51,111,658	
152	19,010	3.64	37,460,786	
182	22,812	2.50	25,668,196	
212	26,614	1.74	17,850,847	
243	30,416	1.33	13,720,149	
273	34,218	1.13	11,583,180	

304	38,020	1.00	10,282,475	← Current size
334	41,822	.93	9,515,878	
364	45,624	.87	8,909,026	
395	49,426	.83	8,495,039	
424	53,228	.79	8,116,496	
456	57,030	.76	7,824,764	
486	60,832	.74	7,563,180	
517	64,634	.71	7,311,729	
547	68,436	.69	7,104,280	
577	72,238	.67	6,895,122	
608	76,040	.66	6,739,731	← 2x size

Here, you can see no peak in total disk I/O and no marginal trends with the addition of more RAM buffers. This is very typical of data warehouse databases that read large tables with full-table scans. Consequently, there is no specific "optimal" setting for the **db_cache_size** parameter. In other words, Oracle has an insatiable appetite for data buffer RAM, and the more you give to **db_cache_size**, the less disk I/O will occur.

As a general rule, all available memory on the host should be tuned, and Oracle should be given to **db_cache_size** up to a point of diminishing returns (see Figure 7-6). There is a point where the addition of buffer blocks will not significantly improve the buffer hit ratio, and these tools give the Oracle DBA the ability to find the optimal amount of buffers.

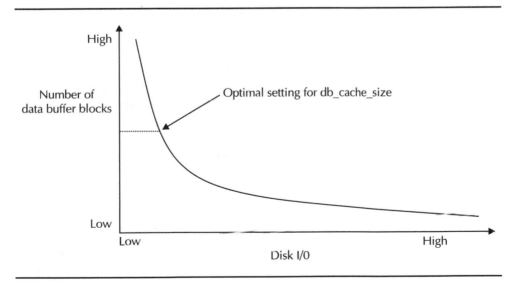

FIGURE 7-6. *Determining the optimal **db_cache_size***

The general rule for adding blocks to **db_cache_size** is simple: as long as marginal gains can be achieved from adding buffers and you have the memory to spare, you should increase the value of **db_cache_size**. Increases in buffer blocks increase the amount of required RAM memory for the database, and it is not always possible to "hog" all of the memory on a processor for the database management system. Therefore, a DBA should carefully review the amount of available memory and determine the optimal amount of buffer blocks.

TIP

*Since you must preallocate the additional RAM data buffers for the **db_cache_size** to use **db_cache_advice**, you may only want to use this utility once to determine an optimal size. Remember, you can also use the data buffer cache hit ratio to gather similar data.*

For more sophisticated Oracle9i databases, you can control not only the number of buffer blocks, but also the block size for each data buffer. For example, you might want to make some of the buffer blocks very large so that you can minimize I/O contention. Remember, the cost for an I/O for a 32K block is not significantly more expensive than an I/O for a 4K block. A database designer might choose to make specific data buffers large to minimize I/O if the application "clusters" records on a database block, while keeping other data blocks small. For more details on using multiple block sizes to reduce disk I/O, see Chapter 8.

When to Trigger a Dynamic Reconfiguration

When your scripts detect a condition where a RAM memory region is overstressed, you are faced with a choice about which region will shrink to provide the RAM for the overstressed area. Table 7-2 provides the threshold condition for triggering a dynamic memory change.

RAM Area	Overstressed Condition	Overallocated Condition
Shared pool	Library cache misses	No misses
Data buffer cache	Hit ratio < 90%	Hit ratio > 95%
PGA aggregate	High multi-pass executions	100% optimal executions

TABLE 7-2. *Threshold Conditions for Dynamic RAM Reallocation*

In practice, the choice of which area to reduce in size is a choice between the shared pool and the PGA aggregate memory (see Figure 7-7). This is because the shared pool is almost always a small region when compared to the regions for the data buffers and PGA session memory.

Now, let's conclude this chapter with a review of the major topics and points.

Conclusion

This chapter has been devoted to illustrating the interaction between UNIX and Oracle connections. You saw differences between dedicated Oracle connections and MTS connections, and a dramatic change in memory management for connections between Oracle8i and Oracle9i. The main concepts in this chapter included the following points:

■ For dedicated connections, the PGA memory is allocated via UNIX in a RAM area outside of Oracle.

■ You can get the UNIX process ID for an Oracle session in the **v$session** view and correlate it to the UNIX task.

■ When using the MTS, Oracle manages the PGA memory demands of connections inside the shared pool or the large pool.

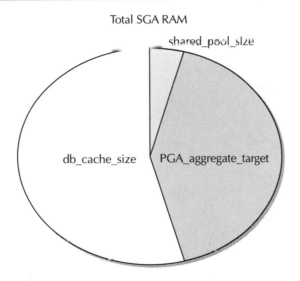

FIGURE 7-7. *A typical RAM configuration for an Oracle database*

■ Starting in Oracle9i, Oracle allows the DBA to dynamically alter SGA and PGA memory regions.

■ In Oracle9i, Oracle has self-tuning features for RAM allocations, and allows the DBA to preallocate PGA RAM by setting the **pga_aggregate_target** parameter.

■ The Oracle9i DBA can dynamically change the RAM region size for the shared pool, **db_cache_size**, and **pga_aggregate_target**. This ability provides the DBA with a vehicle for changing the SGA and PGA RAM sizes depending upon existing processing conditions.

Now that we have exhausted our discussion of Oracle connections and UNIX, let's move on and take a look at file management within a UNIX Oracle environment.

CHAPTER
8

Oracle File
Management in UNIX

his chapter will focus on those UNIX commands that will allow you to manage Oracle files on UNIX. We will explore tools and techniques for monitoring UNIX disk I/O and using Oracle techniques to reduce UNIX disk I/O. This chapter covers the following topics:

- File management in UNIX

- Oracle performance and disk I/O

- Oracle9i and multiple block sizes

- Monitoring Oracle disk I/O with the UNIX **iostat** Utility

- Extending STATSPACK for **iostat** information

Let's begin with an overview of the Oracle Optimal Flexible Architecture (OFA) and see how knowledge of UNIX commands can greatly aid the DBA for an Oracle database.

File Management in UNIX

As you know, the Oracle software resides inside a file system in UNIX in the directory identified by the UNIX $ORACLE_HOME environment variable. Inside this file system structure you find not only the Oracle software, but specialized libraries for trace and dump files (see Figure 8-1).

From this diagram, you see the following important directories in UNIX. In UNIX, the $DBA variable points to the Oracle administrative directory, which might have a name like /u01/app/oracle/admin.

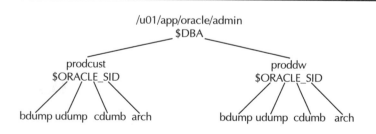

FIGURE 8-1. *The Oracle OFA file system structure*

- **$DBA/$ORACLE_SID/bdump** This directory corresponds to the **background_dump_dest** parameter and serves as the location of the Oracle alert log in UNIX.

- **$DBA/$ORACLE_SID/cdump** This directory is the location of Oracle core dumps.

- **$DBA/$ORACLE_SID/arch** This corresponds to the **log_archive_dest** parameter and is the location of the Oracle archived redo log files. It is critical that the Oracle DBA always ensures that there is free space in this directory because a full UNIX file system can cause a production Oracle outage.

- **$DBA/$ORACLE_SID/udump** This directory corresponds to the **user_dump_dest** parameter and is the location where user trace and dump files are located.

In UNIX, you can easily query the **v$parameter** view to see details on each of these directories:

```
select
    name,
    value,
    description
from
    v$parameter
where
    name like '%dest'
;
```

Here is a listing of all of the UNIX locations:

```
NAME
----------------------------------------------------------------
VALUE
----------------------------------------------------------------
DESCRIPTION
----------------------------------------------------------------
log_archive_dest
/u01/app/oracle/admin/janet1/arch
archival destination text string

standby_archive_dest
?/dbs/arch
standby database archivelog destination text string
```

```
background_dump_dest
/u01/app/oracle/admin/janet1/bdump
Detached process dump directory

user_dump_dest
/u01/app/oracle/admin/janet1/udump
User process dump directory

core_dump_dest
/u01/app/oracle/admin/janet1/cdump
Core dump directory

audit_file_dest
?/rdbms/audit
Directory in which auditing files are to reside
```

You also see important UNIX directories that relate to Oracle. Within UNIX, you see a hierarchy of directory names that are used by the UNIX administrator to manage the UNIX operating system (see Table 8-1).

These files are the most important to the UNIX Oracle DBA because they contain files that must be managed. Let's begin with basic UNIX file system commands and see how they can help you with this task.

General UNIX File Management Commands

The following types of UNIX commands are of the most value to the Oracle DBA:

- **ls command**   This is used to find files within a directory and display files according to dates.

/home	Where the user home directory is located
/bin	Binary or executables directory
/tmp	Temporary files
/dev	Device directory
/etc	System administration files
/var	Where accounting and spooling files are located
/export	Files available to other systems in network

TABLE 8-1.   *Important UNIX Management Directories*

- **du command**   This command quickly computes the used space within a UNIX directory.

- **find command**   The **find** command is great for generating a list of UNIX files that meet specific time and size criteria.

- **xargs and -exec commands**   These commands allow you to pass a list of filenames to a generic command such as the **rm** command.

Let's start with the **ls** command and see how it is used to locate files.

The UNIX ls Command for Oracle

The DBA often needs to see the most recent files in a file system that have been "touched" by a UNIX program. Here you display the most recently touched files in your Oracle bdump directory:

```
root> ls -alt|head
total 820
-rw-r--r--    1 oracle    dba          163272 Oct 22 11:51 alert_janet1.log
drwxrwsr-x    2 oracle    dba            8192 Oct 22 01:55 catalog_export
-rw-r-----    1 oracle    dba           10846 Sep 11 04:00 janet1_snp0_25171.trc
drwxr-xr-x    3 oracle    dba            2048 Jul 29 10:39 .
-rw-r--r--    1 oracle    nofiles      197053 Jul 29 01:34 alert_janet1.log.old
-rw-r-----    1 oracle    dba             573 Jul 16 18:33 janet1_arc2_14380.trc
-rw-r-----    1 oracle    dba             573 Jul 16 18:28 janet1_arc1_14300.trc
-rw-r-----    1 oracle    dba            1224 Jul  4 12:13 janet1_pmon_25159.trc
-rw-r-----    1 oracle    dba             574 Apr 30 10:02 janet1_arc0_25173.trc
```

Note that "touch" is different from "changed." A file is touched any time the file is read by a process, but a file is only changed when it has been written to.

In the following example, you use the **ls** command with other arguments to see the most recently changed files. Note that the **-c** option displays in reverse order and you must pipe to **tail** to see the most recent values:

```
root> ls -alc|tail
drwxrwsr-x    2 oracle    dba            8192 Oct 22 01:55 catalog_export
-rw-r-----    1 oracle    dba             602 Oct 22 02:47 janet1_arc0_25005.trc
-rw-r-----    1 oracle    dba             574 Oct 22 02:47 janet1_arc0_25173.trc
-rw-r-----    1 oracle    dba             600 Oct 22 02:47 janet1_arc0_9312.trc
-rw-r-----    1 oracle    dba             600 Oct 22 02:47 janet1_arc0_9425.trc
-rw-r-----    1 oracle    dba             573 Oct 22 02:47 janet1_arc1_14300.trc
-rw-r-----    1 oracle    dba             573 Oct 22 02:47 janet1_arc2_14380.trc
-rw-r-----    1 oracle    dba            1224 Oct 22 02:47 janet1_pmon_25159.trc
-rw-r-----    1 oracle    dba           10846 Oct 22 02:47 janet1_snp0_25171.trc
-rw-r-----    1 oracle    dba             876 Oct 22 02:47 janet1_snp0_8188.trc
```

Display File Sizes in Kilobytes

The **du** command in UNIX is used to display the amount of occupied space for specific files or a collection of files. The following command will list all the files and sizes in a directory, sorted in ascending order of size:

```
root> du -sk * |sort -n|tail
4        janet1_arc0_9312.trc
4        janet1_arc0_9425.trc
4        janet1_arc1_14300.trc
4        janet1_arc2_14380.trc
4        janet1_pmon_25159.trc
4        janet1_snp0_8188.trc
24       janet1_snp0_25171.trc
336      alert_janet1.log
404      alert_janet1.log.old
2100     catalog_export
```

Note that this command displays the number of kilobyte blocks that are consumed.

Display Total File Space in a Directory

Here is a handy UNIX command to display the total file spaces in any UNIX directory. In the example that follows, you go to the $ORACLE_HOME directory and issue the **du -sk** command. Here you see that the $ORACLE_HOME directory consumes 1450K, or about 1.4 gigabytes of disk space.

```
root> du -sk .
1450    .
```

Remove Elderly Oracle trace, credump, and audit Files

Part of an Oracle DBA's job on a UNIX server is to e-mail current trace and core dump files to Oracle support and e-mail application trace and dump files to code developers. Once problems have been resolved, the DBA must remove unwanted files from the Oracle UNIX file system. These unwanted files may include:

- **Trace files**   Trace files become obsolete as soon as they have been mailed to the developer staff.

- **Core files**   Core files may be removed as soon as Oracle support has received copies of the dump.

- **Audit files**   Audit files are a nuisance that many DBAs remove every day.

The following is a script that will automatically remove all trace files from the background_dump_destination file system in UNIX:

```
# Cleanup trace files more than 7 days old
root> find $DBA/$ORACLE_SID/bdump/*.trc -mtime +7 -exec rm {} \;
root> find $DBA/$ORACLE_SID/udump/*.trc -mtime +7 -exec rm {} \;
root> find $DBA/$ORACLE_SID/cdump/*.trc -mtime +7 -exec rm {} \;
```

Note that the first part of this script (before the **-exec**) displays all trace files that are more than seven days old:

```
root> find $DBA/$ORACLE_SID/bdump/*.trc -mtime +7
```

```
/u01/app/oracle/admin/janet1/bdump/janet1_arc0_25005.trc
/u01/app/oracle/admin/janet1/bdump/janet1_arc0_25173.trc
/u01/app/oracle/admin/janet1/bdump/janet1_arc0_9312.trc
/u01/app/oracle/admin/janet1/bdump/janet1_arc0_9425.trc
/u01/app/oracle/admin/janet1/bdump/janet1_arc1_14300.trc
/u01/app/oracle/admin/janet1/bdump/janet1_arc2_14380.trc
/u01/app/oracle/admin/janet1/bdump/janet1_pmon_25159.trc
/u01/app/oracle/admin/janet1/bdump/janet1_snp0_25171.trc
/u01/app/oracle/admin/janet1/bdump/janet1_snp0_8188.trc
```

Locate Oracle Files that Contain Certain Strings

This is a handy shell command for finding all files that contain a specified string. For example, assume that you are trying to locate a script that queries the v$process table. You can issue the following command, and UNIX will search all subdirectories, looking in all files for the v$process table:

```
root> find . -print|xargs grep v\$process
./TX_RBS.sql:         v$process p,
./UNIX_WHO.sql:from     v$session a, v$process b
./session.sql:from v$session b, v$process a
```

The **grep** utility is always handy, but is especially useful for finding specific strings inside Oracle files.

Locate Recently Created UNIX Files

The following command is useful for finding UNIX files that have been recently added to your server. Part of the job of the Oracle DBA is monitoring the background_dump_dest and the user_dump_dest for trace files, and purging trace files that are no longer required.

The following command lists all files that were created in the past two weeks:

```
root> find . -mtime -14 -print
.
./janet1_ora_27714.trc
```

```
./janet1_ora_27716.trc
./janet1_ora_24985.trc
./janet1_ora_24977.trc
```

This command can easily be expanded with the **xargs** or the **-exec** command to automatically remove the elderly trace files:

```
root> find . -mtime -14 -print|xargs -i rm \;
```

Finding Large Files on a UNIX Server

The following command is very useful in cases where a UNIX file system has become full. As you may know, Oracle will hang whenever Oracle must expand a tablespace, and Oracle cannot extend the UNIX file system.

When a UNIX file become unexpectedly full, it may be because Oracle has written a huge core or trace file into the UNIX file system.

The following script will display all files that are greater than 1 megabyte in size. Note that the **size** parameter is specified in kilobytes.

```
root> find . -size +1024 -print
./prodsid_ora_22951.trc
```

Of course, you can easily append the **xargs** or **-exec** command to automatically remove the large file:

```
root> find . -size +1024 -print|xargs -i rm \;
```

A Step-by-Step Approach to Deleting Unwanted UNIX Files

When writing UNIX scripts to automatically delete obsolete Oracle trace files, audit files, dump files, and archived redo logs, it is a good idea to carefully develop the UNIX script through iteration, getting each piece working. Remember, even seasoned UNIX gurus will not write a complex command until each component is tested.

You start by going to the archived redo log directory and finding all redo log files that are more than seven days old. In this example, you take a cold backup each night, and the DBA has no use for elderly redo log files.

```
root> cd $DBA/$ORACLE_SID/arch
root> find . -mtime +7

./archlog2251.arc
./archlog2252.arc
./archlog2253.arc
./archlog2254.arc
```

Now that you have the list of files, you can add the UNIX **rm** command to this syntax to automatically remove all files that are more than seven days old. In this case, you can use either the **-exec** or the **xargs** commands to remove the files:

```
find . -mtime +7 -exec rm {} \;
```

Delete All Old Oracle Trace and Audit Files More than 14 Days Old

Here is an example of a UNIX script for keeping the archived redo log directory free of elderly files. As you know, it is important to keep room in this directory, because Oracle can lock up if it cannot write a current redo log to the archived redo log file system. This script could be used in coordination with Oracle Recovery Manager (**rman**) to only remove files after a full backup has been taken.

clean_arch.ksh

```
#!/bin/ksh

# Cleanup archive logs more than 7 days old
find /u01/app/oracle/admin/mysid/arch/arch_mysid*.arc -ctime +7 -exec rm {}
;
```

Now that you see how to do the cleanup for an individual directory, you can easily expand this approach to loop through every Oracle database name on the server (by using the oratab file) and remove the files from each directory. If you are using Solaris, the oratab is located in /var/opt/oratab, while HP-UX and AIX have the oratab file in the /etc directory.

clean_all.ksh

```
#!/bin/ksh

for ORACLE_SID in `cat /etc/oratab|egrep ':N|:Y'|grep -v \*|cut -f1 -d':'`
do
 ORACLE_HOME=`cat /etc/oratab|grep ^$ORACLE_SID:|cut -d":" -f2`
 DBA=`echo $ORACLE_HOME | sed -e 's:/product/.*::g'`/admin
 find $DBA/$ORACLE_SID/bdump -name \*.trc -mtime +14 -exec rm {} \;
 $DBA/$ORACLE_SID/udump -name \*.trc -mtime +14 -exec rm {} \;
 find $ORACLE_HOME/rdbms/audit -name \*.aud -mtime +14 -exec rm {} \;
done
```

The above script loops through each database, visiting the bdump, udump and audit directories, removing all files more than two weeks old.

Removing UNIX Files with the dbms_backup_restore Package

Oracle provides a package called **dbms_backup_restore** that can also be used to remove UNIX files. As you may know, you can create a directory entity inside Oracle that contains the location of a UNIX directory.

```
SQL> create or replace directory
     arch_dir
as
     '/u01/oracle/admin/mysid/arch';
```

You can then use a PL/SQL stored procedure to read the UNIX filenames from the **v$archived_log** view. For all files that are more than 30 days old (according to **v$archived_log.completion_time**), you call the **dbms_backup_restore.deletefile** procedure to remove the archived redo log from UNIX.

```
CREATE OR REPLACE PROCEDURE
     remove_elderly_archive_logs
IS
   arc_file      BFILE;
   arc_exist     BOOLEAN;
   arc_name      VARCHAR2(100);
   --***************************************************
   -- Select all files over 30 days old . . .
   --***************************************************
   CURSOR get_archive IS
     SELECT name
       FROM v$archived_log;
      WHERE completion_time < SYSDATE - 30;
BEGIN
  FOR entry IN get_archive LOOP

     --*********************************************************
     -- use the BFILENAME function to get the file name from UNIX
     --*********************************************************
     arc_file  := BFILENAME('arch_dir',entry.name);

     --***************************************************
     -- check to make sure the file still exists in UNIX
     --***************************************************
     arc_file_exists := FALSE;
     arc_file_exists := DBMS_LOB.FILEEXISTS(arc_file) = 1;

     IF arc_file_exists THEN
       dbms_output.put_line('Deleting: ' || entry.name);
```

```
   --**********************************************************
   -- call the DELETEFILE procedure to nuke the UNIX file
   --**********************************************************
   SYS.DBMS_BACKUP_RESTORE.DELETEFILE(entry.name);
  END IF;

 END loop;
END;
/
```

Now you can simply call the procedure from a UNIX **crontab** to periodically remove the files. The **crontab** entry might look like this:

```
#**********************************************************
# Run the archived redo log cleanup Monday at 7:30 AM
#**********************************************************
30 07 1 * * /home/scripts/nuke_logs.ksh mysid > /home/scripts/nuke.lst
```

Here is a sample of the script itself:

nuke_logs.ksh

```
#!/bin/ksh

# First, we must set the environment . . . .
ORACLE_SID=$1
export ORACLE_SID
ORACLE_HOME=`cat /etc/oratab|grep ^$ORACLE_SID:|cut -f2 -d':'`
#ORACLE_HOME=`cat /var/opt/oracle/oratab|grep ^$ORACLE_SID.|cut -f2 -d':'`
export ORACLE_HOME
PATH=$ORACLE_HOME/bin:$PATH
export PATH

$ORACLE_HOME/bin/sqlplus -s /nologin<<!
connect system/manager as sysdba;
set serveroutput on;
exec remove_elderly_archive_logs
exit
!
```

Now that you have seen the host of UNIX commands that can be issued to maintain the file environment, let's move on and take a closer look at minimizing file I/O in a UNIX Oracle environment. Remember, you must actively work to reduce disk I/O to keep the database running at optimal levels.

Oracle Performance and Disk I/O

When a request is made from the Oracle database to fetch a block from a disk, you see sources of latency. This example assumes that you are not using a disk array with caching, and that a physical I/O is required to fetch the data block. When a physical request is made to a disk, the total delay time can be broken into three components:

- **Seek delay (70%)**   The seek delay is the amount of time it takes to move the read-write heads over the appropriate cylinder on the disk device. Seek delay is the largest component of disk delay.

- **Rotational delay (30%)**   Rotational delay is the time that the I/O must wait for the requested block to pass beneath the read-write heads. The average rotational delay for a disk is one-half the rotational speed of the disk.

- **Transmission delay (<1%)**   Transmission delay is the smallest component of Oracle disk response time, and the only one that relates to block size. Transmission time is measured at the speed of light, and the overhead of transmitting a 32K block is not measurable slower than fetching a 2K block.

Once you understand that 99 percent of the disk delay is required whether you read a 2K block or a 32K block, you begin to understand the nature of disk I/O and block sizing.

The seek delay and rotational delay are the same regardless of the size of the block you are reading, and the transmission time differences are so small as to be immeasurable. Once the read-write heads are positioned directly over the cylinder, the only difference in machinery sources is the time required to transmit the larger block across the network back to the Oracle database.

Hence, you can come to an important conclusion:

The database block size does not measurably affect the speed of the block I/O, and fetching a 32K block is no more expensive than fetching a 2K block.

If it takes about the same amount of time to fetch a 2K block as it does to fetch a 32K block, why don't you make all of your database blocks 32K and get as more data for the same I/O cost?

The answer is the expense of potentially wasted RAM storage in the data buffer caches. For example, moving a 32K block into the RAM buffer to retrieve an 80-byte record is a huge waste, unless there are other rows in the 32K block that are likely to be requested by Oracle. Your goal is to manage your precious RAM space and make the most efficient use of your data buffer caches.

While the general rule holds true that the more data you can fetch in a single I/O, the better your overall buffer hit ratio, you have to take a closer look at the multiple data buffer phenomenon to gather a true picture of what's happening under the covers. In general, large blocks are better for sequential data warehouse access, and smaller block sizes are better for random OLTP workloads. Let's start with a simple example.

Reducing Disk I/O in UNIX

When using multiple block sizes, the DBA is given additional control over the UNIX disk I/O subsystem. The Oracle DBA understands the following basic truths about UNIX disk I/O:

- Disk I/O is the largest component of Oracle response time. A reduction in disk I/O will always result in faster performance for that task.

- Creating larger data blocks allows Oracle to access more row data in a single I/O. Oracle9i supports multiple block sizes, and the Oracle9i DBA can move tables easily from one block size to a tablespace with another block size, thereby load-balancing disk I/O.

- The Oracle DBA has tools (in-place table reorgs, CTAS with **order by**) to allow easy table reorganization and can use these tools to resequence table rows in the same order as the primary index to reduce disk I/O on index range scans. For more information, see "Turning the Tables on Disk I/O," January 2000, at Oracle Magazine online (http://www.oramag.com/).

So how do you reduce disk I/O in UNIX? There are three generally accepted techniques for the DBA to reduce disk I/O:

- **Tune SQL statements to retrieve data with a minimum of disk I/O** This is generally performed by finding large-table full-table scans and replacing the full-table scan with an index scan.

- **Change the Oracle SGA** When you increase the shared_pool, large_pool, or db_cache_size, the resulting performance improvement is related to the reduction in disk I/O.

- **Reorganize tables to reduce disk I/O** This is done by selectively moving tables to tablespaces with a different block size, and resequencing table rows into the primary key order.

Let's take a closer look at resequencing table rows to reduce disk I/O, and see how this can help a UNIX-based Oracle system.

Resequencing Table Rows to Reduce Disk I/O

Basically, the **create table as select** (CTAS) statement copies the selected portion of the table into a new table. If you select the entire table with an **order by** clause or an index hint, it will copy the rows in the same order as the primary index. In addition to resequencing the rows of the new table, the CTAS statement coalesces free space and chained rows and resets freelists, thereby providing additional performance benefits. You can also alter table parameters, such as initial extents and the number of freelists, as you create the new table. The steps in a CTAS reorganization include:

1. Define a separate tablespace (maybe with a different block size) to hold the reorganized table.

2. Disable all referential integrity constraints.

3. Copy the table with CTAS (using **order by** or an index hint).

4. Re-enable all referential integrity constraints.

5. Rebuild all indexes on the new table.

The main benefit of CTAS over the other methods is speed. It is far faster to use CTAS to copy the table into a new tablespace (and then re-create all RI and indexes) than it is to use the export/import method. Using CTAS also has the added benefit of allowing the rows to be resequenced into the same order as the primary index, thereby greatly reducing I/O. Within CTAS, there are two general reorganization methods.

Using Oracle9i for In-place Table Reorganizations

Starting in Oracle8i, new **alter table** syntax was introduced to allow you to easily reorganize a table. The syntax for the new command is:

```
alter table
    xxx
move online tablespace
    yyy;
```

Remember that the **alter table move** command requires double the disk space. Because Oracle keeps the old copy of the table until the new table is copied, you must have at least double the space in the tablespace.

While the in-place table reorganization is great for coalescing freelists, removing chained rows and changing the block size for a table, the great downside of in-place table reorganization is the inability to resequence rows.

```
SQL> alter table emp move order by ename tablespace tools;
alter table emp move order by ename tablespace tools
                         *
ERROR at line 1:
ORA-14133: ALTER TABLE MOVE cannot be combined with other operations
```

It is hoped that Oracle9i will be enhanced to allow for row resequencing with the **alter table** syntax, but until that time, the savvy DBA will continue to use the CTAS syntax to reorganize tables.

Two Alternatives for Using CTAS

It is always recommended that you resequence the table rows when performing a table reorganization with CTAS because of the huge I/O benefits. You can use the CTAS statement in one of two ways. Each of these achieves the same result, but they do it very differently:

- Use CTAS in conjunction with the **order by** clause.

- Use CTAS in conjunction with a hint that identifies the index to use.

The approach you choose depends on the size of the table involved, the overall processing power of your environment, and how quickly you must complete the reorganization.

The details of each CTAS approach are discussed more fully in the sections that follow, but in either case, when you create the new table, you can speed the process by using the Oracle **nologging** option (this was called **unrecoverable** in Oracle7). This skips the added overhead of writing to the redo log file. Of course, you cannot use the redo logs to roll forward through a **nologging** operation, and most DBAs take a full backup prior to using CTAS with **nologging**. Let's examine the two methods and see their respective differences.

Using CTAS with the order by Clause

When using CTAS with the **order by** clause, you are directing Oracle to perform the operations shown in Figure 8-2.

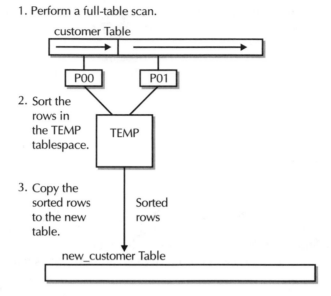

FIGURE 8-2.   *Using CTAS with **order by***

As you can see, the full-table scan can be used with Parallel Query to speed the execution, but you still have a large disk sort following the collection of the rows. Because of the size of most tables, this sort will be done in the TEMP tablespace.

Here is an example of the SQL syntax to perform a CTAS with **order by**:

```
create table new_customer
   tablespace customer_flip
      storage (initial          500m
               next             50m
               maxextents       unlimited)
   parallel (degree 11)
   as select * from customer
   order by customer_number;
```

Using CTAS with **order by** can be very slow without the **parallel** clause. A parallel full-table scan reads the original table quickly (in non-index order).

As you know from Oracle Parallel Query, the CTAS operation will cause Oracle to spawn to multiple background processes to service the full-table scan. This often makes the **order by** approach faster than using the index-hint approach to CTAS. The choice to use **parallel** depends on the database server. If your hardware has multiple CPUs and many (perhaps hundreds of) processes, using **parallel** is likely to be significantly faster. However, if your hardware configuration has a relatively modest number of processes (such as the four specified in the example), the index-hint approach is likely to be faster.

Using CTAS with an Index Hint

The CTAS with an index hint executes quite differently than CTAS with **order by**. When using an index hint, the CTAS begins by retrieving the table rows from the original table using the existing index. Since the rows are initially retrieved in the proper order, there is no need to sort the result set, and the data is used immediately to create the new table, as shown in Figure 8-3.

The syntax for CTAS with an index hint is as follows:

```
create table new_customer
    tablespace customer_flip
        storage  (initial            500m
                    next             50m
                    maxextents       unlimited)
    as select /*+ index(customer customer_primary_key_idx) */  *
    from customer;
```

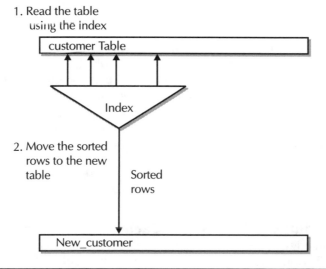

FIGURE 8-3. *Using CTAS with an index hint*

When this statement executes, the database traverses the existing primary-key index to access the rows for the new table, bypassing the sorting operation. Most Oracle DBAs choose this method over the **order by** approach because the runtime performance of traversing an index is generally faster than using the **parallel** clause and then sorting the entire result set.

Now that you see how CTAS works for table reorganizations, let's explore why the database block size can be an important factor in reducing disk I/O.

Oracle9i and Multiple Block Sizes

The ability of Oracle to support multiple block sizes did not get a lot of fanfare during the publicity rollout of Oracle9i. Rather than being touted as an important tool to reduce disk I/O, the multiple block size feature was buried far down on the list of new features of the Oracle9i database. However, for the Oracle administrator, multiple block sizes are extremely important and exciting. For the first time, you will be able to customize your data buffer sizes according to the specific needs of your database.

The ability to support multiple block sizes within Oracle9i opens up a whole new world of disk I/O management. Prior to Oracle9i, your entire Oracle database had to have a single block size and this block size was determined at the time the database was created.

With the introduction of Oracle8i, you received the ability to segregate tables and index blocks into three separate data buffers, but all of the buffer caches had to be the same block size. You had the KEEP pool to store frequently referenced table blocks, the RECYCLE pool to hold blocks from large-table full-table scans, and a DEFAULT pool for miscellaneous object blocks.

With Oracle9i, you can define tablespaces with block sizes of 2K, 4K, 8K, 16K, and 32K, and assign tables and indexes to the best block size to minimize I/O and best manage wasted space in your data buffers. When you combine the new data buffers for these block sizes, you get a total of seven separate and distinct data buffers to segregate your incoming table and index rows.

As you know, disk I/O is the single most expensive operation within an Oracle9i database, and multiple block sizes give you a powerful new tool to manage disk I/O with more power than ever before.

To fully understand the importance of multiple block sizes, it is important to take a look at the basic nature of disk I/O.

Allocating Multiple Data Buffer Caches

Let's see firsthand how the multiple data buffers work. For example, you could define the following buffer cache allocations in your initialization file:

```
db_block_size=32768          -- This is the system-wide
                             -- default block size

db_cache_size=3G             -- This allocates a total of 3 gigabytes
                             -- for all of the 32K data buffers

db_keep_cache_size=1G        -- Here we use 1 gigabyte for the KEEP pool

db_recycle_cache_size=500M   -- Here is 500 meg for the RECYCLE pool
                             -- Hence, the DEFAULT pool is 1,500 meg

-- ************************************************************
-- The caches below are all additional RAM memory (total=3.1 gig)
-- that are above and beyond the allocation from db_cache_size
-- ************************************************************

db_2k_cache_size=200M        -- This cache is reserved for random
                             -- block retrieval on tables that
                             -- have small rows.

dictionary_cache=200m        -- The data dictionary blocks will be 32k

db_4k_cache_size=500M        -- This 4K buffer will be reserved
                             -- exclusively for tables with a small average
                             -- row length and random access

db_8k_cache_size=800M        -- This is a separate cache for
                             -- segregating I/O for specific tables

db_16k_cache_size=1600M      -- This is a separate cache for
                             -- segregating I/O for specific tables
```

From this example, what is the total RAM allocated to the data buffer caches? The total RAM required is the sum of all the named buffer caches, plus **db_cache_size**, in this case, 6,100 megabytes, or 6.1 gigabytes.

Remember that **db_keep_cache_size** and **db_recycle_cache_size** are subtracted from the **db_cache_size**. In the example above, the DEFAULT pool is 1.5 gigabytes, after subtracting the allocation for the KEEP and RECYCLE pools.

Also note that you cannot create a buffer of the same size as your **db_block_size**. In this example, the **db_block_size** is 31768, so you cannot allocate a **db_32k_cache_size**.

Table 8-2 defines seven totally separate data buffers. Let's review the usage for each data buffer, computing the number of data blocks each buffer can hold.

Name	Size	Block Size	Block Space
KEEP pool	1,000M	32K	31,250 blocks
RECYCLE pool	500M	32K	15,625 blocks
DEFAULT pool	1,500M	32K	46,875 blocks
2K cache	200M	2K	100,000 blocks
4K cache	500M	4K	125,000 blocks
8K cache	800M	8K	100,000 blocks
16K cache	1,600M	16K	100,000 blocks

TABLE 8-2.   *Computing the Size and Capacity for Multiple Block Sizes*

Your next step is to create tablespaces using each of these block sizes. Oracle will automatically load a tablespace's blocks into the data buffer of the appropriate block size.

For example, we talked about creating the **db_2k_cache_size** exclusively for tables with small row sizes that are always accessed randomly. Hence, you could define a 2K tablespace as follows:

```
create tablespace
    2k_tablespace
datafile
    '/u01/oradata/mysid/2k_file.dbf'
size
    100M
blocksize
    2k
;
```

Once defined, Oracle will always load block from the **2k_tablespace** into the **db_2k_cache_size** data buffer. Now all you need to do is to move all appropriate tables into the new tablespace using the Create Table As Select (CTAS) command:

```
-- First, disable all RI constraints

create table
    new_customer
as select
    *
from
```

```
    customer
tablespace
2k_tablespace
;

rename customer to old_customer;
rename new_customer to customer;

-- finally, transfer all RI constraints and indexes
```

Now that you see how to create tablespaces with different block sizes, let's explore some other important considerations for determining the tablespace block size.

Large Blocks and Oracle Indexes

Prior to Oracle9i, many Oracle tuning experts recommended that a database be redefined with a larger block size. Many people were mystified when a database with a 2K block size was increased to an 8K block size and the entire database ran faster. A common justification for resisting a block size increase was, "This database randomly fetches small rows. I can't see why moving to a larger block size would improve performance." So what explains the performance improvement with larger block sizes?

When choosing a block size, many DBAs forget about the index trees and how Oracle indexes are accessed sequentially when doing an index range scan. An index range scan is commonly seen in nested loop joins, and the vast majority of row access involved indexes.

Because index range scans involve gathering sequential index nodes, placing the indexes in a larger block size reduces disk I/O and improves throughput for the whole database.

So then, why not create your entire Oracle database with large block sizes and forget about multiple block sizes? The answer is not simple. In order to fully utilize the RAM memory in the data buffers, you must segregate tables according to their distribution of related data:

- **Small blocks**   Tables with small rows that are accessed in a random fashion should be placed onto tablespaces with small block sizes. With random access and small block sizes, more of the RAM in the data buffer remains available to hold frequently referenced rows from other tables.

- **Large blocks**   Indexes, row-ordered tables, single-table clusters, and tables with frequent full-table scans should reside in tablespaces with large block sizes. This is because a single I/O will fetch many related rows and subsequent requests for the "next" rows will already be in the data buffer.

The goal here is simple: you want to maximize the amount of available RAM memory for the data buffers by setting the block sizes according to the amount of I/O experienced by the table or index. Random access of small rows suggests small block sizes, while sequential access of related rows suggests large block sizes.

For example, consider a query that accesses 100 random 80-byte rows from Oracle. Since the accesses are random, you can assume that no two rows exist on the same block, and that 100 block reads are required to access the result set.

If you have 16K blocks, you would need 16MB (16K × 100) of RAM space in the **db_16k_cache_size** data buffer. If you use 2K blocks, your 100 I/Os only use 2MB (2K × 100) in the data buffer. For this query, you would have saved 14 megabytes of RAM to hold other row data.

Waste Not, Want Not – Fully utilizing RAM resources

Until RAM memory becomes cheap enough that you can cache your whole database, you need to manage the RAM that you allocate to your data buffers. The allocation of tables and indexes according to block sizes is a balancing act.

If you allocate the data blocks too large, you waste valuable data buffer space holding row data that Oracle will never reference. If you allocate the data block too small, Oracle will have to do more disk I/Os to satisfy a request. Here are some general rules for allocating data block sizes:

- **Segregate large-table full-table scans** Tables that experience large-table full-table scans will benefit from the largest supported block size and should be placed in a tablespace with your largest block size.

- **Set db_recycle_cache_size carefully** If you are not setting **db_cache_size** to the largest supported block size for your server, you should not use the **db_recycle_cache_size** parameter. Instead, you will want to create a **db_32k_cache_size** (or whatever your max is), and assign all tables that experience frequent large-table full-table scans to the largest buffer cache in your database.

- **The Data Dictionary cache uses the default block size** You should ensure that the data dictionary (that is, your SYSTEM tablespace) is always fully cached in a data buffer pool. Remember, the block size of the data dictionary is not as important as ensuring that the data buffer associated with the SYSTEM tablespace has enough RAM to fully cache all data dictionary blocks.

- **Indexes want large block sizes** Indexes will always favor the largest supported block size. You want to be able to retrieve as many index nodes as possible in a single I/O, especially for SQL that performs index range scans. Hence, all indexes should reside in tablespaces with a 32K block size.

- **Average row length** The block size for a tables' tablespace should always be greater than the average row length for the table (**dba_tables.avg_row_len**). If the average row length is greater than the block size, rows chaining occurs and excessive disk I/O is incurred.

- **Use large blocks for data sorting** Your TEMP tablespace will benefit from the largest supported block size. This allows disk sorting to happen in large blocks with a minimum of disk I/O.

The intent of this section is to give you an idea of the impact of multiple block sizes and multiple RAM caches. Once you are aware of the salient issues surrounding the use of block sizes, you can make intelligent decisions about the proper assignment of block sizes to your tables and indexes.

It is important to note that your tuning changes are never permanent, and you can always move tables from one tablespace to another, experimenting with different block sizes. For example, if you placed a table into a 2K tablespace and the I/O increases, you can simply move the table into a tablespace with a larger block size. Minimizing I/O by adjusting block sizes is a long iterative process.

Now that you know how to reduce UNIX disk I/O, how do you confirm the I/O reduction? The next section will explore how to extend the UNIX **iostat** utility to monitor disk I/O.

Monitoring UNIX Disk I/O

Monitoring disk I/O is a very important UNIX task that is generally performed by the UNIX system administrator or the Oracle DBA. While those who purchase powerful disk array systems such as EMC are limited to proprietary tools such as Open Symmetric Manager or Navistar, those using generic disk can use the **iostat** utility to monitor disk over time.

Since **iostat** measures I/O at the physical disk level, the Oracle DBA must create the mapping between the physical disks, the UNIX mount points, and the Oracle files. Let's see how this is done.

Building the Oracle File-to-Disk Architecture

If you are not using a block-level block striping mechanism such as RAID 0+1, it is a good idea to map each physical disk spindle directly to a UNIX mount point. For example, here is a sample mapping for a set of triple-mirrored disks:

Mount Point	Main Disk	Mirror 1	Mirror 2
/u01	hdisk31	hdisk41	hdisk51
/u02	hdisk32	hdisk42	hdisk52
/u03	hdisk33	hdisk43	hdisk53
/u04	hdisk34	hdisk44	hdisk54
/u05	hdisk35	hdisk45	hdisk55

By mapping the UNIX mount points directly to physical disks, it becomes easy to know the disk location of a hot Oracle datafile. For example, if your STATSPACK hot file report (in the statspack_alert.sql script) indicates that /u03/oradata/prod/books.dbf is consuming an inordinate amount of I/O, you immediately know that /u03 is getting hit, and that /u03 maps directly to disk hdisk33 and its mirrored disks.

Please note that this mapping technology becomes more complex because of the large size of disk spindles. The trend has been toward creating very large disks, and it is not uncommon to find disks that range from 36GB to 72GB. In these cases, many small Oracle databases will reside on a single physical disk, and load balancing becomes impractical. However, this large-disk issue does not imply that the DBA should abandon disk monitoring simply because all of the files reside on a single disk. Remember, high file I/O can be corrected with the judicious use of the Oracle data buffers. For example, a hot table can be moved into the KEEP pool, thereby caching the data blocks and relieving the hot-disk issue.

It is interesting to note that some products such as EMC have developed methods to internally detect hot files and transparently move them to cooler disks. However, this approach has a problem. Blindly moving a hot datafile to a cooler disk is analogous to pressing into an overstuffed pillow: one area goes in, but another area bulges.

It is never simple in the real world. In the real world, the Oracle DBA may find a specific range of data blocks within a datafile that is getting high I/O, and they will segregate these blocks onto a separate datafile. This relates to the point we made earlier in this chapter that the Oracle DBA must always segregate hot tables and indexes onto separate tablespaces.

If you are not using RAID 0+1 or RAID 5, it is simple to write a dictionary query that will display the mapping of tablespaces-to-files and files-to-UNIX mount points. Note that the data selected from the **dba_data_files** view relies on using the Oracle

Optimal Flexible Architecture (OFA). If you use the OFA, the first four characters of the filename represent the UNIX mount point for the file. You can also adjust the substring function in the query to extract the filename without the full disk path to the file.

Reporting on the Oracle Disk Architecture

If your shop follows the OFA standard, you can write a dictionary query that will report on the disk-to-file mapping for your database. This script assumes that you use OFA names for your datafiles (such as /u02/oradata/xxx.dbf), and that your UNIX mount points map to easily identifiable physical disks. The following script queries the **dba_data_files** view and reports the mapping.

rpt_disk_mapping.sql

```
set pages 999;
set lines 80;

column mount_point heading 'MP';

break on mount_point skip 2;

select
   substr(file_name,1,4) mount_point,
   substr(file_name,21,20) file_name,
   tablespace_name
from
   dba_data_files
group by
   substr(file_name,1,4),
   substr(file_name,21,20) ,
   tablespace_name
;
```

Here is the output from this script. Please note that there is a one-to-one correspondence between Oracle tablespaces, physical datafiles, and UNIX mount points.

```
MP    FILE_NAME             TABLESPACE_NAME
----  -------------------   -----------------------------
/u02  annod01.dbf           ANNOD
      arsd.dbf              ARSD
      bookd01.dbf           BOOKD
      groupd01.dbf          GROUPD
      pagestatsd01.dbf      PAGESTATSD
      rdruserd01.dbf        RDRUSERD
```

```
        subscrd01.dbf          SUBSCRD
        system01.dbf           SYSTEM
        userstatsd01.dbf       USERSTATSD

/u03 annox01.dbf               ANNOX
     bookx01.dbf               BOOKX
     groupx01.dbf              GROUPX
     pagestatsx01.dbf          PAGESTATSX
     perfstat.dbf              PERFSTAT
     rbs01.dbf                 RBS
     rdruserx01.dbf            RDRUSERX
     subscrx01.dbf             SUBSCRX
     temp01.dbf                TEMP
     tools01.dbf               TOOLS
     userstatsx01.dbf          USERSTATSX
```

Extending STATSPACK for Disk I/O Data

Our data collection approach relies on I/O information from Oracle and from the physical disks. We will start by using existing STATSPACK tables, but we will also extend STATSPACK to add the disk I/O information. You will use the UNIX **iostat** utility to capture detailed disk I/O because almost every dialect of UNIX has the **iostat** utility. However, there is a dialect issue. Just as **vmstat** has different dialects, **iostat** is slightly different in each version of UNIX, and the Oracle DBA will need to customize a data collection mechanism according to their requirements. Even within the same dialect, there are arguments that can be passed to the **iostat** utility that change the output display.

The UNIX iostat Utility

The UNIX **iostat** command syntax looks like this:

```
iostat <seconds between samples> <number of samples>
```

For example, to request five samples spaced at ten seconds apart, you would issue the command as follows:

```
iostat -t 10 5
```

Unlike the **vmstat** utility, where all of the data is displayed on one line, the **iostat** output will have many lines per snapshot, one for each physical disk. Let's take a short tour of the different dialects of the **iostat** command. We will begin by showing differences between **iostat** for Solaris and HP-UX, and then show a method for extending STATSPACK to capture STATSPACK data for AIX servers.

Using iostat on AIX

root> **iostat 1 1**

tty:	tin	tout	cpu:	% user	% sys	% idle	% iowait
	0.0	73	1.0	44.0	56.0	0.0	0.0

Disks:	% tm_act	Kbps	tps	Kb_read	Kb_wrtn	
hdisk0	17.0	44.0	11.0	44	0	
hdisk1	33.0	100.0	25.0	100	0	
hdisk2	15.0	60.0	14.0	56	4	
hdisk3	16.0	76.0	19.0	76	0	
hdisk4	0.0	0.0	0.0	0	0	
hdisk5	0.0	0.0	0.0	0	0	

Here you see each of the disks displayed on one line. For each disk you see:

- The percentage **tm_act**
- The kilobytes per second of data transfer
- The number of disk transactions per second
- The number of kilobytes read and written during the snapshot period

Using iostat on HP-UX

root> **iostat 1 5**

device	bps	sps	msps
c1t6d0	0	0.0	1.0
c2t6d0	0	0.0	1.0
c11t11d0	0	0.0	1.0
c7t11d0	0	0.0	1.0
c11t10d0	0	0.0	1.0
c7t10d0	0	0.0	1.0
c5t10d0	0	0.0	1.0
c10t10d0	0	0.0	1.0
c11t9d0	0	0.0	1.0
c7t9d0	0	0.0	1.0
c5t9d0	0	0.0	1.0
c10t9d0	0	0.0	1.0

```
    c11t8d0       0      0.0      1.0
     c7t8d0       0      0.0      1.0
     c5t8d0       0      0.0      1.0
    c10t8d0       0      0.0      1.0
    c5t11d0       0      0.0      1.0
   c10t11d0       0      0.0      1.0
    c5t12d0       0      0.0      1.0
    c7t12d0       0      0.0      1.0
   c10t12d0       0      0.0      1.0
   c11t12d0       0      0.0      1.0
```

In the HP-UX output, you see the following columns:

- Device name

- Kilobytes transferred per second

- Number of seeks per second

- Milliseconds per average seek

Using iostat on Solaris

```
root> iostat 1 5
    tty         sd0              sd1              sd6             sd35            cpu
 tin tout kps tps serv  kps tps serv  kps tps serv  kps tps serv  us sy wt id
   0    6  53   6   10    0   0    0    0   0    0    0   0    0    0  0  2 97
   0  234   0   0    0    0   0    0    0   0    0    0   0    0    1  0  0 99
   0   80  24   3   10    0   0    0    0   0    0    0   0    0    0  2  2 97
   0   80 120  15    8    0   0    0    0   0    0    0   0    0    0  0  6 94
   0   80   0   0    0    0   0    0    0   0    0    0   0    0    0  0  0 100
```

Unlike the **iostat** output for HP-UX, here you see each disk presented horizontally across the output. You see disks sd0, sd1, sd6, and sd35.

The **-x** option of the HP-UX **iostat** utility changes the output from vertical to horizontal. For each disk, you report the reads per second, writes per second, and percentage disk utilization.

```
root> iostat -x 1 3
                    extended device statistics
    device    r/s    w/s    kr/s   kw/s wait actv  svc_t  %w  %b
    sd0       0.0    6.5    1.2    51.6  0.0  0.1    9.6   0   4
    sd1       0.0    0.0    0.0     0.0  0.0  0.0    0.0   0   0
    sd6       0.0    0.0    0.0     0.0  0.0  0.0    0.0   0   0
    sd35      0.0    0.0    0.0     0.0  0.0  0.0    0.0   0   0
    nfs1      0.0    0.0    0.0     0.0  0.0  0.0    0.0   0   0
```

```
                  extended device statistics
device      r/s     w/s    kr/s    kw/s wait actv   svc_t   %w   %b
sd0         0.0    16.9     0.0   135.3  0.0  0.2    12.3    0    9
sd1         0.0     0.0     0.0     0.0  0.0  0.0     0.0    0    0
sd6         0.0     0.0     0.0     0.0  0.0  0.0     0.0    0    0
sd35        0.0     0.0     0.0     0.0  0.0  0.0     0.0    0    0
nfs1        0.0     0.0     0.0     0.0  0.0  0.0     0.0    0    0
                  extended device statistics
device      r/s     w/s    kr/s    kw/s wait actv   svc_t   %w   %b
sd0         0.0     0.0     0.0     0.0  0.0  0.0     0.0    0    0
sd1         0.0     0.0     0.0     0.0  0.0  0.0     0.0    0    0
sd6         0.0     0.0     0.0     0.0  0.0  0.0     0.0    0    0
sd35        0.0     0.0     0.0     0.0  0.0  0.0     0.0    0    0
nfs1        0.0     0.0     0.0     0.0  0.0  0.0     0.0    0    0
```

Now that you see the differences between the dialects of **iostat**, let's see how this information can be captured into STATSPACK extension tables.

Defining the STATSPACK Table

Because the **iostat** utility is different on every server, you need to create separate versions of a shell script to capture the disk information. Regardless of the differences in display format, a single Oracle table can be defined to hold the **iostat** information. Here is the syntax for this table:

```
drop table perfstat.stats$iostat;

create table
perfstat.stats$iostat
(
    snap_time           date,
    elapsed_seconds     number(4),
    hdisk               varchar2(8),
    kb_read             number(9,0),
    kb_write            number(9,0)
)
tablespace perfstat
storage (initial 20m next 1m )
;

create index
    perfstat.stats$iostat_date_idx
on
    perfstat.stats$iostat
    (snap_time)
tablespace perfstat
storage (initial 5m next 1m)
```

```
;

create index
   perfstat.stats$iostat_hdisk_idx
on
   perfstat.stats$iostat
   (hdisk)
tablespace perfstat
storage (initial 5m next 1m)
;
```

Capturing the iostat Information

The get_iostat.ksh script is a UNIX shell script that collects disk-level I/O information at five-minute intervals. It runs the **iostat** utility and captures the output into the iostat table, using the data from the vol_grp table to create the sum_iostat table as well. Once you've run this script, you have the data required to identify your system's hot disks and mount points.

get_iostat_solaris.ksh

```ksh
#!/bin/ksh

while true
do
   iostat -x  300 1|\
      sed 1,2d|\
      awk  '{ printf("%s %s %s\n", $1, $4, $5) }' |\
   while read HDISK VMSTAT_IO_R VMSTAT_IO_W
   do

      if [ $VMSTAT_IO_R -gt 0 ] and [ $VMSTAT_IO_W -gt 0 ]
      then
         sqlplus -s perfstat/perfstat <<!
         insert into
            perfstat.stats\$iostat
         values
            (SYSDATE, 5, '$HDISK', $VMSTAT_IO_R,$VMSTAT_IO_W);
         exit
!
      fi
   done
   sleep 300

done
```

Note that this script does not store **iostat** rows where the values for reads and writes are zero. This is because the stats$iostat table will grow very rapidly, and it is only useful to keep nonzero information. To keep the **iostat** utility running, you can add a script to your crontab file:

```
#!/bin/ksh

# First, we must set the environment . . . .
ORACLE_SID=prodz1
ORACLE_HOME=`cat /var/opt/oracle/oratab|grep $ORACLE_SID|cut -f2 -d':'`
PATH=$ORACLE_HOME/bin:$PATH
MON=`echo ~oracle/iostat`

#-----------------------------------------
# If it is not running, then start it . . .
#-----------------------------------------
check_stat=`ps -ef|grep get_iostat|wc -l`;
oracle_num=`expr $check_stat`
if [ $oracle_num -ne 2 ]
 then nohup $MON/get_iostat_solaris.ksh > /dev/null 2>&1 &
fi
```

Once the scripts are created, an entry can be placed into the crontab file to ensure that the **iostat** monitor is always running. The following is a sample of this crontab file:

```
#******************************************************************
# This is the daily iostat collector & report for the DBAs and SAs
#******************************************************************
00 * * * * /home/oracle/iostat/run_iostat_solaris.ksh > \
/home/oracle/iostat/r.lst
```

Generally, you should synchronize the STATSPACK snapshots and get_iostat.ksh so that the file-level and disk-level data are collected during the same time periods. You can run both scripts as often as you like, and you can collect data over long periods of time without adverse effects on database performance. STATSPACK collects file I/O information very quickly from the Oracle database's system global area (SGA) memory. (The actual memory structures that contain the file I/O data are called v$filestat and file$.) The disk I/O data collection is also very fast, usually taking less than one second.

One drawback of this approach is that the data collection tables will eventually become very large. However, you can manage table size by deleting low-I/O datafile entries. For example, you could delete inactive-file entries with the following SQL:

```
delete from perfstat.stats$iostat
where phys_read < 10 and phys_write < 10;
```

Bear in mind that deleting these entries will skew long-term averages, since the averages will be based only on higher-activity entries.

Although the information collected in **stats$iostat** and **stats$filestatxs** is somewhat redundant, the two sets of disk data complement each other. When the **iostat** results identify a hot mount point, you can turn to the **stats$filestatxs** results to look at the activity for each datafile residing on the mount point. The **stats$filestatxs** results also provide more in-depth information, including the overall time required to perform the reads and writes. From elapsed-time information, you can quickly identify the files that are waiting on disk I/O and see the actual number of physical reads and writes.

Now that you see how to extend **iostat** for disk information, let's look at some other useful STATSPACK reports that can provide insight into your I/O subsystem.

Generating iostat Reports

Having a wealth of I/O data will be very useful in the process of disk load balancing, but this data is also useful for spotting trends. An application's disk access patterns can vary greatly according to daily or weekly processing needs, so the optimal file placement may not always be obvious. (For example, hdisk32 might be very busy during evening batch processing but largely idle during daytime processing.) And it's possible that relocating a datafile may relieve I/O contention for one process only to cause contention for an unrelated process.

In practice, disk load balancing takes several iterations of moving files to find the most workable overall file arrangement. Generally, however, the process of load balancing is well worth the time. Once you have achieved a fairly balanced load, you won't need to move the files unless new processes change the I/O pattern for the disks.

Nonetheless, isolating bottlenecks can be time-consuming and elusive. With the scripts and tables detailed in this section, you can quickly set up a procedure to provide the maximum information you can use for balancing your I/O load and minimizing disk I/O, which is key to keeping response times low. Strategies such as load balancing can go a long way toward improving the speed of your applications and keeping users happy across your network.

Using the I/O information from the stats$iostat table, you can generate trend and alert reports. Both types of reports are easy to generate using SQL, and the combination of the reports will help you identify current bottlenecks as well as spot potential future ones:

■ **High disk I/O** For each five-minute interval, this report displays the name of any Oracle database file with an I/O value—defined in this case by number of reads—that is more than 50 percent of the total I/O during that interval.

■ **High file I/O** The alert reports, on the other hand, are intended to identify current bottleneck possibilities—that is, specific datafiles experiencing a disproportionate amount of I/O (for example, those experiencing 20 percent more activity than the average for the mount point).

Often, companies use automated procedures to generate the alert reports and e-mail them to the DBA staff so they can move these files to less-active mount points as soon as possible.

The following script will generate a sum of all of the I/O, summed by day, hour, or every five minutes.

rpt_disk.sql

```
column hdisk              format a10;
column mydate             format a15;
column sum_kb_read        format 999,999;
column sum_kb_write       format 999,999;

set pages 999;

break on hdisk skip 1;

select
   hdisk,
--   to_char(snap_time,'yyyy-mm-dd HH24:mi:ss') mydate,
--   to_char(snap_time,'yyyy-mm-dd HH24') mydate,
   to_char(snap_time,'day') mydate,
   sum(kb_read)  sum_kb_read,
   sum(kb_write) sum_kb_write
from
   stats$iostat
group by
   hdisk
   ,to_char(snap_time,'day')
--   ,to_char(snap_time,'yyyy-mm-dd HH24:mi:ss')
--   ,to_char(snap_time,'yyyy-mm-dd HH24')
;
```

Here is the daily summary of disk activity from this script. Note that you see a clear picture of disk I/O activity by physical disk, and you see the changes by the day of the week:

```
HDISK        MYDATE            SUM_KB_READ SUM_KB_WRITE
----------   ----------------  ----------- ------------
atf0         tuesday                    33        1,749
             wednesday                 150        7,950

atf2         tuesday                     0            4

atf289       tuesday                    33          330
             wednesday                 150        1,500

atf291       tuesday                     0            0

atf293       tuesday                    32        1,696
             wednesday                 150        7,950

atf4         tuesday                     0            0

atf6         tuesday                     1           10

atf8         tuesday                     0            0

sd0          tuesday                    96          160
             wednesday                 450          750
```

Note that this script allows the display of **iostat** information using several different data formats:

```
to_char(snap_time,'day')
to_char(snap_time,'yyyy-mm-dd HH24:mi:ss')
to_char(snap_time,'yyyy-mm-dd HH24')
```

To change the aggregation of the display information, simply substitute the date format. For example, to see the I/O aggregated by the hour of the day, you substitute the 'day' format string with the 'HH24' format string. Here is the same report aggregating by hour of the day:

```
HDISK        MYDATE            SUM_KB_READ SUM_KB_WRITE
----------   ----------------  ----------- ------------
atf0         2000-12-26 21               9          477
             2000-12-26 22              12          636
             2000-12-26 23             112        14636
             2000-12-27 07             382         3636
```

	2000-12-27 08	433	641
atf2	2000-12-26 21	0	4
atf289	2000-12-26 21	9	90
	2000-12-26 22	12	120
	2000-12-26 23	132	5655
atf291	2000-12-26 21	0	0
atf293	2000-12-26 21	8	424
	2000-12-26 22	12	636
	2000-12-26 23	412	1646
	2000-12-27 00	574	4745
	2000-12-27 01	363	3736
	2000-12-27 02	332	432
atf4	2000-12-26 21	23	23
atf6	2000-12-26 21	1	10
atf8	2000-12-26 21	0	9
sd0	2000-12-26 21	24	40
	2000-12-26 22	36	60

Now let's wrap up this chapter with a review of the major concepts regarding UNIX files with Oracle.

Conclusion

This chapter has been concerned with the use of UNIX commands to manage Oracle files and the tools used by the Oracle DBA in UNIX to monitor and reduce disk I/O. The main points of this chapter include the following:

■ The Oracle Optimal Flexible Architecture (OFA) allows for UNIX directories to contain trace files, core dump files, audit files and archived redo log file. It is the job of the Oracle DBA to monitor and manage these UNIX files.

■ UNIX has useful **find** and **grep** commands that can be used to quickly locate specific Oracle files and scripts in UNIX.

■ UNIX provides the **-exec** and **xargs** commands to allow for the deletion of a list of Oracle filenames.

- Many UNIX Oracle DBAs create UNIX crontab files to perform general maintenance on Oracle UNIX files.

- Disk I/O is the single most expensive component of Oracle response time. It is the job of the Oracle DBA to ensure that all SQL executes with a minimum of I/O.

- Oracle DBAs often use the CTAS command to move tables to new tablespaces with different block sizes. The average row length and the nature of SQL queries dictates the optimal block size for rows in an Oracle table.

- The CTAS command can be used with the **order by** clause or an index hint to resequence Oracle rows into the same order as the primary index. This can greatly reduce disk I/O.

- The UNIX **iostat** utility offers details about physical disk I/O.

- UNIX scripts can be written to capture the **iostat** information inside STATSPACK extension tables.

Next, let's look at some very useful server reports that can be generated from Oracle statistics.

CHAPTER
9

Oracle Server
Exception Reports
in UNIX

his chapter is concerned with monitoring UNIX server events for the Oracle DBA. There are several sources of UNIX server information, with some data captured within Oracle, while other data can be captured using UNIX utilities such as the **vmstat** utility. We have already discussed capturing the **vmstat** information inside Oracle in Chapter 3, and we are now ready to broaden the scope and look at scripts to monitoring the UNIX file systems for Oracle. This chapter will cover the following topics:

- Scheduling and customizing Oracle alert reports

- Oracle trace file alert reports

- A real-time check for Oracle problems

Let's start by reviewing how to customize and schedule Oracle alerts for UNIX.

Scheduling and Customizing Oracle Alert Reports

In a UNIX environment, the Oracle DBA can easily control the times when the STATSPACK alert reports are executed. Let's begin by examining a UNIX crontab file that schedules these reports.

Introduction to crontab

The UNIX **crontab** utility is used to schedule Oracle tasks in a UNIX environment. Every UNIX user (as defined in the /etc/passwd file) is allowed to create their own crontab file and schedule UNIX tasks. In an Oracle environment, all Oracle tasks are scheduled on the crontab of the UNIX **oracle** user. There are two main commands that are used in UNIX to view and modify the crontab file:

- **crontab -l**   This lists the contents of the crontab file.

- **crontab -e**   This places you in your default editor (usually vi) and loads the current crontab file for that current UNIX user.

The **crontab** utility has a simple scheduling function, shown in Table 9-1. The best way to understand the **crontab** columns is to use some examples. The following **crontab** entry will submit a job every hour at five minutes past the hour:

```
05 * * * * /home/run_job.ksh > /home/r.1st
```

Column	Function
1	Minute
2	Hour
3	Day
4	Month
5	Weekday

TABLE 9-1. *crontab Scheduling Columns*

This **crontab** entry will submit a task every day at 7:15 A.M.:

```
15 7 * * * /home/run_job.ksh > /home/v.lst
```

This **crontab** entry will submit a task every Tuesday (day 2) at 2:39 P.M.:

```
39 14 2 * * /home/run_job.ksh > /home/v.lst
```

In each column, you can separate executions by placing several values within commas.

In the following example, you schedule a job to run every 15 minutes, at minutes 00, 15, 30 and 45:

```
00,15,30,45 * * * * /home/run_job.ksh > /home/v.lst
```

You can also list ranges of values by using a hyphen. Here, you schedule a task to run at 8:05 A.M. on weekdays (days 1–5):

```
05 8 1-5 * * /home/run_job.ksh > /home/v.lst
```

Here is an example of a task that runs every hour at 15 minutes past each hour, but only on weekends (days 0 and 6):

```
15 * 0,6* * /home/run_job.ksh > /home/v.lst
```

In a more sophisticated example, here you schedule a task to run every five minutes on weekdays (days 1–5):

```
#*************************************************************
# This is the every 5 min. trace file alert report for the DBAs
#*************************************************************
```

```
1,3,5,7,9,11,13,15,17,19,21,23,25,27,29,31,33,35,37,39,41,43,45,
47,49,51,53,5,57,59 * 1-5 * * /home/oracle/check_filesystem_size.ksh >
dev/null >&1
```

Using crontab with Oracle

The following is a sample of a UNIX crontab file that is used to schedule
STATSPACK reports and alert scripts:

```
#***************************************************************
# This is the weekly table and index analyze job for the CBO
#***************************************************************
30 7 1 * * /home/analyze.ksh > /home/analyze.lst
#***************************************************************
# This is the weekly (Monday) object analyze and report for management
#***************************************************************
30 7 * * 1 /home/oracle/obj_stat/get_object_stats.ksh prodb1
00 8 * * 1 /home/obj_stat/run_object_report.ksh prodb1
#***************************************************************
# This is the daily STATSPACK exception report for the DBAs
#***************************************************************
30 7 * * * /home/statspack/statspack_alert.ksh prodsid
#***************************************************************
# This is the daily generic alert report for the DBAs
#***************************************************************
00 7 * * * /home/mon/oracheck.run prodsid > /home/mon/o.lst
#***************************************************************
# This is the daily vmstat collector & report for the DBAs and SAs
#***************************************************************
00 7 * * * /home/vmstat/run_vmstat.ksh > /home/vmstat/r.lst
05 7 * * * /home/vmstat/run_vmstat_alert.ksh prodsid > /home/vmstat/v.lst
09 7 1 * * /home/vmstat/run_vmstat_weekly_alert.ksh prodb1
***************************************************************
# This is the daily iostat collector & report for the DBAs and SAs
#***************************************************************
#00 7 * * * /home/iostat/run_iostat_solaris.ksh > /home/iostat/r.lst
#00 7 * * * /home/iostat/run_iostat.ksh prodsid > /home/iostat/v.lst
#***************************************************************
# This is the every 5 min. trace file alert report for the DBAs
#***************************************************************
1,3,5,7,9,11,13,15,17,19,21,23,25,27,29,31,33,35,37,39,41,43,45,47,49,51,53,
5,57,59 * * * /home/mon/trace_alert.ksh prodsid > /dev/null 2>&1
#***************************************************************
# This code ensures that the daemon to check for buffer busy waits
# is always running.
#***************************************************************
30 7 * * * /home/mon/run_busy.ksh > /dev/null 2>&1
```

You also need to modify these reports to send the information via e-mail to the
appropriate person. The alert reports are designed to spool the output to a known
filename. The DBA just needs to modify the commands that send the e-mail alert to
customize the recipients' e-mail addresses.

Let's look at how this works. The Korn shell code that follows checks the size of
the alert report and mails the report to the DBA if alerts were detected by the script:

```
var=`cat /tmp/statspack_alert.lst|wc -l`

if [[ $var -gt 1 ]];
    then
    echo
    "**********************************************************************"
    echo "There are alerts"
    cat /tmp/statspack_alert.lst|mailx -s "Statspack Alert" \
    don@oracle.com \
    curley@us.oracle.com \
    james@us.oracle.com
    echo
    "**********************************************************************"
 exit
fi
```

Next, let's look at how you can identify and e-mail Oracle trace files to the DBA
and developers.

Oracle Trace File Alert Report

This is a great script for instantly notifying the DBA and developers of the presence
of trace files. In a production environment, this script can be used to alert the DBA
to production aborts, and it is also useful in development environments, where
developers can be e-mailed their trace file dumps when a program aborts. This
script is generally executed every five minutes.

The trace_alert.ksh script interrogates the Oracle datafile systems to find the
locations of all trace and dump files. It then checks these directories and e-mails
any trace files to the appropriate staff member. Let's take a close look at the steps
in this script.

Set the Environment

The first part of the script ensures that a valid ORACLE_SID is passed to the script:

```
#!/bin/ksh

#*******************************************************
# Exit if no first parameter $1 is passed to script
#*******************************************************
if [ -z "$1" ]
```

```
then
   echo "Usage: trace_alert.ksh <ORACLE_SID>"
   exit 99
fi

#*******************************************************
# First, we must set the environment . . . .
#*******************************************************
ORACLE_SID=$1
export ORACLE_SID
ORACLE_HOME=`cat /var/opt/oracle/oratab|grep $ORACLE_SID:|cut -f2 -d':'`
export ORACLE_HOME
ORACLE_BASE=`echo $ORACLE_HOME | sed -e 's:/product/.*::g'`
export ORACLE_BASE
export DBA=$ORACLE_BASE/admin;
export DBA
PATH=$ORACLE_HOME/bin:$PATH
export PATH
MON=`echo ~oracle/mon`
export MON
```

Get Environment Information

Next, you get the name of the database server and the current date:

```
#*******************************************************
# Get the server name & date for the e-mail message
#*******************************************************
SERVER=`uname -a|awk '{print $2}'`

MYDATE=`date +"%m/%d %H:%M"`


#*******************************************************
# Remove the old file list
#*******************************************************
rm -f /tmp/trace_list.lst
touch /tmp/trace_list.lst
```

Get the Names of Any Recent Trace or Dump Files

This section issues the UNIX **find** command to locate any Oracle trace or dump files that were created in the past day:

```
#*******************************************************
# list the full-names of all possible dump files . . . .
#*******************************************************
find $DBA/$ORACLE_SID/bdump/*.trc   -mtime -1 -print >> /tmp/trace_list.lst
find $DBA/$ORACLE_SID/udump/*.trc   -mtime -1 -print >> /tmp/trace_list.lst
find $ORACLE_HOME/rdbms/log/*.trc   -mtime -1 -print >> /tmp/trace_list.lst
```

Exit Immediately If No Files Found

This section exits right away if there are no files to e-mail to the DBA and developers:

```
#*******************************************************
# Exit if there are not any trace files found
#*******************************************************
NUM_TRACE=`cat /tmp/trace_list.lst|wc -l`
oracle_num=`expr $NUM_TRACE`
if [ $oracle_num -lt 1 ]
 then
 exit 0
fi

#echo $NUM_TRACE files found
#cat /tmp/trace_list.lst
```

E-mail the Trace Files

This section of the code extracts the first 100 lines of each trace and dump file and e-mails them to the DBA and developer staff:

```
#*******************************************************
# for each trace file found, send DBA an e-mail message
#  and move the trace file to the /tmp directory
#*******************************************************
cat /tmp/trace_list.lst|while read TRACE_FILE
do

    #*************************************************
    #  This gets the short file name at the end of the full path
    #*************************************************
    SHORT_TRACE_FILE_NAME=`echo $TRACE_FILE|awk -F"/" '{ print $NF }'`
    #*************************************************
    #  This gets the file location (bdump, udump, log)
    #*************************************************
    DUMP_LOC=`echo $TRACE_FILE|awk -F"/" '{ print $(NF-1) }'`

    #*************************************************
    # send an e-mail to the administrator
    #*************************************************

    head -100 $TRACE_FILE|\
    mailx -s "$ORACLE_SID Oracle trace file at $MYDATE."\
       don@remote-dba.net\
       terry@oracle.net\
       tzu@oracle.com
```

Move the Trace File

The final step is to move the trace or dump file from its current location to the UNIX /tmp directory. This keeps the dump file locations from getting clogged and ensures that the trace file is periodically deleted. Most UNIX administrators remove files from the /tmp directory after they are seven days old.

```
#****************************************************
# Move the trace file to the /tmp directory
# This prevents multiple messages to the developers
# and allows the script to run every minute
#****************************************************

cp $TRACE_FILE /tmp/${DUMP_LOC}_${SHORT_TRACE_FILE_NAME}
rm -f $TRACE_FILED
```

```
done
```

Next, let's look at a generic alert script that can be used on non-database servers to e-mail alerts when a program on a Web server aborts.

Web Server Alert Report

In a production Web environment, it is often useful to alert the staff whenever an Oracle-related program aborts. This script is generally executed via a **cron** every five minutes, and this code can be extended to locate core or trace files in any UNIX file location. In this example, the webserver_alert.ksh script can be customized to search the dump file location for any Pro*C, C++, or Perl programs. This script requires the following modifications:

- Change the e-mail addresses to match the people who want to be notified of program dumps.

- Change /usr/src/asp/core to the name and location of core files on your Web server.

This is a simple but quite important script. It searches for a core file and instantly e-mails it to alert the staff about a production abort.

webserver_alert.ksh

```
#!/bin/ksh

MYDATE=`date +"%Y%m%d"`
```

```
SERVER=`uname -a|awk '{print $2}'`

if [ -f /usr/src/asp/core ]
then

    # Move the file to a dated location . . .
    mv /usr/src/asp/core /tmp/core_$MYDATE

    # send an e-mail to the administrator
    head /tmp/core_$MYDATE|\
    mail -s "EMERGENCY - WebServer $SERVER abort in /tmp/core_$MYDATE"\
        don@burleson.cc\
        omar@oracle.com\
        carlos@oracle.com

fi
```

As you can see, this type of script instantly alerts Oracle developers of the presence of trace files, and e-mails them the information that they need to solve the production problem. Next, let's look at a real-time alert script that can warn the DBA about impending problems in the Oracle environment.

A Real-Time Check for Oracle Problems

The oracheck.run script is usually scheduled to run hourly in a production environment to report on any exception condition that may jeopardize the Oracle database. This script is quite sophisticated and contains four parameter files that control the level of reporting. The parameter files for this script include:

■ **parm_mount_point_kb_free.ora** This file contains the threshold for any Oracle mount point. If you are using tablespaces with AUTOEXTEND ON, you must constantly monitor the UNIX mount points to prevent Oracle from hanging on a failure to extend problem.

■ **parm_ts_free.ora** This file contains the threshold for reporting on full tablespaces.

■ **parm_num_extents.ora** This file contains the number by which a table or index's extents cannot exceed. For example, placing 600 in this file will cause the DBA to be e-mailed when any object exceeds 600 extents.

■ **parm_alert_log.ora**   This file contains alert log messages that should be reported to the DBA. The following is a common list for this file:

```
>cat parm_alert_log.ora
ORA-00600
ORA-1631
ORA-1650
ORA-1652
ORA-1653
ORA-00447
ORA-00603
ORA-01092
ORA-02050
ORA-1535
```

■ **oracheck.run**   This is a Korn shell script that reports on anything that might cause the database to hang up or crash. The idea behind this script is to allow the DBA to repair impending problems before that database crashes. Here are the checks that are performed by this script:

■ **Alert log messages**   This script e-mails any alert log messages that are found in the alert log. The parameter file parm_alert_log.ora contains a list of alert log messages to be reported.

■ **Low free space in archived redo log directory**   If the archived redo log directory becomes full, your Oracle database will hang up. This alert allows the Oracle DBA to add space before the database hangs.

■ **UNIX mount point space alert**   This script checks all datafile mount points in Oracle, including the UNIX Oracle home directory. Since most databases now use AUTOEXTEND ON, the DBA must be constantly alert for file systems that may not be able to extend. If the free space in any mount point is less than specified in parm_mount_point_kb_free.ora, an e-mail alert will be sent to the DBA.

■ **Object cannot extend**   This report will alert the Oracle DBA whenever an Oracle table or index does not have room to take another extent. This alert is obsolete if you are using tablespaces with AUTOEXTEND ON, but many DBAs still keep this alert because they want to monitor the growth of the database tables and indexes.

■ **Tablespace > nn% free**   This report sends an e-mail alert whenever any tablespaces contain less space than specified by parm_ts_free.ora.

Again, this alert is obsolete when using AUTOEXTEND ON, but many DBAs still want to see the available space within each tablespace.

- **Object > nnn extents**   This report is very useful for reporting tables and indexes that experience unexpected growth. Whenever a table or index exceeds the number defined in parm_num_extents.ora, an e-mail alert will be sent to the DBA.

Here is an actual sample of the e-mail output from this script:

```
NON-EMERGENCY ALERT. Mount point /usr has less than 250000 K-Bytes free.
```

The full text for the oracheck.run script and the get_dict_parm.sql script is located at the Oracle Press web site at http://www.oraclepressbooks.com/.
For the purpose of illustration, we have broken this script into subcomponents.

Preliminary Checking and Set-up

Here is the first section of the oracheck.run script. This section of the script ensures that a proper $ORACLE_SID has been passed to the script. You do this by comparing the passed value to the $ORACLE_SID in the oratab file. Note that for Solaris, you need to change the /etc directory to the /var/opt/oracle directory.

```ksh
#!/bin/ksh

# Ensure that the parms have been passed to the script
if [ -z "$1" ]
then
    echo "Usage: oracheck.run <ORACLE SID>"
    exit 99
fi

var=`cat /etc/oratab|grep -v "#"|cut -d: -f1|grep ${1}|wc -l`

oracle_num=`expr $var`
if [ $oracle_num -ne 1 ]
 then
 echo "The variable ${1} is not a valid ORACLE_SID.  Please retry."
 exit 0
fi

ORACLE_SID=${1}
export ORACLE_SID

ORACLE_HOME=`cat /etc/oratab|grep ^$ORACLE_SID:|cut -f2 -d':'`
export ORACLE_HOME
```

Get the UNIX Home Directory

This section of the script gets the name of the **oracle** UNIX user home directory. You do this by using the **grep** utility to find the line in /etc/passwd for the **oracle** user.

```
#***************************************************************
# Get the Oracle users home directory from /etc/passwd
#***************************************************************
ora_unix_home_dir=`cat /etc/passwd|grep ^oracle|cut -f6 -d':'`
#echo home dir = $ora_unix_home_dir
```

Get the Free Space Limits

This section of the script gathers the minimum allowed free space from your parm_ts_free.ora file. This value will be used to trigger an e-mail alert if the UNIX directory has too little free space.

```
#***************************************************************
# Here we gather the values from the parm files . . .
#***************************************************************
if [ -f ${ora_unix_home_dir}/mon/parm_ts_free_$ORACLE_SID.ora ]
then
    TS_FREE=`cat ${ora_unix_home_dir}/mon/parm_ts_free_$ORACLE_SID.ora`
else
    TS_FREE=`cat ${ora_unix_home_dir}/mon/parm_ts_free.ora`
fi

if [ -f ${ora_unix_home_dir}/mon/parm_num_extents_$ORACLE_SID.ora ]
then
    NUM_EXTENTS=\
`cat ora_unix_home_dir}/mon/parm_num_extents_$ORACLE_SID.ora`
else
    NUM_EXTENTS=`cat ${ora_unix_home_dir}/mon/parm_num_extents.ora`
fi


if [ -f ${ora_unix_home_dir}/mon/parm_mount_point_kb_free_$ORACLE_SID.ora ]
then
    KB_FREE=\
`cat {ora_unix_home_dir}/mon/parm_mount_point_kb_free_$ORACLE_SID.ora`
else
    KB_FREE=`cat ${ora_unix_home_dir}/mon/parm_mount_point_kb_free.ora`
fi
```

Get the E-mail Lists

This section of the script creates a separate e-mail list based on the $ORACLE_SID.
By allowing different e-mail lists for each database, the same script can be run in
large environments where you have dozens of DBAs, each with many databases.
This section ensures that the appropriate DBA gets the alert e-mail message.

```
#*************************************************************
# E-mailx setup
# Here we setup the $dbalist variable to send messages to the right DBA's
#*************************************************************

case $ORACLE_SID in
     "PRODV" )
                 dbalist='steven@oracle.com, joanne@oracle.com,
ngene@oracle.com' ;;
     "PUMP1" )
                 dbalist='shri@oracle.com, \
                 sash@oracle.com, steven@oracle.com, \
                 richard@oracle.com, engene@oracle.com' ;;
esac
```

Terminate the Script if the Database Is Down

This section of the script skips any database that is not running at the time the script
executes. By doing this, you avoid false error messages in a large environment,
where a database might be down for a cold backup or DBA maintenance.

You perform a double check, the first check to see if the PMON background
process is running, and another that attempts a connection to the database. If either
fails, the script terminates.

```
#*************************************************************
# Let's exit immediately if the database is not running . . .
#*************************************************************
check_stat=`ps -ef|grep ${ORACLE_SID}|grep pmon|wc -l`;
oracle_num=`expr $check_stat`
if [ $oracle_num -lt 1 ]
 then
 exit 0
fi


#*************************************************************
# Test to see if Oracle is accepting connections
#*************************************************************
```

```
$ORACLE_HOME/bin/sqlplus -s /<<! > /tmp/check_$ORACLE_SID.ora
select * from v\$database;
exit
!


#****************************************************************
# If not, exit immediately . . .
#****************************************************************
check_stat=`cat /tmp/check_$ORACLE_SID.ora|grep -i error|wc -l`;
oracle_num=`expr $check_stat`
if [ $oracle_num -gt 0 ]
 then
 exit 0
fi
```

Clean Up Old Holding Files

This section of the script removes all of the UNIX files from the last execution of the script. Note that it is a good idea in UNIX to use the /tmp directory. This is because the UNIX system administrator will periodically remove all files in this directory and you do not have to worry about leaving "junk" files in UNIX directories.

```
#****************************************************************
# Remove the prior files from /tmp . . .
#****************************************************************
rm -f /tmp/alert_log_dir_${ORACLE_SID}.ora
rm -f /tmp/log_archive_start_${ORACLE_SID}.ora
rm -f /tmp/log_archive_dest_${ORACLE_SID}.ora
rm -f /tmp/dump*${ORACLE_SID}.ora
rm -f /tmp/ora600_${ORACLE_SID}.ora
rm -f /tmp/arch_${ORACLE_SID}.ora
```

Get Dictionary File Locations

This section of the script executes get_dict_parm.sql to get the values for the archived redo log directory, the location of the alert log, and whether the database is running in ARCHIVELOG mode:

```
#****************************************************************
# Get details from Oracle dictionary
#****************************************************************
$ORACLE_HOME/bin/sqlplus -s /<<!

@${ora_unix_home_dir}/mon/get_dict_parm $ORACLE_HOME $ORACLE_SID

exit
!
```

Here is a listing of the SQL script. Note that it must be called as a subprogram because of the special characters in the script. Also note how it spools the values from the dictionary into the UNIX /tmp directory, where later sections of the script to read the filenames from the /tmp directory. The UNIX filenames are segregated according to the **&&2** parameter, which is set to the value of the $ORACLE_SID. This allows simultaneous executions of this script on UNIX servers that have multiple Oracle databases.

get_dict_parm.sql

```
set linesize 80
set pagesize 0
set echo off
set space 0;

set termout off
set feedback off;
set verify off;

--*****************************************************
spool /tmp/dump_&&2..ora
select
    'cd '||value||'; df -k .|grep ora|awk ''{print $3}'''
from
    v$parameter
where
    name like '%dump%'
и или
    value like '%/%'
;
spool off;

set linesize 500

--*****************************************************
spool /tmp/alert_log_dir_&&2..ora;

select
    value
from
    v$parameter
where
    name = 'background_dump_dest'
;

spool off;
```

```
--*****************************************************
spool /tmp/log_archive_start_&&2..ora;

select
   value
from
   v$parameter
where
   name = 'log_archive_start'
;

spool off;

--*****************************************************
spool /tmp/log_archive_dest_&&2..ora;
select
   substr(value,1,instr(value,'/',-1))
from v$parameter
where
name = 'log_archive_dest'
;

spool off;
```

Get the Fully Qualified UNIX Path Names for Directories

This section of the script gets the full path name for the UNIX directories. The tricky part of this is when Oracle uses a question mark and not the fully qualified UNIX path name to the directory. In this case, you need to prefix the name with the value from the $ORACLE_HOME variable.

```
#****************************************************************
# If the first character of the dump directory is a question-mark (?)
# then replace it with $ORACLE_HOME
#****************************************************************
sed 's/?/$ORACLE_HOME/g' /tmp/dump_$ORACLE_SID.ora > \
   tmp/dump1_$ORACLE_SID.ora

ALERT_DIR=`cat /tmp/alert_log_dir_${ORACLE_SID}.ora|awk '{print $1}'`
export ALERT_DIR
```

```
#*************************************************************
# If the first character of the alert ora directory is a question-mark (?)
# then prefix with $ORACLE_HOME
#*************************************************************

first_char=`echo $ALERT_DIR|grep ^?|wc -l`
first_num=`expr $first_char`
#echo $first_char
if [ $first_num -eq 1 ]
then
  new=`echo $ALERT_DIR|cut -d? -f2`
  ALERT_DIR=${ORACLE_HOME}$new
fi
```

Alert for Bad Messages in the Alert Log

This section of the script inspects the last 400 lines of the alert log and displays any messages that are listed in the parm_alert_log.ora file. The parm file is used because you do not want to disturb the DBA unless you have an important error. Hence, this parm file should be periodically updated to show the latest important errors.

Note that this script uses the UNIX **diff** command to compare the last error listing to the latest listing. This technique prevents the script from e-mailing the same alert error over and over again.

Also note that you use the UNIX remote shell command called **rsh** to copy all alert log messages into a centralized directory (see Figure 9-1). However, not all

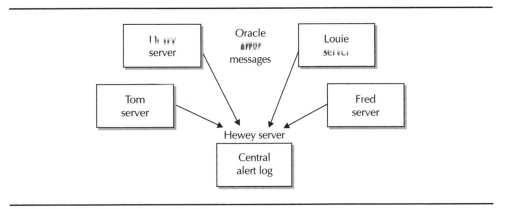

FIGURE 9-1. *Using **rsh** to create a centralized alert file*

environments will allow **rsh** to run on their UNIX servers due to security issues. For these types of Oracle UNIX sites, you can have a server that copies the files via FTP to a centralized directory.

Having a central location for error alerts in a large UNIX environment allows the DBA manager to see exactly what problems are occurring on each UNIX database server:

```
#**********************************************************
# Check alert ora for ORA-600 and other ORA errors
# The list of ORA messages is in the file called parm_alert_log.ora
#**********************************************************

for MSG in `cat ${ora_unix_home_dir}/mon/parm_alert_log.ora`
do
  tail -400 $ALERT_DIR/alert_$ORACLE_SID.log|grep $MSG \
    >> /tmp/ora600_${ORACLE_SID}.ora
done


#**********************************************************
# Only send the alert if there is an error in the output . . . .
#**********************************************************
check_stat=`cat /tmp/ora600_${ORACLE_SID}.ora|wc -l`;
oracle_num=`expr $check_stat`
if [ $oracle_num -ne 0 ]
then
    #**********************************************************
    # Only send the alert if there is a change to the output . . . .
    #**********************************************************
    newm=`diff /tmp/ora600_${ORACLE_SID}.ora \
        /tmp/ora600_${ORACLE_SID}.old|wc -l`
    chgflg=`expr $newm`
    if [ $chgflg -ne 0 ]
    then
        #**********************************************************
        # Mail the message to the DBA's in $dbalist
        #**********************************************************
        cat /tmp/ora600_${ORACLE_SID}.ora|\
            mailx -s "$ORACLE_SID alert log message detected" $dbalist
        #**********************************************************
        # Copy the message to the master log file on sp3db
        #**********************************************************
        echo "$ORACLE_SID ===> `date` - ORA alert log error found." \
          `cat tmp/ora600_${ORACLE_SID}.ora`> logbook/temp$ORACLE_SID
        rcp -p temp$ORACLE_SID  sp3db:/u/oracle/mon/logbook
        rsh sp3db "cat /u/oracle/mon/logbook/temp$host/$ORACLE_SID \
          >> u/oracle/mon/logbook/alert_mon.log"
    fi
```

```
fi

cp /tmp/ora600_${ORACLE_SID}.ora /tmp/ora600_${ORACLE_SID}.old
rm -f /tmp/oracheck_${ORACLE_SID}.ora

# Here we write a blank line to the ora file . . .
echo `date` > /tmp/oracheck_${ORACLE_SID}.ora

#*************************************************************
# Now we run the check, writing errors to the oracheck.ora file
#*************************************************************
~oracle/mon/oracheck.ksh ${ORACLE_SID} ${TS_FREE} ${NUM_EXTENTS} >>
tmp/oracheck_${ORACLE_SID}.ora

#*************************************************************
# This section checks the Oracle mount points
#*************************************************************

#*************************************************************
# Get the Oracle users home directory from /etc/passwd
#*************************************************************
ora_unix_home_dir=`cat /etc/passwd|grep ^oracle|cut -f6 -d':'`
#echo home dir = $ora_unix_home_dir
```

Mark the Dialect Differences for File Space Commands

This section of the script makes the script generic for any UNIX environment. By using the **uname -a** command, you gather the dialect of UNIX and then set an environment variable called **$dialect_df** according to the appropriate space command for that UNIX dialect. This allows the same script to be run in a variety of environments.

```
#*************************************************************
# Set-up the dialect changes for HP/UX and AIX (df -k) vs (bdf)
#*************************************************************
os=`uname -a|awk '{ print $1 }'`
if [ $os = "OSF1" ]
then
    dialect_df="df -k"
fi
if [ $os = "AIX" ]
then
    dialect_df="df -k"
fi
if [ $os = "IRIX64" ]
then
```

```
    dialect_df="df -k"
fi
if [ $os = "HP-UX" ]
then
    dialect_df="bdf"
fi
```

Check the Free Space in the Archived Redo Log Directory

This section of the script checks to see if the database is running in ARCHIVELOG mode, and if so, it uses the UNIX location from **log_archive_dest**, as gathered earlier by the get_dict_parm.sql script:

```
#**************************************************************
# Get the free space from the archived redo log directory
#**************************************************************
LOG_ARCHIVE_START=\
  `cat /tmp/log_archive_start_${ORACLE_SID}.ora|awk '{print $1}'`
export LOG_ARCHIVE_START

#echo $LOG_ARCHIVE_START
if [ $LOG_ARCHIVE_START = 'TRUE' ]
then

    LOG_ARCHIVE_DEST=`cat /tmp/log_archive_dest_${ORACLE_SID}.ora|\
      awk '{print 1}'`
    export LOG_ARCHIVE_DEST

    nohup ${dialect_df} $LOG_ARCHIVE_DEST > \
       /tmp/arch_${ORACLE_SID}.ora 2>&1


    # The above could be not found . . .
    flag1=`cat /tmp/arch_${ORACLE_SID}.ora|grep find|wc -l`
    #**************************************************************
    # If the log archive dest is not found, truncate last entry
    #**************************************************************
    free_space_num=`expr ${flag1}`
    if [ $free_space_num -eq 1 ]
    then
      echo $LOG_ARCHIVE_DEST|sed 's/\/arch//g' > /tmp/arch1_$ORACLE_SID.ora
      LOG_ARCHIVE_DEST=`cat /tmp/arch1_$ORACLE_SID.ora`
    fi
```

```
#  This ugly code is because bdf and df -k
#  have free space in different columns
if [ $os = "IRIX64" ]
then
   arch_dir_mp=`${dialect_df} $LOG_ARCHIVE_DEST|\
       grep -v kbytes|awk '{ print $7 }'`
   arch_free_space=`${dialect_df} ${arch_dir_mp}|\
       grep -v kbytes|awk '{ print $3 }'`
fi
if [ $os = "AIX" ]
then
   arch_dir_mp=`${dialect_df} $LOG_ARCHIVE_DEST|\
       grep -v blocks|awk '{ print $7 }'`
   arch_free_space=`${dialect_df} ${arch_dir_mp}|\
       grep -v blocks|awk '{ print $3 }'`
fi
if [ $os = "OSF1" ]
then
   arch_dir_mp=`${dialect_df} $LOG_ARCHIVE_DEST|\
     grep -v blocks|awk '{ print $7 }'`
   arch_free_space=`${dialect_df} ${arch_dir_mp}|\
     grep -v blocks|awk '{ print $3 }'`
fi
if [ $os = "HP-UX" ]
then
   arch_dir_mp=`${dialect_df} $LOG_ARCHIVE_DEST|\
       grep -v kbytes|awk '{ print $6 }'`
   arch_free_space=`${dialect_df} ${arch_dir_mp}|\
       grep -v kbytes|awk '{ print $4 }'`
fi

#echo $LOG_ARCHIVE_DEST
#echo $arch_dir_mp
#echo $arch_free_space

#*************************************************************
# Now, display if free space is < ${KB_FREE}
#*************************************************************
free_space_num=`expr ${arch_free_space}`
kb_free_num=`expr ${KB_FREE}`
#echo $free_space_num
if [ $free_space_num -lt ${kb_free_num} ]
 then
    #*************************************************************
    # Display a message on the operations console
    #*************************************************************
       echo "NON-EMERGENCY ORACLE ALERT. \
         Mount point ${ora_unix_home_mp1}\
```

```
        has less than ${KB_FREE} K-Bytes free."
   #***************************************************************
      # Copy the message to the master log on sp3db
   #***************************************************************
      echo "$ORACLE_SID ===> `date` - Moint point \
      ${ora_unix_home_mp1} has less than \
      ${KB_FREE} K-bytes free." > logbook/temp$ORACLE_SID
   rcp -p temp$ORACLE_SID  sp3db:/u/oracle/mon/logbook
   rsh sp3db "cat /u/oracle/mon/logbook/temp$ORACLE_SID >> \
      /u/oracle/mon/alert_mon.log"
   exit 67
 fi
fi
```

Check the Free Space
in the UNIX Home Directory

This section of the script gathers the location of the **oracle** user home directory, and then executes the appropriate command, placing the output in a variable called **$ora_unix_home_fr**. This variable can then be interrogated and compared with the allowed value in the parameter file.

```
#***************************************************************
# get the mount point associated with the home directory
#***************************************************************
ora_unix_home_mp=`${dialect_df} ${ora_unix_home_dir}|awk '{ print $7}'`
#echo mp1 = $ora_unix_home_mp
ora_unix_home_mp1=`echo ${ora_unix_home_mp}|awk '{ print $2 }'`

#***************************************************************
# Get the free space for the mount point for UNIX home directory
#***************************************************************
#  This ugly code is because bdf and df -k
#  have free space in different columns
if [ $os = "IRIX64" ]
then
   ora_unix_home_fr=`${dialect_df} ${ora_unix_home_mp1}|awk '{ print $3}'`
fi
if [ $os = "OSF1" ]
then
   ora_unix_home_fr=`${dialect_df} ${ora_unix_home_mp1}|awk '{ print $3}'`
fi
if [ $os = "AIX" ]
then
   ora_unix_home_fr=`${dialect_df} ${ora_unix_home_mp1}|awk '{ print $3}'`
fi
if [ $os = "HP-UX" ]
then
```

```
    ora_unix_home_fr=`${dialect_df} ${ora_unix_home_mp1}|awk '{ print $4}'`
fi
ora_unix_home_fr1=`echo ${ora_unix_home_fr}|awk '{ print $2 }'`
#echo free = $ora_unix_home_fr1

#***************************************************************
# Now, display if free space is < ${KB_FREE}
#***************************************************************
free_space_num=`expr ${ora_unix_home_fr1}`
kb_free_num=`expr ${KB_FREE}`
#echo $free_space_num
if [ $free_space_num -lt ${kb_free_num} ]
 then
    #***********************************************************
    # Display a message on the operations console
    #***********************************************************
    echo "NON-EMERGENCY ORACLE ALERT. Mount point ${ora_unix_home_mp1} \
        has less than ${KB_FREE} K-Bytes free."
    #***********************************************************
    # Copy the message to the master log on sp3db
    #***********************************************************
    echo "$ORACLE_SID ===> `date` - Moint point ${ora_unix_home_mp1}\
        has less than ${KB_FREE} K-bytes free." > logbook/temp$ORACLE_SID
    rcp -p temp$ORACLE_SID  sp3db:/u/oracle/mon/logbook
    rsh sp3db "cat /u/oracle/mon/logbook/temp$ORACLE_SID >>
u/oracle/mon/logbook/alert_mon.log"
    exit 67
fi
```

Check Other UNIX Mount Points

This section of the script executes the commands that you generated in the /tmp/dump1_$ORACLE_SID.ora file. You then loop through the output from this command and send the e-mail alert for any mount point that has less than the accepted value.

```
chmod +x /tmp/dump1_$ORACLE_SID.ora

#***************************************************************
# Now we execute this file to get the free space in the filesystem
#***************************************************************
/tmp/dump1_$ORACLE_SID.ora > /tmp/dump2_$ORACLE_SID.ora

loop-1
#***************************************************************
# Here we loop to get all free space numbers and check each
#***************************************************************
for free_num in `cat /tmp/dump2_$ORACLE_SID.ora`
do
```

```
      #echo loop = $loop
      mp=`cat /tmp/dump1_$ORACLE_SID.ora|awk '{print $2'}`
      mp1=`echo $mp|awk '{print$'$loop'}'`
      #echo point = $mp1
      free_space_num=`expr ${free_num}`
      #echo $free_space_num
      if [ $free_space_num -lt $kb_free_num ]
      then
         #***************************************************************
         # Display a message on the operations console
         #***************************************************************
          echo "NON-EMERGENCY ORACLE ALERT. The mount point for $mp1 has\
              less than ${KB_FREE} K-Bytes free."
         #***************************************************************
         # Copy the message to the master log on sp3db server
         #***************************************************************
          echo "$ORACLE_SID ===> `date` - Moint point ${mp1} less than \
                {KB_FREE} K-Bytes free." > logbook/temp$ORACLE_SID
          rcp -p temp$ORACLE_SID  sp3db:/u/oracle/mon/logbook
          rsh sp3db "cat /u/oracle/mon/logbook/temp$ORACLE_SID >>\
              u/oracle/mon/logbook/alert_mon.log"
          loop="`expr $loop + 1`"
      fi
done


#*****************************************************************
# If errors messages exist (2 or more lines), then go on . . .
#*****************************************************************
if [ `cat /tmp/oracheck_${ORACLE_SID}.ora|wc -l` -ge 2 ]
then
   #***************************************************************
   # Display a message on the operations console
   #***************************************************************
   echo "NON-EMERGENCY ORACLE ALERT. Contact DBA and report error\
       ==>"` cat /tmp/oracheck_${ORACLE_SID}.ora`
   #***************************************************************
   # Copy the message to the master log on sp3db
   #***************************************************************
   echo "$ORACLE_SID ===>" `cat /tmp/oracheck_${ORACLE_SID}.ora`\
       >logbook/temp$ORACLE_SID
   rcp -p temp$ORACLE_SID  sp3db:/u/oracle/logbook
   rsh sp3db "cat /u/oracle/mon/logbook/temp$ORACLE_SID\
       >>u/oracle/mon/logbook/alert_mon.log"
   exit 69
fi
```

Now let's wrap up this chapter with a review of the main concepts.

Conclusion

This chapter has covered the basic tools used by the Oracle DBA to monitor the server environment. In UNIX, there are several file locations that are of interest to the Oracle DBA and developer, and the Oracle DBA can write automated UNIX scripts to locate and e-mail relevant trace files to the DBA and developers.

The main points in this chapter include:

- The Oracle DBA must constantly monitor the production environment for any new trace or dump files, and e-mail them to the appropriate person.

- This monitoring technique can be expanded for application servers, and scripts can be written to capture trace and dump files from Pro*C as well as other app server dump files.

- The Oracle DBA can get many of the UNIX file locations from the Oracle data dictionary and run sophisticated scripts to e-mail the DBA whenever an exception is encountered.

Next, let's move on and take a look at UNIX environmental administration for Oracle.

PART
III

UNIX Administration
for the Oracle DBA

CHAPTER
10

UNIX Environmental
Administration
for Oracle

he following are a collection of useful scripts that will make Oracle administration easier in a UNIX environment. Once the Oracle DBA is comfortable with UNIX programming, there are many great DBA utilities that can be made by combining UNIX commands into scripts. In a large UNIX environment, it is critical that all UNIX servers use the same environmental setting, and the same .profile file for the UNIX **oracle** user. This chapter covers the following topics:

- Managing the UNIX environment for the **oracle** user
- File management commands in UNIX

Managing the UNIX Environment for the oracle User

The Oracle DBA will commonly perform all of their UNIX work when signed on to the UNIX server as the **oracle** user. In large UNIX environments with hundreds of Oracle servers and dozens of Oracle DBAs, it is critical that all UNIX servers have a common look and feel. This is done by creating the following constructs:

- Standard UNIX prompt for the **oracle** user
- Standard command editor
- Standard alias for moving between Oracle directories
- Standard alias name for each $ORACLE_SID

Let's take a look at commands that can be placed into the UNIX .profile script for the **oracle** user. Most large UNIX shops create a standard .profile script for all servers and use the UNIX **rcp** command to distribute the .profile to every Oracle server.

Here is an example of a UNIX script to distribute a standard .profile to every Oracle server:

distr_profile.ksh

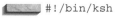
```
#!/bin/ksh

echo 'starting distribution of .profile file'

#*********************************************************************
# We reply on the UNIX /etc/hosts file for a list of Oracle servers
#*********************************************************************
```

```
for host in `cat /etc/hosts|awk '{ print $2 }'`
do
   echo  starting distribution to $host
   rcp -p .profile $host:~oracle/.profile
   rsh $host ls -al ~oracle/.profile
done
```

In this script, you look up each Oracle server name from the /etc/hosts files. Then you loop between each server, using the remote copy command (**rsh**) to copy your standard .profile file to every server. You verify that the copy was successful by using the UNIX **rsh** command to verify the UNIX time and file size for the .profile file. Note that you may need to get your UNIX system administrator to configure the .rhosts files to allow the **rsh** and **rcp** commands to work properly.

A Standard UNIX Prompt

Placing the following setting in your .profile will give you a UNIX prompt that identifies your current server name, the current database name, and current working directory.

This important setting ensures that your Oracle DBA always knows what server and database they are connected to. More important, the Oracle UNIX DBA can easily see the current working directory while still giving the user a full line to enter UNIX commands.

```
#***************************************************************
# Standard UNIX Prompt
#***************************************************************
PS1="
   ꞷꞷꞷ꞉ ꞷꞷꞷ. ꞷ,ꞷ [ꞷꞷꞷꞁꞋꞷ_ꞟꞀꞇ]  \ꞅ{PWD}
>"
```

This prompt has the advantage of displaying the server name, the $ORACLE_SID, and the current directory. It also places the command prompt on the next line so you can have room to type on a new line:

```
diogenes*prodsid-/home/oracle
> pwd

/home/oracle

diogenes*prodsid-/home/oracle
>cd /u01/oradata/prodsid

diogenes*prodsid-/u01/oaradata/prodsid
>
```

Useful UNIX Aliases for Oracle

The following is a list of common UNIX aliases that can be added to the .profile of the UNIX **oracle** user. There are two compelling reasons to use these standard aliases.

In large environments, you may find Oracle file systems that were not installed according to the Oracle Optimal Flexible Architecture (OFA) standard. This is especially true for vendor-installed Oracle systems. The use of standard aliases eliminates the file hunting that commonly occurs on a foreign Oracle server.

For example, once installed, the **alert** alias will reliably display the most recent 100 lines of the alert log file, regardless of the actual location of the file.

```
# UNIX Aliases for the Oracle DBA

    alias alert='tail -100 $DBA/$ORACLE_SID/bdump/alert_$ORACLE_SID.log|more'
    alias arch='cd $DBA/$ORACLE_SID/arch'
    alias bdump='cd $DBA/$ORACLE_SID/bdump'
    alias cdump='cd $DBA/$ORACLE_SID/cdump'
    alias pfile='cd $DBA/$ORACLE_SID/pfile'
    alias rm='rm -i'
    alias sid='env|grep ORACLE_SID'
    alias admin='cd $DBA/admin'
```

To illustrate, here you use the **pfile** alias to quickly change to the UNIX directory that contains the init.ora file:

```
diogenes*prodsid-/home/oracle
> pfile

diogenes*prodsid-/u01/app/oracle/prodsid/pfile
>
```

Standard Aliases for Changing the ORACLE_SID

In environments with older copies of Oracle, you cannot always rely on the **setenv** utility to properly change the $ORACLE_SID. To get around this issue, you can place a loop in your .profile file to loop through every database on your server, creating a UNIX alias with the same name as the $ORACLE_SID:

```
#**************************************************************
# Create an alias for every $ORACLE_SID on the UNIX server
#**************************************************************
```

```
for DB in `cat /var/opt/oracle/oratab|\
    grep -v \#|grep -v \*|cut -d":" -f1`
do
    alias $DB='export ORAENV_ASK=NO; \
    export ORACLE_SID='$DB'; . \
    TEMPHOME/bin/oraenv; \
    export ORACLE_HOME; \
    export ORACLE_BASE=`echo $ORACLE_HOME | sed -e 's:/product/.*::g'`; \
    export DBA=$ORACLE_BASE/admin; \
    export SCRIPT_HOME=$DBA/scripts; export PATH=$PATH:$SCRIPT_HOME; \
    export LIB_PATH=$ORACLE_HOME/lib:$ORACLE_HOME/lib:/usr/lib '
done
```

Once this code is executed, you can use the **alias** command to quickly see the alias for all of the Oracle values on your server:

```
janet*testm1-/export/home/oracle
>alias
alert='tail -100 $DBA/$ORACLE_SID/bdump/alert_$ORACLE_SID.log|more'
arch='cd $DBA/$ORACLE_SID/arch'
bdump='cd $DBA/$ORACLE_SID/bdump'
cdump='cd $DBA/$ORACLE_SID/cdump'
pfile='cd $DBA/$ORACLE_SID/pfile'
sid='env|grep -i sid'
stop='kill -STOP'
suspend='kill -STOP $$'
table='cd $DBA/$ORACLE_SID/ddl/tables'

test9i='export ORAENV_ASK=NO; export ORACLE_SID=test9i; .
TEMPHOME/bin/oraenv; export ORACLE_HOME; export ORACLE_BASE=`echo
ORACLE_HOME | sed -e s:/product/.*::g`; export DBA=$ORACLE_BASE/admin;
xport SCRIPT_HOME=$DBA/scripts; export PATH=$PATH:$SCRIPT_HOME; export
IB_PATH=$ORACLE_HOME/lib:$ORACLE_HOME/lib:/usr/lib '
testmust='export ORAENV_ASK-NO; export ORACLE_SID=testmust; .
TEMPHOME/bin/oraenv; export ORACLE_HOME; export ORACLE_BASE=`echo
ORACLE_HOME | sed -e s:/product/.*::g`; export DBA=$ORACLE_BASE/admin;
xport SCRIPT_HOME=$DBA/scripts; export PATH=$PATH:$SCRIPT_HOME; export
IB_PATH=$ORACLE_HOME/lib:$ORACLE_HOME/lib:/usr/lib '

testm1='export ORAENV_ASK=NO; export ORACLE_SID=testm1; .
TEMPHOME/bin/oraenv; export ORACLE_HOME; export ORACLE_BASE=`echo
ORACLE_HOME | sed -e s:/product/.*::g`; export DBA=$ORACLE_BASE/admin;
xport SCRIPT_HOME=$DBA/scripts; export PATH=$PATH:$SCRIPT_HOME; export
IB_PATH=$ORACLE_HOME/lib:$ORACLE_HOME/lib:/usr/lib '
```

```
testm2='export ORAENV_ASK=NO; export ORACLE_SID=testm2; .
TEMPHOME/bin/oraenv; export ORACLE_HOME; export ORACLE_BASE=`echo
ORACLE_HOME | sed -e s:/product/.*::g`; export DBA=$ORACLE_BASE/admin;
xport SCRIPT_HOME=$DBA/scripts; export PATH=$PATH:$SCRIPT_HOME; export
IB_PATH=$ORACLE_HOME/lib:$ORACLE_HOME/lib:/usr/lib '
```

Once these values are set, you can quickly change your UNIX environment to another $ORACLE_SID. In the following example, you change to the test9i database:

```
janet*testc1-/export/home/oracle
>echo $ORACLE_HOME
/u01/app/oracle/product/8.1.7_64

janet*testc1-/export/home/oracle
>test9i

janet*test9i-/export/home/oracle
>echo $ORACLE_HOME
/u01/app/oracle/product/9.0.1
```

Standard Command History

It is very important to use a common set of UNIX command history and command editing keystrokes. By adding the following command to your .profile, you instruct UNIX to use the **vi** command editor from your UNIX prompt:

```
#****************************************************************
# Keyboard commands
#****************************************************************
stty erase ^?
set -o vi
```

The **set -o vi** command enables the following UNIX keystrokes for quickly locating and re-executing UNIX commands:

- ■ **<esc> k**   Page through previous commands
- ■ **<esc> **   Search the command history for a command with a string
- ■ **<esc> **   Automatic command completion for filenames

Having a common editor between Oracle servers ensures a common look and feel regardless of the current Oracle server.

Next, let's move on and take a closer look at managing UNIX files in the Oracle environment.

File Management Commands in UNIX

There are numerous commands that are required by the Oracle DBA when managing the Oracle files in UNIX. We reviewed the basic UNIX file management commands in Chapter 1, and we are now ready to look at advanced UNIX commands for the Oracle DBA.

Change Default File Permissions with umask

As we noted in Chapter 1, the **umask** and **chmod** commands are often used by the Oracle DBA to allow other UNIX users the ability to read and execute Oracle files.

For example, if you want to create a file with read-write permission for the **oracle** user and read-only permission for everybody else, you can set the **umask** to 022:

```
root> umask 022
root> umask
022

root> touch dumpfile.trc

root> ls -al dumpfile.trc

-rw-r--r--   1 oracle   dba              0 Aug 13 09:36 dumpfile.trc
```

Change File Permissions in UNIX

For another example, say you wanted to allow read-only access to all of the trace files in your user_dump_dest directory in UNIX. This will allow Oracle developers to review their trace files without bothering the Oracle DBA.

```
janet*test9i-/export/home/oracle
>udump

janet*test9i-/u01/app/oracle/admin/test9i/udump
>ls -al
total 76
drwxr-xr-x   2 oracle   dba           2048 Oct 21 01:00 .
drwxr-xr-x   6 oracle   dba             96 Aug 12 19:50 ..
-rw-r-----   1 oracle   dba           2230 Oct  7 01:00 test9i_ora_11777.trc
-rw-r-----   1 oracle   dba           2230 Oct 21 01:00 test9i_ora_14541.trc
-rw-r-----   1 oracle   dba           2230 Sep  9 01:00 test9i_ora_14814.trc
-rw-r-----   1 oracle   dba           2230 Aug 19 01:00 test9i_ora_21031.trc
```

```
-rw-r-----    1 oracle    dba        2230 Oct 14 01:00 test9i_ora_23910.trc
-rw-r-----    1 oracle    dba        2230 Sep 23 01:00 test9i_ora_27041.trc
-rw-r-----    1 oracle    dba        2226 Aug 26 01:00 test9i_ora_517.trc
-rw-r-----    1 oracle    dba        2228 Sep  2 01:00 test9i_ora_6784.trc
-rw-r-----    1 oracle    dba        2228 Sep 30 01:00 test9i_ora_7800.trc

janet*test9i-/u01/app/oracle/admin/test9i/udump
>chmod 644 *.trc

janet*test9i-/u01/app/oracle/admin/test9i/udump
>ls -al
total 76
drwxr-xr-x    2 oracle    dba        2048 Oct 21 01:00 .
drwxr-xr-x    6 oracle    dba          96 Aug 12 19:50 ..
-rw-r--r--    1 oracle    dba        2230 Oct  7 01:00 test9i_ora_11777.trc
-rw-r--r--    1 oracle    dba        2230 Oct 21 01:00 test9i_ora_14541.trc
-rw-r--r--    1 oracle    dba        2230 Sep  9 01:00 test9i_ora_14814.trc
-rw-r--r--    1 oracle    dba        2230 Aug 19 01:00 test9i_ora_21031.trc
-rw-r--r--    1 oracle    dba        2230 Oct 14 01:00 test9i_ora_23910.trc
-rw-r--r--    1 oracle    dba        2230 Sep 23 01:00 test9i_ora_27041.trc
-rw-r--r--    1 oracle    dba        2226 Aug 26 01:00 test9i_ora_517.trc
-rw-r--r--    1 oracle    dba        2228 Sep  2 01:00 test9i_ora_6784.trc
-rw-r--r--    1 oracle    dba        2228 Sep 30 01:00 test9i_ora_7800.trc
```

The **chmod** command also has a set of plus operators (**+**) that can be used to add read (**+r**), write (**+w**), or execute (**+x**) to a file. For example, to make all Korn shell programs in a directory unexecutable for everyone, the following command could be used:

```
root> chmod -x *.ksh

root> ls -al *.ksh

-rw-r--r--    1 oracle    dba         205 Jun 10 09:11 zulu.ksh
-rw-r--r--    1 oracle    dba         303 Jun 10 09:11 alert_ram.ksh
-rw-r--r--    1 oracle    dba         312 Jul 19 11:32 backup_online.ksh
-rw-r--r--    1 oracle    dba         567 Jun 10 09:12 count_rows.ksh
```

Once the maintenance is complete, the script can again be made executable with the **chmod** command:

```
root> chmod +x *.ksh

root> ls -al *.ksh
```

```
-rwxr-xr-x    1 oracle    dba            205 Jun 10 09:11 a.ksh*
-rwxr-xr-x    1 oracle    dba            303 Jun 10 09:11 lert.ksh*
-rwxr-xr-x    1 oracle    dba            312 Jul 19 11:32 back.ksh*
-rwxr-xr-x    1 oracle    dba            567 Jun 10 09:12 coun.ksh*
```

Change File Owners in UNIX

The UNIX **chown** command is used by the Oracle DBA to change the group and owner for UNIX files. There are times when a UNIX developer creates or changes a UNIX file for Oracle and the Oracle DBA must change both the UNIX owner and the UNIX group for a file.

In the following example, you change the owner from **mario** to **oracle** and the UNIX group from **devl** to **dba** for all files in the directory:

```
root> ls -al

total 56
drwxr-sr-x    2 mario     devl           512 Aug 31 1999  ./
drwxr-sr-x    8 mario     devl           512 Apr 13 08:28 ../
-rwxrwxr--    1 mario     devl           819 Jun 23 16:11 initmysid1.ora
-rwxrwxr--    1 mario     devl          4435 Jun 26 15:00 initprodserv1.ora

root> chown oracle:dba *

root> ls -al

total 56
drwxr-sr-x    ? oracle    dba            512 Aug 31 1999  ./
drwxr-sr-x    8 oracle    dba            512 Apr 13 08:00  ./
-rwxrwxr--    1 oracle    dba            819 Jun 23 16:11 initmysid1.ora
-rwxrwxr--    1 oracle    dba          4435 Jun 26 15:00 initprodserv1.ora
```

Create a UNIX Soft Link for Oracle Files

In Oracle environments with multiple $ORACLE_HOME directories, it is often challenging to find certain Oracle parameter files. There are some files such as listener.ora and tnsnames.ora that should only have a single copy on a UNIX server, regardless of how many databases reside on the server.

For example, if you have a UNIX server with Oracle8, Oracle8i, and Oracle9i installed, you may want to create a common location for generic files that are used by every database on the server. These generic files include the following:

- **tnsnames.ora**   Each database server should only have one tnsnames.ora file.

- **listener.ora**   Each server should only have one listener.ora file.

- **sqlnet.ora**   There should only be a single sqlnet.ora file on a server.

To make these singular files, you must trick the Oracle software into thinking that the files are in their default directory ($ORACLE_HOME/network/admin), when in reality they exist in a common directory.

The common directories depend on the dialect of UNIX:

- **/etc**   This is used by HP-UX, Linux, and AIX.

- **/var/opt/oracle**   This directory is used by Solaris.

To create this illusion, the Oracle DBA must use soft links to make each $ORACLE_HOME have access to the proper file (see Figure 10-1).

As we noted, it is important to have a single tnsnames.ora file on each server. In UNIX, the search order for finding the tnsnames.ora file is as follows:

1. Search $TNS_ADMIN.

2. Search /etc (or /var/opt/oracle in Solaris).

3. Search $ORACLE_HOME/network/admin.

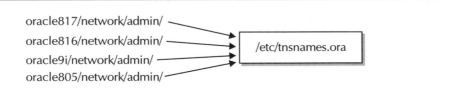

FIGURE 10-1.   *Using the UNIX soft link with Oracle*

The soft links are created by going to each $ORACLE_HOME/network/admin
directory on the UNIX server and using the **ln -s** command to create a soft link for
the tnsnames.ora and listener.ora files:

```
janet*test9i-/export/home/oracle
>cd $ORACLE_HOME/network/admin

janet*test9i-/u01/app/oracle/product/8.1.7_64/network/admin
>ls -al
total 56
drwxr-xr-x   3 oracle    dba            2048 Jul 13 15:43 .
drwxr-xr-x  15 oracle    dba            2048 Jul 12 10:56 ..
-rw-rw-r--   1 oracle    dba             558 Jul 12 10:57 listener.ora
-rw-r--r--   1 oracle    dba             148 Mar  9 2000 shrept.lst
-rw-rw-r--   1 oracle    dba             177 Jul 12 10:57 sqlnet.ora
-rw-rw-r--   1 oracle    dba             348 Jul 12 10:57 tnsname.ora

janet*test9i-/u01/app/oracle/product/8.1.7_64/network/admin
>mv tnsnames.ora tnsnames.old

janet*test9i-/u01/app/oracle/product/8.1.7_64/network/admin
>mv sqlnet.ora sqlnet.old

janet*test9i-/u01/app/oracle/product/8.1.7_64/network/admin
>mv listener.ora listener.old

janet*test9i-/u01/app/oracle/product/8.1.7_64/network/admin
>ln -s /etc/tnsnames.ora

janet*test9i-/u01/app/oracle/product/8.1.7_64/network/admin
>ln -s /etc/sqlnet.ora

janet*test9i-/u01/app/oracle/product/8.1.7_64/network/admin
>ln -s /etc/listener.ora

janet*test9i-/u01/app/oracle/product/8.1.7_64/network/admin
>ls -al
total 56
drwxr-xr-x   3 oracle    dba            2048 Jul 13 15:43 .
drwxr-xr-x  15 oracle    dba            2048 Jul 12 10:56 ..
-rw-rw-r--   1 oracle    dba             558 Jul 12 10:57 listener.old
lrwxrwxrwx   1 oracle    dba              28 Jul 13 15:43 listener.ora ->
```

```
var/opt/oracle/listener.ora
-rw-r--r--   1 oracle    dba              148 Mar  9  2000 shrept.lst
-rw-rw-r--   1 oracle    dba              177 Jul 12 10:57 sqlnet.old
lrwxrwxrwx   1 oracle    dba               26 Jul 13 15:43 sqlnet.ora ->
var/opt/oracle/sqlnet.ora
-rw-rw-r--   1 oracle    dba              348 Jul 12 10:57 tnsname.old
lrwxrwxrwx   1 oracle    dba               28 Jul 13 15:43 tnsnames.ora ->
var/opt/oracle/tnsnames.ora
```

As you can see, these tedious commands can easily be encapsulated into a UNIX script that loops through the /etc/oratab file for each database:

```ksh
#!/bin/ksh
# Loop through each database name on the host /etc/oratab . . .
for db in `cat /etc/oratab|egrep ':N|:Y'|grep -v \*|cut -f1 -d':'`
do
   # Get the ORACLE_HOME for each database
   home=`cat /etc/oratab|egrep ':N|:Y'|grep -v \*|grep ${db}|cut -f2 -d':'`
   echo " "
   echo "database is $db"
   cd $home/dbs
   ln -s /etc/tnsnames.ora
done
```

While this soft link approach is great for multiple Oracle databases in a single UNIX server, most shops have multiple Oracle servers. To keep the standard Oracle files the same on each server, many Oracle DBAs write UNIX scripts to use the **rsh** command to distribute a singular tnsnames.ora file to all Oracle servers.

Copy tnsnames.ora to All UNIX Servers

This is a super-useful UNIX command snippet to distribute common files to all servers. As we have noted, this script requires the .rhosts setup to allow the UNIX **rcp** and **rsh** commands:

```ksh
#!/bin/ksh

echo 'starting distribution of tnanames.ora'

# Note: dbnames file is in the form HOST DATABASE
for host in `cat dbnames|awk '{ print $2 }'`
do
    db=`cat dbnames|awk '{ print $1 }'`
```

```
    echo       starting distr to $host
    rcp -p tnsnames.ora $host:/etc/tnsnames.ora
    rsh $host ls -al /etc/tnsnames.ora
done
```

Note that this script uses a driving file called dbnames that contains a list of hostname and database name pairs. Here is a sample of this file:

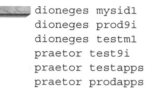

```
dioneges mysid1
dioneges prod9i
dioneges testm1
praetor test9i
praetor testapps
praetor prodapps
```

Make a UNIX Tape Backup

While most DBAs use sophisticated tools such as **ebu** and **rman** to manage Oracle backups, it is important to note that there are easy to use UNIX commands for copying Oracle files onto tape devices. UNIX has two native utilities called **tar** and **cpio** for file copying to tape archives.

Here is an example of a simple Oracle backup to a tape. This script uses the UNIX tape archive **tar** command to copy the tape:

```
#!/bin/ksh

echo Start tar copy at `date`

#***********************************************
# Mount the tape and rewind
#***********************************************
mt -f /dev/rmt/2m rew

#***********************************************
# Copy directories onto /dev/rmt/2m from:
#      /u01/oradata/customer.dbf
#      /u02/oradata/item.dbf
#***********************************************
tar cvf /dev/rmt/2m /u01/oradata/customer.dbf /u02/oradata/item.dbf

echo End `date`
```

Here is an example using the UNIX **dd** command:

```
#!/bin/ksh

echo Start dd copy at `date`

#***********************************************
# Mount the tape and rewind
#***********************************************
mt -f /dev/rmt/2m rew

#***********************************************
# Copy using the dd command:
#    if = input file
#    of = output tape device name
#    BS = blocksize for output device
#***********************************************
dd if=/u1/oradata/customer.dbf of=/dev/rmt/2m BS=32k
echo End dd at `date`
```

A UNIX Script to Detect Listener Failure

Starting in SQL*Net and on into Net8, there are special UNIX conditions that may cause the listener to start refusing Oracle connections. To alleviate these issues with a hanging listener, the Oracle DBA can write a UNIX script to constantly monitor the listener's ability to accept connections. Note that this script is only for Oracle databases that use dedicated connections, and it should not be used if you have installed the multi-threaded server.

This script uses the **ps** and **wc** commands to detect if the listener process is running. If the database is running, it restarts the listener process with the Oracle UNIX **lsnrctl** command:

```
# See if listener is running.

lsnr_up=`ps -eaf |grep lsnr |grep -v grep |wc -l`

# If not, see if database is running . . .
if test $lsnr_up -eq 0 then
        pmon_up=`ps -eaf |grep -i pmon |grep -v grep |wc -l`
        smon_up=`ps -eaf |grep -i smon |grep -v grep |wc -l`
        dbwr_up=`ps -eaf |grep -i dbwr |grep -v grep |wc -l`
        lgwr_up=`ps -eaf |grep -i lgwr |grep -v grep |wc -l`

        # If database is up, restart listener
```

```
        if test $pmon_up -gt 0 &&
           test $smon_up -gt 0 &&
           test $dbwr_up -gt 0 &&
           test $lgwr_up -gt 0
           then # Oracle is up
           lsnrctl start $1 #  Start tnslsnr
           echo 'Started tnslsnr ' `date`
        fi
fi
```

A Simple Script to Exit When the Database Is Not Running

When writing scripts that visit many Oracle servers, it is always a good idea to check if the Oracle database is running before attempting a connection to the database:

```
#************************************************************
# Let's exit immediately if the database is not running . . .
#************************************************************
check_stat=`ps -ef|grep ${ORACLE_SID}|grep pmon|wc -l`;
oracle_num=`expr $check_stat`
if [ $oracle_num -lt 1 ]
 then
 exit 0
fi
```

Detect When Oracle Is Not Accepting Connections

When automating Oracle maintenance with scripts, you should always test to ensure that Oracle is accepting database connections before attempting to perform maintenance on the database. You begin by creating a stand-alone script that connects to the database:

test_connection.ksh

```
#!/bin/ksh
#************************************************************
# Test to see if Oracle is accepting connections
#************************************************************
$ORACLE_HOME/bin/sqlplus -s /<<!
select * from v\$database;
exit
!
```

Once you have this script working, you write another shell script that submits the script in the background using the UNIX **nohup** command. You then wait 30 seconds with the UNIX **sleep** command, and then inspect the messages in the listing file for the connection.

```
#**************************************************************
# Submit the Oracle task in the background
#**************************************************************
nohup test_connection.ksh > /tmp/check_$ORACLE_SID.ora 2>&1 &

#**************************************************************
# Wait for 30 seconds with the UNIX sleep command
#**************************************************************
sleep 30

#**************************************************************
# If the script is done, check for the string "error"
# in the listing file from the prior nohup command:
#**************************************************************
check_stat=`cat /tmp/check_$ORACLE_SID.ora|grep -i error|wc -l`;
oracle_num=`expr $check_stat`

#**************************************************************
# If there is an error, make the script exit with a return code of 99
#**************************************************************
if [ $oracle_num -gt 0 ]
 then
 exit 99
fi
```

Conclusion

This chapter has been concerned with some of the common environmental management and file commands for the UNIX Oracle DBA. The main points for this chapter include:

■ The UNIX **oracle** user should have a set of predefined aliases to make it easy to relocate between Oracle directories in UNIX. These aliases are kept in the ~oracle.profile location on each UNIX server.

■ Many Oracle DBAs create an alias for every $ORACLE_SID on a server to make it easy to change UNIX environments.

■   You can use the **rcp** and **rsh** commands to write scripts that will distribute standard Oracle files such as the tnsnames.ora file to many Oracle servers.

■   UNIX provides soft links that are implemented with the **ln** command. Soft links allow an empty UNIX file to point to the location of the actual file. This is useful in environments where multiple $ORACLE_HOME directories exist.

Next, let's take a look at a summary of task management commands in UNIX.

CHAPTER
11

Oracle Task
Management in UNIX

his chapter deals with the control and submission of Oracle tasks in a UNIX environment. To be an effective UNIX Oracle DBA, you must be able to reliably encapsulate Oracle tasks into UNIX shell scripts, have a means for submitting UNIX scripts, and have a means to check and verify script output. This chapter will cover the following topics:

- Oracle job management in UNIX

- UNIX task management techniques

Let's begin by reviewing how to submit a UNIX script for Oracle.

Oracle Job Management in UNIX

This section describes techniques for submitting and monitoring Oracle tasks that have been placed inside UNIX shell scripts. Let's start by showing how a UNIX shell script is submitted, and then move on to more advanced topics.

Here is an example of a UNIX script that contains SQL*Plus commands to analyze all tables and indexes for an Oracle database. The script accepts the $ORACLE_SID as an input argument.

analyze.ksh

```
#!/bin/ksh

# Validate the Oracle database name with
# lookup in /var/opt/oracle/oratab
TEMP=`cat /var/opt/oracle/oratab|grep \^$1:|\
cut -f1 -d':'|wc -l`
tmp=`expr TEMP`      # Convert string to number
if [ $tmp -ne 1 ]
then
    echo "Your input $1 is not a valid ORACLE_SID."
    exit 99
fi

# First, we must set the environment . . . .
ORACLE_SID=$1
export ORACLE_SID
ORACLE_HOME=`cat /var/opt/oracle/oratab|grep $ORACLE_SID:|cut -f2 -d':'`
export ORACLE_HOME
PATH=$ORACLE_HOME/bin:$PATH
export PATH
```

```
MON=`echo ~oracle/obj_stat`
export MON

# Get the server name
host=`uname -a|awk '{ print $2 }'`

$ORACLE_HOME/bin/sqlplus -s perfstat/perfstat<<!

set heading off;
set feedback off;
set echo off;
set pages 999;
set lines 120;

--*****************************************************************
-- First, let's get the latest statistics for each table
--*****************************************************************
spool $MON/run_analyze.sql
select 'analyze table '||owner||'.'||table_name||' estimate statistics
sample 5000 rows;'
from
   dba_tables
where
   owner not in ('SYS','SYSTEM','PERFSTAT');
--    ****************************
--   Analyze all indexes for statistics
--    ****************************
select 'analyze index '||owner||'.'||table_name||' compute statistics;'
from
   dba_indexes
where
   owner not in ('SYS','SYSTEM','PERFSTAT');
spool off;

set echo on;
set feedback on;

@$MON/run_analyze

exit

!
```

Note that the above script can be split into two separate scripts, and each subscript can be used as a template and called from a master program. Here we have extracted the portion of the code that validates the user input and the code section that calls SQL*Plus. This approach can make the UNIX scripts more modular.

```ksh
#!/bin/ksh

# **********************************************
# Validate the Oracle database name input
# **********************************************
/home/oracle/validate_sid.ksh

# **********************************************
# Execute SQL*Plus script from UNIX call
# **********************************************
/home/oracle/create_table_analyze_syntax.ksh

# **********************************************
# Execute SQL*Plus script from UNIX call
# **********************************************
/home/oracle/execute_table_analyze_syntax.ksh
```

Here you see that your SQL*Plus script is encapsulated inside a UNIX script. You check to ensure that a valid $ORACLE_SID is passed to this script as a parameter, and you then execute SQL*Plus from inside the UNIX script.

Now, let's see how you might submit this task in UNIX as a background job.

Submitting Oracle Jobs in the Background

UNIX provides the **nohup** command to submit a task in the background. This technique is used for long-running Oracle jobs to free up your command line prompt, which is especially useful if you are dialed-in to the UNIX server. In the following example, you have a script that executes a SQL*Plus command, and you submit it for background processing:

```
nohup run_me.ksh > outfile.lst 2>&1 &
```

This command has the following components:

- **nohup**   This directs UNIX to submit the job.
- **run_me.ksh**   This is the name of the UNIX executable script.
- **>**   This redirects the standard output to a UNIX file.
- **outfile.lst**   This is the UNIX file location for the script output.
- **2>&1**   This redirects standard error to standard out, showing any error messages.
- **&**   This submits the job as a background task.

Watch the Execution of a Background Process

In the preceding example, you directed the script output to a file called outfile.lst. You can monitor the execution of the background process by using the UNIX **tail -f** command and see each line of output as it is written to the file:

```
root> tail -f longfile.lst
```

To exit the **tail -f** command, you enter **<crtl> c** at any time to return to the UNIX prompt.

UNIX Task Management Techniques

Now that you understand how to submit a single task, let's look at some more sophisticated UNIX techniques for managing multiple tasks. Here you will look at techniques for verifying the number of input parameters to a UNIX script and also examine techniques for submitting multiple UNIX tasks at the same time.

Parameter Checking for Oracle Shell Scripts

The following code snippet will end a UNIX script with the **exit** command if the appropriate arguments have not been passed to the script. In this example, the run_purge.ksh script requires two parameters, a valid ORACLE_SID and a numeric value, specifying the number of days back to purge. For example:

```
root> run_purge.ksh MYSID 200
```

Here you see that the script will terminate if the appropriate parameters are not passed to the script:

```
# Exit if no first parameter $1
if [ -z "$1" ]
then
   echo "Usage: run_purge.ksh <ORACLE_SID> <#_days> (where value is > 100)"
   exit 99
fi

# Exit if no second parameter $2
if [ -z "$2" ]
then
   echo "Usage: run_purge.ksh <ORACLE_SID> <#_days> (where value is > 100)"
   exit 99
fi
```

```
# Exit is parm is not greater than 100
tmp=`expr $2`              # Convert string to number
if [ $tmp -lt 100 ]
then
    echo
    echo "Argument two is less than 100.  Aborting Script."
    echo
    exit 99
fi
```

Make Sure the UNIX User Is oracle

This statement will ensure that all UNIX scripts are only executed by the **oracle**
UNIX user. This technique offers extra security and protection against unauthorized
execution. Note the use of the UNIX **whoami** command to capture the current user ID.

```
if [ `whoami` != 'oracle' ]
then
    echo "Error: You must be oracle to execute.  Exiting."
    Exit 99
fi
```

Validate an $ORACLE_SID
Being Passed to a UNIX Script

This code snippet is useful when you want to ensure that a valid database name is
passed to a UNIX script. Note that the /etc/oratab file is for HP-UX and AIX, and you
may need to change it to /var/opt/oratab if you are using Solaris.

```
#!/bin/ksh

# Exit if no first parameter $1 passed
if [ -z "$1" ]
then
    echo "Please pass a valid ORACLE_SID to this script"
    exit 99
fi

# Validate the Oracle database name with lookup in /etc/oratab
TEMP=`cat /etc/oratab|grep \^$1:|cut -f1 -d':'|wc -l`
tmp=`expr TEMP`              # Convert string to number
if [ $tmp -ne 1 ]
then
    echo "Your input $1 is not a valid ORACLE_SID.  Retry."
    exit 99
fi
```

Multiplexing Oracle Tasks in UNIX

If you have a large number of tasks to perform in a short amount of time, you can save time by running the jobs simultaneously in UNIX.

A great example is Oracle DBA table reorganizations. When you process table reorganizations in parallel, the total time required to reorganize all the tables is no more than the time required for the largest table. For example, if you need to reorganize 100 gigabytes of table data in a single weekend, the parallel job submission approach is the only way to go.

The following is a Korn shell script you can use to execute the reorganization. The script uses the UNIX **nohup** command to submit simultaneous CTAS reorganizations at the same time.

TIP

*A great benefit of running SQL*Plus in a **nohup** UNIX shell script is that this will allow a desktop computer to disconnect without causing the job to fail. For example, when using the **nohup** command, the DBA can start several jobs and log off their PC without terminating the running jobs.*

master_reorg.ksh

```
#!/bin/ksh
# Written by Donald Keith Burleson
# usage: nohup don_reorg.ksh > don_reorg.lst 2>&1 &

# Ensure that running user is oracle . . . . .
oracle_user=`whoami|grep oracle|grep -v grep|wc -l`;
oracle_num=`expr $oracle_user`
if [ $oracle_num -lt 1 ]
 then echo "Current user is not oracle. Please su to oracle and retry."
 exit
fi

# Ensure that Oracle is running . . . . .
oracle_up=`ps -ef|grep pmon|grep -v grep|wc -l`;
oracle_num=`expr $oracle_up`
if [ $oracle_num -lt 1 ]
 then echo "ORACLE instance is NOT up. Please start Oracle and retry."
 exit
fi

#************************************************************
```

```
# Submit parallel CTAS reorganizations of important tables
#**********************************************************
nohup reorg.ksh CUSTOMER  >customer.lst  2>&1 &
nohup reorg.ksh ORDER     >order.lst     2>&1 &
nohup reorg.ksh ITEM      >item.lst      2>&1 &
nohup reorg.ksh LINE_ITEM >line_item.lst 2>&1 &
nohup reorg.ksh PRODUCT   >product.lst   2>&1 &
```

A UNIX Script to Ensure a Daemon Is Running

The following script is used to ensure that a UNIX **vmstat** monitor is always running. This script can be scheduled via **cron** every 15 minutes. The script checks to see if the UNIX daemon is running and restarts it if it has failed.

In this example, you have a UNIX daemon called get_vmstat_linus.ksh that collects **vmstat** information from UNIX and places it into a STATSPACK extension table called stats$vmstat. You want to make sure that this script is always running, and the following script verifies that it is executing.

run_vmstat.ksh

```
#!/bin/ksh

# First, we must set the environment . . . .
vmstat=`echo ~oracle/vmstat`
export vmstat
ORACLE_SID=`cat ${vmstat}/mysid`
export ORACLE_SID

ORACLE_HOME=`cat /etc/oratab|grep $ORACLE_SID:|cut -f2 -d':'`
export ORACLE_HOME
PATH=$ORACLE_HOME/bin:$PATH
export PATH

#-----------------------------------------
# If it is not running, then start it . . .
#-----------------------------------------
check_stat=`ps -ef|grep get_vmstat|grep -v grep|wc -l`;
oracle_num=`expr $check_stat`
if [ $oracle_num -le 0 ]
 then nohup $vmstat/get_vmstat_linux.ksh > /dev/null 2>&1 &
fi
```

Conclusion

This short chapter has been a review of the basic steps required to create and manage Oracle jobs in UNIX. The main ideas of this chapter include the following points:

- You can encapsulate any SQL*Plus command into a UNIX shell script.

- All UNIX shell scripts should check for the presence of proper parameters and validate all input parameters. You can always exit the script by invoking the UNIX **exit** command.

- You can use the UNIX **nohup** command to submit UNIX shell scripts in the background.

- You can use the UNIX **tail -f** command to monitor the progress of UNIX background tasks.

- You can write a UNIX script to submit multiple **nohup** commands, thereby making Oracle tasks parallel according to the capacity of your UNIX server.

Next, let's wrap up this text with a review of miscellaneous UNIX techniques for the Oracle DBA.

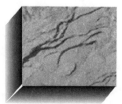

CHAPTER
12

Miscellaneous UNIX
Scripts for Oracle

his chapter serves as an area for miscellaneous topics that did not fit neatly into earlier chapters. Each of the topics in this chapter describes a general technique that can be used in UNIX to improve the workflow and make your UNIX scripts more reliable. These include:

- How to build UNIX commands into scripts

- Using UNIX to locate and examine Oracle SQL

- Miscellaneous UNIX tips and techniques

Let's start with a review of how to stack UNIX commands into powerful single-line scripts.

How to Build UNIX Commands into Scripts

You know that the UNIX **-exec** and **xargs** commands will apply a single UNIX command to a list of inputs, so let's look at how you can quickly generate a UNIX script to perform a powerful task. Suppose you need a UNIX script that searches every file on the UNIX server for a file that contains a reference to the **dba_2pc_pending** view.

You begin by writing a command that will display all filenames on the server. This is quite simple in UNIX and returns a list of every file on the server:

```
root> find . -print
./sql/pl2.sql
./sql/plcur.sql
./sql/check.ksh
./sql/mts.lst
./sql/fix_ts.sql
./sql/d.sql
./tools/sessions.sql
./tools/connections.sql
./tools/flush_shared_pool.sql
./tools/currently_running.sql
./tools/inval_obj.sql
./tools/recomp.sql
./tools/sqlnet.log
./statspack/r.ksh
```

```
./statspack/rpt_8i_bhr_dy.sql
./tmp/t1.sql
./tmp/t2.sql
./tmp/t3.sql
./tmp/n3.sql
./tmp/i2.sql
./ext_routines/common.mk
./ext_routines/common_OCI.c
./ext_routines/common_PROC.pc
```

You now have a complete list of all of the UNIX files. Because you know that the **grep** command accepts filenames as arguments, you can use the UNIX **xargs** command to search each file for your Oracle table name in all SQL files. In this case, you search the whole Oracle UNIX directory structure and quickly find all scripts that reference the **dba_2pc_pending** view:

```
root> find . -print|grep sql|xargs grep -i dba_2pc_pending
./sql/PENDING.sql:from    dba_2pc_pending
```

This ability to take a basic UNIX command and chain it (using a pipe | or redirect >) with other commands is a fundamental principle in UNIX shell programming
for Oracle.

Next, let's examine a UNIX trick that makes it easy to extract and examine all Oracle SQL, directly from the library cache.

Using UNIX to Locate and Tune Oracle SQL

This section describes a UNIX trick commonly used when searching for large-table full-table scans. Of course, not all large-table full-table scans are illegitimate, and you must carefully review the block I/O for the full-table scan versus the block I/O for an index range scan.

In my experience, more than 50 percent of large-table full-table scans are illegitimate, and adding a function-based index will often improve performance by an order of magnitude. For details on this technique, see my Oracle Press book *Oracle High-Performance SQL Tuning*. Remember, the Oracle cost-based optimizer will sometimes give up and invoke a full-table scan when it cannot find a usable index.

Here is a sample of the full-table scan report that is generated by running the access.sql script. Here you see a table called mtl_system_items that is fairly large (5,979 blocks) and has a large amount of full-table scans (575).

```
                        Full table scans and counts

OWNER          NAME                    NUM_ROWS C K   BLOCKS  NBR_FTS
-------------  ----------------------  ------------ - - -------- --------
INV            MTL_SYSTEM_ITEMS              83,432 N K    5,979      575
```

You have at least 5,979 x 575, or more than 3 million logical I/Os per day against this table.

Your first task is to find out if this is a legitimate full-table scan such as a query that requires a count(*), sum or avg, or if the Oracle optimizer is choosing the full-table scan because it cannot find a usable index. You start by extracting all SQL statements that reference the mtl_system_items table.

Finding All SQL Referencing a Specific Table

The first step is to locate all of the SQL in the **v$sql** view that references the mtl_system_items table. Actually, this is done quite easily with a simple script:

get_sql.sql

```
set lines 2000
set heading off
set pages 999

spool items.lst

select
   sql_text
from
   v$sql
where upper(sql_text) like '%MTL_SYSTEM_ITEMS %'
;

spool off;
```

Note that this script will create a spool file with each line containing a complete SQL statement. You can do this by issuing the **set lines 2000** command, which will create a spool file with 2,000 byte line lengths.

Once you run this script, you may be distressed to find that there are more than 100 SQL statements in the library cache that reference this table. How do you find the SQL that is performing the full-table scan?

One approach is to write a UNIX script that will parse the output from the get_sql.sql script and display only those lines that do not contain a reference to an indexed column of the mtl_system_items table. You start by querying the **dba_tab_columns** view to make a list of all columns that are indexed:

get_indexed_cols.sql

```
set pages 999
set heading off
spool get.ksh

select distinct
   column_name
from
   dba_ind_columns
where
   table_name = 'MTL_SYSTEM_ITEMS'
order by
   column_name
;

spool off;
```

Here is the resulting list of indexed columns:

```
ATTRIBUTE1
AUTO_CREATED_CONFIG_FLAG
CATALOG_STATUS_FLAG
DESCRIPTION
INVENTORY_ITEM_ID
INVENTORY_ITEM_STATUS_CODE
ITEM_CATALOG_GROUP_ID
ORGANIZATION_ID
PRODUCT_FAMILY_ITEM_ID
SEGMENT1
SYS_NC00246$
WH_UPDATE_DATE
```

Now, the trick is to write a "filter" that searches through the SQL listing and removes all SQL that references columns that are already indexed.

Sometimes this technique can be used in large databases to quickly find indexing opportunities. Let's take a closer look at how it works.

Using UNIX to Parse the SQL File

The goal is to use the UNIX **grep -v** command. In UNIX, **grep -v** is "anti-**grep**." Whereas **grep** is used to include lines with a matching string, **grep -v** is used to exclude lines that contain a column.

You also need to use the **-i** argument with **grep**, which ignores case sensitivity. This way, you are always sure you get the right answer, regardless of case.

You will alter the preceding script to generate a UNIX script that will perform the following tasks:

■ Read the output from get_sql.sql

■ Exclude all SQL statements that contain a reference to an indexed column

Of course, this script will also exclude all references to a column in the **select** clause, so this approach is not always foolproof.

Here is the modified UNIX script that reads Oracle and generates another UNIX script to issue the appropriate **grep** commands:

filter.ksh

```
#!/bin/ksh

$ORACLE_HOME/bin/sqlplus -s /<<!

set pages 999
set heading off
spool get.ksh

select 'cat items.lst| \' from dual;

select distinct
    'grep -vi '||column_name||'\'
from
    dba_ind_columns
where
    table_name = 'MTL_SYSTEM_ITEMS'
order by
    column_name
;
select '> result.lst' from dual

spool off;
exit
!

chmod +x get.ksh
```

Note the use of the backslash character. This is a common UNIX line continuation character and allows you to build a long UNIX command on multiple lines. Here is the Korn shell script that you have generated:

get.ksh

```
cat items.lst| \
grep -vi ATTRIBUTE1\
grep -vi AUTO_CREATED_CONFIG_FLAG\
grep -vi CATALOG_STATUS_FLAG\
grep -vi DESCRIPTION\
grep -vi INVENTORY_ITEM_ID\
grep -vi INVENTORY_ITEM_STATUS_CODE\
grep -vi ITEM_CATALOG_GROUP_ID\
grep -vi ORGANIZATION_ID\
grep -vi PRODUCT_FAMILY_ITEM_ID\
grep -vi SEGMENT1\
grep -vi SYS_NC00246$\
grep -vi WH_UPDATE_DATE\
> result.lst
```

Now this Korn shell script can be executed to parse through all 100 SQL statements and display only those lines that do not contain a reference to an indexed column.

The final step is to carefully examine the resulting SQL statement and see if it performs an unnecessary full-table scan. If it does, you can add a function-based index of a hint to remove the full-table scan.

Next, let's review some other common UNIX scripts for the Oracle DBA.

Miscellaneous UNIX Tips and Techniques

This section covers miscellaneous tips and techniques for improving the reliability and functionality of your UNIX scripts for Oracle.

Add the UNIX Date to an Oracle Filename

In UNIX, you can simply enter the **date** command to see the current date. You can capture this command inside a UNIX script and use the date as part of a UNIX filename. The following example shows how you can call the UNIX **date** function with date masks to change the display values according to your needs:

```
YEAR=`date +"%Y"`
MONTH=`date +"%m"`
DAY=`date +"%d"`
HOUR=`date +"%H"`
MINUTE=`date +"%M"`
```

In some cases you want to record the current UNIX date inside an Oracle log file. Here you place the date into a log file, indicating the exact time that a UNIX task ended:

```
echo End `date` > /usr/local/bin/scripts/logs/tar_end.lst
```

The following is a clever command that uses the UNIX **tee** command in conjunction with the UNIX **date** command. Note that it appends the current UNIX date and also uses the **tee** command to direct the output both to standard out as well as the progress.log file:

```
echo "Rebuild start for ${TABLESPACE}. . "\
      `date +"%H:%M "`|tee -a progress.log
```

Here is another handy UNIX script to check files with specific dates embedded in the UNIX filename. Once you write files with the UNIX date, you can check UNIX files based on date. The following script takes the current data and displays all files in the /u01/backup/logs directory that have the current day and month:

```
mdate=`date`
mday=`echo $mdate|awk '{print $3}'`
mmonth=`echo $mdate|awk '{print $2}'`

echo  month $mmonth
echo  day $mday

ls -alt /u01/backup/logs|grep `echo $mmonth $mday`
```

Monitor the Performance of Oracle Parallel Server

Here is a handy script to capture DLM performance in an OPS environment and place the output inside an Oracle table for tracking. Note the sophisticated use of the UNIX **date** function in this script.

This script checks the OPS values for locks, resources, and processes using the UNIX Oracle **lkdump** command. Once you have gathered these values, you direct them to the $RPT_FILE UNIX directory and also write them to STATSPACK extension table stats$dlm_stats.

```
DAY_OF_WEEK=`date +"%A"`
MACHINE_NAME=`hostname`
RPT_FILE=/u01/MYSID/reports/dlm_monitor.${MACHINE_NAME}.${DAY_OF_WEEK}.log
```

```
# \
#   Set up the file to log the lock to:
# /
TIMESTAMP=`date +"%C%y.%m.%d-%H:%M:%S"`
DLM_RESOURCES=`/oracle/MYSID/bin/lkdump -a res  | head -2 | awk 'getline'`
DLM_LOCKS=`/oracle/MYSID/bin/lkdump -a lock | head -2 | awk 'getline' `
DLM_PROCESS=`/oracle/MYSID/bin/lkdump -a proc | head -2 | awk 'getline'`
printf "$TIMESTAMP $DLM_RESOURCES  $DLM_LOCKS  $DLM_PROCESS \n" >>
RPT_FILE

RES=`echo $DLM_RESOURCES|cut -f2 -d '='`
LOC=`echo $DLM_LOCKS|cut -f2 -d '='`
PRO=`echo $DLM_PROCESS|cut -f2 -d '='`

ORACLE_SID=MYSID; export ORACLE_SID;
PATH=$PATH:/oracle/MYSID/bin; export PATH;
ORACLE_HOME=/oracle/MYSID; export ORACLE_HOME;

$ORACLE_HOME/bin/sqlplus <<! >> /dev/null

connect system/manager;

insert into perfstat.stats$dlm_stats
 values (
   SYSDATE,
   $PRO,
   $RES,
   $LOC ),

exit;
!
```

UNIX Gotcha: Clobber Your Entire UNIX Server

When folks talk about UNIX security and the tools to prevent mishaps, we are often reminded just how fragile the UNIX environment can be. Most of the job of the UNIX Oracle DBA is keeping the database running, and it does not come as a surprise when they see how easy it is to clobber a server.

The following script cripples the UNIX server by an implosion of incoming jobs. This is known as a denial of service (DOS) attack, and the Oracle DBA should be aware just how easy it is for a hacker to make a mess in UNIX.

Interestingly, the use of a DOS attack is not new, and mainframe programmers have known since the 1960s how to clobber a mainframe job initiator. You can do the same kind of attack on IBM mainframes by creating a recursive IEFBR14 job that directs its SYSOUT to the mainframe internal reader. Here is a section of JCL that illustrates the recursive job submission technique:

```
//EXEC  IEFBR14
//DD SYSIN=IBM.MISC(CRASH),DISP-SHR
//DD SYSOUT=(,,INTRDR)
```

Beware that the following command will clobber any UNIX server in a matter of just a few seconds. *Please note, this script is provided for illustration purposes only and should not be run in a production environment.*

```
nohup /tmp/recursive.ksh > /dev/null 2>&1 &
```

The recursive.ksh file submits two of the same tasks:

```
nohup /tmp/recursive.ksh > /dev/null 2>&1 &
nohup /tmp/recursive.ksh > /dev/null 2>&1 &
```

Because the job submits itself, two jobs submit 4, four submit 16, and so on, until the entire server is unable to accept any work.

Again, this script is described as a warning to any cocky Oracle DBA who assures management that their UNIX server is impervious to DOS attacks.

Looping Between UNIX Servers

UNIX provides a **for** command that can be used to loop for a specific number of iterations. When the **for** command is used to read the /etc/hosts and /etc/oratab files, you can write a script that loops from server to server and database to database.

This is especially useful where all UNIX servers are trusted, by allowing remote shell (**rsh**) commands. This is done by making an entry in the .rhosts file for your **oracle** UNIX user. This is called a *nested loop construct* and is illustrated by the pseudocode that follows:

```
FOR every server defined in .rhosts
     FOR every database defined in the server's /etc/oratab
            connect to SQL*Plus
     END
END
```

This is a very powerful construct, and it can be used to visit every database in your enterprise. In the following example, you perform a double loop, looping from server to server. For each server, you loop from database to database. Here is the actual UNIX code that performs the loops:

```
# Loop through each host name . . .
for host in `cat ~oracle/.rhosts|cut -d"." -f1|awk '{print $1}'|sort -u`
do
   echo " "
   echo "*************************"
   echo "$host"
   echo "*************************"
   # Loop through each database name on the host /etc/oratab . . .
   for db in `rsh $host "cat /etc/oratab|egrep ':N|:Y'|grep -v \*|\
   cut -f1 -':'"`
   do
      # Get the ORACLE_HOME for each database
      home=`rsh $host "cat /etc/oratab|egrep ':N|:Y'|grep -v \*|\
      grep {db}|cut -f2 -d':'"`
      echo " "
      echo "database is $db"
      sqlplus system/manager@$db <<!
      select * from v\$database;
      exit;
!
   done
done
```

In this example, you connected to SQL*Plus using a Net8 connect string for the remote database. However, you can also use the UNIX **rsh** command to directly connect to the SQL*Plus facility on the remote UNIX server.

Let's take a look at how this works.

Executing SQL*Plus on All Remote UNIX Servers

You can expand upon this approach and write a script to visit SQL*Plus on every server and every database on each server. In the following example, you select the name of every database on every server, and display the optimizer_mode for every database:

```
# Loop through each host name . . .
for host in `cat ~oracle/.rhosts|cut -d"." -f1|awk '{print $1}'|sort -u`
do
   echo " "
   echo "*************************"
   echo "$host"
   echo "*************************"
   # loop from database to database
   for db in `cat /etc/oratab|egrep ':N|:Y'|grep -v \*|\
```

```
      grep ${db}|cut -f1 -':'"`
      do
          home=`rsh $host "cat /etc/oratab|egrep ':N|:Y'|\
          grep -v \*|grep {db}|cut -f2 -d':'
          "`echo "***********************"
          echo "database is $db"
          echo "***********************"
          rsh $host "
          ORACLE_SID=${db}; export ORACLE_SID;
          ORACLE_HOME=${home}; export ORACLE_HOME;
          ${home}/bin/sqlplus -s /<<!
          set pages 9999;
          set heading off;
          select value from v"\\""$"parameter where name='optimizer_mode';
          exit
          !"
      done
done
```

In this example, you can quickly get a report of the Oracle optimizer_mode value for all databases in your enterprise. This can make tasks that might take hours into a simple task that takes just a few seconds.

Sending UNIX Files to Internet Mail

As we noted in earlier chapters, it is easy to take a UNIX file such as a trace file and send it to a user via e-mail. This is especially useful for routing Oracle alerts and reports to your e-mail inbox.

NOTE
This script requires your network administrator to set up the e-mail address to be routed to the appropriate e-mail server in your UNIX environment.

In the following example, you e-mail all recorded UNIX commands for the oracle UNIX user. In UNIX, a complete record of every UNIX command is kept in a file called .sh_history in the **oracle** user's home directory.

This is a common script used by an Oracle DBA manager to unobtrusively keep track of what their DBAs are doing, without their knowledge!

```
cat ~oracle/.sh_history|\
    mailx -s "DBA Command Report" don@buleson.cc
```

Changing a String for All Files in a Directory

We took a quick look at this script in Chapter 1, but it is so important that we should review it again here. This is one of the most frequently used UNIX scripts for the Oracle DBA. This script accepts an old string, locates the old string, and changes it to the values of the new string in all files in the directory. One problem with working in UNIX is that it is very hard to perform a global change operation on all files within a directory. The script shown in this section does a search and replace in all files in a directory, replacing one string with another and making a backup of the unaltered files.

The **for** loop that you see in the script causes the **sed** command to be executed for each command in the current directory. Note that the **sed** command does the actual search and replace work, but it does not overlay the files. Instead, **sed** writes the new versions of any affected files to a temporary directory.

This script always makes a backup of the files in a tmp subdirectory before issuing the change, so you can always get back your original files. Also note that this script is defined as a Bourne shell script (.sh file suffix). This is so the script will not change itself when it is executed against Korn shell scripts.

chg_all.sh

```
#!/bin/ksh

tmpdir=tmp.$$

mkdir $tmpdir.new

for f in $*
do
  sed -e 's/oldstring/newstring/g' < $f > $tmpdir.new/$f
done

# Make a backup first!
mkdir $tmpdir.old
mv $* $tmpdir.old/


cd $tmpdir.new
mv $* ../

cd ..
rmdir $tmpdir.new
```

Here you execute this script, passing the file mask as an argument. In the following example, you change the string "oldstring" to "newstring" for all *.sql files in your current directory:

```
> chg_all.sh *.sql
```

Remember that the strings to be changed are specified inside the body of the UNIX script, while the file mask is passed as a parameter. You don't pass the old and new strings as parameters because the **sed** command can be quite tricky, especially if your strings contain special characters.

Let's take a closer look at how this works. The **sed** command that you see in the script invokes the string editor for UNIX. The **sed** command always makes a copy of the changed files, and never changes a file in place. Hence, you see in this example that the **sed** command writes new versions of all changed files to the $tmpdir.new directory. The changes are actually made using **sed** before the backup copies are made. However, the new versions of the files are not copied back from $tmpdir.new until after the old versions have been copied to the backup directory.

How to Use UNIX to Display Row Information

One trick commonly used by UNIX hackers is to leverage the UNIX operating system to probe into the Oracle data blocks. With some knowledge of UNIX and Oracle, the nasty hacker can use UNIX to verify the contents of Oracle data rows. This can be especially useful if a data corruption is causing a data file to go offline or if Oracle data is suspect. Let's see how this is done.

You start by running a SQL query to locate the ROWID of the data block that contains the row you want to investigate. Here you rely on the dbms_rowid package and use the row_block_number procedure to return the data block corresponding to your desired row:

```
select
    dbms_rowid.rowid_block_number(rowid) block
from
    customer
where
    customer_name = 'Burleson';

BLOCK
-----
141
```

Here you see that the customer information for Burleson resides on the 141st block in the data file. You can now go to UNIX and display the contents of this row.

This is a great tool because you can display Oracle data even if the database is shut down. Of course, hackers can also use these tools to bypass the security of the Oracle database, hacking directly into the Oracle data files.

To display block 141, you can use the UNIX **dd** command. The **dd** command accepts a **skip** parameter that tells it how far into a file to travel. To get to block 141, you must allow for 9 blocks in the datafile header. You must also remember that the **skip** statement should take you to the block immediately before your data block.

Hence, your data block is on block 150 (141 + 9) and the **skip** parameter for block 141 will be 141 + 9 - 1 = 149. You also need to specify the blocksize for the **dd** command in the **ibs** parameter.

Once you run the UNIX **dd** command to read the Oracle data block, you can filter the output by piping it to the UNIX **strings** command to only show printable information. Here is the UNIX command and the output showing the displayable data inside the data block:

```
root> dd if=/u01/oradata/prod/customer.dbf \
        ibs=8192 skip=149 count=1|strings

1+0 records in
149+0 records out
Donald Burleson 3/35/56 1401 West Avenue
```

While this technique is most useful in emergency situations when you cannot start the Oracle database, it is important to understand how a UNIX hacker can bypass Oracle and read information directly from your Oracle database files.

Killing UNIX Oracle Processes

We briefly addressed the UNIX **kill** command in Chapter 1, but we should revisit the **kill** command as an emergency tool for the UNIX Oracle DBA. There are times when it is necessary to kill all Oracle processes or a selected set of Oracle processes on your UNIX server. This killing of Oracle processes is required when one of the following conditions occurs:

- You cannot connect to the database with SQL*Plus.

- Parts of the Oracle instance (SGA, background processes) have aborted and the database will not shut down normally.

Of course, Oracle recommends that the background processes only be aborted in emergency situations, but remember that Oracle will always attach warnstart after an abort and roll back any in-flight transactions. Also note that when you kill the Oracle processes you must also issue the **ipcs** command to ensure that all memory segments are removed. To kill all Oracle background processes and connections, you issue the following command:

```
root> ps -ef|grep "ora_"|grep -v grep|awk '{print $2}'|xargs -i kill -9 {}
```

The power of UNIX to quickly cause trouble for your database should be evident by the simplicity of this command. Clearly, access to the UNIX **oracle** account should be tightly controlled.

Conclusion

This text has covered a huge amount of technical material relating to the use of Oracle in a UNIX environment. While there are many dialects of UNIX, there is a central set of commands and techniques that the Oracle DBA must master, and this text has attempted to show all of these commands, techniques, and tools.

As Oracle and UNIX continue to evolve, this text will continue to evolve, and subsequent editions will continue to provide ready-to-use scripts and techniques to assist you in managing Oracle in a UNIX environment.

I make my living using Oracle in a UNIX environment, and I am always excited when I see a new advance in UNIX techniques for the Oracle DBA. As always, I invite reader comments, suggestions, and especially new UNIX tips, scripts, and techniques. Please feel free to e-mail me at don@burleson.cc.

Appendix
of UNIX Scripts

he following pages will include an alphabetical listing of all of the scripts that are referenced in this book. The scripts are available online at the Oracle Press web site at www.oraclepress.com and are reproduced here for your reference. These scripts fall into several topical areas.

Please note that these scripts are not warranteed in any way, and you should use them at your own risk.

■ **Oracle library cache mining scripts**   These are the scripts that can be used to explain all of the SQL in the library cache and produce reports showing the types of table access, and the tables and indexes involved in the access.

■ **STATSPACK extension scripts**   These scripts will be used to extend the standard STATSPACK for disk I/O statistics, UNIX server statistics and Oracle table and index statistics.

■ **Miscellaneous UNIX scripts**   These are miscellaneous UNIX scripts that you can use for Oracle DBA tasks on your UNIX server.

Library Cache Mining Scripts

These scripts are a technique that runs the Oracle9i explain plan statement on all SQL statements in the library cache, analyzes all the execution plans, and provides reports on all table and index access methods. The reports generated by access_reports.sql are invaluable for the following database activities:

■ **Identifying high-use tables and indexes**   See what tables the database accesses the most frequently.

■ **Identifying tables for caching**   You can quickly find small, frequently accessed tables for placement in the KEEP pool (Oracle8) or for use with the CACHE option (Oracle7). You can enhance the technique to automatically cache tables when they meet certain criteria for the number of blocks and the number of accesses. (I automatically cache all tables with fewer than 200 blocks when a table has experienced more than 100 full table scans.)

■ **Identifying tables for row re-sequencing**   You can locate large tables that have frequent index range scans in order to resequence the rows, to reduce I/O.

- **Dropping unused indexes** You can reclaim space occupied by unused indexes. Studies have found that an Oracle database never uses more than a quarter of all indexes available or doesn't use them in the way for which they were intended.

- **Stopping full table scans by adding new indexes** Quickly find the full table scans that you can speed up by adding a new index to a table.

Here are the steps to execute this script:

1. Download the access.sql and access_report.sql scripts.

2. Issue the following statements for the schema owner of your tables:

   ```
   grant select on v_$sqltext to schema_owner;
   grant select on v_$sqlarea to schema_owner;
   grant select on v_$session to schema_owner;
   grant select on v_$mystat to schema_owner;
   ```

3. Go into SQL*Plus, connect as the schema owner, and run access.sql.

You must be signed on as the schema owner in order to explain SQL statements with unqualified table names. Also, remember that you will get statistics only for the SQL statements that currently reside in your library cache. For very active databases, you may want to run this report script several times—it takes less than ten minutes for most Oracle databases.

access.sql

```
--****************************************************************
-- Object Access script
--
-- © 2001 by Donald K. Burleson
--
--    No part of this SQL script may be copied. Sold or distributed
--    without the express consent of Donald K. Burleson
--****************************************************************
set echo on;
--
--*********************************************
--  We must run this script as the SYS user
--*********************************************
accept syspass char prompt "Enter password for SYS user: ";

connect sys/&syspass;
set serveroutput on size 100000

set echo off;
```

```
--****************************************************************
prompt We first gather all SQL in the library cache and run EXPLAIN PLAN.
prompt This takes awhile, so be patient . . .
--****************************************************************

--set echo on
--set feedback on

set feedback off
set echo off
-- Drop and recreate PLAN_TABLE for EXPLAIN PLAN
drop table plan_table;
@$ORACLE_HOME/rdbms/admin/utlxplan

Rem Drop and recreate SQLTEMP for taking a snapshot of the SQLAREA
drop table sys.sqltemp;
create table sys.sqltemp
(
   ADDR            VARCHAR2 (16)
 , HASHVAL         INTEGER
 , SQL_TEXT        VARCHAR2(2000)
 , DISK_READS      NUMBER
 , EXECUTIONS      NUMBER
 , PARSE_CALLS     NUMBER
 , PARSE_USER      VARCHAR2(30)
 , BUFFER_GETS     NUMBER
 , SORTS           NUMBER
 , ROWS_PROCESSED  NUMBER
 , STMT_ID         VARCHAR2(100)
);

--set echo on
set feedback on

CREATE OR REPLACE PROCEDURE do_explain
   (addr IN  VARCHAR2
   , hash IN INTEGER
   , sql_text_IN IN VARCHAR2
   , parse_user_IN IN VARCHAR2
   , stmt_id_IN IN VARCHAR2 )
AS

   dummy     VARCHAR2(32767);

   dummy1    VARCHAR2(100);

   mycursor INTEGER;
   ret       INTEGER;
   my_sqlerrm VARCHAR2 (85);
   signed_hash NUMBER;

   FUNCTION get_sql(addr_IN IN VARCHAR2, hash_IN IN INTEGER)
   RETURN VARCHAR2
   IS
```

```
      temp_return  VARCHAR2(32767);
      CURSOR sql_pieces_cur
      IS
      SELECT sql_text
        FROM v$sqltext
       WHERE address = HEXTORAW(addr_IN)
         AND hash_value = hash_IN
      ORDER BY piece ASC;
   BEGIN
      FOR sql_pieces_rec IN sql_pieces_cur
      LOOP
         temp_return := temp_return||sql_pieces_rec.sql_text;
      END LOOP;

      IF temp_return IS NULL
      THEN
         RAISE_APPLICATION_ERROR(-20000,'SQL Not Found');
      END IF;

      RETURN temp_return;
   END get_sql;

   FUNCTION current_schema RETURN VARCHAR2
   IS
      temp_schema    v$session.schemaname%TYPE;
   BEGIN
      SELECT schemaname
        INTO temp_schema
        FROM v$session
       WHERE sid = (SELECT MAX(sid) FROM v$mystat);
      --
      RETURN temp_schema;
   EXCEPTION
      WHEN OTHERS THEN RETURN NULL;
   END current_schema;

BEGIN
   -- adjust signed_hash if hash > 2**31
   -- (hash type mismatch between v$sqlarea and v$sqltext)
   IF hash > POWER(2,31)
   THEN
      signed_hash := hash - POWER(2,32);
   ELSE
      signed_hash := hash;
   END IF;


   EXECUTE IMMEDIATE 'ALTER SESSION SET CURRENT_SCHEMA='||parse_user_IN;


   dummy:='EXPLAIN PLAN SET STATEMENT_ID='''||stmt_id_IN||''' INTO plan_table FOR
;
   IF LENGTH(sql_text_IN) > 1900
   THEN
```

```
      BEGIN  -- try to get using hash first, and unsigned hash if not found
         dummy:=dummy||get_sql(addr,hash);

      EXCEPTION
         WHEN OTHERS THEN dummy:=dummy||get_sql(addr,signed_hash);

      END;
   ELSE
      dummy := dummy||sql_text_IN;
   END IF;

   -- JB: optimization = only change schema if different from current
   --IF parse_user_IN != current_schema
   --THEN
   --   dbms_output.put_line(current_schema||' '||parse_user_IN);
   --   mycursor := DBMS_SQL.OPEN_CURSOR;
   --   DBMS_SQL.PARSE(mycursor,dummy1,DBMS_SQL.NATIVE);
   --   ret := DBMS_SQL.EXECUTE(mycursor);
   --   DBMS_SQL.CLOSE_CURSOR(mycursor);
   --END IF;

   mycursor := DBMS_SQL.OPEN_CURSOR;
   DBMS_SQL.PARSE(mycursor,dummy,DBMS_SQL.NATIVE);
   ret := DBMS_SQL.EXECUTE(mycursor);


   DBMS_SQL.CLOSE_CURSOR(mycursor);


   COMMIT;
EXCEPTION -- Insert errors into PLAN_TABLE...
   WHEN OTHERS
   THEN
      my_sqlerrm := SUBSTR(sqlerrm,1,80);
      INSERT INTO plan_table(statement_id,remarks) -- change to plan_table (JB)
      VALUES (stmt_id_IN, my_sqlerrm);

      -- cleanup cursor id open
      IF DBMS_SQL.IS_OPEN(mycursor)
      THEN
         DBMS_SQL.CLOSE_CURSOR(mycursor);
      END IF;

EXECUTE IMMEDIATE 'ALTER SESSION SET CURRENT_SCHEMA=SYS';

END;
/


show errors


DECLARE
```

```
     CURSOR  c1
     IS
     SELECT
             RAWTOHEX(SA.address)  addr
           ,SA.hash_value          hash
           ,SA.sql_text            sql_text
           ,SA.DISK_READS          diskrds
           ,SA.EXECUTIONS          execs
           ,SA.PARSE_CALLS         parses
           ,SA.BUFFER_GETS         buffer_gets
           ,SA.SORTS               sorts
           ,SA.ROWS_PROCESSED      rows_processed
           ,DU.username            username
           ,SUBSTR(RAWTOHEX(SA.address)||':'||TO_CHAR(SA.hash_value) , 1,30) stmt_id
       FROM
             v$sqlarea    SA
           ,DBA_USERS     DU
       WHERE
             command_type = 3
         AND
             SA.parsing_schema_id != 0
         AND SA.parsing_schema_id = DU.user_id;

     CURSOR c2
     IS
     SELECT
             addr
           ,hashval
           ,sql_text
           ,parse_user
           ,stmt_id
       FROM
             sqltemp
       ORDER BY parse_user;

BEGIN
EXECUTE IMMEDIATE 'ALTER SESSION SET CURRENT_SCHEMA=SYS';

     FOR c1_rec IN c1
     LOOP
        INSERT INTO
           sqltemp (ADDR
                   ,HASHVAL
                   ,SQL_TEXT
                   ,DISK_READS
                   ,EXECUTIONS
                   ,PARSE_CALLS
                   ,BUFFER_GETS
                   ,SORTS
                   ,ROWS_PROCESSED
                   ,PARSE_USER
                   ,STMT_ID
                   )
           VALUES (c1_rec.addr
```

```
                         ,c1_rec.hash
                         ,c1_rec.sql_text
                         ,c1_rec.diskrds
                         ,c1_rec.execs
                         ,c1_rec.parses
                         ,c1_rec.buffer_gets
                         ,c1_rec.sorts
                         ,c1_rec.rows_processed
                         ,c1_rec.username
                         ,c1_rec.stmt_id
                         );
        END LOOP;
        --
        FOR c2_rec IN c2
        LOOP
           do_explain(c2_rec.addr
                     ,c2_rec.hashval
                     ,c2_rec.sql_text
                     ,c2_rec.parse_user
                     ,c2_rec.stmt_id);
        END LOOP;
END;
/

--show errors

commit;


-- ********************************************************
-- Report section
-- ********************************************************

@access_report
--@/s001/app/oracle/home/sql/access_report

--drop procedure do_explain;
--drop table sqltemp;
--drop table plan_table;
```

access_keep_syntax.sql

```
-- ********************************************************
-- Report section
-- ********************************************************
-- © 2001 by Donald Keith Burleson - All Rights Reserved

set echo off;
set feedback on

column nbr_FTS  format 999,999
```

```
column num_rows format 999,999,999
column blocks    format 999,999
column owner     format a14;
column name      format a25;

set heading off;
set feedback off;
select
   'alter table '||p.owner||'.'||p.name||' storage (buffer_pool keep);'
from
   dba_tables t,
   dba_segments s,
   sqltemp s,
  (select distinct
     statement_id stid,
     object_owner owner,
     object_name name
   from
     plan_table
   where
     operation = 'TABLE ACCESS'
     and
     options = 'FULL') p
where
   s.addr||':'||TO_CHAR(s.hashval) = p.stid
   and
   t.table_name = s.segment_name
   and
   t.table_name = p.name
   and
   t.owner = p.owner
   and
   t.buffer_pool <> 'KEEP'
having
   s.blocks < 50
group by
   p.owner, p.name, t.num_rows, s.blocks
order by
   sum(s.executions) desc;

access_parallel_syntax.sql
-- ********************************************************
-- Report section
-- ********************************************************

set echo off;
set feedback on
```

```
-- © 2001 by Donald Keith Burleson - All Rights Reserved
column nbr_FTS  format 999,999
column num_rows format 999,999,999
column blocks   format 999,999
column owner    format a14;
column name     format a25;

set heading off;
set feedback off;
select
   'alter table '||p.owner||'.'||p.name||' parallel degree 11;'
from
   dba_tables t,
   dba_segments s,
   sqltemp s,
  (select distinct
     statement_id stid,
     object_owner owner,
     object_name name
   from
      plan_table
   where
      operation = 'TABLE ACCESS'
      and
      options = 'FULL') p
where
   s.addr||':'||TO_CHAR(s.hashval) = p.stid
   and
   t.table_name = s.segment_name
   and
   t.table_name = p.name
   and
   t.owner = p.owner
   and
   t.degree = 1
having
   s.blocks > 1000
group by
   p.owner, p.name, t.num_rows, s.blocks
order by
   sum(s.executions) desc;
access_recycle_syntax.sql

-- ********************************************************
-- Report section
-- ********************************************************

set echo off;
```

```
set feedback on

-- © 2001 by Donald Keith Burleson - All Rights Reserved
column nbr_FTS   format 999,999
column num_rows  format 999,999,999
column blocks    format 999,999
column owner     format a14;
column name      format a25;

set heading off;
set feedback off;
select
    'alter table '||p.owner||'.'||p.name||' storage (buffer_pool recycle);'
from
    dba_tables t,
    dba_segments s,
    sqltemp s,
  (select distinct
      statement_id stid,
      object_owner owner,
      object_name name
    from
       plan_table
    where
       operation = 'TABLE ACCESS'
       and
       options = 'FULL') p
where
    s.addr||':'||TO_CHAR(s.hashval) = p.stid
    and
    t.table_name = s.segment_name
    and
    t.table_name = p.name
    and
    t.owner = p.owner
    and
    t.buffer_pool <> 'RECYCLE'
having
    s.blocks > 1000
group by
    p.owner, p.name, t.num_rows, s.blocks
order by
    sum(s.executions) desc;
```

access_report.sql

```
-- ********************************************************
-- Report section
-- ********************************************************
-- © 2001 by Donald Keith Burleson - All Rights Reserved

set echo off;
set feedback on

column nbr_FTS   format 999,999
column num_rows  format 999,999,999
column blocks    format 999,999
column owner     format a14;
column name      format a24;
column ch        format a1;
column K         format a1;

--spool access.lst;

set heading off;
set feedback off;
ttitle 'Total SQL found in library cache'
select count(distinct statement_id) from plan_table;

ttitle 'Total SQL that could not be explained'
select count(distinct statement_id) from plan_table where remarks is not null;

set heading on;
set feedback on;
ttitle 'full table scans and counts|  |Note that "?" indicates in the table is
ached.'
select
   p.owner,
   p.name,
   t.num_rows,
   ltrim(t.cache) ch,
   decode(t.buffer_pool,'KEEP','K','DEFAULT',' ') K,
   s.blocks blocks,
   sum(s.executions) nbr_FTS
from
   dba_tables t,
   dba_segments s,
   sqltemp s,
  (select distinct
     statement_id stid,
     object_owner owner,
```

```
      object_name name
   from
      plan_table
   where
      operation = 'TABLE ACCESS'
      and
      options = 'FULL') p
where
   s.addr||':'||TO_CHAR(s.hashval) = p.stid
   and
   t.owner = s.owner
   and
   t.table_name = s.segment_name
   and
   t.table_name = p.name
   and
   t.owner = p.owner
having
   sum(s.executions) > 9
group by
   p.owner, p.name, t.num_rows, t.cache, t.buffer_pool, s.blocks
order by
   sum(s.executions) desc;

column nbr_RID  format 999,999,999
column num_rows format 999,999,999
column owner       format a15;
column name        format a25;

ttitle 'Table access by ROWID and counts'
select
   p.owner,
   p.name,
   t.num_rows,
   sum(s.executions) nbr_RID
from
   dba_tables t,
   sqltemp s,
   (select distinct
      statement_id stid,
      object_owner owner,
      object_name name
   from
      plan_table
   where
      operation = 'TABLE ACCESS'
      and
      options = 'BY ROWID') p
```

```
where
   s.addr||':'||TO_CHAR(s.hashval) = p.stid
   and
   t.table_name = p.name
   and
   t.owner = p.owner
having
   sum(s.executions) > 9
group by
   p.owner, p.name, t.num_rows
order by
   sum(s.executions) desc;


--************************************************
--  Index Report Section
--************************************************

column nbr_scans  format 999,999,999
column num_rows   format 999,999,999
column tbl_blocks format 999,999,999
column owner      format a9;
column table_name format a20;
column index_name format a20;

ttitle 'Index full scans and counts'
select
   p.owner,
   d.table_name,
   p.name index_name,
   seg.blocks tbl_blocks,
   sum(s.executions) nbr_scans
from
   dba_segments seg,
   sqltemp s,
   dba_indexes d,
   (select distinct
      statement_id stid,
      object_owner owner,
      object_name name
   from
      plan_table
   where
      operation = 'INDEX'
      and
      options = 'FULL SCAN') p
where
   d.index_name = p.name
   and
```

```
   s.addr||':'||TO_CHAR(s.hashval) = p.stid
   and
   d.table_name = seg.segment_name
   and
   seg.owner = p.owner
having
   sum(s.executions) > 9
group by
   p.owner, d.table_name, p.name, seg.blocks
order by
   sum(s.executions) desc;


ttitle 'Index range scans and counts'
select
   p.owner,
   d.table_name,
   p.name index_name,
   seg.blocks tbl_blocks,
   sum(s.executions) nbr_scans
from
   dba_segments seg,
   sqltemp s,
   dba_indexes d,
   (select distinct
      statement_id stid,
      object_owner owner,
      object_name name
    from
       plan_table
    where
       operation = 'INDEX'
       and
       options = 'RANGE SCAN') p
where
   d.index_name = p.name
   and
   s.addr||':'||TO_CHAR(s.hashval) = p.stid
   and
   d.table_name = seg.segment_name
   and
   seg.owner = p.owner
having
   sum(s.executions) > 9
group by
   p.owner, d.table_name, p.name, seg.blocks
order by
```

```
   sum(s.executions) desc;


ttitle 'Index unique scans and counts'
select
   p.owner,
   d.table_name,
   p.name index_name,
   sum(s.executions) nbr_scans
from
   sqltemp s,
   dba_indexes d,
   (select distinct
      statement_id stid,
      object_owner owner,
      object_name name
   from
      plan_table
   where
      operation = 'INDEX'
      and
      options = 'UNIQUE SCAN') p
where
   d.index_name = p.name
   and
   s.addr||':'||TO_CHAR(s.hashval) = p.stid
having
   sum(s.executions) > 9
group by
   p.owner, d.table_name, p.name
order by
   sum(s.executions) desc;
```

STATSPACK Extension Scripts

vmstat Scripts

create_vmstat_table.sql

```
connect perfstat/perfstat;

drop table stats$vmstat;
create table stats$vmstat
(
     start_date           date,
```

```
    duration              number,
    server_name           varchar2(20),
    runque_waits          number,
    page_in               number,
    page_out              number,
    user_cpu              number,
    system_cpu            number,
    idle_cpu              number,
    wait_cpu              number
)
tablespace perfstat
storage (initial 10m
        next      1m
        pctincrease 0)
;
```

get_vmstat_aix.ksh

```
#!/bin/ksh

# First, we must set the environment . . . .
ORACLE_SID=PCT9
export ORACLE_SID
ORACLE_HOME=`cat /etc/oratab|grep \^$ORACLE_SID:|cut -f2 -d':'`
export ORACLE_HOME
PATH=$ORACLE_HOME/bin:$PATH
export PATH

SERVER_NAME=`uname -a|awk '{print $2}'`
typeset -u SERVER_NAME
export SERVER_NAME

# sample every five minutes (300 seconds) . . . .
SAMPLE_TIME=300

while true
do
   vmstat ${SAMPLE_TIME} 2 > /tmp/msg$$

# This script is intended to run starting at 7:00 AM EST Until midnight EST
cat /tmp/msg$$|sed 1,4d | awk  '{ printf("%s %s %s %s %s %s %s\n", $1, $6, $7,
14, $15, $16, $17) }' | while read RUNQUE PAGE_IN PAGE_OUT USER_CPU SYSTEM_CPU
DLE_CPU WAIT_CPU
   do

      $ORACLE_HOME/bin/sqlplus -s / <<EOF
      insert into perfstat.stats\$vmstat
                       values (
```

```
                                    sysdate,
                                    $SAMPLE_TIME,
                                    '$SERVER_NAME',
                                    $RUNQUE,
                                    $PAGE_IN,
                                    $PAGE_OUT,
                                    $USER_CPU,
                                    $SYSTEM_CPU,
                                    $IDLE_CPU,
                                    $WAIT_CPU
                                        );
        EXIT
EOF
    done
done

rm /tmp/msg$$
```

get_vmstat_linux.ksh

```
#!/bin/ksh

# This is the linux version

# First, we must set the environment . . . .
#ORACLE_SID=edi1
#export ORACLE_SID
#ORACLE_HOME=`cat /etc/oratab|grep \^$ORACLE_SID:|cut -f2 -d':'`
#export ORACLE_HOME

ORACLE_HOME=/usr/app/oracle/admin/product/8/1/6
export ORACLE_HOME

PATH=$ORACLE_HOME/bin:$PATH
export PATH

SERVER_NAME=`uname -a|awk '{print $2}'`
typeset -u SERVER_NAME
export SERVER_NAME

# sample every five minutes (300 seconds) . . . .
SAMPLE_TIME=300
SAMPLE_TIME=3

while true
do
    vmstat ${SAMPLE_TIME} 2 > /tmp/msg$$


# run vmstat and direct the output into the Oracle table . . .
```

```
cat /tmp/msg$$|sed 1,3d | awk  '{ printf("%s %s %s %s %s %s\n", $1, $8, $9, $14,
15, $16) }' | while read RUNQUE PAGE_IN PAGE_OUT USER_CPU SYSTEM_CPU IDLE_CPU
   do

     $ORACLE_HOME/bin/sqlplus -s perfstat/perfstat@testb1<<EOF
     insert into perfstat.stats\$vmstat
                           values (
                              sysdate,
                              $SAMPLE_TIME,
                              '$SERVER_NAME',
                              $RUNQUE,
                              $PAGE_IN,
                              $PAGE_OUT,
                              $USER_CPU,
                              $SYSTEM_CPU,
                              $IDLE_CPU,
                              0
                                   );
     EXIT
EOF
   done
done

rm /tmp/msg$$
```

get_vmstat_solaris.ksh

```
#!/bin/ksh

# First, we must set the environment . . . .
ORACLE_SID=prodb1
export ORACLE_SID
ORACLE_HOME=`cat /var/opt/oracle/oratab|grep \^$ORACLE_SID:|cut -f2 -d':'`
export ORACLE_HOME
PATH=$ORACLE_HOME/bin:$PATH
export PATH

SERVER_NAME=`uname -a|awk '{print $2}'`
typeset -u SERVER_NAME
export SERVER_NAME

# sample every five minutes (300 seconds) . . . .
SAMPLE_TIME=300

while true
do
   vmstat ${SAMPLE_TIME} 2 > /tmp/msg$$

# Note that Solaris does not have a wait CPU column
cat /tmp/msg$$|sed 1,3d | \
```

```
awk '{ printf("%s %s %s %s %s %s\n", $1, $8, $9, $20, 21, $22) }'\
 | while read RUNQUE PAGE_IN PAGE_OUT USER_CPU SYSTEM_CPU IDLE_CPU
   do

       $ORACLE_HOME/bin/sqlplus -s / <<EOF
       insert into perfstat.stats\$vmstat
                        values (
                           SYSDATE,
                           $SAMPLE_TIME,
                           '$SERVER_NAME',
                           $RUNQUE,
                           $PAGE_IN,
                           $PAGE_OUT,
                           $USER_CPU,
                           $SYSTEM_CPU,
                           $IDLE_CPU,
                           0
                                );
       EXIT
EOF
   done
done

rm /tmp/msg$$
```

get_vmstat_solaris_remote.sql

```
#!/bin/ksh

# First, we must set the environment . . . .
ORACLE_SID=prodb1
export ORACLE_SID
ORACLE_HOME=`cat /var/opt/oracle/oratab|grep \^$ORACLE_SID:|cut -f2 -d':'`
export ORACLE_HOME
PATH=$ORACLE_HOME/bin:$PATH
export PATH

SERVER_NAME=`uname -a|awk '{print $2}'`
typeset -u SERVER_NAME
export SERVER_NAME

# sample every five minutes (300 seconds) . . . .
SAMPLE_TIME=300
SAMPLE_TIME=3

while true
do
   vmstat ${SAMPLE_TIME} 2 > /tmp/msg$$
```

```
# Note that Solaris does not have a wait CPU column
cat /tmp/msg$$|sed 1,3d | \
awk '{ printf("%s %s %s %s %s %s\n", $1, $8, $9, $20, 21, $22) }' \
| while read RUNQUE PAGE_IN PAGE_OUT USER_CPU SYSTEM_CPU IDLE_CPU
   do

      $ORACLE_HOME/bin/sqlplus -s perfstat/perfstat@prodb1<<EOF
      insert into perfstat.stats\$vmstat
                         values (
                           SYSDATE,
                           $SAMPLE_TIME,
                           '$SERVER_NAME',
                           $RUNQUE,
                           $PAGE_IN,
                           $PAGE_OUT,
                           $USER_CPU,
                           $SYSTEM_CPU,
                           $IDLE_CPU,
                           0
                                 );
      EXIT
EOF
   done
done

rm /tmp/msg$$
```

rpt_vmstat.sql

```
connect perfstat/perfstat;
-- © 2001 by Donald Keith Burleson - All Rights Reserved

set feedback off;
set verify off;

column my_date heading 'date' format a20
column c2         heading runq   format 999
column c3         heading pg_in  format 999
column c4         heading pg_ot  format 999
column c5         heading usr    format 999
column c6         heading sys    format 999
column c7         heading idl    format 999
column c8         heading wt     format 999


select
 to_char(start_date,'yyyy-mm-dd') my_date,
-- avg(runque_waits)      c2
-- avg(page_in)          c3,
-- avg(page_out)         c4,
avg(user_cpu + system_cpu)          c5,
-- avg(system_cpu)       c6,
```

```
-- avg(idle_cpu)             c7,
avg(wait_cpu)              c8
from
    stats$vmstat
group  BY
 to_char(start_date,'yyyy-mm-dd')
order by
 to_char(start_date,'yyyy-mm-dd')
 ;
```

rpt_vmstat_dy.sql

```
connect perfstat/perfstat;
-- © 2001 by Donald Keith Burleson - All Rights Reserved

set feedback off;
set verify off;

column my_date heading 'date' format a20
column c2        heading runq    format 999
column c3        heading pg_in   format 999
column c4        heading pg_ot   format 999
column c5        heading usr     format 999
column c6        heading sys     format 999
column c7        heading idl     format 999
column c8        heading wt      format 999


select
 to_char(start_date,'day') my_date,
-- avg(runque_waits)        c2
-- avg(page_in)             c3,
-- avg(page_out)            c4,
avg(user_cpu + system_cpu)             c5,
-- avg(system_cpu)          c6,
-- avg(idle_cpu)            c7,
avg(wait_cpu)              c8
from
    stats$vmstat
group  BY
 to_char(start_date,'day')
order by
 to_char(start_date,'day')
 ;
```

rpt_vmstat_hr.sql

```
connect perfstat/perfstat;
-- © 2001 by Donald Keith Burleson - All Rights Reserved

set feedback off;
```

```
set verify off;

column my_date heading 'date' format a20
column c2       heading runq    format 999
column c3       heading pg_in   format 999
column c4       heading pg_ot   format 999
column c5       heading usr     format 999
column c6       heading sys     format 999
column c7       heading idl     format 999
column c8       heading wt      format 999


select
 to_char(start_date,'day') my_date,
-- avg(runque_waits)        c2
-- avg(page_in)             c3,
-- avg(page_out)            c4,
avg(user_cpu + system_cpu)           c5,
-- avg(system_cpu)          c6,
-- avg(idle_cpu)            c7,
avg(wait_cpu)              c8
from
    stats$vmstat
group  BY
 to_char(start_date,'day')
order by
 to_char(start_date,'day')
;
```

run_vmstat.ksh

```
#!/bin/ksh

# First, we must set the environment . . . .
vmstat=`echo ~oracle/vmstat`
export vmstat
ORACLE_SID=`cat ${vmstat}/mysid`
export ORACLE_SID
ORACLE_HOME=`cat /etc/oratab|grep $ORACLE_SID:|cut -f2 -d':'`
export ORACLE_HOME
PATH=$ORACLE_HOME/bin:$PATH
export PATH


#---------------------------------------
# If it is not running, then start it . . .
#---------------------------------------
check_stat=`ps -ef|grep get_vmstat|grep -v grep|wc -l`;
oracle_num=`expr $check_stat`
if [ $oracle_num -le 0 ]
 then nohup $vmstat/get_vmstat.ksh > /dev/null 2>&1 &
fi

HOUR=`date +"%H"`
```

```
#if [ $HOUR -gt 19 ]
#then
    #myvar=`ps|grep get_vmstat|awk '{print $1 }'|wc -l`
    #if [ $myvar -gt 0 ]
    #then kill -9 `ps|grep get_vmstat|awk '{print $1 }'` > /dev/null
    #fi
#fi
```

run_vmstat_alert.ksh

```
#!/bin/ksh

# First, we must set the environment . . . .
ORACLE_SID=$1
export ORACLE_SID
ORACLE_HOME=`cat /var/opt/oracle/oratab|grep $ORACLE_SID:|cut -f2 -d':'`
export ORACLE_HOME
PATH=$ORACLE_HOME/bin:$PATH
export PATH
vmstat=`echo ~oracle/vmstat`
export vmstat

sqlplus /<<!
spool /tmp/vmstat_$1.lst
@$vmstat/vmstat_alert 7
spool off;
exit;
!

# Mail the report
check_stat=`cat /tmp/vmstat_$1.lst|wc -l`;
oracle_num=`expr $check_stat`
if [ $oracle_num -gt 3 ]
 then
    cat /tmp/vmstat_$1.lst|mailx -s "Oracle vmstat alert" don@remote-dba.net
erry.oakes@worldnet.att.net adamf@oracle.com
fi
```

run_vmstat_linux.ksh

```
#!/bin/ksh

# First, we must set the environment . . . .
vmstat=`echo ~oracle/vmstat`
export vmstat
ORACLE_SID=`cat ${vmstat}/mysid`
export ORACLE_SID

ORACLE_HOME=`cat /etc/oratab|grep $ORACLE_SID:|cut -f2 -d':'`
export ORACLE_HOME
```

```
PATH=$ORACLE_HOME/bin:$PATH
export PATH

#----------------------------------------
# If it is not running, then start it . . .
#----------------------------------------
check_stat=`ps -ef|grep get_vmstat|grep -v grep|wc -l`;
oracle_num=`expr $check_stat`
if [ $oracle_num -le 0 ]
 then nohup $vmstat/get_vmstat_linux.ksh > /dev/null 2>&1 &
fi
```

run_vmstat_rpt.ksh

```
#!/bin/ksh

# First, we must set the environment . . . .
ORACLE_SID=mon1
export ORACLE_SID
ORACLE_HOME=`cat /etc/oratab|grep $ORACLE_SID:|cut -f2 -d':'`
export ORACLE_HOME
PATH=$ORACLE_HOME/bin:$PATH
export PATH
vmstat=`echo ~oracle/vmstat`
export vmstat

echo 'Starting Reports'

for db in `cat ${vmstat}/dbnames|awk '{ print $1 }'`
do
    host=`cat ${vmstat}/dbnames|grep $db|awk '{ print $2 }'`
sqlplus /<<!

select count(*) from perfstat.stats\$vmstat;
exit;
!
done
```

run_vmstat_solaris.ksh

```
#!/bin/ksh

# First, we must set the environment . . . .
vmstat=`echo ~oracle/vmstat`
export vmstat
ORACLE_SID=`cat ${vmstat}/mysid`
export ORACLE_SID
ORACLE_HOME=`cat /var/opt/oracle/oratab|grep $ORACLE_SID:|cut -f2 -d':'`
export ORACLE_HOME
PATH=$ORACLE_HOME/bin:$PATH
```

```
export PATH

#----------------------------------------
# If it is not running, then start it . . .
#----------------------------------------
check_stat=`ps -ef|grep get_vmstat|grep -v grep|wc -l`;
oracle_num=`expr $check_stat`
if [ $oracle_num -le 0 ]
 then nohup $vmstat/get_vmstat_solaris.ksh > /dev/null 2>&1 &
fi

HOUR=`date +"%H"`

#if [ $HOUR -gt 19 ]
#then
    #myvar=`ps|grep get_vmstat|awk '{print $1 }'|wc -l`
    #if [ $myvar -gt 0 ]
    #then kill -9 `ps|grep get_vmstat|awk '{print $1 }'` > /dev/null
    #fi
#fi
```

vmstat.cron.txt

```
00 7 * * * /export/run_vmstat.ksh > /export/home/oracle/vmstat/r.lst
00 7 * * * /export/run_vmstat_alert.ksh prodb1 > /export/home/oracle/vmstat/v.lst
```

vmstat_alert.sql

```
set lines 80;
-- © 2001 by Donald Keith Burleson - All Rights Reserved
set feedback off;
set verify off;

column my_date heading 'date        hour' format a20
column c2        heading runq    format 999
column c3        heading pg_in   format 999
column c4        heading pg_ot   format 999
column c5        heading usr     format 999
column c6        heading sys     format 999
column c7        heading idl     format 999
column c8        heading wt      format 999


ttitle 'run queue > 2|May indicate an overloaded CPU|When runqueue exceeds the
number of CPUs| on the server, tasks are waiting for service.';


select
 server_name,
 to_char(start_date,'YY/MM/DD    HH24') my_date,
 avg(runque_waits)        c2,
```

```
 avg(page_in)               c3,
 avg(page_out)              c4,
 avg(user_cpu)              c5,
 avg(system_cpu)            c6,
 avg(idle_cpu)              c7
from
perfstat.stats$vmstat
WHERE
runque_waits > 2
and start_date > sysdate-&1
group by
 server_name,
 to_char(start_date,'YY/MM/DD    HH24')
ORDER BY
 server_name,
 to_char(start_date,'YY/MM/DD    HH24')
;

ttitle 'page_in > 1|
May indicate overloaded memory|
Whenever Unix performs a page-n, the RAM memory |
on the server has been exhausted and swap pages are being used.';

select
 server_name,
 to_char(start_date,'YY/MM/DD    HH24') my_date,
 avg(runque_waits)         c2,
 avg(page_in)              c3,
 avg(page_out)             c4,
 avg(user_cpu)             c5,
 avg(system_cpu)           c6,
 avg(idle_cpu)             c7
from
perfstat.stats$vmstat
WHERE
page_in > 1
and start_date > sysdate-&1
group by
 server_name,
 to_char(start_date,'YY/MM/DD    HH24')
ORDER BY
 server_name,
 to_char(start_date,'YY/MM/DD    HH24')
;

ttitle 'user+system CPU > 70%|
Indicates periods with a fully-loaded CPU subssystem.|
Periods of 100% utilization are only a |
concern when runqueue values exceeds the number of CPs on the server.';


select
 server_name,
 to_char(start_date,'YY/MM/DD    HH24') my_date,
```

```
    avg(runque_waits)      c2,
    avg(page_in)           c3,
    avg(page_out)          c4,
    avg(user_cpu)          c5,
    avg(system_cpu)        c6,
    avg(idle_cpu)          c7
from
perfstat.stats$vmstat
WHERE
(user_cpu + system_cpu) > 70
and start_date > sysdate-&1
group by
 server_name,
 to_char(start_date,'YY/MM/DD    HH24')
ORDER BY
 server_name,
 to_char(start_date,'YY/MM/DD    HH24')
;
```

Table and Object Extension Scripts for STATSPACK

create_object_tables.sql

```
connect perfstat/perfstat;

drop table perfstat.stats$tab_stats;

create table perfstat.stats$tab_stats
(
    snap_time         date,
    server_name       varchar2(20),
    db_name           varchar2(9),
    tablespace_name   varchar2(40),
    owner             varchar2(40),
    table_name        varchar2(40),
    num_rows          number,
    avg_row_len       number,
    next_extent       number,
    extents           number,
    bytes             number
)
tablespace perfstat
storage (initial 1m next 1m maxextents unlimited)
;

drop table perfstat.stats$idx_stats;


create table perfstat.stats$idx_stats
```

```
(
    snap_time          date,
    server_name        varchar2(20),
    db_name            varchar2(9),
    tablespace_name    varchar2(40),
    owner              varchar2(40),
    index_name         varchar2(40),
    clustering_factor  number,
    leaf_blocks        number,
    blevel             number,
    next_extent        number,
    extents            number,
    bytes              number
)
tablespace perfstat
storage (initial 1m next 1m maxextents unlimited)
;


drop index
    perfstat.tab_stat_date_idx;

create index
    perfstat.tab_stat_date_idx
on
    perfstat.stats$tab_stats
( snap_time )
tablespace perfstat
storage (initial 1m next 1m maxextents unlimited)
;


drop index
    perfstat.idx_stat_date_idx;
create index
    perfstat.idx_stat_date_idx
on
    perfstat.stats$idx_stats
( snap_time )
tablespace perfstat
storage (initial 1m next 1m maxextents unlimited)
;
```

get_object_stats.ksh

```ksh
#!/bin/ksh

# Validate the Oracle database name with
# lookup in /var/opt/oracle/oratab
TEMP=`cat /var/opt/oracle/oratab|grep \^$1:|\
cut -f1 -d':'|wc -l`
tmp=`expr TEMP`     # Convert string to number
if [ $tmp -ne 1 ]
```

```
then
    echo "Your input $1 is not a valid ORACLE_SID."
    exit 99
fi

# First, we must set the environment . . . .
ORACLE_SID=$1
export ORACLE_SID
ORACLE_HOME=`cat /var/opt/oracle/oratab|grep $ORACLE_SID:|cut -f2 -d':'`
export ORACLE_HOME
PATH=$ORACLE_HOME/bin:$PATH
export PATH
MON=`echo ~oracle/obj_stat`
export MON

# Get the server name
host=`uname -a|awk '{ print $2 }'`

$ORACLE_HOME/bin/sqlplus -s perfstat/perfstat<<!

set heading off;
set feedback off;
set echo off;
-- © 2001 by Donald Keith Burleson - All Rights Reserved
set lines 120;

--*****************************************************************
-- First, let's get the latest statistics for each table
--*****************************************************************
spool $MON/run_analyze.sql
select 'analyze table '||owner||'.'||table_name||' estimate statistics sample 50
rows;'
from
    dba_tables
where
    owner not in ('SYS','SYSTEM','PERFSTAT');
--    ****************************
--   Analyze all indexes for statistics
--    ****************************
select 'analyze index '||owner||'.'||table_name||' compute statistics;'
from
    dba_indexes
where
    owner not in ('SYS','SYSTEM','PERFSTAT');
spool off;

set echo on;
set feedback on;

@@$MON/run_analyze

connect perfstat/perfstat;

--*****************************************************************
-- Now we grab the table statistics
--*****************************************************************
```

```
insert into perfstat.stats\$tab_stats
(
 . select
      SYSDATE,
      lower('${host}'),
      lower('${ORACLE_SID}'),
      t.tablespace_name,
      t.owner,
      t.table_name,
      t.num_rows,
      t.avg_row_len,
      s.next_extent,
      s.extents,
      s.bytes
from
   dba_tables    t,
   dba_segments s
where
   segment_name = table_name
   and
   s.tablespace_name = t.tablespace_name
   and
   s.owner = t.owner
   and
   t.owner not in ('SYS','SYSTEM')
--    and
--    num_rows > 1000
);


--****************************************************************
-- Now we grab the index statistics
--****************************************************************
insert into perfstat.stats\$idx_stats
(
   select
      SYSDATE,
      lower('${host}'),
      lower('${ORACLE_SID}'),
      i.tablespace_name,
      i.owner,
      i.index_name,
      i.clustering_factor,
      i.leaf_blocks,
      i.blevel,
      s.next_extent,
      s.extents,
      s.bytes
   from dba_indexes  i,
        dba_segments s,
        dba_tables   t
   where
      i.table_name = t.table_name
   and
      segment_name = index_name
   and
```

```
        s.tablespace_name = i.tablespace_name
    and
        s.owner = i.owner
    and
        i.owner not in ('SYS','SYSTEM')
--    and
--        t.num_rows > 1000
);

exit
!
```

rpt_bytes.sql

```
--**********************************************************
-- First we need to get the second-highest date in tab_stats
--**********************************************************
set lines 80;
-- © 2001 by Donald Keith Burleson - All Rights Reserved
set feedback off;
set verify off;
set echo off;

drop table d1;

create table d1 as
select distinct
    to_char(snap_time,'YYYY-MM-DD') mydate
from
    stats$tab_stats
where
    to_char(snap_time,'YYYY-MM-DD') <
      (select max(to_char(snap_time,'YYYY-MM-DD')) from stats$tab_stats)
;


--**********************************************************
-- The second highest date is select max(mydate) from d1;
--**********************************************************

set heading off;

prompt Object growth - Comparing last two snapshots
prompt
prompt This report shows the growth of key tables
prompt for the past week.


select 'Old date = '||max(mydate) from d1;
select 'New date = '||max(to_char(snap_time,'YYYY-MM-DD')) from stats$tab_stats;

break on report ;
compute sum of old_bytes on old.table_name;
```

```
set heading on;

column old_bytes format 999,999,999
column new_bytes format 999,999,999
column change    format 999,999,999

select
   new.table_name,
   old.bytes              old_bytes,
   new.bytes              new_bytes,
   new.bytes - old.bytes  change
from
   stats$tab_stats old,
   stats$tab_stats new
where
   old.table_name = new.table_name
and
   new.bytes > old.bytes
and
   new.bytes - old.bytes > 10000
and
   to_char(new.snap_time, 'YYYY-MM-DD') =
         (select max(to_char(snap_time,'YYYY-MM-DD')) from stats$tab_stats)
and
   to_char(old.snap_time, 'YYYY-MM-DD') =
           (select max(mydate) from d1)
and
   new.table_name not like 'STATS$%'
order by
   new.bytes-old.bytes desc
;

--************************************************************
   First we need to get the second-highest date in idx_stats
--************************************************************
set lines 80;
-- © 2001 by Donald Keith Burleson - All Rights Reserved
set feedback off;
set verify off;
set echo off;

drop table d1;

create table d1 as
select distinct
   to_char(snap_time,'YYYY-MM-DD') mydate
from
   stats$idx_stats
where
   to_char(snap_time,'YYYY-MM-DD') <
     (select max(to_char(snap_time,'YYYY-MM-DD')) from stats$idx_stats)
;

--************************************************************
```

```
-- The second highest date is select max(mydate) from d1;
--*********************************************************

set heading off;

prompt Object growth - Comparing last two snapshots
prompt
prompt This report shows the growth of key indexes
prompt for the past week.


select 'Old date = '||max(mydate) from d1;
select 'New date = '||max(to_char(snap_time,'YYYY-MM-DD')) from stats$idx_stats;

break on report ;
compute sum of old_bytes on old.table_name;

set heading on;

column old_bytes format 999,999,999
column new_bytes format 999,999,999
column change    format 999,999,999

select
   new.index_name,
   old.bytes               old_bytes,
   new.bytes               new_bytes,
   new.bytes - old.bytes   change
from
   stats$idx_stats old,
   stats$idx_stats new
where
   old.index_name = new.index_name
and
   new.bytes > old.bytes
and
   new.bytes - old.bytes > 10000
and
   to_char(new.snap_time, 'YYYY-MM-DD') =
          (select max(to_char(snap_time,'YYYY-MM-DD')) from stats$idx_stats)
and
   to_char(old.snap_time, 'YYYY-MM-DD') =
           (select max(mydate) from d1)
and
   new.index_name not like 'STATS$%'
order by
   new.bytes-old.bytes desc
;
```

rpt_obj_stats.sql

```
connect perfstat/perfstat;
```

```
set lines 80;
-- © 2001 by Donald Keith Burleson - All Rights Reserved
set feedback off;
set verify off;
set echo off;

--*********************************************************
-- This report compares the max(snap_time) to the second-highest date
--*********************************************************

--*********************************************************
-- First we need to get the second-highest date in tab_stats
--*********************************************************
drop table d1;

create table d1 as
select distinct
   to_char(snap_time,'YYYY-MM-DD') mydate
from
   stats$tab_stats
where
   to_char(snap_time,'YYYY-MM-DD') <
    (select max(to_char(snap_time,'YYYY-MM-DD')) from stats$tab_stats)
;

--*********************************************************
-- The second highest date is select max(mydate) from d1;
--*********************************************************

set heading off;

prompt '*********************************************'
select '  Most recent date '||
         max(to_char(snap_time,'YYYY-MM-DD'))
from stats$tab_stats;
select '  Older date '||
         max(mydate)
from d1;
prompt '*********************************************'

set heading on;

drop table t1;
drop table t2;
drop table t3;
drop table t4;


create table t1 as
select db_name, count(*) tab_count, snap_time from stats$tab_stats
where    to_char(snap_time, 'YYYY-MM-DD') =
          (select max(to_char(snap_time,'YYYY-MM-DD')) from stats$tab_stats)
group by db_name, snap_time;
```

```
create table t2 as
select db_name, count(*) idx_count, snap_time from stats$idx_stats
where    to_char(snap_time, 'YYYY-MM-DD') =
            (select max(to_char(snap_time,'YYYY-MM-DD')) from stats$idx_stats)
group by db_name, snap_time;

create table t3 as
select db_name, sum(bytes) tab_bytes, snap_time from stats$tab_stats
where    to_char(snap_time, 'YYYY-MM-DD') =
            (select max(to_char(snap_time,'YYYY-MM-DD')) from stats$tab_stats)
group by db_name, snap_time;

create table t4 as
select db_name, sum(bytes) idx_bytes, snap_time from stats$idx_stats
where    to_char(snap_time, 'YYYY-MM-DD') =
            (select max(to_char(snap_time,'YYYY-MM-DD')) from stats$idx_stats)
group by db_name, snap_time;

--*********************************************************
-- This report displays the most recent counts & size totals
--*********************************************************

column tab_bytes format 999,999,999,999
column idx_bytes format 999,999,999,999
column tab_count format 99,999
column idx_count format 99,999

clear computes;
compute sum label "Total" of tab_count on report;
compute sum label "Total" of idx_count on report;
compute sum label "Total" of tab_bytes on report;
compute sum label "Total" of idx_bytes on report;

break on report;

ttitle 'Most recent database object counts and sizes'

select
   a.db_name,
   tab_count,
   idx_count,
   tab_bytes,
   idx_bytes
from
   perfstat.t1 a,
   perfstat.t2 b,
   perfstat.t3 c,
   perfstat.t4 d
where
   a.db_name = b.db_name
and
   a.db_name = c.db_name
and
   a.db_name = d.db_name
```

```
;
--************************************************************
-- These temp tables will compare size growth since last snap
--************************************************************
drop table t1;
drop table t2;
drop table t3;
drop table t4;

create table t1 as
select db_name, sum(bytes) new_tab_bytes, snap_time from stats$tab_stats
where    to_char(snap_time, 'YYYY-MM-DD') =
           (select max(to_char(snap_time,'YYYY-MM-DD')) from stats$tab_stats)
group by db_name, snap_time;

create table t2 as
select db_name, sum(bytes) new_idx_bytes, snap_time from stats$idx_stats
where    to_char(snap_time, 'YYYY-MM-DD') =
           (select max(to_char(snap_time,'YYYY-MM-DD')) from stats$idx_stats)
group by db_name, snap_time;

create table t3 as
select db_name, sum(bytes) old_tab_bytes, snap_time from stats$tab_stats
where    to_char(snap_time, 'YYYY-MM-DD') =
           (select max(mydate) from d1)
group by db_name, snap_time;

create table t4 as
select db_name, sum(bytes) old_idx_bytes, snap_time from stats$idx_stats
where    to_char(snap_time, 'YYYY-MM-DD') =
           (select max(mydate) from d1)
group by db_name, snap_time;

--************************************************************
-- This is the size comparison report
--************************************************************
column old_bytes format 999,999,999,999
column new_bytes format 999,999,999,999
column change    format 999,999,999,999

compute sum label "Total" of old_bytes on report;
compute sum label "Total" of new_bytes on report;
compute sum label "Total" of change    on report;

break on report;
ttitle 'Database size change|comparing the most recent snapshot dates';

select
   a.db_name,
   old_tab_bytes+old_idx_bytes old_bytes,
   new_tab_bytes+new_idx_bytes new_bytes,
   (new_tab_bytes+new_idx_bytes)-(old_tab_bytes+old_idx_bytes) change
from
```

```
      perfstat.t1 a,
      perfstat.t2 b,
      perfstat.t3 c,
      perfstat.t4 d
where
   a.db_name = b.db_name
and
   a.db_name = c.db_name
and
   a.db_name = d.db_name
;


--***********************************************************
-- This is the standard chained row report
--
-- This is for columns without long columns
-- because long columns often chain onto adjacent data blocks
--***********************************************************

column c1 heading "Owner"    format a9;
column c2 heading "Table"    format a12;
column c3 heading "PCTFREE" format 99;
column c4 heading "PCTUSED" format 99;
column c5 heading "avg row" format 99,999;
column c6 heading "Rows"     format 999,999,999;
column c7 heading "Chains"   format 999,999,999;
column c8 heading "Pct"      format .99;

set heading off;
select 'Tables with > 10% chained rows and no LONG columns.' from dual;
set heading on;

select
   owner            c1,
   table_name       c2,
   pct_free         c3,
   pct_used         c4,
   avg_row_len      c5,
   num_rows         c6,
   chain_cnt        c7,
   chain_cnt/num_rows c8
from
   dba_tables
where
   owner not in ('SYS','SYSTEM','PERFSTAT')
and
   chain_cnt/num_rows > .1
and
table_name not in
 (select table_name from dba_tab_columns
   where
 data_type in ('RAW','LONG RAW','CLOB','BLOB')
 )
and
```

```
chain_cnt > 0
order by chain_cnt desc
;

--********************************************************
-- This chained row report is for tables that have long
-- columns.  The only fix for this chaining is increasing
-- the db_block_size
--********************************************************
set heading off;
select 'Tables with > 10% chained rows that contain LONG columns.' from dual;
set heading on;

select
   owner             c1,
   table_name        c2,
   pct_free          c3,
   pct_used          c4,
   avg_row_len       c5,
   num_rows          c6,
   chain_cnt         c7,
   chain_cnt/num_rows c8
from
   dba_tables
where
   owner not in ('SYS','SYSTEM','PERFSTAT')
and
   chain_cnt/num_rows > .1
and
table_name in
 (select table_name from dba_tab_columns
   where
 data_type in ('RAW','LONG RAW','CLOB','BLOB')
 )
and
chain_cnt > 0
order by chain_cnt desc
;

--********************************************************
-- This report will show all objects that have extended
-- between the snapshot period.
-- The DBA may want to increase the next_extent size
-- for these objects
--********************************************************
column db format a10
column owner format a10
column tab_name format a30

break on db;


ttitle 'Table extents report|Where extents > 200 or table extent changed|comparing
```

```
most recent snapshots'

select /*+ first_rows */
distinct
   a.db_name       db,
   a.owner         owner,
   a.table_name    tab_name,
   b.extents       old_ext,
   a.extents       new_ext
from
   PERFSTAT.stats$tab_stats a,
   PERFSTAT.stats$tab_stats b
where
   a.db_name = b.db_name
and
   a.owner = b.owner
and
   a.table_name = b.table_name
and
(
   b.extents > a.extents
   or
   a.extents > b.extents
   or
   a.extents > 200
)
and
   a.owner not in ('SYS','SYSTEM','PERFSTAT')
and
   a.table_name not in ('PLAN_TABLE')
and
   to_char(a.snap_time, 'YYYY-MM-DD') =
           (select max(to_char(snap_time,'YYYY-MM-DD')) from stats$tab_stats)
and
   to_char(b.snap_time, 'YYYY-MM-DD') =
           (select max(mydate) from d1)
order by
   a.db_name,
   a.extents
;

column db format a10
column owner format a10
column idx_name format a30

break on db;


ttitle 'Index extents report|Where extents > 200 or index extent changed|Comparing
past two snapshots'

select /*+ first_rows */
distinct
   a.db_name       db,
```

```
        a.owner         owner,
        a.index_name    idx_name,
        b.extents       old_ext,
        a.extents       new_ext
from
        PERFSTAT.stats$idx_stats a,
        PERFSTAT.stats$idx_stats b
where
        a.owner not in ('SYS','SYSTEM','PERFSTAT')
and
        a.db_name = b.db_name
and
        a.owner = b.owner
and
        a.index_name = b.index_name
and
(
        b.extents > a.extents
        or
        a.extents > b.extents
        or
        a.extents > 200
)
and
        to_char(a.snap_time, 'YYYY-MM-DD') =
                (select max(to_char(snap_time,'YYYY-MM-DD')) from stats$idx_stats)
and
        to_char(b.snap_time, 'YYYY-MM-DD') =
                (select max(mydate) from d1)
order by
        a.db_name,
        a.extents
;
```

rpt_tab.sql

```
column c1  heading "TABLE NAME"       format a15;
column c2  heading "EXTS"             format 999;
column c3  heading "FL"               format 99;
column c4  heading "# OF ROWS"        format 99,999,999;
column c5  heading "#_rows*row_len"   format 9,999,999,999;
column c6  heading "SPACE ALLOCATED"  format 9,999,999,999;
column c7  heading "PCT USED"         format 999;

-- © 2001 by Donald Keith Burleson - All Rights Reserved
set lines 80;

spool tab_rpt.lst

select
        table_name          c1,
        b.extents           c2,
        b.freelists         c3,
```

```
        num_rows              c4,
        num_rows*avg_row_len  c5,
        blocks*16384          c6,
        ((num_rows*avg_row_len)/(blocks*16384))*100 c7
from
   perfstat.stats$tab_stats a,
   dba_segments b
where
 b.segment_name = a.table_name
and
    to_char(snap_time,'yyyy-mm-dd') =
       (select max(to_char(snap_time,'yyyy-mm-dd')) from perfstat.stats$tab_stats)
and
    avg_row_len > 500
order by c5 desc
;

spool off;
```

rpt_table_rows.sql

```
--**********************************************************
-- First we need to get the second-highest date in tab_stats
--**********************************************************
set lines 80;
-- © 2001 by Donald Keith Burleson - All Rights Reserved
set feedback off;
set verify off;
set echo off;

drop table d1;

create table d1 as
select distinct
   to_char(snap_time,'YYYY-MM-DD') mydate
from
   stats$tab_stats
where
   to_char(snap_time,'YYYY-MM-DD') <
     (select max(to_char(snap_time,'YYYY-MM-DD')) from stats$tab_stats)
;

--**********************************************************
-- The second highest date is select max(mydate) from d1;
--**********************************************************

ttitle 'Oracle Object growth|Comparing last two snapshots'

prompt This report shows the growth of key tables within the RovOracle

prompt for the past week.

column old_rows format 9,999,999
```

```
column new_rows format 9,999,999

select
   new.table_name,
   old.num_rows                old_rows,
   new.num_rows                new_rows,
   new.num_rows - old.num_rows change
from
   stats$tab_stats old,
   stats$tab_stats new
where
   new.num_rows > old.num_rows
and
   old.table_name = new.table_name
and
   to_char(new.snap_time, 'YYYY-MM-DD') =
           (select max(to_char(snap_time,'YYYY-MM-DD')) from stats$tab_stats)
and
   to_char(old.snap_time, 'YYYY-MM-DD') =
           (select max(mydate) from d1)
;
```

run_object_report.ksh

```
#!/bin/ksh

# Validate the Oracle database name with
# lookup in /var/opt/oracle/oratab
TEMP=`cat /var/opt/oracle/oratab|grep \^$1:|\
cut -f1 -d':'|wc -l`
tmp=`expr TEMP`      # Convert string to number
if [ $tmp -ne 1 ]
then
   echo "Your input $1 is not a valid ORACLE_SID."
   exit 99
fi


# Here we must set the environment . . . .
ORACLE_SID=$1
export ORACLE_SID
ORACLE_HOME=`cat /var/opt/oracle/oratab|grep $ORACLE_SID:|cut -f2 -d':'`
export ORACLE_HOME
PATH=$ORACLE_HOME/bin:$PATH
export PATH
MON=`echo /export/home/oracle/obj_stat`
export MON


sqlplus perfstat/perfstat<<!
spool ${MON}/stats_rpt.lst
@${MON}/rpt_oracle
@${MON}/rpt_object_stats
```

```
spool off;
exit;
!

#*************************************
# Mail the Object Statistics Reports
#*************************************
cat $MON/stats_rpt.lst|mailx -s "Oracle Weekly Statistics Summary" \
   don@remote-dba.net
# \
#   terry.oakes@worldnet.att.net
```

iostat Reports

create_iostat.sql

```
drop table perfstat.stats$iostat;

create table
perfstat.stats$iostat
(
snap_time          date,
elapsed_seconds    number(4),
hdisk              varchar2(8),
kb_read            number(9,0),
kb_write           number(9,0)
)
tablespace perfstat
storage (initial 20m next 1m )
;

create index
perfstat.stats$iostat_date_idx
on
perfstat.stats$iostat
(snap_time)
tablespace perfstat
storage (initial 5m next 1m)
;

create index
perfstat.stats$iostat_hdisk_idx
on
perfstat.stats$iostat
(hdisk)
tablespace perfstat
storage (initial 5m next 1m)
;
```

get_iostat_aix.ksh

```
#!/bin/ksh

while true
do
    iostat 300 1 | awk  '{ printf("%s ,%s ,%s\n", $1, $5, $6) }' |\
    while read    HDISK VMSTAT_IO_R VMSTAT_IO_W
    do
    if (echo $HDISK|grep -cq hdisk );then

        sqlplus -s / <<EOF
        insert into iostat values
        (SYSDATE, 5, '$HDISK', $VMSTAT_IO_R,$VMSTAT_IO_W);
        EXIT
        EOF
    fi
    done
done
```

get_iostat_solaris.ksh

```
#!/bin/ksh

while true
do
    iostat -x  300 1|\
        sed 1,2d|\
        awk  '{ printf("%s %s %s\n", $1, $4, $5) }' |\
    while read HDISK VMSTAT_IO_R VMSTAT_IO_W
    do

        echo $HDISK
        echo $VMSTAT_IO_R
        echo $VMSTAT_IO_W

        sqlplus -s / <<!
        insert into
            perfstat.stats\$iostat
        values
            (SYSDATE, 300, '$HDISK', $VMSTAT_IO_R,$VMSTAT_IO_W);
        exit
!

    done
    sleep 300

done
```

rpt_disk.sql

```
column hdisk            format a10;
column mydate           format a15;
column sum_kb_read      format 999,999;
column sum_kb_write     format 999,999;

-- © 2001 by Donald Keith Burleson - All Rights Reserved

break on hdisk skip 1;

select
   hdisk,
--   to_char(snap_time,'yyyy-mm-dd HH24:mi:ss') mydate,
--   to_char(snap_time,'yyyy-mm-dd HH24') mydate,
   to_char(snap_time,'day') mydate,
   sum(kb_read)  sum_kb_read,
   sum(kb_write) sum_kb_write
from
   stats$iostat
group by
   hdisk
   ,to_char(snap_time,'day')
--   ,to_char(snap_time,'yyyy-mm-dd HH24:mi:ss')
--   ,to_char(snap_time,'yyyy-mm-dd HH24')
   ;
```

rpt_hot.sql

```
-- © 2001 by Donald Keith Burleson - All Rights Reserved
set feedback off;
set verify off;

--prompt *********************************************************
--prompt  This will identify any single disk who's read I/O
--prompt  is more than 25% of the total read I/O of the database.
--prompt
--prompt  The "hot" disk should be examined, and the hot table/index
--prompt  should be identified using STATSPACK.
--prompt
--prompt *********************************************************
column mydate format a16
column hdisk format a40
column reads  format 999,999,999

select
   to_char(new.snap_time,'yyyy-mm-dd HH24')  mydate,
   new.hdisk                                  file_name,
   new.kb_read-old.kb_read                    reads
from
   perfstat.stats$iostat old,
   perfstat.stats$iostat new
```

```
where
   new.snap_time > sysdate-&1
and
   old.snap_time = new.snap_time-1
and
   new.hdisk = old.hdisk
and
   (new.kb_read-old.kb_read)*10 >
(
select
   (newreads.kb_read-oldreads.kb_read) reads
from
   perfstat.stats$iostat oldreads,
   perfstat.stats$iostat newreads
where
   new.snap_time = newreads.snap_time
and
   newreads.snap_time = new.snap_time
and
   oldreads.snap_time = new.snap_time-1
and
   (newreads.kb_read-oldreads.kb_read) > 0
)
;
--prompt ************************************************************
--prompt  This will identify any single disk who's write I/O
--prompt  is more than 10% of the total write I/O of the database.
--prompt ************************************************************
--prompt
column mydate format a16
column file_name format a40
column writes   format 999,999,999

select
   to_char(new.snap_time,'yyyy-mm-dd HH24')  mydate,
   new.hdisk                                 file_name,
   new.kb_write-old.kb_write                 writes
from
   perfstat.stats$iostat old,
   perfstat.stats$iostat new
where
   new.snap_time > sysdate-&1
and
   old.snap_time = new.snap_time-1
and
   new.hdisk = old.hdisk
and
   (new.kb_write-old.kb_write)*10 >
(
select
   (newwrites.kb_read-oldwrites.kb_read) writes
from
   perfstat.stats$iostat oldwrites,
   perfstat.stats$iostat newwrites
```

```
where
   new.snap_time = newwrites.snap_time
and
   newwrites.snap_time = new.snap_time
and
   oldwrites.snap_time = new.snap_time-1
and
  (newwrites.kb_read-oldwrites.kb_read) > 0
);
```

run_iostat_aix.ksh

```
#!/bin/ksh

# First, we must set the environment . . . .
ORACLE_SID=xxxx
ORACLE_HOME=`cat /etc/oratab|grep $ORACLE_SID|cut -f2 -d':'`
PATH=$ORACLE_HOME/bin:$PATH
MON=`echo ~oracle/mon`

#---------------------------------------
# If it is not running, then start it . . .
#---------------------------------------
check_stat=`ps -ef|grep get_iostat_aix|wc -l`;
oracle_num=`expr $check_stat`
if [ $oracle_num -ne 2 ]
 then nohup $MON/get_iostat_aix.ksh > /dev/null 2>&1 &
fi
```

run_iostat_solaris.ksh

```
#!/bin/ksh

# First, we must set the environment . . . .
ORACLE_SID=prodb1
ORACLE_HOME=`cat /var/opt/oracle/oratab|grep $ORACLE_SID|cut -f2 -d':'`
PATH=$ORACLE_HOME/bin:$PATH
MON=`echo ~oracle/iostat`

#---------------------------------------
# If it is not running, then start it . . .
#---------------------------------------
check_stat=`ps -ef|grep get_iostat|grep -v grep|wc -l`;
oracle_num=`expr $check_stat`
if [ $oracle_num -lt 1 ]
 then nohup $MON/get_iostat_solaris.ksh > /dev/null 2>&1 &
fi
```

Miscellanous UNIX Scripts

These scripts are provided as examples of actual UNIX scripts that you may modify for your environment.

apps_start.ksh

```ksh
#!/bin/ksh

#*******************************************************************
#
# Copyright (c) 2002 by Donald K. Burleson
#
# Licensing information may be found at www.dba-oracle.com
#
#*******************************************************************

# Exit if no first parameter $1
if [ -z "$1" ]
then
   echo "ERROR: Please pass a valid ORACLE_SID to this script"
   exit 99
fi


# Validate Oracle

TEMP=`cat /etc/oratab|grep \^$1:|cut -f1 -d':'|wc -l`
tmp=`expr TEMP`            # Convert string to number
if [ $tmp -ne 1 ]
then
   echo
   echo "ERROR: Your input parameter $1 is invalid.  Please Retry"
   echo
   exit 99
fi

if [ `whoami` != 'root' ]
then
   echo "Error: You must be root to execute the script.  Exiting."
   exit
fi

# First, we must set the environment . . . .
ORACLE_SID=$1
export ORACLE_SID

ORACLE_HOME=`cat /etc/oratab|grep ^$ORACLE_SID:|cut -f2 -d':'`
export ORACLE_HOME
PATH=$ORACLE_HOME/bin:$PATH:$ORACLE_HOME/lib
export PATH
```

```
APPL_TOP=`cat /etc/oratab|grep ^$ORACLE_SID|cut -d":" -f5`;
export APPL_TOP

. $ORACLE_HOME/$ORACLE_SID.env
. $APPL_TOP/APPL$ORACLE_SID.env

DB_NAME=$ORACLE_SID
export DB_NAME


#********************************************************
# Stop the Forms Server
#********************************************************
su - applmgr -c "/usr/local/bin/scripts/forms_server_start.ksh $1" >
usr/local/bin/scripts/logs/forms_server_start_$1

#Check for errors
test=`grep -i error /usr/local/bin/scripts/logs/forms_server_start_$1|wc -l`
val=`expr $test`

if [ $val -gt 0 ]
then
    echo
    echo "ERROR: Errors found in
usr/local/bin/scripts/logs/forms_server_start_$1."
    grep -i error /usr/local/bin/scripts/logs/forms_server_start_$1|mailx -s "$1
orm shutdown error detected" dhurley@custom.com dburleson@custom.com
fi


#********************************************************
# Stop the Concurrent manager
#********************************************************
su - applmgr -c "/usr/local/bin/scripts/conc_mgr_start.ksh $1" >
usr/local/bin/scripts/logs/conc_mgr_start_$1

#Chek for errors
test=`grep -i error /usr/local/bin/scripts/logs/conc_mgr_start_$1|wc -l`
val=`expr $test`

if [ $val -gt 0 ]
then
    eho
    eho "ERROR: Errors found in /usr/local/bin/scripts/logs/conc_mgr_start_$1."
    grep -i error /usr/local/bin/scripts/logs/conc_mgr_start_$1|mailx -s "$1
oncurrent manager shutdown error detected" dhurley@custom.com dburleson@custom.com
fi


#********************************************************
# Stop the Webserver
#********************************************************
su - oracle -c "/usr/local/bin/scripts/webserver_start.ksh $1" >
usr/local/bin/scripts/logs/webserver_start_$1

#Chek for errors
```

```
test=`grep -i error /usr/local/bin/scripts/logs/webserver_start_$1|wc -l`
val=`expr $test`

if [ $val -gt 0 ]
then
    eho
    eho "ERROR: Errors found in /usr/local/bin/scripts/logs/webserver_start_$1."
    grep -i error /usr/local/bin/scripts/logs/webserver_start_$1|mailx -s "$1
ebserver shutdown error detected" dhurley@custom.com dburleson@custom.com
fi


#*********************************************************
# Stop the listeners
#*********************************************************
su - oracle -c "/usr/local/bin/scripts/listener_start.ksh $1" >
usr/local/bin/scripts/logs/listener_start_$1

#Chek for errors
test=`grep -i error /usr/local/bin/scripts/logs/listener_start_$1|wc -l`
val=`expr $test`

if [ $val -gt 0 ]
then
    eho
    eho "ERROR: Errors found in /usr/local/bin/scripts/logs/listener_start_$1."
    grep -i error /usr/local/bin/scripts/logs/listener_start_$1|mailx -s "$1
ebserver shutdown error detected" dhurley@custom.com dburleson@custom.com
fi



#!/bin/ksh

# Exit if no first parameter $1
if [ -z "$1" ]
then
    echo "ERROR: Please pass a valid ORACLE_SID to this script"
    exit 99
fi

# Validate Oracle

TEMP=`cat /etc/oratab|grep \^$1:|cut -f1 -d':'|wc -l`
tmp=`expr TEMP`                # Convert string to number
if [ $tmp -ne 1 ]
then
    echo
    echo "ERROR: Your input parameter $1 is invalid.  Please Retry"
    echo
    exit 99
fi

if [ `whoami` != 'root' ]
then
    echo "Error: You must be root to execute the script.  Exiting."
```

```
    exit
fi

# First, we must set the environment . . . .
ORACLE_SID=$1
export ORACLE_SID

ORACLE_HOME=`cat /etc/oratab|grep ^$ORACLE_SID:|cut -f2 -d':'`
export ORACLE_HOME
PATH=$ORACLE_HOME/bin:$PATH:$ORACLE_HOME/lib
export PATH

APPL_TOP=`cat /etc/oratab|grep ^$ORACLE_SID|cut -d":" -f5`;
export APPL_TOP

. $ORACLE_HOME/$ORACLE_SID.env
. $APPL_TOP/APPL$ORACLE_SID.env

DB_NAME=$ORACLE_SID
export DB_NAME


#*******************************************************
# Stop the Forms Server
#*******************************************************
su - applmgr -c "/usr/local/bin/scripts/forms_server_stop.ksh $1" >
/usr/local/bin/scripts/logs/forms_server_stop_$1

#Check for errors
test=`grep -i error /usr/local/bin/scripts/logs/forms_server_stop_$1|wc -l`
val=`expr $test`

if [ $val -gt 0 ]
then
    echo
    echo "ERROR: Errors found in /usr/local/bin/scripts/logs/forms_server_stop_$1."
    grep -i error /usr/local/bin/scripts/logs/forms_server_stop_$1|mailx -s "$1
orm shutdown error detected" dhurley@custom.com dburleson@custom.com
fi

#*******************************************************
# Stop the Concurrent manager
#*******************************************************
su - applmgr -c "/usr/local/bin/scripts/conc_mgr_stop.ksh $1" >
usr/local/bin/scripts/logs/conc_mgr_stop_$1

#Chek for errors
test=`grep -i error /usr/local/bin/scripts/logs/conc_mgr_stop_$1|wc -l`
val=`expr $test`

if [ $val -gt 0 ]
then
    eho
    eho "ERROR: Errors found in /usr/local/bin/scripts/logs/conc_mgr_stop_$1."
```

```
    grep -i error /usr/local/bin/scripts/logs/conc_mgr_stop_$1|mailx -s "$1
oncurrent manager shutdown error detected" dhurley@custom.com dburleson@custom.com
fi

#*******************************************************
# Stop the Webserver
#*******************************************************
su - oracle -c "/usr/local/bin/scripts/webserver_stop.ksh $1" >
usr/local/bin/scripts/logs/webserver_stop_$1

#Chek for errors

test=`grep -i error /usr/local/bin/scripts/logs/webserver_stop_$1|wc -l`
val=`expr $test`

if [ $val -gt 0 ]
then
    eho
    eho "ERROR: Errors found in /usr/local/bin/scripts/logs/webserver_stop_$1."
    grep -i error /usr/local/bin/scripts/logs/webserver_stop_$1|mailx -s "$1
ebserver shutdown error detected" dhurley@custom.com dburleson@custom.com
fi

#*******************************************************
# Stop the listeners
#*******************************************************
su - oracle -c "/usr/local/bin/scripts/listener_stop.ksh $1" >
usr/local/bin/scripts/logs/listener_stop_$1

#Chek for errors
test=`grep -i error /usr/local/bin/scripts/logs/listener_stop_$1|wc -l`
val=`expr $test`

if [ $val -gt 0 ]
then
    eho
    eho "ERROR: Errors found in /usr/local/bin/scripts/logs/listener_stop_$1."
    grep -i error /usr/local/bin/scripts/logs/listener_stop_$1|mailx -s "$1
ebserver shutdown error detected" dhurley@custom.com dburleson@custom.com
fi
```

apps_stop.ksh

```
#!/bin/ksh

#*****************************************************************
#
# Copyright (c) 2002 by Donald K. Burleson
#
# Licensing information may be found at www.dba-oracle.com
#
#*****************************************************************
```

```
# Exit if no first parameter $1
if [ -z "$1" ]
then
   echo "ERROR: Please pass a valid ORACLE_SID to this script"
   exit 99
fi

# Validate Oracle

TEMP=`cat /etc/oratab|grep \^$1:|cut -f1 -d':'|wc -l`
tmp=`expr TEMP`              # Convert string to number
if [ $tmp -ne 1 ]
then
   echo
   echo "ERROR: Your input parameter $1 is invalid.  Please Retry"
   echo
   exit 99
fi

if [ `whoami` != 'root' ]
then
   echo "Error: You must be root to execute the script.  Exiting."
   exit
fi

# First, we must set the environment . . . .
ORACLE_SID=$1
export ORACLE_SID

ORACLE_HOME=`cat /etc/oratab|grep ^$ORACLE_SID:|cut -f2 -d':'`
export ORACLE_HOME
PATH=$ORACLE_HOME/bin:$PATH:$ORACLE_HOME/lib
export PATH

APPL_TOP=`cat /etc/oratab|grep ^$ORACLE_SID|cut -d":" -f5`;
export APPL_TOP

. $ORACLE_HOME/$ORACLE_SID.env
. $APPL_TOP/APPL$ORACLE_SID.env

DB_NAME=$ORACLE_SID
export DB_NAME


#********************************************************
# Stop the Forms Server
#********************************************************
su - applmgr -c "/usr/local/bin/scripts/forms_server_stop.ksh $1" >
usr/local/bin/scripts/logs/forms_server_stop_$1

#Check for errors
test=`grep -i error /usr/local/bin/scripts/logs/forms_server_stop_$1|wc -l`
val=`expr $test`
```

```
if [ $val -gt 0 ]
then
   echo
   echo "ERROR: Errors found in
usr/local/bin/scripts/logs/forms_server_stop_$1."
   grep -i error /usr/local/bin/scripts/logs/forms_server_stop_$1|mailx -s
$1 form shutdown error detected" dhurley@custom.com dburleson@custom.com
fi


#*******************************************************
# Stop the Concurrent manager
#*******************************************************
su - applmgr -c "/usr/local/bin/scripts/conc_mgr_stop.ksh $1" >
usr/local/bin/scripts/logs/conc_mgr_stop_$1

#Chek for errors
test=`grep -i error /usr/local/bin/scripts/logs/conc_mgr_stop_$1|wc -l`
val=`expr $test`

if [ $val -gt 0 ]
then
   eho
   eho "ERROR: Errors found in
usr/local/bin/scripts/logs/conc_mgr_stop_$1."
   grep -i error /usr/local/bin/scripts/logs/conc_mgr_stop_$1|mailx -s "$1
oncurrent manager shutdown error detected" dhurley@custom.com
burleson@custom.com
fi


#*******************************************************
# Stop the Webserver
#*******************************************************
su - oracle -c "/usr/local/bin/scripts/webserver_stop.ksh $1" >
usr/local/bin/scripts/logs/webserver_stop_$1

#Chek for errors
test=`grep -i error /usr/local/bin/scripts/logs/webserver_stop_$1|wc -l`
val=`expr $test`

if [ $val -gt 0 ]
then
   eho
   eho "ERROR: Errors found in
usr/local/bin/scripts/logs/webserver_stop_$1."
   grep -i error /usr/local/bin/scripts/logs/webserver_stop_$1|mailx -s "$1
ebserver shutdown error detected" dhurley@custom.com dburleson@custom.com
fi


#*******************************************************
# Stop the listeners
#*******************************************************
su - oracle -c "/usr/local/bin/scripts/listener_stop.ksh $1" >
usr/local/bin/scripts/logs/listener_stop_$1
```

```
#Chek for errors
test=`grep -i error /usr/local/bin/scripts/logs/listener_stop_$1|wc -l`
val=`expr $test`

if [ $val -gt 0 ]
then
    eho
    eho "ERROR: Errors found in
usr/local/bin/scripts/logs/listener_stop_$1."
    grep -i error /usr/local/bin/scripts/logs/listener_stop_$1|mailx -s "$1
ebserver shutdown error detected" dhurley@custom.com dburleson@custom.com
fi
```

check_db.ksh

```
#!/bin/ksh

#*******************************************************************
#
# Copyright (c) 2002 by Donald K. Burleson
#
# Licensing information may be found at www.dba-oracle.com
#
#*******************************************************************

# Loop through each host name . . .
for host in `cat ~oracle/.rhosts|cut -d"." -f1|awk '{print $1}'|sort -u`
do
  echo " "
  echo "************************"
  echo "$host"
  echo "************************"
  # Loop through each database name on the host. . .
  for db in `rsh $host "cat /etc/oratab|egrep ':N|:Y'|grep -v \*|cut -f1 -
':'"`
  do
    # Get the ORACLE_HOME for each database
    home=`rsh $host "cat /etc/oratab|egrep ':N|:Y'|grep -v \*|grep
{db}|cut -f2 -d':'"`
    echo " "
    echo "database is $db"
    #echo "home is is $home"
    rsh $host "
    ORACLE_SID=${db}; export ORACLE_SID;
    ORACLE_HOME=${home}; export ORACLE_HOME;
    ${home}/bin/sqlplus -s /<<!
    set pages 9999;
    set heading off;
    --*************************************************
    --  Here is the SQL
    --*************************************************
    select * from v"\\""$"database;
    select value from v"\\""$"parameter where name = 'optimizer_mode';
```

```
   --*************************************************
     exit
     !"
  done
done
```

check_filesystem_size.ksh

```
#!/bin/ksh

#*********************************************************************
#
# Copyright (c) 2002 by Donald K. Burleson
#
# Licensing information may be found at www.dba-oracle.com
#
#*********************************************************************

for i in `df -k|grep /u0|awk '{ print $4 }'`
do
   # Convert the file size to a numeric value
   filesize=`expr i`

   # If any filesystem has less than 100k, issue an alert
   if [ $filesize  -lt 100 ]
   then
      mailx -s "Oracle filesystem $i has less than 100k free."\
         don@burleson.cc\
         lawrence@oracle.com
   fi
done
```

check_initora.ksh

```
#!/bin/ksh

#*********************************************************************
#
# Copyright (c) 2002 by Donald K. Burleson
#
# Licensing information may be found at www.dba-oracle.com
#
#*********************************************************************

# Loop through each host name . . .
for host in `cat ~oracle/.rhosts|cut -d"." -f1|awk '{print $1}'|sort -u`
#for host in `echo sp2mr1 sp2mr2 sp2pr2`
do
  echo " "
  echo "************************"
  echo "$host"
```

```
    echo "************************"
    # Loop through each database name on the host. . .
    for db in `rsh $host "cat /etc/oratab|egrep ':N|:Y'|grep -v \*|cut -f1 -
':'"`
    do
        # Get the ORACLE_HOME for each database
        home=`rsh $host "cat /etc/oratab|egrep ':N|:Y'|grep -v \*|grep
{db}|cut -f2 -d':'"`
        echo " "
        echo "    -----------------------"
        echo "    Database is $db"
        echo "    -----------------------"
        #echo "home is is $home"
        rsh $host "
        ORACLE_SID=${db}; export ORACLE_SID;
        ORACLE_HOME=${home}; export ORACLE_HOME;
        ${home}/bin/sqlplus -s /<<!
        set pages 9999;
        set heading off;
        set echo off;
        set feedback off;
        column c1 format a30;
        column c2 format a40;
        select name c1, value c2 from v"\\""$"parameter where
        name in (
            'hash_joined_enabled ',
            'hash_area_size',
            'hash_multiblock_io_count',
            'v733_plans_enabled',
            'create_bitmap_area_size',
            'b_tree_bitmap_plans',
            'partition_view_enabled',
            'optimizer_percent_parallel',
            'fast_full_scan_enabled',
            'always_anti_join'
        );
        exit
        !"
    done
done
```

check_log_switch.ksh

```
#!/bin/ksh

#*******************************************************************
#
# Copyright (c) 2002 by Donald K. Burleson
#
# Licensing information may be found at www.dba-oracle.com
#
#*******************************************************************
```

```
# Loop through each host name . . .
for host in `cat ~oracle/.rhosts|cut -d"." -f1|awk '{print $1}'|sort -u`
do
  echo " "
  echo "*************************"
  echo "$host"
  echo "*************************"
  # Loop through each database name on the host. . .
  for db in `rsh $host "cat /etc/oratab|egrep ':N|:Y'|grep -v \*|cut -f1 -
':'"`
  do
      # Get the ORACLE_HOME for each database
      home=`rsh $host "cat /etc/oratab|egrep ':N|:Y'|grep -v \*|grep
{db}|cut -f2 -d':'"`
      echo " "
      echo "database is $db"
      #echo "home is is $home"
      rsh $host "
      ORACLE_SID=${db}; export ORACLE_SID;
      ORACLE_HOME=${home}; export ORACLE_HOME;
      ${home}/bin/sqlplus -s /<<!
      set pages 9999;
      select * from v"\\""$database;
break on DB_NAME skip 2;

select   name DB_NAME,
         count(distinct tablespace_name) NUM_TS,
         count(distinct file_id) NUM_FILES,
         round(avg(switches)) AVG_LOGS
from     v"\""$database,
         dba_data_files,
         (select substr(first_time,1,8) day,
               count(*) switches
          from v"\""$"loghist
          group by substr(first_time,1,8))
group by name;
      exit
      !"
  done
done
```

check_max_extents.ksh

```
#!/bin/ksh
#****************************************************************
#
# Copyright (c) 2002 by Donald K. Burleson
#
# Licensing information may be found at www.dba-oracle.com
#
#****************************************************************

# Loop through each host name . . .
```

```
for host in `cat ~oracle/.rhosts|cut -d"." -f1|awk '{print $1}'|sort -u`
do
  echo " "
  echo "************************"
  echo "$host"
  echo "************************"
  # Loop through each database name on the host. . .
  for db in `rsh $host "cat /etc/oratab|egrep ':N|:Y'|grep -v \*|cut -f1 -
':'"`
  do
     # Get the ORACLE_HOME for each database
     home=`rsh $host "cat /etc/oratab|egrep ':N|:Y'|grep -v \*|grep
{db}|cut -f2 -d':'"`
     echo " "
     echo "database is $db"
     #echo "home is is $home"
     rsh $host "
     ORACLE_SID=${db}; export ORACLE_SID;
     ORACLE_HOME=${home}; export ORACLE_HOME;
     ${home}/bin/sqlplus -s /<<!
     set pages 9999;
     set heading off;
     --************************************************
     --  Here is the SQL
     --************************************************
     select
        owner,
        table_name,
        max_extents
     from
        dba_tables
     where
        max_extents < 2000;
     --************************************************
     exit
     !"
  done
done
```

check_optimizer_mode.ksh

```
#!/bin/ksh
#*****************************************************************
#
# Copyright (c) 2002 by Donald K. Burleson
#
# Licensing information may be found at www.dba-oracle.com
#
#*****************************************************************

# Loop through each host name . . .
for host in `cat ~oracle/.rhosts|cut -d"." -f1|awk '{print $1}'|sort -u`
do
```

```ksh
   echo " "
   echo "***********************"
   echo "$host"
   echo "***********************"
   # Loop through each database name on the host. . .
   for db in `rsh $host "cat /etc/oratab|egrep ':N|:Y'|grep -v \*|cut -f1 -
':'"`
   do
      # Get the ORACLE_HOME for each database
      home=`rsh $host "cat /etc/oratab|egrep ':N|:Y'|grep -v \*|grep
{db}|cut -f2 -d':'"`
      echo " "
      echo "database is $db"
      #echo "home is is $home"
      rsh $host "
      ORACLE_SID=${db}; export ORACLE_SID;
      ORACLE_HOME=${home}; export ORACLE_HOME;
      ${home}/bin/sqlplus -s /<<!
      set pages 9999;
      set heading off;
      select value from v"\\""$"parameter where name='optimizer_mode';
      exit
      !"
   done
done
```

check_oraenv.ksh

```ksh
#!/bin/ksh

#*******************************************************************
#
# Copyright (c) 2002 by Donald K. Burleson
#
# Licensing information may be found at www.dba-oracle.com
#
#*******************************************************************

# Loop through each host name . . .
for host in `cat temphosts|cut -d"." -f1|awk '{print $1}'|sort -u`
do
  echo " "
  echo "***********************"
  echo "$host"
  echo "***********************"
      rsh $host "ls -al /usr/local/bin/oraenv"
      rsh $host "ls -al /usr/lbin/oraenv"
done
```

check_tnsnames.ksh

```ksh
#!/bin/ksh
#********************************************************************
#
# Copyright (c) 2002 by Donald K. Burleson
#
# Licensing information may be found at www.dba-oracle.com
#
#********************************************************************

# Loop through each host name . . .
for host in `cat ~oracle/.rhosts|cut -d"." -f1|awk '{print $1}'|sort -u`
do
  echo " "
  echo "************************"
  echo "$host"
  echo "************************"
  # Loop through each database name on the host. . .
  for db in `rsh $host "cat /etc/oratab|egrep ':N|:Y'|grep -v \*|cut -f1 -
':'"`
  do
    # Get the ORACLE_HOME for each database
    home=`rsh $host "cat /etc/oratab|egrep ':N|:Y'|grep -v \*|grep
{db}|cut -f2 -d':'"`
    echo " "
    echo "database is $db"
    #echo "home is is $home"
    # check the size of the tnsnames.ora file
    rsh $host "ls -al ${home}/network/admin/tnsnames.ora"
#    sqlplus -s /<<!
#    set pages 9999;
#
#from v\$parameter@$db
#where name  in ('nls_date_format','nls_language');
#    exit
#!
  done
done
```

chg_all.sh

```ksh
#!/bin/ksh


tmpdir=tmp.$$

mkdir $tmpdir.new

for f in $*
do
  sed -e 's/oldstring/newstring/g' < $f > $tmpdir.new/$f
```

```
done

# Make a backup first!
mkdir $tmpdir.old
mv $* $tmpdir.old/


cd $tmpdir.new
mv $* ../

cd ..
rmdir $tmpdir.new
```

chg_sys_system_password.ksh

```
#!/bin/ksh

#*********************************************************************
#
# Copyright (c) 2002 by Donald K. Burleson
#
# Licensing information may be found at www.dba-oracle.com
#
#*********************************************************************

# Loop through each host name . . .
for host in `cat ~oracle/.rhosts|cut -d"." -f1|awk '{print $1}'|sort -u`
do
  echo " "
  echo "*************************"
  echo "$host"
  echo "*************************"
  # Loop through each database name on the host. . .
  for db in `rsh $host "cat /etc/oratab|egrep ':N|:Y'|grep -v \*|cut -f1 -
':'"`
  do
     # Get the ORACLE_HOME for each database
     home=`rsh $host "cat /etc/oratab|egrep ':N|:Y'|grep -v \*|grep
{db}|cut -f2 -d':'"`
     echo " "
     echo "database is $db"
     #echo "home is is $home"
     rsh $host "
     ORACLE_SID=${db}; export ORACLE_SID;
     ORACLE_HOME=${home}; export ORACLE_HOME;
     ${home}/bin/sqlplus -s /<<!
     set pages 9999;
     set feedback on;
     set echo on;
     --*************************************************
     alter user sys    identified by xxx;
     alter user system identified by xxx;
     --*************************************************
```

```
    exit
    !"
  done
done
```

conc_mgr_start.ksh

```
#!/bin/ksh

#*******************************************************************
#
# Copyright (c) 2002 by Donald K. Burleson
#
# Licensing information may be found at www.dba-oracle.com
#
#*******************************************************************

if [ `whoami` != 'applmgr' ]
then
   echo "Error: You must be applmgr to execute the script.  Exiting."
   exit
fi

# Exit if no first parameter $1
if [ -z "$1" ]
then
   echo "ERROR: Please pass a valid ORACLE_SID to this script"
   exit 99
fi

# Validate Oracle

TEMP=`cat /etc/oratab|grep \^$1:|cut -f1 -d':'|wc -l`
tmp=`expr TEMP`            # Convert string to number
if [ $tmp -ne 1 ]
then
   echo
   echo "Your input parameter $1 is invalid.  ERROR: Please Retry"
   echo
   exit 99
fi

# First, we must set the environment . . . .
ORACLE_SID=$1
export ORACLE_SID

ORACLE_HOME=`cat /etc/oratab|grep ^$ORACLE_SID:|cut -f2 -d':'`
export ORACLE_HOME
PATH=$ORACLE_HOME/bin:$PATH:$ORACLE_HOME/lib
export PATH

APPL_TOP=`cat /etc/oratab|grep ^$ORACLE_SID|cut -d":" -f5`;
```

```
export APPL_TOP

. $ORACLE_HOME/$ORACLE_SID.env;
. $APPL_TOP/APPL$ORACLE_SID.env

echo "Starting concurrent manager for $DB_NAME ..."

DB_NAME=$ORACLE_SID
export DB_NAME
if [ $DB_NAME = "PROD" ]
then
   $FND_TOP/bin/startmgr sysmgr=apps/appsmwc mgrname=$DB_NAME
else
   $FND_TOP/bin/startmgr sysmgr=apps/apps mgrname=$DB_NAME
fi

jre oracle.apps.fnd.tcf.SocketServer $TCF_PORT &

exit_code=$?
```

conc_mgr_stop.ksh

```
#!/bin/ksh

#******************************************************************
#
# Copyright (c) 2002 by Donald K. Burleson
#
# Licensing information may be found at www.dba-oracle.com
#
#******************************************************************

if [ `whoami` != 'applmgr' ]
then
   echo "Error: You must be applmgr to execute the script.  Exiting."
   exit
fi

# Exit if no first parameter $1
if [ -z "$1" ]
then
   echo "ERROR: Please pass a valid ORACLE_SID to this script"
   exit 99
fi

# Validate Oracle

TEMP=`cat /etc/oratab|grep \^$1:|cut -f1 -d':'|wc -l`
tmp=`expr TEMP`             # Convert string to number
if [ $tmp -ne 1 ]
then
   echo
```

```
      echo "Your input parameter $1 is invalid.  ERROR: Please Retry"
      echo
      exit 99
fi

# First, we must set the environment . . . .
ORACLE_SID=$1
export ORACLE_SID

ORACLE_HOME=`cat /etc/oratab|grep ^$ORACLE_SID:|cut -f2 -d':'`
export ORACLE_HOME
PATH=$ORACLE_HOME/bin:$PATH:$ORACLE_HOME/lib
export PATH

APPL_TOP=`cat /etc/oratab|grep ^$ORACLE_SID|cut -d":" -f5`;
export APPL_TOP

. $ORACLE_HOME/$ORACLE_SID.env
. $APPL_TOP/APPL$ORACLE_SID.env

DB_NAME=$ORACLE_SID
export DB_NAME


echo "Shutting down concurrent managers for $DB_NAME ..."

echo $FND_TOP


if [ $DB_NAME = "PROD" ]; then
     $FND_TOP/bin/CONCSUB apps/appsmwc SYSADMIN 'System Administrator'
YSADMIN CONCURRENT FND SHUTDOWN
else
     $FND_TOP/bin/CONCSUB apps/apps SYSADMIN 'System Administrator' SYSADMIN
ONCURRENT FND SHUTDOWN
fi
```

core_alert.ksh

```
#!/bin/ksh

#*******************************************************************
#
# Copyright (c) 2002 by Donald K. Burleson
#
# Licensing information may be found at www.dba-oracle.com
#
#*******************************************************************

MYDATE=`date +"%Y%m%d"`

SERVER=`uname -a|awk '{print $2}'`
```

```ksh
if [ -f /usr/local/src/rsp_server-0.01/inetd_copy/core ]
then

   # Move the file to a dated location . . .
   mv /usr/local/src/rsp_server-0.01/inetd_copy/core /tmp/core_$MYDATE

   # send an e-mail to the administrator
   head /tmp/core_$MYDATE|\
   mail -s "EMERGENCY - WebServer $SERVER abort in /tmp/core_$MYDATE"\
      don@remote-dba.net\
      omar@rovia.com\
      carlos@rovia.com

   # Remove all connections for this WebServer from the testb1 database
   su - oracle -c "/usr/app/oracle/admin/product/8/1/6/bin/sqlplus
eader/reader@testb1<<!
   select count(*) from current_logons;
   delete from current_logons where webserver_name = '$SERVER';
   select count(*) from current_logons;
   exit
!"

   # Remove all connections for this WebServer from the testb2 database
   su - oracle -c "/usr/app/oracle/admin/product/8/1/6/bin/sqlplus
eader/reader@testb2<<!
   select count(*) from current_logons;
   delete from current_logons where webserver_name = '$SERVER';
   select count(*) from current_logons;
   exit
!"

fi
```

distr_files.ksh

```ksh
#!/bin/ksh

#******************************************************************
#
# Copyright (c) 2002 by Donald K. Burleson
#
# Licensing information may be found at www.dba-oracle.com
#
#******************************************************************

# Loop through each host name . . .
for host in `cat ~oracle/.rhosts|cut -d"." -f1|awk '{print $1}'|sort -u`
do
  echo " "
  echo "************************"
  echo "$host"
  echo "************************"
  #
```

```
#***************************************************
#   Add your rcp command below . . .
#***************************************************
 rcp -p /etc/xxxx ${host}:/etc/xxxx
done
```

distr_hp_kshrc.ksh

```
#!/bin/ksh

#********************************************************************
#
# Copyright (c) 2002 by Donald K. Burleson
#
# Licensing information may be found at www.dba-oracle.com
#
#********************************************************************

# Loop through each host name . . .
for host in `echo spp01 spp02 spp03 dtsgdev`
do
  echo " "
  echo "************************"
  echo "$host"
  echo "************************"
  #
  #***************************************************
  #   Add your rcp command below . . .
  #***************************************************
  rsh $host "ls -al .k*"
  rsh $host "chmod 700 .kshrc"
  rcp -p /u/oracle/all/.kshrc_hp ${host}:~oracle/.kshrc
  echo " "
  rsh $host "chmod 500 .kshrc"
  rsh $host "ls -al .k*"
done
```

distr_profile.ksh

```
#!/bin/ksh

#********************************************************************
#
# Copyright (c) 2002 by Donald K. Burleson
#
# Licensing information may be found at www.dba-oracle.com
#
#********************************************************************


# Loop through each host name . . .
```

```
for host in `echo dssseth sg40 ssev1 sss01 spdd02 sdds03` do
  echo " "
  echo "************************"
  echo "$host"
  echo "************************"
  #
  #**************************************************
  #  Add your rcp command below . . .
  #**************************************************
  rsh $host "ls -al .p*"
  rsh $host "chmod 700 .profile"
  rcp -p /u/oracle/.profile ${host}:~oracle/.profile
  echo " "
  rsh $host "chmod 500 .profile"
  rsh $host "ls -al .p*"
done
```

distr_rhosts.ksh

```
#!/bin/ksh

#*********************************************************************
#
# Copyright (c) 2002 by Donald K. Burleson
#
# Licensing information may be found at www.dba-oracle.com
#
#*********************************************************************


filetag=`date +"%y%m%d"`

# Loop through each host name . . .
for host in `cat ~oracle/.rhosts|cut -d"." -f1|awk '{print $1}'|sort -u`
do
  echo " "
  echo "************************"
  echo "$host"
  echo "************************"
  #
  #
  rsh $host "ls -al .r*"
  rsh $host "cp .rhosts .rhosts_${filetag}"
  echo "************************"
  rsh $host "ls -al .r*"
  echo "************************"
  rcp -p ~oracle/.rhosts $host:
  rsh $host "ls -al .r*"
done
```

distr_sql_login.ksh

```ksh
#!/bin/ksh

#********************************************************************
#
# Copyright (c) 2002 by Donald K. Burleson
#
# Licensing information may be found at www.dba-oracle.com
#
#********************************************************************


# Loop through each host name . . .
for host in `cat .rhosts|cut -d"." -f1|awk '{print $1}'|sort -u`
do
  echo " "
  echo "************************"
  echo "$host"
  echo "************************"
  #
  #**************************************************
  #  Add your rcp command below . . .
  #**************************************************
  rsh $host "ls -al /u01/app/oracle/admin/site/login.sql"
  rsh $host "chmod 700 /u01/app/oracle/admin/site/login.sql"
  rcp -p /u01/app/oracle/admin/site/login.sql
{host}:/u01/app/oracle/admin/site/login.sql
  echo " "
  rsh $host "chmod 500 /u01/app/oracle/admin/site/login.sql"
  rsh $host "ls -al /u01/app/oracle/admin/site/login.sql"
done
```

get_busy.ksh

```ksh
#!/bin/ksh

#********************************************************************
#
# Copyright (c) 2002 by Donald K. Burleson
#
# Licensing information may be found at www.dba-oracle.com
#
#********************************************************************


# First, we must set the environment . . . .
ORACLE_SID=PROD
export ORACLE_SID
ORACLE_HOME=`cat /etc/oratab|grep \^$ORACLE_SID:|cut -f2 -d':'`
export ORACLE_HOME
PATH=$ORACLE_HOME/bin:$PATH
```

```
export PATH
MON=`echo ~oracle/mon`
export MON
ORA_ENVFILE=${ORACLE_HOME}/${ORACLE_SID}.env
. $ORA_ENVFILE

SERVER_NAME=`uname -a|awk '{print $2}'`
typeset -u SERVER_NAME
export SERVER_NAME

# sample every 10 seconds
SAMPLE_TIME=10

while true
do

   #**************************************************************
   # Test to see if Oracle is accepting connections
   #**************************************************************
   $ORACLE_HOME/bin/sqlplus -s /<<! > /tmp/check_$ORACLE_SID.ora
   select * from v\$database;
   exit
!

   #**************************************************************
   # If not, exit . . .
   #**************************************************************
   check_stat=`cat /tmp/check_$ORACLE_SID.ora|grep -i error|wc -l`;
   oracle_num=`expr $check_stat`
   if [ $oracle_num -eq 0 ]
      then


      rm -f /home/oracle/statspack/busy.lst

      $ORACLE_HOME/bin/sqlplus -s / <<!>/home/oracle/statspack/busy.lst

      set feedback off;
      select
         to_char(sysdate,'yyy-mm-dd HH24:mi:ss'),
         event,
         substr(tablespace_name,1,14),
         p2
      from
         v\$session_wait a,
         dba_data_files  b
      where
         a.p1 = b.file_id
      and
         event in
         (
           'buffer busy waits',
           'enqueue'
```

```
        )
    ;

!

    var=`cat /home/oracle/statspack/busy.lst|wc -l`

    if [[ $var -gt 1 ]];
      then
        echo
**************************************************************"
        echo "There are waits"
        cat /home/oracle/statspack/busy.lst|\
            mailx -s "Monona block wait found"\
        dburleson@mline.com
#       dhurley@mline.com \
        echo
**************************************************************"
      exit
    fi

    sleep $SAMPLE_TIME
  fi
done
```

get_idlm.ksh

```
#*********************************************************************
#
# Copyright (c) 2002 by Donald K. Burleson
#
# Licensing information may be found at www.dba-oracle.com
#
#*********************************************************************

# Capture IDLM statistics - (c) 1998 by Donald Keith Burleson
DAY_OF_WEEK=`date +"%A"`
MACHINE_NAME=`hostname`
REPORT_FILE=/oracle/HOME/dba_reports/dlm_monitor.${MACHINE_NAME}.${DAY_OF_WE
K}.l
og
#
# Set up the file to log the lock to:
#
TIMESTAMP=`date +"%C%y.%m.%d-%H:%M:%S"`
DLM_RESOURCES=`/oracle/HOME/bin/lkdump -a res | head -2 | awk 'getline'`
DLM_LOCKS=`/oracle/HOME/bin/lkdump -a lock | head -2 | awk 'getline' `
DLM_PROCESS=`/oracle/HOME/bin/lkdump -a proc | head -2 | awk 'getline'`
printf "$TIMESTAMP  $DLM_RESOURCES  $DLM_LOCKS  $DLM_PROCESS \n" >>
REPORT_FILE

RES=`echo $DLM_RESOURCES|cut -f2 -d '='`
LOC=`echo $DLM_LOCKS|cut -f2 -d '='`
```

```
PRO=`echo $DLM_PROCESS|cut -f2 -d '='`

ORACLE_SID=HOME; export ORACLE_SID;
PATH=$PATH:/oracle/HOME/bin; export PATH;
ORACLE_HOME=/oracle/HOME; export ORACLE_HOME;
/oracle/HOME/bin/sqlplus <<! >> /dev/null

connect perfstat/perfstat;

insert into perfstat.stats$idlm_stats
 values (
   SYSDATE,
   $PRO,
   $RES,
   $LOC );

exit;
!
```

master_reorg.ksh

```
#!/bin/ksh

#*********************************************************************
#
# Copyright (c) 2002 by Donald K. Burleson
#
# Licensing information may be found at www.dba-oracle.com
#
#*********************************************************************

# usage: nohup don_reorg.ksh > don_reorg.lst 2>&1 &


# Ensure that running user is oracle . . . . .
oracle_user=`whoami|grep oracle|grep -v grep|wc -l`;
oracle_num=`expr $oracle_user`
if [ $oracle_num -lt 1 ]
 then echo "Current user is not oracle. Please su to oracle and retry."
 exit
fi

# Ensure that Oracle is running . . . . .
oracle_up=`ps -ef|grep pmon|grep -v grep|wc -l`;
oracle_num=`expr $oracle_up`
if [ $oracle_num -lt 1 ]
 then echo "ORACLE instance is NOT up. Please start Oracle and retry."
 exit
fi

#***********************************************************
# Submit parallel CTAS reorganizations of important tables
#***********************************************************
```

```
nohup reorg.ksh CUSTOMER   >customer.lst  2>&1 &
nohup reorg.ksh ORDER      >order.lst     2>&1 &
nohup reorg.ksh ITEM       >item.lst      2>&1 &
nohup reorg.ksh LINE_ITEM  >line_item.lst 2>&1 &
nohup reorg.ksh PRODUCT    >product.lst   2>&1 &
```

oracheck_solaris_run.ksh

```
#!/bin/ksh

#*********************************************************************
#
# Copyright (c) 1999 by Donald K. Burleson
# Licensing information may be found at www.dba-oracle.com
#
#*********************************************************************

# Ensure that the parms have been passed to the script
if [ -z "$1" ]
then
   echo "Usage: oracheck.run <ORACLE_SID>"
   exit 99
fi

var=`cat /var/opt/oracle/oratab|grep -v "#"|cut -d: -f1|grep ${1}|wc -l`

oracle_num=`expr $var`
if [ $oracle_num -ne 1 ]
 then
 echo "The variable ${1} is not a valid ORACLE_SID.  Please retry."
 exit 0
fi

ORACLE_SID=${1}
export ORACLE_SID

ORACLE_HOME=`cat /var/opt/oracle/oratab|grep ^$ORACLE_SID:|cut -f2 -d':'`
export ORACLE_HOME
#*************************************************************
# Get the Oracle users home directory from /etc/passwd
#*************************************************************
ora_unix_home_dir=`cat /etc/passwd|grep ^oracle|cut -f6 -d':'`
#echo home dir = $ora_unix_home_dir

#*************************************************************
# Here we gather the values from the parm files . . .
#*************************************************************
if [ -f ${ora_unix_home_dir}/mon/parm_ts_free_$ORACLE_SID.ora ]
then
   TS_FREE=`cat ${ora_unix_home_dir}/mon/parm_ts_free_$ORACLE_SID.ora`
else
   TS_FREE=`cat ${ora_unix_home_dir}/mon/parm_ts_free.ora`
fi
```

```
if [ -f ${ora_unix_home_dir}/mon/parm_num_extents_$ORACLE_SID.ora ]
then
   NUM_EXTENTS=`cat
{ora_unix_home_dir}/mon/parm_num_extents_$ORACLE_SID.ora`
else
   NUM_EXTENTS=`cat ${ora_unix_home_dir}/mon/parm_num_extents.ora`
fi


if [ -f ${ora_unix_home_dir}/mon/parm_mount_point_kb_free_$ORACLE_SID.ora ]
then
   KB_FREE=`cat
${ora_unix_home_dir}/mon/parm_mount_point_kb_free_$ORACLE_SID.ora`
else
   KB_FREE=`cat ${ora_unix_home_dir}/mon/parm_mount_point_kb_free.ora`
fi

#**************************************************************
# E-mailx setup
# Here we setup the $dbalist variable to send messages to the right DBA's
#**************************************************************

case $ORACLE_SID in
     "readprod" )
        dbalist='don@remote-dba.net, terry.oakes@worldnet.att.net' ;;
esac

#**************************************************************
# Let's exit immediately if the database is not running . . .
#**************************************************************
check_stat=`ps -ef|grep ${ORACLE_SID}|grep pmon|wc -l`;
oracle_num=`expr $check_stat`
if [ $oracle_num -lt 1 ]
 then
 exit 0
fi

#**************************************************************
# Test to see if Oracle is accepting connections
#**************************************************************
$ORACLE_HOME/bin/sqlplus -s /<<! > /tmp/check_$ORACLE_SID.ora
select * from v\$database;
exit
!

#**************************************************************
# If not, exit immediately . . .
#**************************************************************
check_stat=`cat /tmp/check_$ORACLE_SID.ora|grep -i error|wc -l`;
oracle_num=`expr $check_stat`
if [ $oracle_num -gt 0 ]
 then
 exit 0
fi
```

```
#echo db is up


rm -f /tmp/alert_log_dir_${ORACLE_SID}.ora
rm -f /tmp/log_archive_start_${ORACLE_SID}.ora
rm -f /tmp/log_archive_dest_${ORACLE_SID}.ora
rm -f /tmp/dump*${ORACLE_SID}.ora
rm -f /tmp/ora600_${ORACLE_SID}.ora
rm -f /tmp/arch_${ORACLE_SID}.ora

#**************************************************************
# Get details from Oracle dictionary
#**************************************************************
$ORACLE_HOME/bin/sqlplus -s /<<!

@${ora_unix_home_dir}/mon/get_dict_parm $ORACLE_HOME $ORACLE_SID

exit
!
#cat /tmp/dump*

#**************************************************************
# If the first character of the dump directory is a question-mark (?)
# then replace it with $ORACLE_HOME
#**************************************************************
sed 's/?/$ORACLE_HOME/g' /tmp/dump_$ORACLE_SID.ora >
tmp/dump1_$ORACLE_SID.ora

ALERT_DIR=`cat /tmp/alert_log_dir_${ORACLE_SID}.ora|awk '{print $1}'`
export ALERT_DIR

#**************************************************************
# If the first character of the alert ora directory is a question-mark (?)
# then prefix with $ORACLE_HOME
#**************************************************************

first_char=`echo $ALERT_DIR|grep ^?|wc -l`
first_num=`expr $first_char`
#echo $first_char
if [ $first_num -eq 1 ]
then
  new=`echo $ALERT_DIR|cut -d? -f2`
  ALERT_DIR=${ORACLE_HOME}$new
fi



#**************************************************************
# Check alert ora for ORA-600 and other ORA errors
# The list of ORA messages is in the file called parm_alert_log.ora
#**************************************************************

for MSG in `cat ${ora_unix_home_dir}/mon/parm_alert_log.ora`
do
```

```
   tail -400 $ALERT_DIR/alert_$ORACLE_SID.log|grep $MSG >>
tmp/ora600_${ORACLE_SID}.ora
done

#***************************************************************
# Only send the alert if there is an error in the output . . . .
#***************************************************************
check_stat=`cat /tmp/ora600_${ORACLE_SID}.ora|wc -l`;
oracle_num=`expr $check_stat`
if [ $oracle_num -ne 0 ]
then
    #***************************************************************
    # Only send the alert if there is a change to the output . . . .
    #***************************************************************
    newm=`diff /tmp/ora600_${ORACLE_SID}.ora /tmp/ora600_${ORACLE_SID}.old|wc
l`
    chgflg=`expr $newm`
    if [ $chgflg -ne 0 ]
    then
        #***************************************************************
        # Mail the message to the DBA's in $dbalist
        #***************************************************************
        cat /tmp/ora600_${ORACLE_SID}.ora|mailx -s "$ORACLE_SID alert log
    essage detected" $dbalist
    fi
fi

cp /tmp/ora600_${ORACLE_SID}.ora /tmp/ora600_${ORACLE_SID}.old
rm -f /tmp/oracheck_${ORACLE_SID}.ora

# Here we write a blank line to the ora file . . .
echo `date` > /tmp/oracheck_${ORACLE_SID}.ora

#***************************************************************
# Now we run the check, writing errors to the oracheck.ora file
#***************************************************************
~oracle/mon/oracheck.ksh ${ORACLE_SID} ${TS_FREE} ${NUM_EXTENTS} >>
tmp/oracheck_${ORACLE_SID}.ora

#***************************************************************
# This section checks the Oracle mount points
#***************************************************************


#***************************************************************
# Get the Oracle users home directory from /etc/passwd
#***************************************************************
ora_unix_home_dir=`cat /etc/passwd|grep ^oracle|cut -f6 -d':'`
#echo home dir = $ora_unix_home_dir


#***************************************************************
# Set-up the dialect changes for HP/UX and AIX (df -k) vs (bdf)
#***************************************************************
```

```
dialect_df="df -k"

#***************************************************************
# Get the free space from the archived redo log directory
#***************************************************************
LOG_ARCHIVE_START=`cat /tmp/log_archive_start_${ORACLE_SID}.ora|awk '{print
1}'`
export LOG_ARCHIVE_START

#echo $LOG_ARCHIVE_START
if [ $LOG_ARCHIVE_START = 'TRUE' ]
then

   LOG_ARCHIVE_DEST=`cat /tmp/log_archive_dest_${ORACLE_SID}.ora|awk '{print
1}'`
   export LOG_ARCHIVE_DEST

   nohup ${dialect_df} $LOG_ARCHIVE_DEST > /tmp/arch_${ORACLE_SID}.ora 2>&1


   # The above could be not found . . .
   flag1=`cat /tmp/arch_${ORACLE_SID}.ora|grep find|wc -1`
   #***************************************************************
   # If the log archive dest is not found, truncate last entry
   #***************************************************************
   free_space_num=`expr ${flag1}`
   if [ $free_space_num -eq 1 ]
   then
     echo $LOG_ARCHIVE_DEST|sed 's/\/arch//g' > /tmp/arch1_$ORACLE_SID.ora
     LOG_ARCHIVE_DEST=`cat /tmp/arch1_$ORACLE_SID.ora`
   fi

   #  This ugly code is because bdf and df -k have free space in different
columns
   if [ $os = "IRIX64" ]
   then
     arch_dir_mp=`${dialect_df} $LOG_ARCHIVE_DEST|grep -v kbytes|awk '{
print $7 }'`
     arch_free_space=`${dialect_df} ${arch_dir_mp}|grep -v kbytes|awk '{
print $3 }'`
   fi
   if [ $os = "AIX" ]
   then
     arch_dir_mp=`${dialect_df} $LOG_ARCHIVE_DEST|grep -v blocks|awk '{
print $7 }'`
     arch_free_space=`${dialect_df} ${arch_dir_mp}|grep -v blocks|awk '{
print $3 }'`
   fi
   if [ $os = "OSF1" ]
   then
     arch_dir_mp=`${dialect_df} $LOG_ARCHIVE_DEST|grep -v blocks|awk '{
print $7 }'`
     arch_free_space=`${dialect_df} ${arch_dir_mp}|grep -v blocks|awk '{
print $3 }'`
```

```
   fi
   if [ $os = "HP-UX" ]    then
       arch_dir_mp=`${dialect_df} $LOG_ARCHIVE_DEST|grep -v kbytes|awk '{
print $6 }'`
       arch_free_space=`${dialect_df} ${arch_dir_mp}|grep -v kbytes|awk '{
print $4 }'`
   fi

   #echo $LOG_ARCHIVE_DEST
   #echo $arch_dir_mp
   #echo $arch_free_space

   #**************************************************************
   # Now, display if free space is < ${KB_FREE}
   #**************************************************************
   free_space_num=`expr ${arch_free_space}`
   kb_free_num=`expr ${KB_FREE}`
   #echo $free_space_num
   if [ $free_space_num -lt ${kb_free_num} ]
     then
       #**************************************************************
       # Display a message on the operations console
       #**************************************************************
         echo "NON-EMERGENCY ORACLE ALERT. Mount point ${ora_unix_home_mp1}
as less than ${KB_FREE} K-Bytes free."|mailx -s "Rovia Alert Detected"
dbalist
       exit 67
   fi
fi
#**************************************************************
# get the mount point associated with the home directory
#**************************************************************

#echo $ora_unix_home_dir
#df  k $ora_unix_home_dir

ora_unix_home_mp=`${dialect_df} ${ora_unix_home_dir}|sed 1,1d|awk '{ print
6}'`
#echo mp1 = $ora_unix_home_mp
ora_unix_home_mp1=`echo ${ora_unix_home_mp}|awk '{ print $2 }'`

#**************************************************************
# Get the free space for the mount point for UNIX home directory
#**************************************************************

ora_unix_home_fr1=`${dialect_df} ${ora_unix_home_mp}|sed 1,1d|awk '{ print
4}'`

#echo free = $ora_unix_home_fr1

#**************************************************************
# Now, display if free space is < ${KB_FREE}
#**************************************************************
free_space_num=`expr ${ora_unix_home_fr1}`
```

```
kb_free_num=`expr ${KB_FREE}`
#echo $free_space_num
if [ $free_space_num -lt ${kb_free_num} ]
 then
    #*************************************************************
    # Display a message on the operations console
    #*************************************************************
    echo "NON-EMERGENCY ORACLE ALERT. Mount point ${ora_unix_home_mp1} has
ess than ${KB_FREE} K-Bytes free." |mailx -s "Rovia Alert Detected" $dbalist
    exit 67
fi

chmod +x /tmp/dump1_$ORACLE_SID.ora

#****************************************************************
# Now we execute this file to get the free space in the filesystem
#****************************************************************
/tmp/dump1_$ORACLE_SID.ora > /tmp/dump2_$ORACLE_SID.ora

loop=1
#****************************************************************
# Here we loop to get all free space numbers and check each
#****************************************************************
for free_num in `cat /tmp/dump2_$ORACLE_SID.ora`
do
    #echo loop = $loop
    mp=`cat /tmp/dump1_$ORACLE_SID.ora|awk '{print $2'}`
    mp1=`echo $mp|awk '{print$'$loop'}'`
    #echo point = $mp1
    free_space_num=`expr ${free_num}`
    #echo $free_space_num
    if [ $free_space_num -lt $kb_free_num ]
    then
        #*************************************************************
        # Display a message on the operations console
        #*************************************************************
        echo "NON-EMERGENCY ORACLE ALERT. The mount point for $mp1 has less
han ${KB_FREE} K-Bytes free."|mailx -s "Rovia Alert Detected" $dbalist
        loop="`expr $loop + 1`"
    fi
done

#****************************************************************
# If errors messages exist (2 or more lines), then go on . . .
#****************************************************************
if [ `cat /tmp/oracheck_${ORACLE_SID}.ora|wc -l` -ge 2 ]
then
    #*************************************************************
    # Display a message on the operations console
    #*************************************************************
    echo "NON-EMERGENCY ORACLE ALERT. Contact the DBA and report this error
==>"` cat /tmp/oracheck_${ORACLE_SID}.ora`|mailx -s "Rovia Alert Detected"
dbalist
```

```
    exit 69
fi
```

pin_packs.ksh

```
#!/bin/ksh

sqlplus /<!
set heading off;
set echo off;
set feedback off;

spool /tmp/msg$$

select
'execute dbms_shared_pool.keep('''||name||''');'
from
    v\$db_object_cache
where
    type in ('PACKAGE')
and
    kept='NO'
and
  executions >
  (select
      avg(executions)-(avg(executions)*.7)
      from
    v\$db_object_cache
    where
      type in ('PACKAGE')
  )
order by
    executions desc;

spool off;

-- Execute the pin command
--@/tmp/msg$$
!
```

profile.ksh

```
#!/bin/ksh

#*****************************************************************
#
# Copyright (c) 2002 by Donald K. Burleson
#
# Licensing information may be found at www.dba-oracle.com
#
#*****************************************************************
```

```
#**************************************************************
#  DO NOT customize this .profile script.
#  The directive below will allow to you add customizations
#  to the .kshrc file.  All host-specific profile customizations
#  should be placed in the .kshrc file.
#**************************************************************

ENV=.kshrc; export ENV


#******************************************************************
#  These are generic UNIX set-up commands
#******************************************************************
umask 022

DBABRV=ora; export DBABRV
ORACLE_TERM=vt100; export ORACLE_TERM
TERM=vt100; export TERM
wout=`who am i`DISPLAY=`expr "$wout" : ".*\(\([0-9]*\.[0-9]*\.[0-9]*\.[0-
9]*\)\)"`
DISPLAY="${DISPLAY}:0"; export DISPLAY
ORAENV_ASK=NO; export ORAENV_ASK
export EDITOR=vi

PATH=$PATH:$OBK_HOME/bin:/legato/bin:/usr/lbin:/usr/sbin:.
export PATH

SQLPATH=/export/home/oracle/admin:/u01/app/oracle/admin/sql:/u01/app/oracle/
admin/scripts/dba:/export/home/oracle/tools
export SQLPATH

#TNS_ADMIN=/u01/app/oracle/admin/site
#export TNS_ADMIN

#******************************************************************
# Keyboard
#******************************************************************
stty erase ^?
set -o vi

#******************************************************************
# Standard UNIX Prompt
#******************************************************************
ORACLE_SID=readtest
export ORACLE_SID

PS1="
`hostname`*\${ORACLE_SID}-\${PWD}
>"

export PS1

    TEMPHOME=`cat /var/opt/oracle/oratab|egrep ':N|:Y'|grep -v \*|cut -f2 -
```

```
':'|head -1`
   export TEMPHOME

   #*****************************************************************
   # For every Oracle_SID in /var/opt/oracle/oratab, create an alias using
the SID name.
   # Now, entering the ORACLE_SID at the UNIX prompt will completely set the
   # UNIX environment for that SID
   #*****************************************************************


   for DB in `cat /var/opt/oracle/oratab|grep -v \#|grep -v \*|cut -d":" -
1`
   do
      alias $DB='export ORAENV_ASK=NO; export ORACLE_SID='$DB'; .
TEMPHOME/bin/oraenv; export ORACLE_HOME; export ORACLE_BASE=`echo
ORACLE_HOME | sed -e 's:/product/.*::g'`; export DBA=$ORACLE_BASE/admin;
xport SCRIPT_HOME=$DBA/scripts; export PATH=$PATH:$SCRIPT_HOME; export
IB_PATH=$ORACLE_HOME/lib64:$ORACLE_HOME/lib '
   done

   #*************************************************************
   #  Here we set a default database SID and get an ORACLE_HOME
   #*************************************************************

   ORACLE_HOME=`cat /var/opt/oracle/oratab|grep -v \#|grep -v \*|cut -d":" -
2|head -1`
   export ORACLE_HOME
   ORACLE_BASE=`echo $ORACLE_HOME | sed -e 's:/product/.*::g'`
   export ORACLE_BASE
   DBA=$ORACLE_BASE
   export DBA

ATH=$PATH:$ORACLE_HOME/bin:$ORACLE_HOME:/usr/ccs/bin:/usr/local/bin:/usr/ucb
/export/home/oracle/tools
   export PATH

   ORACLE_SID=`cat /var/opt/oracle/oratab|grep -v \#|grep -v \*|cut -d":" -
1|head -1`
   export ORACLE_SID

#PATH=$PATH:$ORACLE_HOME/bin:$ORACLE_HOME:/usr/ccs/bin:/usr/ucb:/usr/include
   #
   # Aliases
   #
   alias tools='cd /export/home/oracle/tools'
   alias listbk='ls /export/home/oracle/book/Chapter8'
   alias table='cd $DBA/$ORACLE_SID/ddl/tables'
   alias index='cd $DBA/$ORACLE_SID/ddl/indexes'
   alias plsql='cd $DBA/$ORACLE_SID/ddl/plsql'
   alias ts='cd $DBA/$ORACLE_SID/ddl/tablespaces'
   alias precomp='cd $ORACLE_HOME/precomp/demo/proc/terrydir'
   alias alert='tail -100 $DBA/$ORACLE_SID/bdump/alert_$ORACLE_SID.log|more'
   alias arch='cd $DBA/$ORACLE_SID/arch'
```

```
        alias bdump='cd $DBA/$ORACLE_SID/bdump'
        alias cdump='cd $DBA/$ORACLE_SID/cdump'
        alias pfile='cd $DBA/$ORACLE_SID/pfile'
        alias udump='cd $DBA/$ORACLE_SID/udump'
        alias arsd='cd $DBA/$ORACLE_SID/arsd'
        alias rm='rm -i'
        alias sid='env|grep -i sid'
        alias admin='cd $DBA/admin'
        alias logbook='/u01/app/oracle/admin/$ORACLE_SID/logbook'

NLS_LANG='english_united kingdom.we8iso8859p1'
ORA_NLS33=$ORACLE_HOME/ocommon/nls/admin/data
ORACLE_TERM=vt100
LD_LIBRARY_PATH=/usr/lib:$ORACLE_HOME/lib64:$ORACLE_HOME/lib
PATH=$PATH:$ORACLE_HOME/bin
export NLS_LANG ORA_NLS33 PATH LD_LIBRARY_PATH

export JAVA_HOME=/usr/local/jre
export PATH=$JAVA_HOME/bin:$PATH

#readprod
readtest
```

sprem.ksh

```
#!/bin/ksh
# *********************************************
#
#  This will purge the 168 oldest snapshots
#  (7 oldest days worth @ one snapshot per hour)
#
#  This should be cronned weekly
#
#  sample crontab entry
#
#  00 7 1 * * /export/home/oracle/sprem.ksh > /export/home/r.lst
#
#   4/3/01 By Donald K. Burleson
#
# *********************************************

# First, we must set the environment . . . .
ORACLE_SID=$ORACLE_SID
export ORACLE_SID
#ORACLE_HOME=`cat /etc/oratab|grep ^$ORACLE_SID:|cut -f2 -d':'`
ORACLE_HOME=`cat /var/opt/oracle/oratab|grep ^$ORACLE_SID:|cut -f2 -d':'`
export ORACLE_HOME
PATH=$ORACLE_HOME/bin:$PATH
export PATH

for i in `echo 1 2 3 4 5 6 7`
do
$ORACLE_HOME/bin/sqlplus -s perfstat/perfstat<<!
```

```
select min(snap_id) + 24
   from
      perfstat.stats\$snapshot;


delete from
   perfstat.stats\$snapshot
where
  snap_id <
  (select
      min(snap_id)+24
   from
      perfstat.stats\$snapshot)
;
commit;
exit
!
done
```

tar_all.ksh

```
#!/bin/ksh

echo Start `date` > /usr/local/bin/scripts/logs/tar_start.lst

#***********************************************
# Mount the tape and rewind
#***********************************************
mt -f /dev/rmt/2m rew

#***********************************************
# Copy directories onto /dev/rmt/2m
#***********************************************
tar cvf /dev/rmt/2m /u03/oradata/PROD /u04/oradata/PROD /u01/oradata/PROD
u02/oradata/PROD /u01/app/oracle/admin/PROD/arch /u02/oradata/TEST
u03/oradata/TEST /u02/app/applmgr/1103/PROD /u01/app/oracle/product/8.0.5
u01/app/oracle/admin/PROD/arch

echo End `date` > /usr/local/bin/scripts/logs/tar_end.lst
```

trace_alert.ksh

```
#!/bin/ksh

#******************************************************************
#
# Copyright (c) 2002 by Donald K. Burleson
#
# Licensing information may be found at www.dba-oracle.com
#
#******************************************************************
```

```
#********************************************************
# Exit if no first parameter $1 is passed to script
#********************************************************
if [ -z "$1" ]
then
    echo "Usage: trace_alert.ksh <ORACLE_SID>"
    exit 99
fi


#********************************************************
# First, we must set the environment . . . .
#********************************************************
ORACLE_SID=$1
export ORACLE_SID
ORACLE_HOME=`cat /var/opt/oracle/oratab|grep $ORACLE_SID:|cut -f2 -d':'`
export ORACLE_HOME
ORACLE_BASE=`echo $ORACLE_HOME | sed -e 's:/product/.*::g'`
export ORACLE_BASE
export DBA=$ORACLE_BASE/admin;
export DBA
PATH=$ORACLE_HOME/bin:$PATH
export PATH
MON=`echo ~oracle/mon`
export MON
#********************************************************
# Get the server name & date for the e-mail message
#********************************************************
SERVER=`uname -a|awk '{print $2}'`

MYDATE=`date +"%m/%d %H:%M"`



#********************************************************
# Remove the old file list
#********************************************************
rm -f /tmp/trace_list.lst
touch /tmp/trace_list.lst


#********************************************************
# list the full-names of all possible dump files . . . .
#********************************************************
find $DBA/$ORACLE_SID/bdump/*.trc    -mtime -1 -print >> /tmp/trace_list.lst
find $DBA/$ORACLE_SID/udump/*.trc    -mtime -1 -print >> /tmp/trace_list.lst
find $ORACLE_HOME/rdbms/log/*.trc    -mtime -1 -print >> /tmp/trace_list.lst


#********************************************************
# Exit if there are not any trace files found
#********************************************************
NUM_TRACE=`cat /tmp/trace_list.lst|wc -l`
oracle_num=`expr $NUM_TRACE`
if [ $oracle_num -lt 1 ]
 then
 exit 0
fi
```

```
#echo $NUM_TRACE files found
#cat /tmp/trace_list.lst


#****************************************************
# for each trace file found, send DBA an e-mail message
#  and move the trace file to the /tmp directory
#****************************************************
cat /tmp/trace_list.lst|while read TRACE_FILE
do

   #****************************************************
   #  This gets the short file name at the end of the full path
   #****************************************************
   SHORT_TRACE_FILE_NAME=`echo $TRACE_FILE|awk -F"/" '{ print $NF }'`
   #****************************************************
   #  This gets the file location (bdump, udump, log)
   #****************************************************
   DUMP_LOC=`echo $TRACE_FILE|awk -F"/" '{ print $(NF-1) }'`

   #****************************************************
   # send an e-mail to the administrator
   #****************************************************

   head -100 $TRACE_FILE|\
   mailx -s "$ORACLE_SID Oracle trace file at $MYDATE."\
      don@remote-dba.net\
      terry.oakes@worldnet.att.net\
      tzumainn@arsdigita.com
   #****************************************************
   # Move the trace file to the /tmp directory
   # This prevents multiple message to the developers
   # and allows the script to run every minute
   #****************************************************

   mv $TRACE_FILE /tmp/${DUMP_LOC}_${SHORT_TRACE_FILE_NAME}

done
```

userid.sh

```
#******************************************************************
#
# Copyright (c) 2002 by Donald K. Burleson
#
# Licensing information may be found at www.dba-oracle.com
#
#******************************************************************

for HOST1 in `cat /usr/local/dba/sh/userid| cut -d":" -f1`
do
        echo " "
        echo "==============="
```

```
          echo "HOST= $HOST1"
          echo "==============="
          # Now, get the database names on each box...
          for DB in `remsh $HOST1 -n "cat /etc/oratab | grep :Y|cut -d":" -f1"`
          do
                  echo "        "
                  echo "        --------------"
                  echo "        DB= $DB"
                  echo "        -------------"
                  #Now, we log into the database
                  TWO_TASK=t:$HOST1:$DB
                  export TWO_TASK DB
     su oracle -c "/usr/oracle/bin/sqlplus /<<!
select username from dba_users where username like '%UGA%';
exit;
!"
          done
done
exit
```

webserver_start.ksh

```
#!/bin/ksh

#*******************************************************************
#
# Copyright (c) 2002 by Donald K. Burleson
#
# Licensing information may be found at www.dba-oracle.com
#
#*******************************************************************

if [ `whoami` != 'oracle' ]
then
   echo "Error: You must be oracle to execute the script.  Exiting."
   exit
fi

# Exit if no first parameter $1
if [ -z "$1" ]
then
   echo "ERROR: Please pass a valid ORACLE_SID to this script"
   exit 99
fi

# Validate Oracle

TEMP=`cat /etc/oratab|grep \^$1:|cut -f1 -d':'|wc -l`
tmp=`expr TEMP`            # Convert string to number
if [ $tmp -ne 1 ]
then
```

```
    echo
    echo "Your input parameter $1 is invalid.  ERROR: Please Retry"
    echo
    exit 99
fi

# First, we must set the environment . . . .
ORACLE_SID=$1
export ORACLE_SID

ORACLE_HOME=`cat /etc/oratab|grep ^$ORACLE_SID:|cut -f2 -d':'`
export ORACLE_HOME
PATH=$ORACLE_HOME/bin:$PATH:$ORACLE_HOME/lib
export PATH

APPL_TOP=`cat /etc/oratab|grep ^$ORACLE_SID|cut -d":" -f5`;
export APPL_TOP

. $ORACLE_HOME/$ORACLE_SID.env;
. $APPL_TOP/APPL$ORACLE_SID.env


owsctl start wrb
FORMS_PORT=`cat /etc/oratab|grep ^$ORACLE_SID | awk -F: '{print $6}' -`
TCF_PORT=`cat /etc/oratab|grep ^$ORACLE_SID | awk -F: '{print $7}' -`
NLS_FORMS_PORT=`cat /etc/oratab|grep ^$ORACLE_SID | awk -F: '{print $8}' -`

DB_NAME=$ORACLE_SID
export DB_NAME

owsctl start wrb
owsctl start admin
owsctl start lprd
```

webserver_stop.ksh

```
#!/bin/ksh

#*******************************************************************
#
# Copyright (c) 2002 by Donald K. Burleson
#
# Licensing information may be found at www.dba-oracle.com
#
#*******************************************************************

if [ `whoami` != 'oracle' ]
then
    echo "Error: You must be oracle to execute the script.  Exiting."
    exit
```

```
fi

# Exit if no first parameter $1
if [ -z "$1" ]
then
   echo "ERROR: Please pass a valid ORACLE_SID to this script"
   exit 99
fi

# Validate Oracle

TEMP=`cat /etc/oratab|grep \^$1:|cut -f1 -d':'|wc -1`
tmp=`expr TEMP`             # Convert string to number
if [ $tmp -ne 1 ]
then
   echo
   echo "Your input parameter $1 is invalid.  ERROR: Please Retry"
   echo
   exit 99
fi

# First, we must set the environment . . . .
ORACLE_SID=$1
export ORACLE_SID

ORACLE_HOME=`cat /etc/oratab|grep ^$ORACLE_SID:|cut -f2 -d':'`
export ORACLE_HOME
PATH=$ORACLE_HOME/bin:$PATH:$ORACLE_HOME/lib
export PATH

APPL_TOP=`cat /etc/oratab|grep ^$ORACLE_SID|cut -d":" -f5`;
export APPL_TOP

. $ORACLE_HOME/$ORACLE_SID.env;
. $APPL_TOP/APPL$ORACLE_SID.env


FORMS_PORT=`cat /etc/oratab|grep ^$ORACLE_SID | awk -F: '{print $6}' -`
TCF_PORT=`cat /etc/oratab|grep ^$ORACLE_SID | awk -F: '{print $7}' -`
NLS_FORMS_PORT=`cat /etc/oratab|grep ^$ORACLE_SID | awk -F: '{print $8}' -`

DB_NAME=$ORACLE_SID
export DB_NAME


owsctl stop lprd
owsctl stop admin
owsctl stop wrb
```

Index

D

P

S

W

X

INTERNATIONAL CONTACT INFORMATION

AUSTRALIA
McGraw-Hill Book Company Australia Pty. Ltd.
TEL +61-2-9417-9899
FAX +61-2-9417-5687
http://www.mcgraw-hill.com.au
books-it_sydney@mcgraw-hill.com

CANADA
McGraw-Hill Ryerson Ltd.
TEL +905-430-5000
FAX +905-430-5020
http://www.mcgrawhill.ca

GREECE, MIDDLE EAST,
NORTHERN AFRICA
McGraw-Hill Hellas
TEL +30-1-656-0990-3-4
FAX +30-1-654-5525

MEXICO (Also serving Latin America)
McGraw-Hill Interamericana Editores S.A. de C.V.
TEL +525-117-1583
FAX +525-117-1589
http://www.mcgraw-hill.com.mx
fernando_castellanos@mcgraw-hill.com

SINGAPORE (Serving Asia)
McGraw-Hill Book Company
TEL +65-863-1580
FAX +65-862-3354
http://www.mcgraw-hill.com.sg
mghasia@mcgraw-hill.com

SOUTH AFRICA
McGraw-Hill South Africa
TEL +27-11-622-7512
FAX +27-11-622-9045
robyn_swanepoel@mcgraw-hill.com

UNITED KINGDOM & EUROPE
(Excluding Southern Europe)
McGraw-Hill Education Europe
TEL +44-1-628-502500
FAX +44-1-628-770224
http://www.mcgraw-hill.co.uk
computing_neurope@mcgraw-hill.com

ALL OTHER INQUIRIES Contact:
Osborne/McGraw-Hill
TEL +1-510-549-6600
FAX +1-510-883-7600
http://www.osborne.com
omg_international@mcgraw-hill.com

Get Your FREE Subscription to *Oracle Magazine*

Oracle Magazine is essential gear for today's information technology professionals. Stay informed and increase your productivity with every issue of *Oracle Magazine*. Inside each **FREE,** bimonthly issue you'll get:

- Up-to-date information on Oracle Database Server, Oracle Applications, Internet Computing, and tools
- Third-party news and announcements
- Technical articles on Oracle products and operating environments
- Development and administration tips
- Real-world customer stories

Three easy ways to subscribe:

1. Web Visit our Web site at www.oracle.com/oramag/. You'll find a subscription form there, plus much more!

2. Fax Complete the questionnaire on the back of this card and fax the questionnaire side only to **+1.847.647.9735.**

3. Mail Complete the questionnaire on the back of this card and mail it to P.O. Box 1263, Skokie, IL 60076-8263.

If there are other Oracle users at your location who would like to receive their own subscription to *Oracle Magazine*, please photocopy this form and pass it along.

☐ YES! Please send me a FREE subscription to *Oracle Magazine*.   ☐ NO

To receive a free bimonthly subscription to *Oracle Magazine*, you must fill out the entire card, sign it, and date it (incomplete cards cannot be processed or acknowledged). You can also fax your application to **+1.847.647.9735. Or subscribe at our Web site at www.oracle.com/oramag/**

SIGNATURE (REQUIRED) X _____   DATE _____

NAME _____   TITLE _____

COMPANY _____   TELEPHONE _____

ADDRESS _____   FAX NUMBER _____

CITY _____   STATE _____   POSTAL CODE/ZIP CODE _____

COUNTRY _____   E-MAIL ADDRESS _____

☐ From time to time, Oracle Publishing allows our partners exclusive access to our e-mail addresses for special promotions and announcements. To be included in this program, please check this box.

You must answer all eight questions below.

1 What is the primary business activity of your firm at this location? *(check only one)*
- ☐ 03 Communications
- ☐ 04 Consulting, Training
- ☐ 06 Data Processing
- ☐ 07 Education
- ☐ 08 Engineering
- ☐ 09 Financial Services
- ☐ 10 Government—Federal, Local, State, Other
- ☐ 11 Government—Military
- ☐ 12 Health Care
- ☐ 13 Manufacturing—Aerospace, Defense
- ☐ 14 Manufacturing—Computer Hardware
- ☐ 15 Manufacturing—Noncomputer Products
- ☐ 17 Research & Development
- ☐ 19 Retailing, Wholesaling, Distribution
- ☐ 20 Software Development
- ☐ 21 Systems Integration, VAR, VAD, OEM
- ☐ 22 Transportation
- ☐ 23 Utilities (Electric, Gas, Sanitation)
- ☐ 98 Other Business and Services
  _____

2 Which of the following best describes your job function? *(check only one)*
CORPORATE MANAGEMENT/STAFF
- ☐ 01 Executive Management (President, Chair, CEO, CFO, Owner, Partner, Principal)
- ☐ 02 Finance/Administrative Management (VP/Director/ Manager/Controller, Purchasing, Administration)
- ☐ 03 Sales/Marketing Management (VP/Director/Manager)
- ☐ 04 Computer Systems/Operations Management (CIO/VP/Director/ Manager MIS, Operations)

IS/IT STAFF
- ☐ 07 Systems Development/ Programming Management
- ☐ 08 Systems Development/ Programming Staff
- ☐ 09 Consulting
- ☐ 10 DBA/Systems Administrator
- ☐ 11 Education/Training
- ☐ 14 Technical Support Director/ Manager
- ☐ 16 Other Technical Management/Staff
- ☐ 98 Other _____

3 What is your current primary operating platform? *(check all that apply)*
- ☐ 01 DEC UNIX
- ☐ 02 DEC VAX VMS
- ☐ 03 Java
- ☐ 04 HP UNIX
- ☐ 05 IBM AIX
- ☐ 06 IBM UNIX
- ☐ 07 Macintosh
- ☐ 09 MS-DOS
- ☐ 10 MVS
- ☐ 11 NetWare
- ☐ 12 Network Computing
- ☐ 13 OpenVMS
- ☐ 14 SCO UNIX
- ☐ 24 Sequent DYNIX/ptx
- ☐ 15 Sun Solaris/SunOS
- ☐ 16 SVR4
- ☐ 18 UnixWare
- ☐ 20 Windows
- ☐ 21 Windows NT
- ☐ 23 Other UNIX _____
- ☐ 98 Other _____
- 99 ☐ **None of the above**

4 Do you evaluate, specify, recommend, or authorize the purchase of any of the following? *(check all that apply)*
- ☐ 01 Hardware
- ☐ 02 Software
- ☐ 03 Application Development Tools
- ☐ 04 Database Products
- ☐ 05 Internet or Intranet Products
- 99 ☐ **None of the above**

5 In your job, do you use or plan to purchase any of the following products or services? *(check all that apply)*
SOFTWARE
- ☐ 01 Business Graphics
- ☐ 02 CAD/CAE/CAM
- ☐ 03 CASE
- ☐ 05 Communications
- ☐ 06 Database Management
- ☐ 07 File Management
- ☐ 08 Finance
- ☐ 09 Java
- ☐ 10 Materials Resource Planning
- ☐ 11 Multimedia Authoring
- ☐ 12 Networking
- ☐ 13 Office Automation
- ☐ 14 Order Entry/Inventory Control
- ☐ 15 Programming
- ☐ 16 Project Management

- ☐ 17 Scientific and Engineering
- ☐ 18 Spreadsheets
- ☐ 19 Systems Management
- ☐ 20 Workflow
HARDWARE
- ☐ 21 Macintosh
- ☐ 22 Mainframe
- ☐ 23 Massively Parallel Processing
- ☐ 24 Minicomputer
- ☐ 25 PC
- ☐ 26 Network Computer
- ☐ 28 Symmetric Multiprocessing
- ☐ 29 Workstation
PERIPHERALS
- ☐ 30 Bridges/Routers/Hubs/Gateways
- ☐ 31 CD-ROM Drives
- ☐ 32 Disk Drives/Subsystems
- ☐ 33 Modems
- ☐ 34 Tape Drives/Subsystems
- ☐ 35 Video Boards/Multimedia
SERVICES
- ☐ 37 Consulting
- ☐ 38 Education/Training
- ☐ 39 Maintenance
- ☐ 40 Online Database Services
- ☐ 41 Support
- ☐ 36 Technology-Based Training
- ☐ 98 Other _____
- 99 ☐ **None of the above**

6 What Oracle products are in use at your site? *(check all that apply)*
SERVER/SOFTWARE
- ☐ 01 Oracle8
- ☐ 30 Oracle8*i*
- ☐ 31 Oracle8*i* Lite
- ☐ 02 Oracle7
- ☐ 03 Oracle Application Server
- ☐ 04 Oracle Data Mart Suites
- ☐ 05 Oracle Internet Commerce Server
- ☐ 32 Oracle *inter*Media
- ☐ 33 Oracle JServer
- ☐ 07 Oracle Lite
- ☐ 08 Oracle Payment Server
- ☐ 11 Oracle Video Server
TOOLS
- ☐ 13 Oracle Designer
- ☐ 14 Oracle Developer
- ☐ 54 Oracle Discoverer
- ☐ 53 Oracle Express
- ☐ 51 Oracle JDeveloper
- ☐ 52 Oracle Reports
- ☐ 50 Oracle WebDB
- ☐ 55 Oracle Workflow
ORACLE APPLICATIONS
- ☐ 17 Oracle Automotive

- ☐ 35 Oracle Business Intelligence System
- ☐ 19 Oracle Consumer Packaged Goods
- ☐ 39 Oracle E-Commerce
- ☐ 18 Oracle Energy
- ☐ 20 Oracle Financials
- ☐ 28 Oracle Front Office
- ☐ 21 Oracle Human Resources
- ☐ 37 Oracle Internet Procurement
- ☐ 22 Oracle Manufacturing
- ☐ 40 Oracle Process Manufacturing
- ☐ 23 Oracle Projects
- ☐ 34 Oracle Retail
- ☐ 29 Oracle Self-Service Web Applications
- ☐ 38 Oracle Strategic Enterprise Management
- ☐ 25 Oracle Supply Chain Management
- ☐ 36 Oracle Tutor
- ☐ 41 Oracle Travel Management
ORACLE SERVICES
- ☐ 61 Oracle Consulting
- ☐ 62 Oracle Education
- ☐ 60 Oracle Support
- ☐ 98 Other _____
- 99 ☐ **None of the above**

7 What other database products are in use at your site? *(check all that apply)*
- ☐ 01 Access
- ☐ 02 Baan
- ☐ 03 dbase
- ☐ 04 Gupta
- ☐ 05 IBM DB2
- ☐ 06 Informix
- ☐ 07 Ingres
- ☐ 08 Microsoft Access
- ☐ 09 Microsoft SQL Server
- ☐ 10 PeopleSoft
- ☐ 11 Progress
- ☐ 12 SAP
- ☐ 13 Sybase
- ☐ 14 VSAM
- ☐ 98 Other _____
- 99 ☐ **None of the above**

8 During the next 12 months, how much do you anticipate your organization will spend on computer hardware, software, peripherals, and services for your location? *(check only one)*
- ☐ 01 Less than $10,000
- ☐ 02 $10,000 to $49,999
- ☐ 03 $50,000 to $99,999
- ☐ 04 $100,000 to $499,999
- ☐ 05 $500,000 to $999,999
- ☐ 06 $1,000,000 and over

If there are other Oracle users at your location who would like to receive a free subscription to *Oracle Magazine*, please photocopy this form and pass it along, or contact Customer Service at +1.847.647.9630

Form 5

OPRESS